Biometric and Auditing Issues Addressed in a Throughput Model

Biometric and Auditing Issues Addressed in a Throughput Model

by

Waymond Rodgers
University of California

Information Age Publishing, Inc.
Charlotte, North Carolina • www.infoagepub.com

Library of Congress Cataloging-in-Publication Data

Rodgers, Waymond.
  Biometric and auditing issues addressed in a throughput model / edited by
Waymond Rodgers.
      p. cm.
  Includes bibliographical references.
  ISBN 978-1-61735-653-7 (pbk.) -- ISBN 978-1-61735-654-4 (hbk.) --
ISBN 978-1-61735-655-1 (ebook)
  1. Business--Data processing--Security measures. 2. Biometric identification.
3. Computers--Access control. 4. Computer networks--Security measures.
5. Auditing, Internal. 6. Business enterprises--Security measures. I Title.
  HF5548.37.R63 2011
  658.4'78--dc23   2011039435

Printed in the United States of America

CONTENTS

PREFACE

Cyber-related security intimidations have the makings for highly debilitating consequences for organizations. Nonetheless, many entities do not have effective security control systems in place to mitigate such threats. Cyber-fraud and lost productivity from cyber-attacks are also significant threats to economic activity. An underlying reason of such losses is the absence or breakdown of identification and verification systems.

Hence, today's world has an unprecedented need for security and asset protection systems. These systems include restricting access to physical resources, such as buildings and facilities, to controlling access to information technology resources such as computers and networks. Identity and verification procedures provide knowing exactly who is attempting to gain access or execute a transaction. These procedures are fundamental to any security system. To date, the most common approaches have relied on access cards and user name/password combinations techniques that have proven to be insecure and complex for both users and the organization.

Biometrics may seem novel; however, they represent one of the oldest forms of identification and verification. Animals such as lions, bears, and foxes recognize each other's scent; penguins recognize calls. People recognize each other by sight from across the street, voices on the telephone, signatures on contracts and photographs on driver's licenses. Fingerprints have been used to identify individuals at crime scenes for more than 1000 years.

What is innovative about biometrics is that technology is now employed in order to identify and verify. Various means such as fingerprints, palm prints, facial recognition, iris scans, voice recognition, and key board dynamics are a few of the technology-based biometric tools implemented in practice today.

One of the most promising approaches for reliable identification or verification is biometrics, since it identifies users based on something that they are—an innate biological characteristic—not something that can be shared or stolen like a card, a password or a PIN. Sound identification and verification devices are often an essential prerequisite for mitigating threats to other key security services such as confidentiality, nonrepudiation, data integrity, and data availability.

In view of recent widespread security and safeguarding of assets concerns, there has been a surge of interest in biometric devices as a way of intensifying identification and authentication control systems. A biometric is a distinguishable physiological or behavioral feature that can be implemented to automatically verify and authenticate a user's identity. Some of the accepted biometrics include fingerprints, palm prints, hand geometry, vein analysis, voice patterns, iris and retinal scans, signature verification, and keystroke analysis. Since a biometric is associated to a person, its misuse (from loss or theft) is more difficult, although not impossible.

Security has always been a major concern for managers and information technology professionals of all entities. An internal control biometrics system that is appropriately implemented can provide unparalleled security, enhanced convenience, heightened accountability, better fraud detection, and is very effective in depressing fraud. Controlling right of entry to physical assets of an organization is not the only concern that must be dealt with by managers. Organizations, executives, and security managers must also take into account security of the biometric data (template).

Many organizations have implemented internal control biometrics systems to meet regulatory mandates related to security audits and access control. Internal control biometrics systems provide the robust identity verification needed to support audit trails and satisfy many regulations.

Unlike the use of proxy-type credentials such as cards, passwords or PINs, which can be easily shared or stolen, internal control biometrics systems provide nonreputable evidence of the user's identity and confirms that the intended user was present for an access transaction.

This book proposes a *Throughput Model* that draws from computer science, economic and psychology literatures to model perceptual and judgmental processes whereby biometrics might be implemented to reduce risks to an organization's internal control. Despite its potential strengths, biometric tools is not a universal remedy and represents one factor in a portfolio of security apparatuses needed to safeguard information resources and other intangible assets. The book discusses challenges in employing biometric technology and pinpoints avenues for future research.

The *Throughput Modeling* process enables organizations to employ trust systems in assisting transactions that are motivated by ethical considerations. Auditing systems are by far based on trust.

Many issues arising due to privacy of information, security of that information, and payment details, whether or not payment details (e.g., credit card details) will be misused, identity theft, contracts, and, whether we have one or not, what laws and legal jurisdiction apply. Concepts of ethics and trust are aided by the employment of biometrics technology, which enhances the transactions between individuals and organizations in an internal control environment. Issues pertaining to sustainability are also examined with the assistance of the *Throughput Model*. Biometrics is the examination of measurable biological characteristics. In organizational security, biometrics refers to tools that rely on measurable physical and behavioral characteristics that can be automatically checked.

Finally, this book examines the potential use of an internal control biometrics system to lessen threats to identification and verification procedures. This book proposes an *"Throughput Model* framework" that considers both exposure and information risks as fundamental factors in classifying applications and organizational processes that might be candidates for the type of internal control biometrics system that biometrics can offer. This framework utilizes concepts of information risk and exposure risk, as well as the interaction of information systems and strategy, to model potential accounting applications and organizational processes that can benefit from an application of biometrics to reduce risk. Information risk refers to the level of information technology content in an organization's product/service and value chain. Information risk is high when the information content of both the product/service and the value chain is high. Similarly, information risk is low in situations where the reverse occurs. Exposure risk refers to potential losses that an organization can suffer in the absence of sufficient internal control biometrics system.

ACKNOWLEDGMENTS

The writing of this book, similar to any other production, involves a cast of thousands. Additionally, this work owes a great debt to those researchers whose efforts laid the groundwork of areas in auditing, ethics, trust, biometrics, sustainability issues, decision making, and internal control systems. Most of the research during the last six years has been supported by contracts from the Department of Defense. Further support was provided by the Department of Homeland Security Science and Technology University Programs Division and the Federal Bureau of Investigation Criminal Justice Information Services Division. Finally, my own research efforts have naturally fueled how I think about many of the aforementioned topics.

CHAPTER 1

INTRODUCTION TO AUDITING AND BIOMETRICS APPLICATIONS

Plato is my friend—Aristotle is my friend—but my greatest friend is truth (1664)
—Isaac Newton

If I have seen further it is by standing on the shoulders of giants (1676)
—Isaac Newton

If you have ever taken a long trip anywhere, you can have your good things and your bad things occurring along the way. All things about that trip, the good and the bad, they are all bits and pieces of the experience. They are the parts of a whole. It is all a part of the experience of the trip.

The journey of life could be thought of as a process. A process is not complete without all its parts. Auditing uses *processes*, which are sets of questions asked or directions given by an auditor to help an organization find out things about its operations and improve its financial condition. In financial statement auditing, the audit process begins from the planning stage, proceeds to the performance stage, and arrives at the opinion forming stage.

An individual trained and qualified in applying auditing to organizations for their betterment is called an *auditor*. *Auditor* is defined as *one who listens*, from the Latin *audire* meaning to *hear or listen*. There are many, many

Biometric and Auditing Issues Addressed in a Throughput Model, pp. 1–35
Copyright © 2012 by Information Age Publishing
All rights of reproduction in any form reserved.

different auditing processes, and each one may improve an organization's ability to confront and handle part of its existence. When the specific objective of any one process is attained, the process is ended and another can then be run to address a different part of an organization's operations.

A summary of the audit process follows, in describing the three main stages of planning, performing, and providing an opinion in a financial audit. In practice, there are a few more processes in between; however, these three stages represent the most significant parts of the audit.

In planning an audit, it is necessary to gain an understanding of the client's business and its environment. Further, an understanding and documentation of the working papers is necessary in each significant business cycle (e.g., revenue, expenditure, fixed assets, payroll, cash, and intangible property rights). After gaining an understanding of the client's business cycles, identification and documentation of the auditor's understanding of the client's internal controls is required for each of the business cycles.

Subsequently, compliance testing such as walk-through tests is required in order to determine if the controls are properly designed and implemented, and test of controls to test operational effectiveness of controls. If the internal controls are reliable, the auditor can seek to rely on them and perform a lesser degree of substantive testing. If the controls are not reliable, then the auditor should perform a higher level of substantive testing.

Compliance testing is a way of providing reasonable assurance that internal accounting control procedures are being employed as prescribed so that the auditor is confident of the validity of supporting evidence. Any oversights to compliance must be noted. Supporting evidence encompasses an examination of the accounts themselves as well as reviewing the journals, ledgers, and worksheets. If the compliance tests offer evidence that controls are functioning appropriately, the supporting evidence is considered reliable, and the Certified Public Accountant (CPA) can lessen the degree of validation and analytical review procedures. The following three audit procedures are normally implemented in conducting compliance tests: (1) inquiry of personnel regarding the performance of their duties; (2) observing personnel actions; and (3) inspecting documentation for evidence of performance in conducting employee functions. An example is examining invoices to assure that receiving documents and proof of delivery are affixed when the invoices are offered for payment. Tests of compliance should be applied to transactions during the year under audit as the financial statements reflect transactions and events for the whole year. Compliance tests may be carried out on a subjective or statistical basis.

Substantive testing is the test of account balances to confirm the correctness of the amounts. The three types of substantive tests include (1) tests of transactions (which are often carried out concomitantly with compliance test); (2) tests of balances; and (3) analytical review procedures. Tests of transactions and balances bring together evidence of the soundness of the accounting treatment of transactions and balances. They are intended to identify errors and irregularities. Statistical sampling may be implemented in establishing the correctness of financial statement numbers. Tests of transactions may be performed repeatedly throughout the audit year or at or close to the balance sheet date.

When the CPA traces a sales invoice from the journal to the ledger for correctness, it is called a transaction test. When the CPA compares the book balance of cash to the book balance, it is a test of balances. This test is done near or at the year-end reporting date. Another substantive test is calculating i nterest revenue on marketable securities and making sure the amount in the financial records. Analytical review procedures entail examining the reasonableness of relationships in financial statement items and uncovering variations from trends. The procedures may be applied to financial information taken as a whole, financial data of segments, and individual elements. If relationships appear reasonable, evidence corroborating the account balance exists.

Analytical review procedures test relationships among accounts and detect material changes. It necessitates analyzing significant ratios and trends for unusual change and questionable items. Integrated in the analytical review process are: (1) reading important documents and analyzing their accounting and financial effects; (2) reviewing the activity in an account between interim and year-end, in particular noting entries out of the ordinary; and (3) comparing current period account balances to previous periods as well as to budgeted amounts, noting reasonableness of account balances by evaluating logical relationships among them (i.e., relating payables to expenses, accounts receivable to sales). Fundamentally, analytical review entails reading the financial statement, scanning the figures, making comparisons to previous periods, appraising logical relationships among accounts, tracing financial statement items to the financial statements, and evaluating the overall process. The degree of analytical review required is based on the materiality of the item, available supporting data, and the quality of the internal control system. Analytical review aids in ascertaining the correctness and reliability of the accounts.

Performing the audit is the stage where most of the audit work is performed. Auditors gather audit evidence by performing substantive testing (test of details and substantive analytical procedures) on each significant account balances and class of transactions.

Further, importance in identifying risk areas of the client at an early stage and focusing more attention on these areas is required.

The work performed will be documented in the auditors' working papers, for review by seniors and managers. Auditors will be clearing review notes and comments on their working papers after review by superiors on an ongoing basis.

Finally, the partner forms an opinion based on audit evidence obtained from the earlier stages, and signs on the audit report. This is done after all significant outstanding matters have been cleared (i.e., review notes on working papers, pending items and other issues with the client).

Stakeholders such as investors, creditors, managers, regulators, and society are very much interested in the auditing standard-setting process that produces high-quality audits. In general, the purpose of the "audit" is to provide an independent opinion to stakeholders on the reasonableness and fairness of the financial statements. In addition, audits serve a vital role in the society in that it helps to enforce accountability and promote confidence in financial reporting. Although there is a great movement for international accounting standards, unfortunately, there is neither a guiding framework nor any fundamental principles for auditing.

The primary purpose of auditing standards is to enable auditors to perform high-quality audits. In addition, auditing standards can be helpful to regulators in their quest for monitoring the fairness of financial statements. Auditing standards dealing with different issues encompassing the collection of appropriate audit evidence are useful, however are becoming less clear than they used to be in many complex areas. The changing measurement, disclosure and reporting procedures have an impact on the evidence auditors need to accumulate.

Auditing standards require auditors to acquire a suitable understanding of the business and financial risks before providing an opinion. Also, auditors must consider the inherent limitations of an audit while obtaining sufficient relevant and reliable evidence on which to base their opinion. When auditors formulate an opinion on the financial statements, they consider the appropriateness of management's use of the going concern assumption. Auditors determine their audit procedures by evaluating internal controls and the potential existence of fraud in terms of risk that there may be material misstatements.

INTERNAL CONTROL DEFINED

The accounting system depends upon internal control procedures to ensure the reliability of accounting data. Many internal control procedures, on the other hand, make use of accounting data in keeping track of assets and monitoring the performance of departments.

The need for adequate internal control explains the nature and the very existence of many accounting records, reports, documents, and procedures. Thus, the topic of internal control and the study of accounting go hand-in-hand.

Internal controls fall into two broad categories: accounting controls and administrative controls. Accounting controls are measures that relate directly to the protection of assets or to the reliability of accounting information. An example would be the utilization of cash registers to create an immediate record of cash receipts. Another example would be the policy of making an annual physical count of inventory even though when a perpetual inventory system is in use.

Administrative controls are measures designed to enhance operational efficiency; they have no direct bearing upon the reliability of the accounting records. An example of an administrative control is a requirement that traveling salespeople submit reports displaying customers names contacted on a given day. Another example is the condition that airline pilots have annual medical examinations.

Internal accounting controls are those controls that have a direct bearing upon the reliability of accounting records, financial statements, and other accounting reports. In addition, sound administrative controls also contribute an essential role in the successful operation of an organization.

INTERNAL CONTROL PROCESS

An internal control is a process designed to provide reasonable assurance regarding the achievement of objectives in the following categories (Messier, Glover, & Prawitt, 2009):

1. Effectiveness and efficiency of operations.
2. Reliability of financial reporting.
3. Compliance with applicable laws and regulations.

Several significant aspects should be made about this definition:

1. **Individuals at every level of an organization affect internal control.** Internal control is, comparatively, everyone's responsibility. Within an organization, employees at the department-level are primarily responsible for internal control in their departments.

2. **Effective internal control assists an organization achieve its operations, financial reporting, and compliance objectives.** Effective internal control is an integrated part of the management process (i.e., plan, organize, direct, and control). Internal control directs an organization on course toward its objectives and the realization of its mission, and curtails problems along the way. Internal control encourages effectiveness and efficiency of operations, lessens the risk of asset loss, and assists to guarantee compliance with laws and regulations. In addition, internal controls also make sure the reliability of financial reporting. That is, all transactions are recorded and that all recorded transactions are genuine, suitably valued,

recorded on a timely basis, appropriately classified, and in the approved manner summarized and posted.

3. **Internal control can provide only reasonable assurance (not absolute assurance) pertaining to the attainment of an organization's objectives.** Effective internal control assists an organization to achieve its objectives; it does not guarantee success. There are quite a few explanations why internal control cannot provide absolute assurance that objectives will be accomplished. For example, cost/benefit realities, collusion among employees, and external events outside an organization's control.

BIOMETRICS DECISION-MAKING MODELING

Although some human interaction can be made possible through the web, organizations cannot provide the richness of interaction provided by personal service. For most organizations, biometric techniques provide the equivalent of an information-rich counter attendant rather than a salesperson. This also means that feedback about how users react to product and service offerings also tends to be rougher or perhaps lost using organizational approaches. If an organization's only feedback is that individuals are (or are not) buying its products or services online, this is inadequate for evaluating how to change or improve their organizational strategies and/or product and service offerings. The *Throughput Modeling* approach can assist organizations to understand, anticipate and meet changing online customer needs and preferences, which is critical for decision making in a rapidly ongoing Internet-based changing global environment.

Understanding how to utilize *Throughput Modeling* for organizational transactions will undoubtedly assist in making improved decision choices. Four major concepts help guide our decisions. They are *perception* (*P*), *information* (*I*), *judgment* (*J*), and *decision choice* (*D*). These four concepts combine in various ways to provide us with six different pathways to making a decision (Rodgers, 1997). Typically, one of the six pathways provides us with the most successful, appropriate and constructive decision (Figure 1.1).

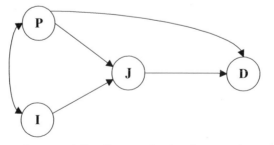

Figure 1.1. Throughput modeling for organizational transactions

Perception includes classification and categorization (pattern recognition) of knowledge structures to be retrieved from memory in order to frame or structure a problem. The classification and categorization of knowledge typically is induced by education, experience, and training. Conditions in organizational transactions can induce either *patterns* or *functional relations* in a situation. Pattern seeking is stimulated if the circumstances impart information that is highly organized (e.g., a wel-designed company's webpage) and if an individual is required to produce coherent explanations of how to go from one location on the webpage to another. Information is converted to knowledge once it is processed in the mind of people and knowledge becomes information once it is communicated and presented in the form of text, graphics words, or other symbolic forms. Incoming data sources are considered as facts and information is processed, interpreted data. Finally, knowledge is personalized information (Rodgers, 2006).

Functional relations seeking are induced if the information is not organized in a reasoned manner and if one is required to provide descriptions or predictions (e.g., a speculation on the location of the description of a product on a company's webpage). Employment of this concept to external information can generate a likelihood of blunders, resulting in biases of one's perception and/or a mismatch to external information. The closer the complement, the more relevant is the coherence between perception and information sources. If the coherence between the two is weak, then one of the following possible scenarios may exist:

1. Framing of the problem may diverge with external information.
2. The information may be imparting perplexing signals that cannot accurately match perception.
3. The external information is not comprehended.
4. There may be inadequate reliance in the quality of the information.

Judgment entails a more detailed examination whereby a person uses an adequate set of operations. This concept provides for the analysis of individuals' perception and information. Finally, perception and judgment can affect decision choice.

Throughput modeling portrays the theoretical underpinnings necessary to understand, explain, and predict decision choices related to organizational transactions. Past research has centered upon input—output relations between information and the resultant action or decision. Throughput modeling goes one step further by emphasizing that information and decision processes of perception and judgment do not occur at the same time or within the same space. That is, information is reanalyzed, resorted, and reconfigured in subsequent stages of information processing. In addition, people put into action different stages of cognitive processing (perception and judgment) that brings forth diverse and similar knowledge structures applied to a problem at hand. Therefore, throughput modeling enables us to examine information and cognitive processes in multiple stages before arriving at a decision. This procedure provides for a more in-depth analysis of the varying stages affecting decisions. By opening up the so-called "black box" we can become more knowledgeable about the steps people employed to make useful decision choices. In this manner, we may be able to improve upon knowledge acquisition, learning behavior, problem solving, and decision making in general as it applies to organizational transactions.

Throughput modeling requires researchers and practitioners to think in terms of systems or models. This book incorporates an explicit representation of a distinction between observed (measured) and unobserved (latent) variables, and its use in hypotheses testing. The basic statistic in structural equation modeling is the covariance. It compares the observed covariance matrix with the predicted covariance matrix that is based on a tested model. It is also possible, however to analyze other data types such as means. Causal modeling can also be implemented for not only non-experimental (correlational) data, but also for data from experiments (laboratory settings). Special cases of this model include ANOVA, multiple regression, canonical correlation, discriminant analysis, factor analysis, etc. Causal modeling is typically based upon large samples and it is possible to test parts of a model as well as testing the entire model (Rodgers, 1997).

Throughput modeling also enables us to design an ethical theoretical structure, propose a series of relationships, or develop a system of equations and test them in its entirety (Rodgers, 2010). Whereas previous procedures only allowed for testing of parts of a theory or conceptual framework, throughput model allows for detail and global scrutiny of a theory in the most rigorous manner. Testing only parts of a system does not convey whether or not the entire system or conceptual framework is acceptable. For example, only testing one page in a webpage does not indicate that the webpage is sufficient for information, service, and system quality. Therefore, a conceptual or theoretical model should go hand in glove with a methodology that allows for simultaneous testing of the complete model. Simultaneous testing of the model depicts the interrelationships of the concepts understudy. For exampe, if we hold nonfinancial information constant and increase the influence of financial information, what changes will occur in later processes such as the judgment or analysis stage (Rodgers, 1997, 2010).

ETHICAL SYSTEMS IN AUDITING

In a global economy where legal and ethical limits are pushed to the maximum and how the attitude pervades those around us that if there are no rules against something then it is tolerable to do, make ethical decision making for organizational transactions extremely important since it affects all users. Along with the wireless web mail from cellular telephones and other PDA communication devices, e-commerce is affecting more lives than ever before. Security and privacy concerns along with regulatory issues will become more widespread. Apparently, it is becoming more difficult to determine who you can trust online; especially with all the unethical, illegal, and Internet marketing and online advertising frauds and email scams.

Other ethical issues include what is communicated in an ecommerce website is a reflection of how the organization is viewed to the rest of the world. For example, negative or defamatory articles published about various people and organizations on other websites, if not properly researched, could possibly have legal consequences of libel that can extend across countries. In addition, Weblogs or Blogs may also fall into the legal liability zone. A blog is a website where daily, weekly, or monthly personal or corporate thoughts, ideas, and happenings can be published and shared with others. If webmasters perform unethical optimization of a client's website, it could have long-lasting negative business consequences and the trust level may not be easily repaired or restored.

When dealing with ethics in business transactions, there is a foremost degree of trust that is imparted to an individual or group that maintains the website. It is imperative from an ethical values based in an internal control perspective to make sure that the written words and what is represented about a company are factual. That is, issues involving ethics for marketing issues and advertising purposes is very paramount. For example, there are potential areas for revealing trade secrets or knowledge-based assets (this issue is discussed in more detail in Chapter 5—*Ethical Issues addressed in Biometrics Management* and in Chapter 6—*Biometrics Legal and Ethical Issues*) if proper ethical behavior is not followed. In addition, email correspondence should be private and confidential. Knowledge-based assets (or intellectual assets) include patents, brands, trademarks, and digital content that can be specified, protected, and traded. Knowledge-based assets that cannot be bought or sold include human capital, know-how, and organizational culture (Rodgers, 2003, 2007). Some knowledge-based assets are hardly "intellectual," for example, those that involve reproductions of sounds or images with nothing but entertainment value.

While certain people might not see any harm extracting it on the Web from an email sent, it is always advisable to get an individual's consent previous to publishing anything. While an individual might give consent, he or she might not realize the full implications. This leads to the book definition of ethics as employed in a security system transactions. Ethics refers to the principles or rules of moral conduct. Ethics suggests a social institution, composed of a set of standards pervasively acknowledged by the members of a culture. Therefore, ethics is concerned with internal control system security practices defined by right and wrong (Rodgers, 2009).

Different kinds of customs, rules, and mores, are transmitted within cultures and institutions from generation to generation. Ethical behavior is a precondition for internal control systems to function in a disciplined way. Therefore, it can be argued that ethics is the glue that binds organization's transactions globally. Ethics can then be classified as a set of moral principles or values.

The need for ethics in organizational settings is such a vital factor that many commonly held ethical values are incorporated into guidelines and procedures when navigating a particular organization's website. However, many ethical values of a society cannot be incorporated into organizational rules due to the perceived view and judgmental nature of certain values. For example, it is impractical to have e-commerce-based rules that deal with friendliness, honor and commitment. This does not imply that these principles are less important for an orderly organizational setting. We each have a set of values, even though we may or may not have considered them openly. In Chapter 5, a deeper exploration of dominate ethical positions that can be implemented in organizational setting will be considered and discussed.

This book underscores the notion that ethical positions depicted in a Throughput Model can be depicted in three primary pathways of *preferences, rules, and principles* (Rodgers, 2009). Each of these pathways differs by how much weight one puts on his or her perception or available information. Building on these three primary ethical pathways led to three secondary pathways of relativism, virtue ethics, and ethics of care pathways. Although we may be more apt to align to a distinct type of ethical position, the dictates of whether information is available, reliable or relevant, will influence our capability to achieve a secondary level of ethical decision making.

In addition, time pressures, changing or shifting environments, and our level of expertise in collecting and employing knowledge effectively, efficiently and wisely can thrust us into another ethical position in terms of describing the decision-making processes used to arrive at a decision choice.

TRUST SYSTEMS IN AUDITING

Establishing individual identity ("oneness" with a person already known to the internal control system) reliably and conveniently has become one of the foremost challenges in an information and knowledge society. The fast growth in Internet connectivity and mobility of people has led to new models of person-to-person interaction that necessitate novel means of proving identity, establishing trust, and authorizing access. Biometric tools developed in response to this growing global demand for automated individual identification include a variety of biometric tools such as finger, palm, vein, face, hand, iris, and other identifiers. These tools depend on the science of pattern recognition in order to determine a people identity based on stable physical patterns on their body. Today's technology has reached a level of trust whereby biometrics are now relied upon by an increasing number of applications in security, identity programs, and identity management systems.

For example, returning goods online can be an area of trust complexity. The uncertainties surrounding the initial payment and delivery of goods can aggravate this process. Will the goods get back to their source? Who pays for the return postage? Will the refund be paid? Will I be left with nothing? How long will it take? Contrast this with the offline experience of returning goods to a physical storefront.

Trust behavior is a necessary condition in order for transactions to be performed in an efficient and effective manner. These trust behaviors consist of decision-making perceptions that include the following concepts of the:

1. Level of increasing one's vulnerability in an organizational transaction.
2. Extend user's behavior loses control.
3. Amount of a penalty (disutility) one suffers if a party to the transaction abuses that vulnerability, which is greater than the benefit (utility).

Trust includes feelings, values, beliefs, and risk. Individuals' perceptions of others' ability, benevolence, and integrity account for a major segment of the discrepancy in perceived trust. Ability relates to a set of skills or competencies that allow an organizational user perform in some area. Benevolence implies a yearning to care for the protection of another, and the perception of integrity supports the notion that another attributes to a set of principles that one finds satisfactory (Vatanasombut, Igbaria, Stylianou, & Rodgers, 2008).

Trust also stems from judgments about integrity that are based on the perceived consistency of another's actions and the extent to which another's actions are harmonious with his or her words. Trust can develop over time from relational bonds, resulting in psychological contracts between the organizational users even though they have not personally met one another face to face. These implicit notions are for the most part taken for granted and unrecognized until violated. When a psychological contract breach occurs, however, it may place into awareness a question regarding the validity of these implicit assumptions. Unfortunately, these events may weaken and undermine the foundation of organizational transactions.

Trust positions follow an assumption that organizational transactions are underlined that both parties want to cooperate to find an ethically acceptable solution (this issued is discussed in more detail in Chapter 7— *Auditing Secured Biometric Transactions: Trust Issues*). Each of these roles has a set of preferences, rules, and/or principles.

BIOMETRICS AND AUDITING APPLICATIONS

Paper forms of singling out an individual rely heavily on the skills and ability of a person to recognize potential fraud and risk. Training personnel can assist with fraud triggered by paper records; however, there is still a customary level of human error that is tolerable. By placing less reliance on people to perform an identification check and more reliance on biometrics technology, the human error factor is lessened and elevated efficiency rates can be accomplished.

Biometrics is the study of measurable biological characteristics (Jain, Flynn, and Ross, 2008). In organizational security, biometrics refers to authentication technologies that rely on measurable physical and behavioral characteristics that can be automatically checked. Authentication (or verification) biometrics makes sure you are who you claim to be. In general, this sort of system requires two informational sources: (1) a depiction of one's identity (e.g., user name to retrieve your biometric template implanted inside of it), and (2) one's biometric information, such as your finger to create one's fingerprint template.

In general, identification is a much more demanding problem since it involves 1:N matching compared with 1:1 matching for verification (Table 1.1).

In identification, the system has to recognize a person (*Who am I?*) from a list of N users in the template database (Figure 1.2).

Verification, on the other hand (*Am I who I claim I am?*) requires substantiating or rejecting a person's *claimed identity* (Figure 1.3).

Progressing away from a paper-based identity verification system to one that is biometric oriented is a matter of accuracy. Organizations providing

Table 1.1.   Biometric Classification for Identification and Verification Systems

Recognition	Identification	Verification
Procedure	Who is this INDIVIDUAL?	Is this INDIVIDUAL who she says She is?
Matching type	1:N	1:1
Databank required?	Yes, Databank with linked personal information	No Databank
Kind of action	Overt or Covert	Covert

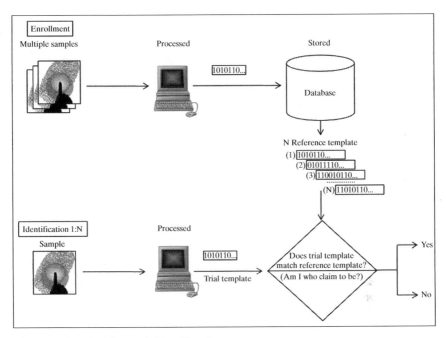

Figure 1.2. The biometric identification process
Source: GAO, 2003.

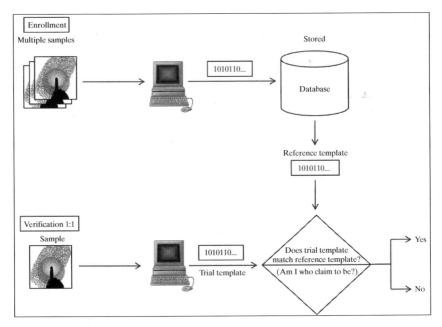

Figure 1.3. The biometric verification process
Source: GAO, 2003.

their customers with a biometric form of identity authentication are providing better customer service and an added advantage of lower costs. Also, a biometric-oriented system increases accuracy which can further reduce costs that are passed on by identity fraud. Moving towards a biometric authentication system suggests the addition of hardware and software can replace the human error factor that occurs by human-only verification. For example, fingerprint sensors eradicate the need for the user to write down passwords, greatly reduce calls to help desks and ensure that only a preenrolled and authorized user gains access to a PC or cellular phone, the data stored on the device, and the network to which it connects.

Like many forms of communication, a transition is occurring to move paper records to a biometric stored format. Paper identification methods have a shortcoming of being open to tampering. To stay ahead of offenders in quest of committing identity fraud a company should have an identity authentication process in place. Progressing from a dependency of paper to a streamlined biometric system is one-way identity fraud risk patterns that can be identified and mitigated. Identity fraud is a crime that costs all of organizational participants. As procedures have been enhanced in recent years to diminish identity fraud, so too has the level of sophistication of the fraudulent acts. Individuals dedicated to committing fraud had the upper hand for some time, but technology is now catching up to these intruders.

Conventional personal authentication systems that are centered on knowledge (e.g., password) or physical tokens (e.g., identification card) are not able to meet stringent security performance requirements for organizational applications. Biometrics-based authentication systems that use physiological and/or behavioral traits (see Table 1.2) are good

Table 1.2.   Different Types of Physiological and Behavioral Biometrics

Physiological	Behavioral
Fingerprint	Speaker recognition
Palm print	Gait
Hand geometry	Dynamic signature
Vein patterns	Keystroke dynamics
DNA	
Retina scan	
Iris scan	
Face recognition	
Face thermography	
Ear recognition	
Body odor recognition	

alternatives to conventional techniques. These systems are more reliable (biometric data cannot be lost, forgotten, or guessed) and more user-friendly (there is nothing to remember or carry). Despite these biometrics improvements over conventional systems, there are many unresolved issues associated with its employment (a detailed discussion of these issues is provided in Chapter 7—*Auditing Secured Biometric Transactions: Trust Issues*).

Advances in biometrics technology include measurable physiological and/or behavioral characteristics can be utilized to verify the identity of an individual, which offers inherently stronger security than previous approaches. When used in combination with the other measures (what you know/have), biometrics takes individual identity verification and non-refutation to very high levels of accuracy.

The next section provides a brief review of physiological and behavioral biometrics. These different types of biometrics will be discussed in more detail in Chapter 2.

PHYSIOLOGICAL BIOMETRICS

Fingerprint

Fingerprint technology can be used for both verification (1:1) matching as well as for Identification (1:n) matching. Electronic fingerprint matching can be attained through one of two procedures. The first implements the ridge endings and bifurcation's on an individual's finger to plot points known as minutiae (Minutiae-based approach). These minutiae allow for the comparison of two fingerprints to be achieved electronically. The second procedure utilizes a pattern-based approach. This comparison technique (Pattern based) is performed in two fundamental blocks called image Enhancement and distortion Removal, respectively. In each case a finger is touchedon a fingerprint device, the ridge pattern displays a distinct degree of distortion.

Palm Print (palm scan)

Palm recognition performs in the same manner as fingerprint recognition, by measuring the pattern, ridge endings and splits in ridge paths of the raised portion of the print. Each palm print is unique to the person and the mathematical formulas are fairly easy to store in a large database. The result is a stronger internal control biometrics system to capture and link palm prints to a single record, which will increase fraud prevention and help ensure impostors do not attempt to use multiple identities.

Hand Geometry

Hand geometry systems are typically available in two main forms. Full hand geometry systems take an image of the entire hand for comparison while a "two finger" reader only image two fingers of the hand. Hand recognition systems are especially useful in outdoor environments. Hand recognition templates are also extremely small, a characteristic that makes the templates very portable.

Vein Patterns

The pattern of blood vessels is captured by transmitting near-infrared light at different hand vascular patterns of veins present at the back of a hand. Veins are inside the body, invisible to the eye, it is extremely difficult to forge and impossible to manipulate. There are different types of vein recognition technology, which include finger vein, wrist vein, palm, and back-hand vein recognition. The underlying concept of scanning remains the same with each of these techniques.

DNA

DNA (deoxyribonucleic acid) is the well-known double-helix structure present in every human cell. A DNA sample is used to produce either a DNA fingerprint or a DNA profile. In addition, DNA can be collected from any number of sources: blood, hair, finger nails, mouth swabs, blood stains, saliva, straws, and any number of other sources that has been attached to the body at some time. The main problems surrounding DNA biometrics is that it is not a quick process to identify someone by his/her DNA. The process is also a very costly one.

Retina Scan

Retina scanning is very accurate and distinctive to each person, and it typically requires the user to look into a receptacle and focus on a given point for the user's retina to be scanned. This tool is more intrusive than other biometric techniques; therefore, retina scanning is not the friendliest process even though the tool itself is very accurate for use in identification, verification, and authentication.

Iris Scan

Iris recognition is a method of biometric authentication that uses pattern recognition techniques based on high-resolution images of the iris of a person's eye. Iris recognition uses camera technology, and subtle irradiance illumination to reduce specular reflection from the convex cornea to create images of the detail-rich, intricate structures of the iris. These distinct structures transformed into digital templates, provide mathematical representations of the iris that produce unambiguous positive identification of a person.

Face Recognition

Face recognition uses an image or series of images either from a camera or photograph to recognize an individual. Face recognition is a passive biometrics and does not require an individual's cooperation. It can recognize people from a distance even without them being aware that they are being analyzed. This tool has advanced from a simple geometric recognition pattern to matching complex points on the face. Facial recognition is used most widely in passport identification, missing person's identification and other areas of law enforcement. This advancement in technology there is still a problem with accuracy.

Face Thermography (thermoimaging recognition)

Facial thermography detects heat patterns shaped by the sectioning of blood vessels and emitted from the skin. These patterns, called thermograms, are very diffferent. Thermography operates similarly to face recognition, except that an infrared camera is utilized to import the images. The advantages of facial thermography over other biometric technologies are that no physical contact is required and that every individual presents a usable image, and the image can be collected on the quickly.

Ear Recognition

Ear shape recognition is based on the distinctive shape of each individual's ears and the structure of the largely cartilaginous, projecting portion of the outer ear. Unlike faces, ears are remarkably consistent, in that they do not change shape with different expressions or age, and remain fixed in the middle of the side of the head against a predictable background. In addition, hair is not a problem in covering the ear in that infrared images can be implemented.

Body Odor (scent) Recognition

Body odor technology is new and it would use an odor-sensing instrument (an electronic "nose") to capture the volatile chemicals that skin pores all over the body emit to make up an individual's smell. Distinguishing one individual from another by odor may eventually be feasible, the fact that personal habits such as the use of deodorants and perfumes, diet, and medication influence a person's body odor causes the progress of this technology to be quite complex.

BEHAVIORAL BIOMETRICS

Speaker (Voice) Recognition

Speaker recognition biometric readers are used to recognize a particular speaker's voice. Speaker recognition and speech recognition are not to be confused with one another. Speaker recognition relies on the physical structure of a person's vocal tract and their personality. Speech recognition simply recognizes certain words. Speaker recognition can be implemented, as a way of isolating a person while speech recognition cannot. There are two key defects in speaker recognition tools. The first is that it is dependent on a scripted text. The second major flaw is that the biometric readers can be fooled by a recording of the voice or may not recognize the voice of a individual with a cold.

Gait Recognition

Gait recognition is a method of recognizing people by their unique walk, and it captures a sequence of images to derive and analyze motion characteristics. An individual's gait can be difficult to disguise since a person's musculature essentially limits the variation of motion, and measuring it requires no contact with the individual. However, gait can be obscured or disguised if the person is injured, wearing loose fitting clothes or deliberately changes their walk.

Dynamic Signature

Biometric signatures are based upon recording various characteristics of one's signing style to carry out the process of identification in the future. Amount of pressure employed, angle of writing, formation of letters and other traits, which are categorized as behavioral biometrics, form the basis of biometric signature recognition technology.

Keystroke Dynamics

Keystroke dynamics is a detailed account of the timing of key-down and key-up procedures when users enter usernames, passwords, or any other string of characters. Since user's keystroke timings are as personal as hand-writing or a signature, keystroke dynamics can be utilized as part of a method to verify a user's identity.

CONCLUSION

A while back, an information systems professional was needed to operate a computer.

Today organizational personnel can obtain and use information, as well as biometric data, on the computer themselves. Some of the general applications implemented to generate reports by organizations are word processing, desktop publishing, spreadsheets, database management systems, graphics programs, electronic mail, project management, scheduling software, and mainframe-based query systems, voice mail and video conferencing. Moreover, to computer applications, organizations utilize other information systems applications such as fingerprinting, facial recognition and voice recognition.

Advancing technology enables organizations to purchase or develop internal control biometrics systems and applications, shifting certain common control responsibilities from the centralized information systems department to end-user departments. This often happens in the move from the mainframe to a client-server environment.

Biometrics are automated methods of recognizing an individual based on a physiological or behavioral characteristic. Among the features measured include fingerprint, palm print, hand geometry, vein patterns, DNA, retina scan, iris scan, face recognition, face thermography, ear recognition, body odor recognition, speaker recognition, gait, dynamic signature, and keystroke dynamics. Biometric tools are becoming the foundation of an extensive array of safeguarding of assets, highly secure identification and verification methods. As the level of security breaches and transaction fraud increases, the need for highly secure identification and verification tools is becoming apparent.

Biometrics-based authentication applications comprise of workstation, network, and domain access, single sign-on, application logon, data protection, remote access to resources, transaction security and Web security. Trust in these electronic transactions is critical to the healthy growth of the world-wide economy. Biometrics tools implemented alone or integrated with other technologies such as smart cards, encryption keys and digital signatures, biometrics are set to permeate nearly all facets of the economy and our daily lives. Using biometrics for authentication is becoming more expedient and significantly more precise than contemporary methods (such as the utilization of passwords or PINs). The primary reason for the aforementioned is that biometrics connects the event to a particular person (a password or token may be used by someone other than the authorized user), is convenient (there is nothing to carry or remember), precise (it provides for positive authentication), can make available an audit trail and is becoming socially acceptable and inexpensive.

Further, the biometrics setting provides access to a wide range of information, and enables individuals to communicate without the limitations of physical distance. However, finding the information needed, with a high degree of confidence that the information is correct, can be a tedious job. This book provides a conceptual framework called "*Throughput Modeling*," which enables one to depict the various stages influenced by one's ethical and trust positions when buying or selling products/services in an organizational atmosphere. In the context of auditing transactions, biometrics technology will be discussed and examined in later chapters as it relates to ethical and trust systems employed by organizational users.

The following array of ethical concerns with biometric identification methods has been acknowledged:

- Some biometric identification methods are relatively intrusive (e.g., retina scans).
- The gathering of biometric information like fingerprints is linked with criminal behavior in the minds of many people.
- Usually, detailed biometric information has been gathered by large institutions, like the military or police; people may feel a loss of privacy or personal dignity.
- Individuals feel embarrassed when rejected by a public sensor.
- Automated face recognition in public places could be implemented to track everyone's movements without their knowledge or consent.

In addition, there are also a variety of questions regarding how this data will be stored and utilized:

- How will loads of biometric data be stored? These are not fingerprint cards stored in a secured building; this is easily moved and duplicated electronic information. How will this information be protected?
- Who will have access to this information? Will organizations be permitted access to facial biometrics, allowing them to utilize security cameras to positively identify customers on a routine basis? How would you feel about walking into a department store you've never been in before, only to be greeted by name by a sales associate who has just read a summary of all of your recent purchases?

- Are we trying to identify or authenticate? In the great majority of cases, biometrics can be implemented to assist *authenticate* an assertion by a person: for example, "I am the legitimate holder of this token." However, slack system design, or a desire to use every part of the technology system, or a misconceived desire to future-proof the technology investment, means that organizations instead set out to *identify* the user: rather than test an assertion, they try to single out a person from a database. An example is an immigration system, which selects the person out from its database of enrolled users by the biometric alone. As opposed to asking them to present a machine-readable document and then confirming that the holder has the associated biometrics.

The stronger the ethical and trust positions in an auditing environment provides a platform whereby a large numbers of organizations can be serviced for confirmation and assurance purposes. People operating in a strong ethical and trust environment will be more relaxed in exploring financial and investment opportunities, mergers and acquisitions, commercial lending, and using numerous other value added features.

Biometric verification can help resolve the problem of identification fraud and provide the point of service person that the customer presented is the actual person represented on the identification. The benefit of a biometric verification is that legitimate multiple identifications can be linked to a single person through one unique biometric fingerprint records. The additional benefit is that these unique biometric tools cannot be utilized in multiple fraudulent identifications. In sum, biometric-based methods are able to provide for safeguarding of assets, confidential financial transactions and personal data privacy. The need for biometrics can be found in various government levels, in the military, and in commercial applications. Organizations' security infrastructures, government IDs, secure electronic banking, investing and other financial transactions, retail sales, law enforcement, and health and social services are already benefiting from these tools.

REFERENCES

GAO. (2003). United States General Accounting Office. *Information Security Challenges in Using Biometrics*. www.gao.gov/cgi-bin/getrpt?GAO-03-1137T.

Jain, A. K., Flynn, P., & Ross, A. (2008). *Handbook of biometrics*. New York, NY: Springer.

Messier, W. F., Glover, S., & Prawitt, D. (2009). *Auditing & assurance services: A systematic approach*. New York, NY: McGraw-Hill/Irwin.

Rodgers, W. (1997). *Throughput modeling: Financial information used by decision makers*. Greenwich, CT: JAI Press.

Rodgers, W. (2003). Measurement and reporting of knowledge-based assets. *Journal of Intellectual Capital 4*, 181–190.

Rodgers, W. (2007). Problems and resolutions to future knowledge-based assets reporting. *Journal of Intellectual Capital, 8*, 205–215.

Rodgers, W. (2009). *Ethical beginnings: preferences, rules and principles*. New York, NY: iUniverse.

Rodgers, W. (2010). *E-commerce and biometric issues addressed in a Throughput Model*. Hauppauge, NY: Nova Publication.

University of California. (2010). *Understanding internal controls. A reference guide for managing university business practices*. http://www.ucop.edu/ctlacct/under-ic.pdf

Vatanasombut, B., Igbaria, M., Stylianou, A. C., & Rodgers, W. (2008). Information systems continuance intention of web-based applications customers: The case of online banking, *Information and Management, 45*, 419–428.

APPENDIX A

Internal control includes five interconnected components as follows (Messier, Glover, & Prawitt, 2009; University of California, 2010):

1. Control (or Operating) environment
2. Risk assessment
3. Control activities
4. Information and communication
5. Monitoring

All five internal control components must be present to conclude that internal control is effective (University of California, 2010).

CONTROL ENVIRONMENT

The control environment is the control awareness of an organization. Further, it is the surroundings in which individuals conduct their activities and carry out their control responsibilities. An effective control environment is an environment where proficient individuals understand their responsibilities, the restrictions to their authority, and are knowledgeable, mindful, and committed to doing what is correct. In addition, these employees are unswerving to following an organization's policies and procedures and its ethical guidelines.

The control environment includes technical competence and ethical commitment. This type of intangible asset is indispensable to effective internal control. A governing board and management augment an organization's control environment when they institute and effectively communicate written policies and procedures, a code of ethics, and standards of conduct. Furthermore, a governing board and management augment the control environment when they behave in an ethical manner generating a constructive "tone at the top," as well as requiring the same standard of conduct from everyone in the organization.

Hence, management is responsible for "setting the tone" for their organization. Therefore, management should encourage a control environment that encourages:

a. the utmost levels of integrity and personal and professional standards,
b. a leadership philosophy and operating approach that endorse internal controls throughout the organization, and
c. assignment of authority and responsibility.

Effective human resource policies and procedures enhance an organization's control environment. These policies and procedures should speak to hiring, orientation, training, evaluations, counseling, promotions, compensation, and disciplinary actions. When it turns out that an employee does not comply with an organization's policies and procedures or behavioral standards, an organization must take suitable disciplinary action to maintain an effective control environment. The control environment is very much inspired by the degree to which people acknowledge that they will be held accountable.

RISK ASSESSMENT

Risk assessment forms a basis for determining how those risks should be managed. Therefore, risk assessment is the detection and analysis of risks associated with the achievement of operations, financial reporting, and compliance goals and objectives.

Two of the major features of internal control are to identify risks to the achievement of an organization's objectives and to manage those risks. Therefore, setting goals and objectives is a prerequisite to internal controls. Utmost, goals and objectives should be presented in a strategic plan that embraces a mission statement and broadly defined strategic initiatives. At the department level, goals and objectives should sustain the organization's strategic plan. The categorization of goals and objectives are as follows:

Operation objectives relate to the attainment of the basic mission(s) of an organization and the effectiveness and efficiency of its operations, including performance standards and safeguarding resources against loss.

Financial reporting objectives relate to the organization of reliable financial reports, taking into account the deterrence of fraudulent public financial reporting.

Compliance objectives relate to adherence to germane laws and regulations.

A clear set of goals and objectives is essential to the success of an organization. Particularly, an organization should have

a.   a mission statement,
b.   written goals and objectives for the department as a whole, and
c.   written goals and objectives for each significant activity in the department

Moreover, goals and objectives should be articulated in terms that provide vital performance measurements.

To properly manage their operations, managers need to ascertain operation levels, financial and compliance risk they are willing to assume. Risk assessment is one of management's responsibilities and facilitates management to act proactively in reducing unwelcomed surprises. Failure to purposely manage these risks can result in a lack of confidence that operation, financial and compliance goals will be realized.

Furthermore, a risk is anything that could make vulnerable the attainment of an objective. For each of the organization's objectives, risks should be acknowledged. The following questions clarify risks identification:

1. What is inappropriate?
2. How could the organization go out of business?
3. What must go right for the organization to succeed?
4. What decision choices necessitate the most judgment (analysis)?
5. How do we know whether we are accomplishing our objectives?
6. What aspects of the organization are vulnerable?
7. What tangible and intangible assets need protection?
8. What is the greatest legal exposure?
9. What activities are regulated?
10. What are the largest organization's monetary expenditures?
11. How does the organization bill and collect revenue?
12. How could someone pilfer from the organization?
13. How could someone upset organizational operations?
14. Does the organization have liquid assets or assets with alternative uses?
15. What are the information drivers that we most rely upon?
16. What organizational activities are most complex?

It is essential that risk identification be wide-ranging at the activity or process level, for operations, financial reporting, and compliance objectives. Both external and internal risk aspects need to be well thought-out. By and large, several risks can be identified for each objective.

When evaluating the potential impact of risk, both quantitative and qualitative costs need to be addressed. Quantitative costs include the cost of buildings, land, machinery, computers, equipment, inventory, monetary losses, damage and repair costs, defending a lawsuit costs, etc. Qualitative costs can have wide-ranging implications to an organization's intangible assets. For example, these costs may include: loss of investors and public trust, harm to the organization's image and reputation, increased legislation violation of laws, etc.

After risks have been acknowledged, a risk analysis should be executed to prioritize those risks in the following manner:

a.   assess the probability (or frequency) of the risk occurring;
b.   approximate the possible effect if the risk were to transpire; consider both quantitative and qualitative costs; and
c.   ascertain how the risk should be managed; decide what actions are necessary.

CONTROL ACTIVITIES

Control activities are actions buttressed by policies and procedures that when performed appropriately and in a timely approach can cope with or diminish risks. In the similar manner that managers are chiefly accountable for recognizing the financial and compliance risks for their operations, they also have line responsibility for outlining, executing and scrutinizing their internal control system.

Preventive and detective controls are two ways to handle risks. Preventive controls attempt to discourage or thwart detrimental events from happening. They are proactive controls that facilitate to avoid losses. Examples of preventive controls are separation of duties, proper authorization, adequate documentation, and physical control over assets.

Alternatively, detective controls attempt to detect undesirable acts. This control provides evidence that a loss has occurred, however do not prevent a loss from occurring. Examples of detective controls are analyses, reviews, variance analyses, reconciliations, physical inventories, and audits. Both kinds of controls are vital to an effective internal control system. From a quality perspective, preventive controls are indispensable since they are proactive and accentuate quality. Nevertheless, detective controls play a important role offering evidence that the preventive controls are functioning and preventing losses. Control activities include approvals, authorizations, verifications, reconciliations, reviews of performance, security of intangible and tangible assets, segregation of duties, and controls over information systems.

Approvals, Authorizations, and Verifications (Preventive)

Management authorizes employees to perform certain activities and to execute certain transactions within limited parameters. In addition, management specifies those activities or transactions that need supervisory approval before they are performed or executed by employees. A supervisor's approval (manual or electronic) implies that he or she has verified and validated that the activity or transaction conforms to established policies and procedures.

Reconciliations (Detective)

An employee relates different sets of data to one another, identifies and investigates differences, and takes corrective action, when necessary.

Reviews of Performance (Detective)

Management compares information about current performance to budgets, forecasts, prior periods, or other benchmarks to measure the extent to which goals and objectives are being achieved and to identify unexpected results or unusual conditions that require follow-up.

Security of Assets (preventive and detective)

Access to equipment, inventories, securities, cash and other assets is restricted; assets are periodically counted and compared to amounts shown on control records.

Segregation of Duties (preventive)

Duties are segregated among different people to reduce the risk of error or inappropriate action. Normally, responsibilities for authorizing transactions, recording transactions (accounting), and handling the related asset (custody) are divided.

Controls over Information Systems (preventive and detective)

Controls over information systems are grouped into two broad categories: general controls and application controls. General controls typically comprise of controls over data center operations, system software acquisition and maintenance, access security, and application system development and maintenance. Application controls such as computer matching and edit checks are programmed steps within application software. These controls are designed help make certain the completeness and accuracy of transaction processing, authorization, and validity. General controls are required to support the functioning of application controls. Both general and application controls are required to make certain complete and accurate information processing.

Control activities must be put into practice thoughtfully, conscientiously, and consistently. Further, a procedure will not be effective if performed mechanically without any intelligent continuing focus on conditions to which the policy is directed. Finally, it is crucial that unusual conditions identified as a result of performing control activities be investigated and suitable corrective action be taken.

Control Activities—Approvals (preventive)

1. Written policies and procedures
2. Restriction to authority
3. Supporting documentation
4. Question abnormal items
5. No "rubber stamps"
6. No blank signed forms

A critical control activity is authorization/approval. Authorization is the handing over of authority; it may be general or specific. Providing a department permission to expend funds from an approved budget is an example of general authorization. Specific authorization relates to distinctive transactions; it necessitates the signature or electronic approval of a transaction by an individual with approval authority. Approval of a transaction entails that the approver has reviewed the supporting documentation and is assured that the transaction is proper, accurate and abides with applicable laws, regulations, policies, and procedures. Approvers ought to review supporting documentation, question abnormal items, and make sure that essential information is present to validate the transaction it is signed. Finally, signing blank forms should never be allowed.

Approval authority could be tied to a particular dollar level. Transactions that exceed the stipulated dollar level would necessitate approval at an upper level. An approver should never convey to someone that they could sign the approver's name on behalf of the approver. Likewise, an approver with electronic approval authority should not share her or his password with another person. To make certain proper segregation of duties, an individual initiating a transaction should not be the person who approves the transaction. A department's approval levels should be spelled out in a departmental policies and procedures manual.

Control Activities—Reconciliations (detective)

Reconciliation is a comparison of different sets of data to one another, recognizing and inspecting differences, and taking remedial action, when required to resolve differences. For example, verifying charges in the subsidiary accounts payable ledger to file copies of approved invoices. This control activity helps to ensure the accuracy and completeness of transactions that have been charged to a department's accounts. To ensure proper segregation of duties, the person who approves transactions or handles cash receipts should not be the individual who performs the reconciliation.

A critical component of the reconciliation process is to resolve differences. Differences should be identified, investigated, and explained. For example, if an expenditure is incorrectly charged to a department's accounts, then the approver should request a correcting journal entry; the reconciler should ascertain that the correcting journal entry was posted. Reconciliations should be documented and endorsed by management.

Control Activities—Reviews (detective)

Reviewing reports, statements, reconciliations, and other information by management is a vital control activity; management should assess such information for consistency and reasonableness. Reviews of performance offer a basis for discovering problems such as:

a. budget to actual comparison,

b. current to prior period comparison,

c. performance indicators, and

d. follow-up on unexpected results or unusual items.

Management should contrast information about current performance to budgets, forecasts, prior periods or other benchmarks to measure the degree that goals and objectives are being achieved and to identify unexpected results or unusual conditions which require follow-up. Management's assessment of reports, statements, reconciliations, and other information ought to be documented as well as the resolution of items noted for follow-up.

Control Activities—Asset Security (preventive and detective)

Liquid assets, assets with alternative uses, risky assets, vital documents, critical systems, and confidential information must be safeguarded against unauthorized acquisition, utilization, or disposition. As a rule, access controls are the paramount means to safeguard these assets. Examples of access controls such as fingerprints, palm print, facial recognition are as follows: locked door, key pad systems, card key system, badge system, locked filing cabinet, guard, terminal lock, computer password, menu protection, automatic callback for remote access, smart card, and data encryption. Preventive and detective procedures include but are not limited to:

a.   Security of physical an intangible assets (knowledge-based assets),
b.   Physical safeguards,
c.   Perpetual records are maintained,
d.   Periodic counts/physical inventories,
e.   Compare counts to perpetual records, and
f.   Investigate/correct differences.

Departments with capital assets or significant inventories should establish perpetual inventory control over these items by recording purchases and issuances. Periodically, the items should be physically counted by an individual who is independent of the purchase, authorization and asset custody functions, and the counts should be compared with balances as per the perpetual records. Missing items should be scrutinized, resolved, and analyzed for potential control deficiencies; perpetual records should be adjusted to physical counts if missing items are not tracked down.

Control Activities—Segregation of Duties (preventive and detective)

Segregation of duties is vital to effective internal control; it diminishes the risk of both incorrect and unacceptable actions. By and large, the approval function, the accounting/reconciling function and the asset custody function ought to be separated among employees. For example, no one individual should...

a.   initiate the transaction
b.   approve the transaction
c.   record the transaction
d   reconcile balances
e.   handle assets
f.   review reports

When these functions cannot be disconnected, due to insignificant department size, a detailed supervisory review of related activities is necessary as a compensating control activity. Segregation of duties is a prevention measure to fraud since it calls for collusion with another individual to perpetrate a fraudulent act.

Specific examples of segregation of duties are as follows:

1. The individual who requisitions the purchase of goods or services should not be the person who approves the purchase.
2. The individual who approves the purchase of goods or services should not be the person who reconciles the monthly financial reports.
3. The individual who approves the purchase of goods or services should not be able to get hold of custody of checks.
4. The individual who maintains and reconciles the accounting records should not be able to obtain custody of checks.
5. The individual who opens the mail and organizes a listing of checks received should not be the person who makes the deposit.
6. The individual who opens the mail and sets up a listing of checks received should not be the person who keeps the accounts receivable records.

Control Activities—Information Systems

An organization's employees may use different types of information systems such as mainframe computers, local area and wide area networks of minicomputers and personal computers, single-user workstations and personal computers, telephone systems, video conference systems, etc. Therefore, the need for internal control over these systems depends on the essential and discretionary nature of the information as well as the complexity of the applications that is inherent in the systems. There are basically two categories of controls over information systems: general controls and application controls.

General Controls

General controls apply to entire information systems and to all the applications that reside on the systems. These systems are as follows:

a. Access Security, Data & Program Security, Physical Security.
b. Software Development & Program Change Controls.
c. Data Center Operations.
d. Disaster Recovery.

General controls consist of practices intended to preserve the integrity and availability of information processing functions, networks, and associated application systems. These controls pertain to business application processing in computer centers by ensuring complete and accurate processing. These controls ensure that correct data files are processed, processing diagnostics and errors are noted and resolved, applications and functions are processed according to recognized schedules, file backups are taken at suitable intervals, recovery procedures for processing breakdowns are recognized, software development and change control procedures are dependably applied, and actions of computer operators and system administrators are reviewed.

Moreover, these controls ensure that physical security and environmental measures are taken to reduce the risk of sabotage, vandalism and destruction of networks and computer processing centers. Finally, these controls make certain the acceptance of disaster planning to escort the successful recovery and continuity of networks and computer processing in the aftermath of a disaster.

Application Controls

Applications are the computer programs and processes, including manual processes, which enable organizations to conduct vital activities; buying products, paying people, accounting for research costs, and forecasting and monitoring budgets. Application controls pertain to computer application systems and include input controls (e.g., edit checks), processing controls (e.g., record counts), and output controls (e.g., error listings), they are particular to distinct applications.

Application controls include the following programmed procedures within application software:

1. input controls (data entry)
    (a) authorization
    (b) validation
    (c) error notification and correction
2. processing controls
3. output controls

Application controls consist of the devices in place over each independent computer system that make certain that authorized data is completely and accurately processed. They are designed to prevent, detect, and correct errors and irregularities as transactions flow through the business system. They guaranteed that the transactions and programs are protected;

the systems can continue processing after some business disruption, all transactions are adjusted and explained for when errors occur, and the system processes data in an efficient manner.

Electronic data interchange, voice response, and expert systems are types of applications that may necessitate certain controls in addition to common application controls. When an organization decides to purchase or develop an application, organization personnel must make sure the application contains sufficient application controls for:

1. input controls
2. processing controls
3. output controls

Input controls make sure the entire and accurate recording of authorized transactions by only approved users; detect rejected, suspended, and duplicate items; and make sure resubmission of rejected and suspended items. Examples of input controls are error listings, field checks, limit checks, self-checking digits, sequence checks, validity checks, key verification, matching, and completeness checks.

Processing controls make sure the complete and precise processing of authorized transactions. Examples of processing controls are run-to-run control totals, posting checks, end-of-file procedures, concurrency controls, control files, and audit trails.

Output controls make certain that a inclusive and precise audit trail of the results of processing is conveyed to proper people for review. Examples of output controls are listings of master file changes, error listings, distribution registers, and reviews of output.

If an organization has applications that are essential to its success, then organizational personnel must make certain that application controls lessen input, processing, and output risks to tolerable levels.

The end-user department becomes accountable for segregation of duties within the department's information systems environment, backup and recovery procedures, program development and documentation controls, hardware controls, and access controls. If a department has end-user information systems that are essential to its success, then department personnel must ensure that application and general controls reduce information systems risks to reasonable levels.

INFORMATION AND COMMUNICATION

Information and communication are necessary in order to effect control. Information pertaining to an organization's plans, control environment, risks, control activities, and performance should require to be communicated up, down, and across an organization. Reliable and relevant information from both internal and external sources ought to be identified, captured, processed, and communicated to the individuals who require it; in a form and timeframe that is constructive. Information systems generate reports, include operational, financial, and compliance-related information that makes it possible to operate and control an organization.

Information and communication systems can be formal or informal. Formal information and communication systems can range from complex computer technology to straightforward staff meetings. These systems should offer input and feedback data relative to operations, financial reporting, and compliance objectives; such systems are vital to an organization's success.

When considering internal control biometric systems over a significant activity (or process), the key questions to ask about information and communication are as follows:

a.   Does the department receive the information it needs from internal and external sources in a form and timeframe that is useful?

b.   Does the department receive information that signals it to internal or external risks (*e.g.*, legislative, regulatory, and developments)?

c.   Does the department receive information that measures its performance-information that informs the department whether it is achieving its operations, financial reporting, and compliance objectives?

d.   Does the department identify, capture, process, and communicate the information that others need (e.g., information utilized by customers or suppliers) in a mode and timeframe that is practical?

e.   Does the department offer information to others that alarms them to internal or external risks?

f.   Does the department communicate effectively both internally and externally?

MONITORING

Monitoring is the evaluation of internal control performance over time. This procedure is achieved by ongoing monitoring activities and by distinct evaluations of internal control such as self-assessments, peer reviews, and internal audits. The rationale of monitoring is to ascertain whether internal control is satisfactorily designed, properly executed, and effective. Internal control is sufficiently designed and properly executed if all five internal control components (Control Environment, Risk Assessment, Control Activities, Information and Communication, and Monitoring) are at hand and functioning as designed.

Internal control is efficient if management and interested stakeholders have reasonable assurance that:

1. They understand the degree to which operations objectives are being achieved.
2. Published financial statements are being organized reliably.
3. Applicable laws and regulations are being accumulated.

Although internal control is a process, its effectiveness is an assessment of the condition of the process at one or more points in time. Similar to control activities, monitoring assists to ensure that control activities and other planned actions to effect internal control are carried out properly and in a timely manner and that the end result is effective internal control.

Ongoing monitoring activities comprises of various management and supervisory activities that evaluate and improve the design, execution, and effectiveness of internal control. On the other hand, separate evaluations such as self-assessments and internal audits, are periodic evaluations of internal control components resulting in a formal report on internal control.

Management's role in an internal control biometrics system is essential to its effectiveness. Similarly to managers, auditors do not have to examine every single piece of information to conclude that the controls are functioning and should focus their monitoring activities in high-risk areas. The use of spot checks of transactions or basic sampling techniques can offer a reasonable level of assurance that the controls are carried out as intended.

CHAPTER 2

DECISION-MAKING TECHNIQUES IN AUDITING AND BIOMETRICS

"The essence of ultimate decisions remains impenetrable to the observer - often, indeed to the decider himself . . ."

—(John F. Kennedy, cited in Sorensen, Theodore C. 1963. Decision Making in the White House: The Olive Branch and the Arrows. New York).

Biometrics technology provides a more robust level of security and protection achieved in the identification component of access control, ID, and verification programs.

A security system can implement three different types of authentication:

1. Something you know such as a password, PIN, or piece of personal information (such as your mother's maiden name).
2. Something you have similar to a card key, smart card, or token (e.g., security identification card); and/or
3. Something you are such as a biometric.

For the most part of the three types, a biometric is the most secure and convenient authentication tool. It cannot be borrowed, stolen, or forgotten,

Biometric and Auditing Issues Addressed in a Throughput Model, pp. 37–54
Copyright © 2012 by Information Age Publishing
All rights of reproduction in any form reserved.

and forging one is basically impossible. This robustness is due to the fact that biometrics measures a person's unique physical or behavioral characteristics in order to recognize or authenticate his or her identity.

The term "biometrics" is drawn from the meaning of measuring biological characteristics. For purposes of this book, biometrics is used to generally describe the art and science of capturing an individual's characteristic feature, or trait, for subsequent use in a system or subsystem designed for automated human identification or recognition. As in so many other disciplines, advances in computer technology also accelerated the capabilities and quality of biometric technology. In studying its potential and considering particular applications for use, it is essential to recognize the value of its substantive qualities and inherent limitations.

There is no equivalent alternate for biometrics in the automated individual identification function, and any claim to the contrary, including those who assert we can rely on "something we have" or "something we know" without biometrics, should be viewed with great skepticism.

In terms of safeguarding assets for stronger internal control systems, biometrics are here to stay as the preeminent component of an automated identification program. In addition, organizations' internal control systems have hardly begun to scratch the surface in responding to the need for the ultimate measure and validation of our unique individual nature.

Automated methods of recognizing a person based on a biological or behavioral characteristic is the basic tenet underlying biometrics. Authentication (or verification) biometrics makes sure you are who you claim to be. In general, this sort of system requires two informational sources: (1) a depiction of one's identity, for example, user name to retrieve your biometric template implanted inside of it and (2) one's biometric information, such as your finger to create one's fingerprint template.

In general, identification is a much more demanding problem since it involves 1:N matching compared to 1:1 matching for verification. Verification (*Am I who I claim I am?*) requires substantiating or rejecting a person's *claimed identity*. Whereas, in identification, the system has to recognize a person (*Who am I?*) from a list of N users in the template database (see Tabe 2.1).

Table 2.1.   Recognition: Identification versus Verification of Individuals

Identification	*Verification*
Who is this PERSON?	Is this PERSON who she says she is?
1:N	1:1
Databank connected to personal information	No Databank
Overt or Covert	Overt

Identification and verification of individuals are crucial to eradicating threats to national security and public safety, and securing business transactions. As technology advances and public policy debates continue over the strengths and weaknesses of national identity programs, the state of the identity management industry continues to develop and transform. Specific to biometric tools, increased attention to homeland security, for example, has spurred significant growth in biometrics.

As a "contemporary tool," biometrics has been around since the 1960s. Biometric authentication is the "automatic," "real-time," "nonforensic" subset of the broader field of human identification. People recognize each other according to their mixture of characteristics. For instance, friends, family, and coworkers recognize each other by faces and voices.

A biometric internal control system is basically a pattern recognition system that recognizes an individual by comparing the binary code of a distinctively specific biological or physical characteristic with the binary code of the stored characteristic. Samples are taken from people in order to determine if there is match to biometric references previously taken from known individuals. The internal control system then put into operation a specific mathematical algorithm to the sample and alters it into a binary code and then contrasts it to the template sample to determine if the person can be recognized.

In terms of accessing through a strong internal control system, an individual applying for access will be asked to submit a sample and (often, but not always) claim an "identity" or "oneness of source" with a template previously stored. If the acquired sample is satisfactorily comparable to the claimed stored template, the access authorizations for the template can be verified and applied to the individual seeking access. A reference model or reference containing the biometric attributes of individuals is collected in the internal control system (generally after data compression) by recording their characteristics. These characteristics may be obtained several times during enrollment in order to get a reference profile that matches up most with reality.

PERCEPTION AND JUDGMENT USE OF BIOMETRICS

Several key considerations need to be addressed before a decision is made to design, develop, and implement biometrics into an internal control security system. Therefore, the *Throughput Model* is introduced, which separates the decision-making process into its four main parts: *perception* (*P*), *information* (*I*), *judgment* (*J*) and *decision choice* (*D*).

In the *Throughput Model*, perception (in Figure 2.1) entails a phase of framing and editing (i.e., perception), followed by judgment (in Figure 2.1) which is a phase of evaluation and analysis. The first phase consists of a

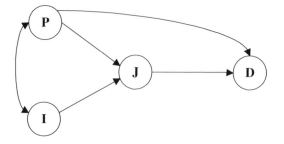

Figure 2.1. Throughput modeling of individuals' decision processes diagram.
P = perception, I = information, J = judgment, and D = decision choice

preliminary analysis of the decision problem, which frames the outcomes. Framing is part of the editing or screening process (coding) in which problem presentation is impacted by the manner in which, for example, an investment or loan is presented as well as by expectancies of a person. Thus, perception provides a screening, which is a special case of sorting and categorizing. The target or information (in Figure 2.1) is evaluated by categorizing its similarities and its dissimilarities to standards or templates. Further screening is based upon evaluation of a particular kind of dissimilarity or incompatibility between the characteristics of an option and internally or externally criteria.

In the second phase, the framed prospects are evaluated (judgment), and the prospect is accepted or rejected. Individuals' perceptual apparatus is attuned to the evaluation of changes or differences based upon information sources. It follows that individuals' perception and judgment are crucial in evaluating or predicting events when making a decision choice. Understanding decision-making processes requires an understanding of these two different processes and the ways in which the integration between them shapes peoples' cognitive processes.

Figure 2.1 illustrates how the process of an individual's decision choice is made. If perceived causality is an important determinant of how an individual represents a problem and uses the information, it is necessary to know what determines the perception of causality in the Throughput Model. Since information typically is processed subjectively by individuals, it is interdependent with perception in the model. The situational information and the person's prior expectations or beliefs about the information are relevant to perceiving the degree of covariation between them. Both of these information sources jointly determine covariation perception. Ignoring covariation perception may lead to conceptual difficulties in understanding and interpreting results. The execution of a person's decision choice may be made ambiguous and difficult due to redundancy of information (i.e., prior expectation of information). In particular, the fact that information sources are related not only to perceptions but to each other, as well, means that the role of interdependency of perception and information should be considered in a model. For example, individuals' perceptions result from an integration of diverse pieces of information. The interdependency and redundancy of perceptual effects and presented information have important effects on the kinds of judgment and decision choice strategies individuals use.

In the Throughput Model, information also affects judgment. For example, information stored in memory affects individuals' evaluations of framed prospects. Typically, before a person can make a decision choice, that person encodes the information and develops a representation for the problem. Finally, perception and judgment can affect decision choice. That is, both automatic, perception-like heuristics and more deliberate information processing strategies (judgment) are involved in most decision choices. Errors, biases, and context-dependent heuristics may result from cognitive mechanisms of which individuals are largely unaware, and these may have a direct impact on decision choice (Rodgers, 1997; 2006). The strategies of judgment that influence decision choice are under a person's deliberate control. Finally, the Throughput Model posits feedback loops from the interaction of perception and information, which allows the perceptual processes to update and discharge concepts that are inappropriate for future decision making. This interactive loop permits the modeling of learning effects; that is, the changes in knowledge bases and decision strategies.

At their most basic level, biometric technologies are similar to people's perceptual processes in that its pattern recognition systems use either image-acquisition devices, such as scanners or cameras in the case of fingerprint or iris recognition technologies. For example, sound or movement acquisition devices (microphones or platens in the case of voice recognition or signature recognition technologies) use to collect the biometric patterns or characteristics.

The implementation of biometrics in an organization's internal control system has major implications regarding privacy issues that pertain to interacting parties. Although the U.S. Constitution does not overtly indicate that "privacy" is an individual right, interpretation of the First, Third, Fourth, Fifth, Ninth, and Fourteenth amendments by the Supreme Court support privacy as a constitutional right. This right extends to informational, physical, decisional, and communications privacy.

Informational privacy and physical privacy symbolize the two most principal areas. Informational privacy allows individuals to be in command of their own personal data. While it may be open to question whether a biometric is personal data, biometrics is often associated with other information that is personal data. For that reason, biometrics is organized under the informational privacy category, which is the freedom to control access to information about oneself. Physical privacy take into consideration the right to control access to one's body and personal space, which would perhaps consist of the right to be in charge of access to one's biometric information. The two other forms of privacy rights acknowledged by the courts are decisional privacy and communications privacy, which represent the freedom to make choices in personal matters and freedom to write or speak without being burdened. These two privacy rights could also influence the use of biometrics, but to a much lesser degree.

Privacy concerns become more prominent when it comes to utilizing biometric internal control systems in private, consumer-facing applications. Biometric data are separate and different from personal information and templates (a mathematical representation of biometric data) have been resilient to being reverse-engineered to reconstruct this information. Primarily due to these inherent attributes, biometrics is a constructive way to further secure privacy and discourage identity theft; however, its application must be cautiously designed to attain that objective. For example, biometrics can be implemented for computer and network access control purposes, thereby impeding unauthorized personnel from acquiring access to sensitive business and personal information. With the improvement in technology and decrease in prices, the use of biometrics can be expected to increase at a fast rate for internal control purposes.

Organizations are seeking ways to increase the levels of accountability and security among employees, suppliers, partners, and customers. The most effective way to do this is to centralize identity management functions in a single location whereby it can be effectively managed and the suitable level of trust can be maintained in the authentication process. Biometrics impart one of the most secure and effective means of authenticating a person, whether through the biometric itself or in combination with a PIN, password, or other token. Designed properly, biometric identity management addresses the proper management of biometric identities, particularly for large-scale enrollment (database) populations.

FOUR STAGES OF THE THROUGHPUT MODEL

This section depicts each of the four primary concepts of perception, information, judgment, and decision choice relationship with internal control biometrics systems.

Perpetual Processes

Individuals' perceptual frames are diverse and are subject to many barriers, theories, concepts, and practices that stem from the relative culture (i.e., stigma, dignity or heritage) and experiences/ training (i.e., religion or philosophical) of the international community. The successful utilization of an internal control biometrics system in part depends on how individuals relate to this technology. That is, people may feel uneasy working with biometric technology that they have to touch (e.g., fingerprints, hand geometry), or feel that their privacy has been invaded due to the closeness of the tool (e.g., retina scan). Therefore, the foremost consideration in the implementation of an internal control biometrics system involves examining the relationship of people, processes (information examined), and technology (biometrics tools). People inability to understand the security aspect of biometrics may make them skeptical of the technology. The perceived benefits, levels of comfort, and acceptance of biometrics can also change depending on the context. Hence, apparent benefits and lows risks may lead to greater perceptions of usability and higher acceptance opinions of biometrics than situations where there are minimum benefits and high risks.

One of the prime purposes of any internal control biometrics system is keeping under control of people into or out of protected areas, such as physical buildings, information systems, and a nation. Individuals' security perceptions are influenced by three fundamental ways: (1) by something they know, (2) something they have, or (3) something they are. People and systems regularly use these methods to identify individuals in everyday life. For example, members of a neighborhood typically perceive one another by how they look, how their voices sound or by something they are.

Technology such as automated teller machines (ATM) identifies customers from their presentation of a bank card, something they have by their entering a personal identification number (PIN) or something they know. Another example of utilizing something you have is employing keys to enter a locked building. More secure internal control biometrics systems may combine two or more of these tools.

Perceived security concerns need to be balanced with sensible cost and operational deliberations as well as political and economic interests. A throughput modeling approach can assist organizations to identify and address security concerns. As organizations consider the development of internal control biometrics systems, they need to define what the mission goals of this system will be and develop the concept of operations that will exemplify the people, process, and technologies required to obtain these goals. Addressing these issues will better provide the perceived role of biometric tools in the prevention of fraud and safeguarding assets. If these details are not resolved, the estimated cost and performance of the resulting system will be at risk.

In summary, the perceived use of an internal control biometrics system includes:

a. Decisions that must be made on how the technology will be used.

b. A detailed cost-benefit analysis must be conducted to determine that the benefits gained from a system outweigh the costs.

   c.   A trade-off analysis must be conducted between the increased security, the usefulness biometrics would provide, and the effect on areas such as privacy and convenience.

Information

The information regarding biometric tools is to assist controlled access to applications, networks, personal computers (PCs), and physical facilities. An internal control biometrics system is fundamentally a procedure of ascertaining an individual's identity by comparing the binary code of a distinctively specific biological or physical characteristic with the binary code of an electronically stored characteristic called a biometric. The critical aspect for putting into operation an internal control biometrics system is that it cannot be infiltrated by hackers. That is, it cannot be shared, lost, or guessed. That is, an internal control biometrics system is an effective way to replace the customary password-based authentication system. While there are a range of potential biometrics tools, at least 15 biometric authentication technologies have been deployed or pilot-tested in applications in the public and private sectors and are grouped into two as given (Rodgers, 2010) below.

- Contact Biometric Technologies
  - fingerprint
  - palm print
  - hand geometry
  - vein patterns
  - DNA
  - dynamic signature verification
  - keystroke dynamics

- Contactless Biometric Technologies
  - Iris scan
  - Retinal scan
  - facial recognition
  - facial thermography
  - ear recognition
  - body odor recognition
  - speaker recognition
  - gait

Contact biometric technologies

A biometric tool requires a person to make direct contact with an electronic device (scanner) or object and is described as a contact biometric. Given that the very nature of a contact biometric is that an individual aspires admission is obligated to make direct contact with an electronic device for the purpose of attaining logical or physical access. Due to the intrinsic need of an individual not to make direct contact, many people have come to deem a contact biometric to be a tool that trespasses on personal space and to be alarming to personal privacy.

Finger print.   A fingerprint consists of several ridges and valleys on the surface of the finger. Ridges are the upper skin layer parts of the finger and valleys are the lower portions. The ridges form the minutia points: ridge endings (where a ridge end) and ridge bifurcations (where a ridge splits in two). The fingerprint biometric tool is an automated digital version of the old ink-and-paper technique put into practice by law enforcement agencies. The biometric device necessitates users placing their finger on a platen for the print to be read. The minutiae are then extracted by the vendor's algorithm, which in addition makes a fingerprint pattern analysis. With the arrival of computing and scanning technology it is much simpler to scan and store fingerprint information and assign that information to people by the use of name, age, and other biometric data. Fingerprint biometrics tools have three primary application parts: large-scale Automated Finger Imaging Systems (AFIS) generally used for law enforcement purposes, fraud prevention in entitlement programs, and physical and computer access.

Palm print.   Similar to fingerprints, palms of hands have epidermal ridges, considered to provide a friction surface to assist with gripping and object of surface. The biometric uses of palm prints uses ridge patterns to identify a person. Comparable in many aspects to fingerprint identification, palm print identification systems measure and compare ridges, lines and minutiae located on the palm. Each palm print is unique to the individual and the mathematical formulas are fairly easy to store in a large database.

Hand geometry.   Hand geometry is a biometric that classifies users by the shape of their hands. Its readers measure an individual's hand along many dimensions and contrast those measurements to measurements situated in a file. This technique takes the hand spatial geometry on the sensor's surface and implements guiding poles between the fingers to appropriately place the hand and initiate the reading. Hand geometry is very dependable in conjunction with other identification methods, such as identification cards or personal identification numbers. Hand geometry is a highly developed technology that has been methodically field-tested and is without nuisance accepted by users.

Vein patterns.   Each person has a distinct set of blood veins in his/her hand. Veins are very complicated therefore contain a wealth of different features that help to identify a person. In addition, it will not vary during an individual's lifetime. It is a very secure method of authentication since the blood vein pattern lies under the skin. This makes it almost unattainable for others to read or copy.

A person's vein pattern image is depicted by radiating the hand with near-infrared rays. The reflection technique illuminates the palm implementing an infrared ray and captures the light given off by the region after diffusion through the palm. The deoxidized hemoglobin in the vein vessels absorbs the infrared ray, thereby decreasing the reflection rate and causing the veins to appear as a black pattern. This vein pattern is then confirmed against a preregistered pattern to authenticate the person.

There are distinct types of vein recognition technology, which include finger vein, wrist vein, palm, and backhand vein recognition. Security systems, log-in control, healthcare, and banking and financial services presently implement the vein biometric system.

DNA.   Deoxyribonucleic acid (DNA) Biometrics could be the most exact form of identifying any given individual. Each individual has 23 pairs of chromosomes that contain their DNA blueprint. Each pair has one member from the person's mother and one from the father. Since DNA is the structure that defines who we are physically and intellectually, it is unlikely that any other individual will have the same exact set of genes. There are different procedures of collecting an individual's DNA. Some are collected by gaining a strand of hair, a mouth swab, or blood work.

The essential problems surrounding DNA biometrics is that it is not a quick process to identify someone by their DNA. The process is also a very expensive procedure.

The current uses of DNA technology is generally to compare DNA between suspects 1 and suspect 2 against DNA discover at a crime scene, in law enforcement and court. Further, DNA is utilized in paternity testing, and identification of a missing person.

Retinal scan.   The retinal scan uses a low-intensity light source and a delicate sensor to scan the pattern of blood vessels at the back of the retina, a pattern unique to each individual. This tool is considered a "contact biometric tool" since an individual must place his/her head against a machine. In addition, during the retinal scan, the person must remove glasses, stare at a specific point, and hold their head still for the 10–15 s against the machine until the scan is complete.

The retina scan maps the different patterns of an individual's retina. The blood vessels within the retina absorb light more readily than the surrounding tissue and are easily identified with appropriate lighting. A retinal scan is performed by casting an undetectable ray of low-energy infrared light into a person's eye as they look through the scanner's eyepiece. This beam of light outlines a circular path on the retina. Since retinal blood vessels are more sensitive to light than the rest of the eye, the amount of reflection fluctuates. The outcomes of the retina scan are converted to computer code and stored in a database.

A person retina is a thin tissue composed of neural cells that is located in the posterior portion of the eye. Due to its complex capillaries structure that supplies the retina with blood, each individual's retina is distinct. The network of blood vessels in the retina is very complex whereby identical twins do not share comparable patterns. A retinal scan is very difficult to deceive since no technology exists that allows the imitation of a human retina. Further, the retina of a deceased person decays too rapidly to be used to fraudulently bypass a retinal scan.

Although retinal patterns may be altered in cases of diabetes, glaucoma, retinal degenerative disorders or cataracts, the retina typically remains unchanged from birth until death. Due to its distinct and unchanging nature, the retina appears to be a very accurate and reliable biometric.

Dynamic signature verification.   Signature biometrics procedures are done by analyzing the stroke order, the pressure applied, and the speed. In addition, this tool examines the time that the stylus is in and out of contact with the "paper"; the total time taken to make the signature; and where the stylus is raised from and lowered onto the "paper." The signature image is also analyzed. A scanner is implemented to record the manner in which an individual writes on tablet. Yet, another method of capturing a signature biometric is by utilizing ultrasonic sensing. Once the signature is captured, it is confirmed against the database.

Online signature verification is presently used by some organizations to confirm an accurate signature from a false one. Camera verification is another present implementation of signature biometrics. Individuals utilize signature biometrics everyday when they sign their names to make a purchase. Contract execution, access to controlled documents, and acknowledgement of services are some of the more popular and current utilization of signature biometrics.

Keystroke dynamics.   Keystroke dynamics is an automated biometric identification tool that examines the way in which a person types on a keyboard. This tool inspects such dynamics as speed and pressure, the total time of typing a specific password, and the time a user takes between hitting certain keys. Keystroke dynamics' algorithms are still being developed in order to make better robustness and distinctiveness. Useful promising applications of this tool comprised authenticating computer access, where this biometric could be employed to substantiate the computer user's identity continuously.

The behavioral biometric of keystroke dynamics implements the style and rhythm in which an individual types characters on a keyboard or keypad. The keystroke rhythms of a person are measured to develop a distinctive biometric template of the users typing pattern for future authentication. Raw measurements accessible from most every keyboard can be recorded to ascertain "dwell time" (the time a key pressed) and "flight time" (the time between "key down" and the next "key down" and the time between "key up" and the next "key up"). The recorded keystroke timing data is then handled through a distinctive neural algorithm, which establishes a primary pattern for future comparison.

While the user is typing a phrase with the keyboard, the internal control biometrics system records the timing of the typing. This typically has to be done a number of times in order to confirm that the keystrokes are distinctive. It is compared against the database to confirm and identify the user.

Contactless biometric technologies

A contactless biometric can either come in the mold of a passive (biometric tool continuously monitors for the correct activation frequency) or active (user commences activation at will) biometric. In either method, authentication of the user biometric should not take place until the person voluntarily consents to present the biometric for sampling. A contactless biometric can be used to validate a person identity and offers at least two fundamentals that contact biometric technologies cannot match imitate. A contactless biometric is one that does not necessitate disagreeable contact in order to take out the essential data sample of the biological characteristic. Consequently, a contactless biometric is most flexible to people of dissimilar ability levels.

Facial recognition.   Facial recognition registers the spatial geometry of distinguishing facial appearance. Different vendors utilize distinctive methods of facial recognition, however, all focus on measures of key features. Facial recognition tools can come across performance problems resulting from such aspects as no obliging behavior of the user, lighting, and other environmental variables. Facial recognition has been implemented in projects to identify card counters in casinos, shoplifters in stores, criminals in targeted urban areas, and terrorists overseas.

Ear.   It is based on the distinctive shape of each individual's ears and the structure of the largely cartilaginous, projecting portion of the outer ear.

It is known from prior art that the acoustical properties of the ear can be used to identify people uniquely. This kind of biometric feature cannot easily be copied, and can easily be implemented in a mobile phone for remote identification, thus replacing conventional, less reliable methods of identification such as the PIN code. In the case of acoustic ear canal biometrics, what is of interest is the topology of the ear canal, which is unique for every human. An incoming sound signal is reflected and otherwise modified by the ear canal to give an aurally reflected signal which exits the ear canal.

A sound signal is directed into the ear of a user, and the frequency response of the ear canal is measured and analyzed to extract a feature vector unique to this user. However, since the microphone used to detect the response from the ear canal must also pick up any surrounding sound signals, such a measurement system is particularly prone to error owing to background noise. These unwanted background noise signals can really only be excluded from the measurement described by, for example, enclosing the microphone and the ear in headphones of a size large enough to encompass the entire ear. Since such headphones are generally cumbersome to use and awkward to transport, they are impractical for frequent use, and unsuited to user identification for applications such as telephone banking, telephone brokerage, etc., which a user generally wishes to carry out with a mobile phone, whether at home or underway.

Odor.   The body odor biometrics is based on the fact that virtually each human smell is unique. The smell is captured by sensors that are capable to obtain the odor from nonintrusive parts of the body such as the back of the hand. Methods of capturing a person's smell are being explored by Mastiff Electronic Systems. Each human smell is made up of chemicals known as volatiles. They are extracted by the system and converted into a template.

The use of body odor sensors brings up the privacy issue as the body odor carries a significant amount of sensitive personal information. It is possible to diagnose some diseases or activities in the last hours (like sex, for example) by analyzing the body odor.

Speaker recognition.   Voice or speaker recognition uses vocal features to identify people by means of a pass-phrase. Voice recognition can be influenced by such environmental factors as background noise. Moreover, it is unclear whether the tools essentially recognize the voice or just the pronunciation of the pass-phrase (password) utilized. This technology has been the center of considerable efforts on the part of the telecommunications industry and National Security Agency (NSA), which maintain working on improving reliability. A telephone or microphone can operate as a sensor that makes it a comparatively inexpensive and easily deployable tool.

There is a difference between *speaker recognition* (recognizing **who** is speaking) and *speech recognition* (recognizing **what** is being said). These two terms are commonly confused, as is *voice recognition*. Voice recognition is a synonym for speaker, and accordingly not speech recognition.

Speaker recognition has a history dating back some four decades, where the output of several analog filters was averaged in due course for matching. Speaker recognition implements the acoustic characteristics of speech that have been found to differ between people. These acoustic patterns reveal both anatomy (e.g., size and shape of the throat and mouth) and learned behavioral patterns (e.g., voice pitch, speaking style). This amalgamation of learned patterns into the voice templates (the latter called "*voiceprints*") has earned speaker recognition its classification as a "behavioral biometric."

Iris scan.   Iris scanning measures the iris pattern in the colored part of the eye, though the iris color has nothing to do with the biometric. Iris patterns are shaped indiscriminately. Consequently, the iris patterns in the left and right eyes are distinctive. Iris scanning can be implemented promptly for both identification and verification.

Iris recognition is a method of biometric authentication that utilizes pattern recognition procedures established on high-resolution images of the irides of a person's eyes. Iris recognition uses camera technology, and subtle infrared illumination (IR) to reduce specular reflection from the convex cornea to create images of the detail-rich, intricate structures of the iris. These distinctive structures converted into digital templates, provide mathematical representations of the iris that yield unambiguous positive identification of an individual.

Gait.   Gait biometrics identifies a person by the way the walk, run, or any other type of motion of the legs. A person's gait is the way in which they move on their feet. Gait biometrics can be used to identify everything from the length and thickness of individuals' legs to the stride of their step. Unlike some other, more researched and identifiable methods of biometrics, gait biometric technology faces the difficulty of identifying not only a particular body part but a motion (World Information, 2003).

At Georgia Tech University, professors and students are developing a system that will be able to recognize a persons gait by radar signals. This Doppler effect is 80–95% effective in identifying an individual. Research Engineer Bill Marshall explains that they can decode radio signals reflecting of a person's walking stride, as they walk toward the signal. This signal pattern is converted to an individual's audio signature, which can be catalogued for later use. Marshall is sure to include that audio signals, decoded from an individual's gait, are not unique to a particular person. Any given number of people may have the same audio signature, but unlike the unique DNA or finger prints, gait biometrics can catalog an individual without them being aware that they were ever being observed.

Gait biometrics would be particularly beneficial in identifying criminal suspects. Police could scan a large crowd for a suspect without them knowing they were on to them. Gait biometrics can also be used to identify shoplifters, particularly 'pregnant' women. Women pretending to be pregnant will walk differently then women who are actually pregnant. This would be a large advancement in technology if introduced to common retail stores.

Some sources recognize what gait biometrics says it can do, but doubts its ability to perform. A gait system can easily be deceived because walking patterns can be sometimes be altered. Skeptics also doubt gait biometrics ability to perform in real-life scenarios, such as airports and large crowds. Regardless of what critics say, gait biometrics will have to prove its capabilities in action.

Judgment

Effective use of perception and information provides for a comprehensive understanding of the value of the internal control systems and information being assessed. Judgment can be expressed in terms of the degree of perception of the systems and information relative to integrity, confidentiality, availability, authenticity, and nonrepudiation.

Integrity indicates that information must be protected from unauthorized, unanticipated, or unintentional modification. This includes, but is not limited to:

1. Confidentiality relating to the information that requires protection from unauthorized disclosure.
2. Authenticity, which asserts that a third party must be able to confirm that the content of a message has not been changed in transit.
3. Nonrepudiation that involves the origin or the receipt of a specific message verifiable by a third party.
4. Accountability relates to a security goal that produces the necessity for decision choices of an organization to be traced uniquely to that organization.
5. Availability involves the information technology resource (system or data) that should be available on a timely basis to meet mission requirements or to avoid substantial losses. Availability also includes ascertaining that resources are implemented only for intended purposes.

When determining the value, consider any laws, regulations, or policies that establish specific requirements for integrity, confidentiality, authenticity, availability, and nonrepudiation of data and information in the system.

The "judgment" stage considers the perception and information processed by the internal control biometrics systems associated with the need for security and safeguarding of assets measures. Both the perceived risks and the information processed should relate to each of the three basic protection requirements of *confidentiality*, *integrity*, and *availability*. In addition, it is instrumental to categorize the internal control biometrics systems or group of systems by sensitivity level. Three examples of such categories for sensitive information are described below:

1. High—extremely grave injury accrues to organizations's assets (e.g., patents, software, procedures, etc.) if the information is compromised; could cause major financial loss or require legal action for correction.
2. Medium—serious damage accrues to organization's interests if the information is compromised; could cause significant financial loss or require legal action for correction.
3. Low—injury accrues to organization's interests if the information is compromised; would cause only minor financial loss or require only administrative action for correction.

For example, an internal control biometrics system and its information may require a high degree of integrity and availability, yet have no need for confidentiality.

Regardless of the method used, management is responsible for determining the sensitivity of the internal control biometrics system and information. The sensitivity should be considered as each control objective relates to security and safeguarding of assets. The determination for lesser or more stringent protection should be made due to either the sensitivity of the data and operations affected or because there are compensating controls that lessen the need for this particular control methods. It should be noted that the system security plan contains supporting documentation as to why the specific control has or has not been implemented.

Decision Choice

Decision choices are formulated on perception and information inputs as well as the assessment (judgment) of cost, risk, and mission impact on people, processes and technology.

The consideration of a strong internal control biometric system for security and safeguarding of assets should be implemented and enforced as an ongoing agenda to identify and institutionalize best practices of the organization. Active support from senior management is necessary for the success of internal control biometrics systems. Decisions choices based on the internal control biometrics systems should include at least:

a.   Improving security program,

b.   Improving security program procedures,

c.   Improving or refining security controls,

d.   Adding security controls,

e.   Integrating security within existing and evolving information technology architecture, and

f.   Improving organizational mission processes and risk management activities.

The decision choice stage results from a continuous improvement and refinement agenda instilled within the organization. Understanding of organizational mission-related risks and its associated costs of reducing these risks are considered with a full range of implementation options to achieve maximum mission cost-effectiveness of security and safeguarding of assets measures. Organizations should be influence by selecting controls that offer the lowest cost implementation while offering adequate risk mitigation, versus high-cost implementation and low-risk mitigation.

CONCLUSIONS

In the *Throughput Model*, perception entails framing informational sources. The double-ended arrow connecting perception and information in Figure 2.1 represents this coherence relationship. Further, information and perception are interdependent because information is dependent on how individuals, influenced by their framing, interpret it and information can transformed individuals' frames. In the *first stage*, perception and information affect judgment; while in the *second stage* perception and judgment affect the decision choice. Judgment, the next step in the decision-making process, requires more analysis of the information and the perceptual processes. It is in the judgment stage where analytical tools and deeper insights are used for the interpretation of information.

Three key considerations need to be addressed before a decision choice is made to design, develop, and implement biometrics into an internal control biometric system:

1. Perception on how the technology will be implemented, and what is available (information).
2. A detailed cost-benefit analysis (judgment) must be conducted to determine that the benefits gained from a system outweigh the costs.
3. A decision choice must be conducted between the increased safe-guarding of assets/security issues, which the use of biometrics would provide, and the effect on areas such as performance, privacy and convenience.

In sum, biometric templates are collected in a database or on a smart card hardware and software, allowing for fast and real-time technologies. They all vary in performance, capabilities, unique limitations as well as operating methodologies. These characteristics of the attained samples are considered the most distinctive between users and the most stable for each user are extracted and encoded into a biometric reference or template that is a mathematical representation of an individual's biometric feature. These or other tokens are implemented for comparison when recognition is warranted. Biometric internal control systems are automated by decision making in identification situations. Different biometrics tools offer differ-ent features and benefits and are analyzed based on how and why they are being implemented. They all vary in infrastructure requirements, cost per-formance, capabilities, unique limitations, and operating methodologies.

REFERENCE

Rodgers, W. (2010). *E-commerce and biometric issues addressed in a Throughput Model.* Hauppauge, NY: Nova Publication, 2010.

CHAPTER 3

INTERNAL CONTROL BIOMETRICS SYSTEMS

As I have said, the first thing is to be honest with yourself. You can never have an impact on society if you have not changed yourself ... Great peacemakers are all people of integrity, of honesty, but humility.

—Nelson Mandela
South African Statesman—b 1918—Nobel Prize Winner 1993

Upholding effective internal controls is a basic element of financial management, mandated by both accounting guidelines and federal regulations. Biometrics is a promising technology that has the potential to augment the effectiveness of internal controls for organizations by strengthening control over access to assets and information systems, enhancing the reliability of financial data and ensuring greater compliance with laws and regulations.

The objectives of understanding internal controls are that:

1. Management is responsible for ensuring that internal controls are established, properly documented, maintained and adhered to in each unit, department or area of an organization.
2. Employees are responsible for compliance with internal controls.
3. Establishing, properly documenting, maintaining, and adhering to an organization's system of internal controls is essential.

Biometric and Auditing Issues Addressed in a Throughput Model, pp. 55–103
Copyright © 2012 by Information Age Publishing
All rights of reproduction in any form reserved.

Over time, controls may be expected to change to reflect changes in an organization's operating environment. An effective internal control system provides reasonable, but not absolute assurance for the reliability of financial information, the protection of assets, and the compliance with laws and regulations. Reasonable assurance is a concept that recognizes that internal control systems should be developed and employed to provide management with the suitable balance between risk of a specific organizational practice and the level of control required to ensure organizational objectives are met.

The cost of a control should not go beyond the benefit to be derived from it. The degree of control utilized is a matter of sound perceptual and judgmental processes. When organizational controls are found to have weaknesses, the following alternatives maybe employed:

1. increase supervision and monitoring,
2. introduce additional or compensating controls, and/or
3. accept the risk intrinsic with the control weakness (assuming management approval).

Verification is often referred to as 1:1 (one-to-one) matching. Verification systems can contain databases ranging from dozens to millions of enrolled templates but are always predicated on matching an individual's presented biometric against his or her reference template. Nearly all verification systems can render a match–no-match decision in less than a second. An example of a verification application system is one that requires employees to authenticate their claimed identities before granting them access to secure buildings or to computers.

In identification systems, the step after enrollment is to identify who the individual is. Unlike verification systems, no identifier is provided. To find a match, instead of locating and comparing the user's reference template in contrast to his or her presented biometric, the trial template is evaluated against the stored reference templates of all individuals enrolled in the system. Identification systems are referred to as 1:N (one-to-N, or one-to many) matching since a person's biometric is compared against many biometric templates in the system's database.

Essentially, there are two types of identification systems: positive and negative. Positive identification systems are designed to ensure that an individual's biometric is enrolled in the database. The expected result of a search is a match. A typical positive identification system controls access to a protected structure or secure computer is by checking anyone who seeks access against a databank of enrolled employees. The objective is to establish whether a user seeking access can be identified as having been enrolled in the system.

Negative identification systems are designed to ensure that an individual's biometric information is not present in a database. The expected result of a search is a nonmatch. Comparing an individual's biometric information in contrast to a databank of all who are registered in a health plan, for example, can ensure that this person is not "double dipping" by utilizing fraudulent documentation to register under multiple identities.

Another type of negative identification system is a watch list system. Such systems are designed to identify people on the watch list and alert authorities for proper action. For all other people, the system is to check that they are not on the watch list and permit them normal passage.

The individuals whose biometrics features are in the database in these systems may not have provided them voluntarily. For example, for a surveillance system, the biometric may be faces captured from mug shots provided by a law enforcement agency.

No match is ever perfect in either verification or identification system, since every time a biometric is captured, the template is likely to be distinctive. Consequently, internal control biometrics systems can be configured to make a match or no-match decision, based on a predefined number, referred to as a threshold, that institutes the satisfactory extent of similarity between the trial template and the enrolled reference template. After the comparison, a score representing the degree of similarity is produced, and this score is compared with the threshold to make a match or no-match decision choice. Depending on the setting of the threshold in identification systems, sometimes several reference templates can be considered matches to the trial template, with the improved scores corresponding to enhanced matches.

WHY USE INTERNAL CONTROL BIOMETRICS SYSTEMS?

Financial sector institutions have engaged a range of methods productively for many years to identify, verify, and authenticate new and continuing customers and their transactions. PIN and password protections and point-of-sale authorization procedures remain the most widely implemented applications for discouraging identity theft.

"Identity theft" is the stealing of personally identifying information of another person (e.g., a Social Security number or credit card account number) to commit fraud or theft. Children and the public have been victimized by crooks that reportedly paid money to hospital employees for every Social Security number the trusted workers provided. The workers stole information about child patients, which the fraudsters implemented to file fraudulent tax returns (Davis and Stevenson, 2004). In addition, thieves also have stolen patient information from pediatricians' offices to open credit card accounts under the children's identity, or to start a new life or build a new credit history (Davis, 2004).

American soldiers on active duty are at vulnerable as well. One explanation is that career officers tend to have very good credit histories, and they may earn the higher credit limits that appeal to thieves. If soldiers are absent from home on active duty, they may not be able to maintain and detect details to bank account statements, credit card statements, and other records that may divulge personal information or provide evidence of identity theft. When soldiers are abroad and has their identity stolen, the theft can cause severe troubles for family members back home. Concern over such family problems only heightens the anxiety a soldier in a combat environment already faces (Department of the Treasury, 2005).

Thieves have stolen information about individuals in order to reroute the victims' mail and attempt to take ownership of the victims' houses to sell or utilize for home-equity loans. Fraudsters also have instituted websites using the names of legitimate securities brokerage firms.

Victims frequently may not learn for weeks, months, or even years that someone has been utilizing information relating to them for financial gain since it may take a while before warning signs to become apparent. For example, identity theft may occur, by means of:

- theft and unauthorized use of a credit card, debit card, or ATM card;
- skimming of credit card account numbers from the magnetic stripe, by criminals serving customers in a retail business;
- impersonation of a lawful account holder or his representative, over the telephone or online, to attain account or other personal identifying information;
- "dumpster diving" to acquire account or other personal identifying information from discarded statements, bills, or solicitations;
- computer hacking of databases whereby personal identifying information or account numbers are amassed;
- eavesdropping and interception of an account number during transmission over phone lines or Internet;
- exploitation of information from credit reports; and
- mail theft of credit cards, modification of address forms, checks, or applications (Department of the Treasury, 2005).

Government and commercial enterprises are increasingly adopting internal control biometrics systems to address heightened security and safeguarding of assets requirements. Biometric tools provide an optimal security tool to protect against identity theft, unauthorized access to borders and restricted facilities, network systems and critical data. Moreover, several legislative acts, government mandates and compliance requirements are driving the demand for biometrics to be integrated into control systems.

Internal control biometrics systems are implemented not only at a data center/co-location facility, but also for laptop access. Fingerprints, palm prints, and vein analysis can provide access to critical information. Furthermore, retinal/iris scans and other facial recognition scans provide the credentials required to prevent forgery.

Sustaining effective internal controls is a primary element of management, required by both accounting guidelines and federal regulations. Biometrics is a promising technology that has the potential to enhance the effectiveness of internal controls for organizations by strengthening control over access to assets and information systems, improving the reliability of financial data and ensuring greater compliance with laws and regulations.

Frauds and misappropriation of assets cannot be completely eliminated; however, biometrics controls can be put in place in order to minimize these threats. The risk of theft of assets can be mitigated with the introduction of biometric controls as part of the internal control system. Biometrics uniquely identifies an individual by comparing distinctive biometrics features of a person with a previously created digital template of those features and clearly rejects unauthorized users. For example, implementing biometric authentication in an organization such as a USB fingerprint scanner connected to desktops can store passwords on personal computers. For user authentication, the user would scan his or her finger and the software (that comes with biometric device) would translate his or her finger print into a password that would be sent across the network to server.

The term biometrics covers a wide range of tools that can be implemented to confirm identity by measuring and analyzing human characteristics. This technique relies on attributes of the individual instead of things the individual may have or know. Different methods can be utilized to obtain a person password. Some of these methods include: looking under the keyboard, calling for a password reset, using password sniffers and crackers, and looking over an employee's shoulder (i.e., shoulder surfing). Management must be sure that no one has been able to make improper changes.

Biometrics can be used for much more than augmenting or replacing passwords. Implementing biometrics can make possible to document when management and employees saw and when they saw it in an organization setting. For example, while the focus of firewalls was keeping unauthorized users from destroying or stealing data, the information security issues need to be quite different. Organizations and external auditors ought to document which authorized users of segments of an internal control system attempted to aggregate or modify data.

Lastly, some people, especially those with disabilities may have problems with contact biometrics. Not because they do not want to use it, but because they endure a disability that either prevents them from maneuvering into a position that will allow them to make use the biometric or because the internal control biometrics system is not adaptable to the user. For example, if the user is blind, a voice biometric tool may be more suitable.

SECURITY ISSUES

The most widespread standardized encryption method used to protect an organization's infrastructure is the Public Key Infrastructure (PKI) approach. This routine comprises two keys with a binary string ranging in size from 1024-bits to 2048-bits, the first key is a public key (widely known) and the second key is a private key (only known by the owner). In spite of this, the PKI must also be stored and inherently it too can become target to the same authentication limitation of a password, PIN, or token. In addition, it can be guessed, lost, stolen, shared, hacked, or thwarted; this is even further justification for an internal control biometrics system. For the reason of the technology industry configuration, making biometric security a characteristic of embedded systems, such as cellular phones, may be more straightforward than adding similar features to personal computers. Unlike the personal computer, the cell phone is a fixed-purpose apparatus. To integrate biometrics successfully, cell-phone developers need not put together support from nearly as many groups as PC-application developers must.

Securitizing an organization infrastructure, can be performed by implementing a smart card. A smart card is a portable device with an implanted central processing unit (CPU). The smart card can either be produced to look like a credit card, identification card, radio frequency identification (RFID), or a Personal Computer Memory Card International Association (PCMCIA) card. The smart card can be utilized to store data of all kinds; however, it is generally implemented to store encrypted data, human resources data, medical data, financial data, and biometric data (template).

Gaining access to a smart card can be performed by the use of a card reader, PCMCIA slot, or proximity reader. Quite a few internal control biometrics systems determine the identity of people that present themselves to the system. Typically, the identity is furnished to the system, often by presenting a machine-readable ID card, and then the system asked to verify. This technique is "one-to-one matching." Personal computers can conduct a one-to-one match in a few seconds. One-to-one matching differs considerably from one-to-many matching. In a system that stores a million sets of fingerprints, a one-to-many match requires contrasting the presented fingerprint with 10 million prints (1 million sets times 10 prints/set). Smart cards hold the fundamental essentials of a computer (interface, processor, and storage); hence, are very capable of achieving authentication operations on the card.

The function of performing authentication within the limits of the card is known as "Matching on the Card (MOC)". MOC is ideal for security since the biometric template, biometric sampling and associated algorithms do not leave the card. Therefore, it cannot be intercepted or spoofed by others. The problem with smart cards is the public-key infrastructure certificates built into the card does not resolve the issue of someone stealing the card or reproducing one. A TTP (Trusted Third Party) can be implemented to confirm the authenticity of a card by means of an encrypted MAC (Media Access Control).

Sarbanes-Oxley Act

The United States Congress passed the Sarbanes-Oxley Act of 2002 (SOX) in the wake of a myriad of corporate scandals. What these scandals had in common was skewed reporting of selected financial transactions. For instance, entities such as Enron, WorldCom, and Tyco covered up or distorted a range of questionable transactions, resulting in enormous losses to stakeholders and a crisis in investor confidence. The act aims to improve corporate governance and strengthen corporate accountability by:

a.   formalizing and intensifying internal checks and balances within corporations,
b.   establishing a range of new levels of control and sign-off designed to,
c.   ensure that financial reporting exercises full disclosure, and
d.   corporate governance is carried out with full transparency.

The Act covers a whole range of governance issues, many covering the types of trade that are allowed within an entity, with an emphasis upon keeping everything transparent. The enactment of SOX inserted legal obligations to diminish fraud from external auditors, corporate attorneys, directors, and managements of large companies. SOX applies to all public companies in the United States and international companies that have registered equity or debt securities with the Securities and Exchange Commission and the accounting firms that provide auditing services to them.

This Act also created the Public Company Accounting Oversight Board (PCAOB) for setting auditing standards for public companies. Smaller companies continue to utilize Statements on Auditing Standards from the American Institute of Certified Public Accountants (AICPA). Sections 302, 404 and 906 of the Sarbanes Oxley enhanced the responsibilities of corporate managements and of auditors with respect to fraud mitigation.

Section 302 mandates corporate responsibility for financial reporting and internal controls. It necessitates the chief executive officer (CEO) and the chief financial officer (CFO) to attest that they have reviewed the report for the periodic filing and that the financial statements and disclosures in all material aspects correctly embody the operational results and financial conditions of the company. [Sarbanes-Oxley Act Section 302. Retrieved September 2007 from http://www.sox-online.com/act_section_302.html]

Section 404 compels management's assessment of internal controls. It calls for each annual report filed with security exchange commission (SEC) to contain a report on its internal controls. This report should state management's responsibility to establish and maintain internal control procedures for financial reporting and also evaluate the effectiveness of these internal controls. A registered public accounting firm must evaluate management's assessment of their internal controls. [Sarbanes-Oxley Act Section 404. Retrieved September, 2007 from http://www.sox-online.com/act_section_404.html]

Section 906 amplifies corporate responsibility for financial reporting by involving the CEO and the CFO to certify financial statements filed with SEC. These certifications must maintain compliance with Securities Exchange Act and also state that all material aspects accurately represent the operational results and financial conditions of the company. [The Sarbanes-Oxley Act of 2002. Retrieved September, 2007 from http://www.sox-online.com/soxact.html#sec906]

To fulfill with the Sarbanes-Oxley Act, organizations need to improve documentation and internal controls for financial reporting. These internal controls should be tested and monitored to make financial reporting transparent. Unfortunately, the same old way of usernames and passwords are used for security. This is just a false impression of security. There are many methods to ascertain passwords, ranging from casual conversation to more advanced software which arrests passwords. If the password requirements become more complex, to enhance security people typically write down this password someplace so that they do not forget the complex password. Whoever has access to this written password is a security risk.

The Sarbanes-Oxley Act of 2002 and other compliance measures have augmented the need for service organizations to report on their internal controls. SAS 70 became the de facto standard for such reporting. However, Standards for Attestation Engagements No. 16 (SSAE 16) modified Statement on Auditing Standards, No. 70, Service Organizations (SAS 70) for attestation purposes. While SAS 70 was also implemented for service organization reporting in other countries, it remained a U.S. standard. To make available a global standard for service organization reporting, the International Auditing and Assurance Standards Board (IAASB) of the International Federation of Accountants (IFAC) developed the International Standard on Assurance Engagements No. 3402 (ISAE 3402).

For an audit, critical areas to review related to biometrics are as follows:

1. enrollment process for a new user,
2. accuracy and monitoring of the biometric device, and
3. termination of users.

During enrollment, a user's biometric template is generated in a database. There must be in place a documented process for adding and authorizing new users to the database. Documentation includes who may authorize access, and how much access to give the new employee.

The audit must determine the accuracy and monitoring of biometric usage. A review is conducted in terms of using the biometric device, as well as reviewing the logs to identify any unusual activity. For example, if a certain employee has entered the facility four times and there is no exit, then the device may not be working properly. Another example, involves the resignation of an employee. How do you know to delete the employee credentials from the system? Do Human Resources have a policy to notify management immediately when a person needs to be removed from the system. The internal control biometrics system should have a checklist of items/inventory to be returned when employee exits and the form should include a sign-off to indicate removal from the biometric device.

Management is obliged to provide a report on its internal controls. An independent auditor has to appraise management's assessment of its internal controls and provide a report. Hence, the external auditors now have added responsibility for fraud mitigation. Frauds cannot be entirely eradicated, but controls can be put in place to curtail frauds. An organization has to have stringent controls over the user's system access rights, limit access to sensitive data centered on user role, and observe who tried to access sensitive data. In its place of using a weak password control system, organizations can implement a user access authentication system with these characteristics: unique identification of each user and controls extending to the transaction and field levels.

While organizations require integrated data, individual users of computer systems should not be able to access data for which they lack authorizations. Biometrics can offer this solution. Biometrics implements particular characteristics of a person such as fingerprints, iris pattern, or facial recognition to uniquely identify an individual grant access for an authorized user and clearly reject unauthorized users.

There is a tendency to think of the internal control security of an application, in terms of technical security measures implemented by an information technology system that drives the application. Internal control security includes human and procedural measures, and physical and environmental security. Reliance upon solely on technology to provide security is not sufficient. Technology is in general unlikely to address the full spectrum of internal control security issues. Achieving security includes an understanding of people, processes and technology threats, as well as a risk management approach to implementing an appropriate collection of mutually supportive countermeasures. As a matter of course this will include technical and nontechnical elements.

People, processes and technology must work together as part of an overall security process. Weaknesses in any of these areas decrease the effectiveness of the internal control security process. The security process needs to depict the limitations in biometric tools. For instance, some individuals cannot enroll in a biometrics system. Likewise, errors sometimes occur during matching operations. Procedures need to be cultivated in order to handle these situations.

SOX Compliance Requirements for Management

The need for companies to ensure their internal controls has never been greater since SOX:

a. individuals expect the institutions they interact with to guarantee the security of their payments and the privacy of their personal and financial information;

b. organizations are looking to protect their operations, build trust with customers and decrease the risk of financial losses caused by events such as identity theft and financial fraud; and

c. governments are examining improved measures to ensure the security and privacy of their citizens, borders and infrastructure, while at the same time providing services in expedient and available venues.

To comply with the SOX, organizations must improve documentation and internal controls for financial reporting. These internal controls need to be examined and monitored in order to convey transparency in financial reporting. Management is mandated to issue a report on its internal controls. In addition, independent auditors have to assess management's judgment of its internal controls and provide a report. Hence, the external auditors now have added responsibility for fraud mitigation along with the following controls.

1. assess risk and design controls,
2. segregate duties,
3. place internal controls for processes and system access,
4. monitor controls and follow up to check if controls are in place,
5. document and test the controls,
6. management has to provide a report on its internal controls,
7. independent auditor evaluating management's assessment of its internal controls and providing a report.

Just as it is prudent to stop at a red light when attempting to travel through a busy intersection despite local legal requirements, it is prudent to use biometrics to enhance internal controls and to lessen fraud regardless of whether organizations are large enough to be subject to SOX or to other mandatory laws, regulations, standards, or to codes. Laws epitomize minimum standards. Organizations may still suffer large losses from frauds even if their internal control systems meet minimum standards.

While organizations develop measures to protect their assets, they must at the same time be able to meet the requirements of their stakeholders: investors, customers, alliances, community, suppliers and employees. In essence, no stakeholder will trust an organization that they perceive to be insecure; regardless of the services they provide or how innovative they are.

Up to now internal control biometrics systems have been operating in various closed environments. In contrast, their employment in private transactions will be based on consent. The existing legal frame does not deter public and private actors from putting into practice applications. The installment of an internal control biometrics system does not threaten procedural rights (i.e., rights in a court of law); their use is deemed intrusive but within reasonable limits. Nonetheless, their widespread implementation and the fear of a "surveillance" society may have a psychological effect. The following four themes are depicted in order to provide a better understanding of the legal implications of an internal control biometrics system:

Facilitating legal environment. The existing legal environment (privacy and data protection) is accommodating in that it allows legislation legitimizing the *de facto* business use of personal data. Data protection rules regulate the utilization of biometrics tools; however, they lack normative content and ethical debate.

Opacity/transparency rules compulsory enforced. Data protection (transparency rules) does not spell out what the limits of use and abuse of biometrics tools are. Opacity (privacy) rules may forbid use in cases where there is the need to guarantee against outside lop-sided power balances.

Wide-ranging putting into operation raises basic concerns. As biometrics tools are disseminated in society some concerns are gaining in significance. For example, concerns about (a) power buildup, (b) further use of existing data, (c) specific threats related to the use of biometrics tools by the public sector, (d) the failure to guard people from their inclination to trade their own privacy with what appears to be a very inexpensive convenience.

Employment of biometrics in law enforcement. It is essential that biometrics evidence be regulated when presented as evidence in courts of Law so as to protect suspects adequately (e.g., being heard, right to counter-expertise).

ORGANIZATIONAL AND ECONOMIC ASPECTS

Apart from organizational biometrics use, these tools are most identified with government agencies. For example, border control and transport agencies use facial recognition technology; fingerprint and iris scanning to guard national and border security. Governments globally have already put into practice or begun to take into account biometrics in functions such as social security, hospital/medical identification and access management. With identity theft on the rise, strict control over passports as well as other official documents such as National ID cards, driver's licenses and visas has become an important issue for quite a few nations. Biometrics provides customs/immigration officials the capacity to compare data against both country-specific and global databases, helping to authenticate the identity of the passport and visa holder.

Apart from the enhanced security attained through substantiating identity based on objectively measured physical characteristics (rather than an item a person remembers, hence can forget), biometrics also can offer cost and process benefits, improved privacy protection, time reduction, and increased convenience for affected individuals. Everyone needs to be able to trust in identity, and this is why biometrics is imperative at this moment in time.

For instance, the use of biometrics is appropriate where it is vital for transactional businesses, such as retailers and banks, to be able to rapidly, accurately and easily ascertain a customer's identity, whether online, in a store or branch office. For retailers, the processing for a biometric payment contrast to a PIN transaction is faster. In addition, transaction costs can also be lower compared with a traditional debit card payment. A speedier and protected transaction generates trust between the customer and an organization by improving the quality of service. Further, it also produces immense value to an organization by dropping costly ID fraud and the number of erroneous transactions. Biometric tools also facilitate organizations to have access to more precise data on which to profile their customers and hence personalize services.

Yet, another example is the transport sector, biometrics linked to human resource systems can ensure improved passenger safety through substantiating driver training is up to date (such as trains and heavy machinery). Biometrics tied to intelligent observation can assist with capacity and volume planning at commuter stations.

Internal control biometrics systems are resilient identification technologies and as such influence the level of 'trust' in economic transactions. That is, they can assist in the lessening of fraud; thereby, helping to materialize the efficiency and equity gains of the biometrics tools. Further, these biometric tools assist to make things easier from the user viewpoint, thereby decreasing the likelihood of error. At the same time, their widespread deployment in companies will make identification over the Internet transactions network simpler, more secure and may bring down costs per secure transaction. This in turn will assist consumers to make more efficient transactions. Standards and interoperability issues, however, determine widespread adoption and shape economic challenges. The following five themes summarize the economic implications of biometrics:

The concept of the best internal control biometrics system. The economic importance of identity is rising in a digital society, but the strongest internal control biometrics system protection is not necessarily the optimal one.

Negative implications of stronger internal control biometrics system. Identity errors and abuse may become less frequent; however, when they occur, they could possibly be more perilous. For example, identity theft may become less frequent but more serious and with wider social repercussions.

Interoperability is essential for market operation. There is a grave peril that the biometrics identification market as well as markets that depend on identity, may fragment into groups that will not interoperate, thereby resulting into a in a weaker position to monopolization or dominance by a few entities.

Biometrics-related intellectual property rights threaten open competition. The unregulated exploitation of intellectual property rights to facets of biometrics can appreciably reduce competition in biometrics and/or distort development, direction and speed of adoption.

Public sector interest will shape the market. The utilization of biometrics in government initiatives and associated large-scale public obtainment could be critical factors to guarantee open and competitive markets, and rapid and socially productive innovation.

TECHNOLOGICAL ASPECTS OF INTERNAL CONTROL
BIOMETRICS SYSTEMS

Internal control biometrics systems are still largely undergoing development and are not yet mature enough for widespread use in society. Enrollment is the first and most important stage of any internal control biometrics systems since the overall efficiency, accuracy and usability of a system depends on this stage. Re-enrollment during the life-cycle of an application is not only essential because of natural and accidental changes to biometric attributes, but also to make certain that the acquisition of the sample patterns is performed using state-of-the-art sensor technology. Biometric sample or template storage and their safeguard are also very central issues. Storing can be performed in centralized databases or on portable media such as smart cards or tokens. The following four technological concerns for an internal control biometrics system are (1) performance/accuracy, (2) biometric privacy, (3) interoperability, and (4) multimodality. These four technical issues will be addressed later by the "internal control" features to ensure the stability of the technological concerns.

Performance/Precision

There will always be a compromise between the precision level that can be attained from an internal control biometric system and the level of performance obtained in operating such a system with a threshold based on operator- or application-defined constraints.

Biometric Privacy

Biometrics could be implemented in the future to enhance privacy by means of a biometric characteristic to encode a security key, for example a PIN code that allows access to a bank account. There are many benefits to biometrics utilization. First and foremost that keys thus developed are not associated to the original patterns, are not stored and can be rescinded at will.

Interoperability

Technical interoperability and the availability of commonly acknowledged standards and specifications are issues that are presently being researched. They are for the most part important in finger print identification applications, in which different provinces are inevitably involved but are also increasingly the case with worldwide consumer applications (e.g., bank ATMs).

Multimodality

Combining several modalities (e.g., facial recognition and iris) in sequence can result in the enhancement of an internal control biometrics systems overall efficiency. While combining them in parallel enriches an internal control biometrics systems' flexibility by making available alternative modes for the verification/identification process. The choice of which modalities to combine is motivated by the particular application design. This amalgamation may be performed at distinct stages of the process, resulting in a variety of benefits. Multimodality could also be viewed as an internal control biometrics systems security augmentation. For example, by having the internal control biometrics system request alternative modalities to be tested at random may discourage potential impostors.

The four technological concerns for an internal control biometrics system of (1) performance/accuracy, (2) biometric privacy, (3) interoperability, and (4) multimodality should be addressed by internal control characteristics. These characteristics can be underscored by: Access control; Audit controls; Authorization control; Data authentication; and Entity authentication. Each of these areas is discussed below.

Access control

Internal control biometrics systems, especially when combined with other identification methods, ensure the highest level of accuracy and data protection by confirming individuals' rights and permissions. Biometric identifiers cannot be lost, forgotten, shared, stolen or counterfeited, which is quite critical for access control applications. Access controls requirement include features for emergency access procedures and provisions for context-based, role-based, and/or user-based access of different biometrics tools (i.e., multimodality). For example, a two-factor identification feature can also be implemented by embedding the biometric data into a contactless card. In this case, two digital fingerprint templates are compared: the previously enrolled template and the newly produced one.

For internal control biometrics systems that involve very valuable intangible assets (such as formulas, patents, and software code) the use of encryption may be necessary as a means of providing access control. Hence, access control can augment performance/precision of an internal control biometrics system.

Access controls are necessary under emergency conditions, although they may be very different from those used in normal operational circumstances. For example, in a situation when normal environmental systems, including electrical or other forms of energy power, have been severely damaged or rendered inoperative due to a natural or man-made disaster, procedures should be established in advance to provide direction on possible means to gain access to required electronic protected private information (i.e., enhancing biometric privacy).

Encryption provides confidentiality, which is a form of an internal control feature. The use of encryption, for the purpose of access control of data at rest, should be based upon an organization's risk analysis. The combination of unique user identification and provision for emergency access procedures, as well as encryption may be a requirement for an organization implementation specification.

Efficient and reliable access control procedures for sensitive areas and facilities present a challenge to any business, regardless of its nature and scale (Table 3.1).

Table 3.1.   Access Control Features

Access Control capability	Safety of employees and visitors Protection of inventory, equipment, property and other assets Streamlined personnel management
Key functions performed by access control	1. Identification of employees coming to or leaving the company's offices or facilities. 2. Identification of visitors following a specified route within a protected area. 3. Access restriction to highly secure areas (zones) (production facilities, inventories, etc.). 4. Access to depositary boxes and safes. 5. Identification of visitors and simplified servicing (frequent visitor privileges, prevention of access by malicious persons).
Popular technologies	Contact and contactless cards, tokens, etc. PIN-code Biometric identifiers
key access control functions	Biometric identification method is biometrics (e.g., fingerprint, iris, face). Biometric identification can be supplemented with PIN-codes and/or contactless cards. Access control features are can be fully integrated with time and attendance tracking options.
Interaction with standard access control tools	Electro-mechanic and electromagnetic door-locks, turnstiles and gateways that are managed by end-device controllers.

Multimodality	Accelerating the flow of employees through a main entrance during peak periods (start and end of business)—a PIN-code + facial recognition.
	Additional access restriction to highly secure premises—a contactless card + palm print.
Internal control biometrics system	Access control checkpoints and user rights are managed centrally
	Individuals' biometric and other related data (full name, position, etc.) are enrolled just once, and users can be granted assigned access rights as soon as they have enrolled
	Opening a door-lock or turnstile come with the recording of the employee's arrival/departure event
	A variety of reports can be generated: indicating the employee's actually worked hours, whereabouts in the office area or facilities (if biometric terminals are installed in the vicinity of internal areas), etc.
	Enclosed security contours can be generated, allowing an employee to pass through all security contours; employees have not registered their check-in event at the entrance, they are not allowed to enter the internal facilities.

Audit controls

Audit control mechanisms should be in place to record and examine system activity (e.g., precision and performance criteria). This requirement includes the capability to record and examine system activity. This audit internal control feature is a type of technical safeguard (i.e., biometric privacy). Security standards in this rule establish a minimum level of security that covered organizations must meet for federal or state requirements. For example, although a federal or state "privacy rule" does not incorporate a requirement for an "audit trail" task, it does call for providing an accounting of certain disclosures of protected private information (e.g., health) to an individual upon request. While audit trails are basically implemented to record uses within an electronic information system, the "privacy rule" requirement for accounting applies to certain disclosures outside of the covered entity (e.g., to public health authorities).

A biometric audit trail can be implemented to increase the accountability levels linked with people, processes and technology that are critical to an organization' operations. For example, pharmaceutical companies could use biometrics to make certain they have indubitably documented who played a role in producing drugs for their customers. Aircraft maintenance would undoubtedly benefit from an unquestionable audit trail associated with the employees who took a replacement fan blade out of inventory, installed it in an aircraft engine and conducted the final inspection before releasing the aircraft to service. Finally, the U.S. Food and Drug Administration, as well as the Federal Aviation Administration would embrace an irrefutable audit trail which documents the individuals involved in these activities. In these examples, multiple stakeholders could pay a very high price for accountability lapses which lead to errors.

Integrity

Each organization should corroborate that data in its possession have not been altered or destroyed in an unauthorized manner and provided examples of mechanisms that could be used to accomplish this task. In addition, an internal control biometrics system should be able to communicate with different systems outside of the organization domain (i.e., an interoperability component). Error-correcting memory and magnetic disc storage are examples of the built-in data authentication mechanisms that are omnipresent in hardware and operating systems today. A risk analysis process will address what data must be authenticated and should provide answers appropriate to the different situations confronted by organizations.

Person or entity authentication

"Automatic logoff" and "Unique user identification" are specified as mandatory features, and should be attached with at least one of the following features: (1) a "biometric" identification system; (2) a "password" system; (3) a "personal identification number"; and (4) "telephone callback," or a "token" system that utilizes a physical device for user identification. These authentication procedures ought to enhance biometric privacy issues.

Transmission security

Due to organizational practices and technology change, situations may arise where transmitted electronic protected information from a particular organization may be at significant risk of being accessed by unauthorized entities. "Transmission security" controls should be mandatory to protect the security of information when it is transmitted electronically from one point to another over open networks, along with a combination of mandatory and optional implementation features (i.e., an interoperability component). When electronic protected information is transmitted from one point to another, it must be protected in a manner commensurate with the associated risk (i.e., biometric privacy). For example, encryption may not be a mandatory requirement for transmission over dial-up lines, since these lines have a very small probability of interception. However, where risk analysis demonstrate such risk to be significant, then encryption may be advisable.

BIOMETRIC APPLICATIONS

Most biometric applications fall into one of nine general categories:

- Financial and investment services (e.g., ATMs and kiosks).
- Immigration and border control (e.g., points of entry, advance cleared frequent travelers, passport and visa issuance, asylum cases).
- Social services (e.g., fraud deterrence in entitlement programs).
- Health care (e.g., security measure for privacy of medical records).
- Physical right of entry control (e.g., institutional, government, and residential).
- Time and attendance (e.g., replacement of time punch card).
- Computer security (e.g., personal computer access, network access, Internet utization, e-commerce, e-mail, encryption).
- Telecommunications (e.g., mobile phones, call center technology, phone cards, televised shopping).
- Law enforcement (e.g., criminal investigation, national ID, driver's license, correctional institutions/prisons, home confinement, smart gun).

Biometric features include a range of body features; however, not all such subsets are appropriate for identification purposes. For example, a photograph of one specific body part (the face) is sufficient for various purposes, while a photograph of other body parts (say, elbows or feet) is useless. The evaluation whether a particular body characteristic is suitable for biometric use can be done on the following seven *criteria* (Table 3.2) (Jain, Jain, & Pankanti, 1999):

Table 3.2.   Seven Pillars of Biometric Wisdom

Universality	All individuals are endowed with the same physical features—such as fingers, iris, ears, face, veins, DNA—which can be used for identification
Distinctiveness	For each individual these features are distinct, and therefore represent a unique aspect
Permanence	These features remain largely unchanged throughout an individual's life
Collectability	An individual's distinctive physical features need to be collected in a reasonably effortless manner for rapid identification
Performance	The degree of precision of identification must be quite high before the system can be operational
Acceptability	Applications will not be worthwhile if employees, suppliers, customers, management etc. offers resilient and continuous resistance to biometrics
Resistance to Circumvention	In order to provide additional security and safeguarding of assets, an internal control biometric system needs to be difficult to elude than existing identity management systems.

Behavioral Aspects

Biometric technologies are just a tool, but their behavior implications for employees, suppliers, customers, and others may be far-reaching. Organizations are confronted with understanding the longer-term implications of large-scale deployment of internal control biometrics systems so as to make certain their beneficial implementation. Table 3.3 illustrates four dominant themes identified as the main behavioral issues. Issues addressed should include the following:

a. Clarity of purpose in regards to an internal control biometrics system application. Therefore, it is important to be unambiguous about what the needs of the application are and how biometrics will be able to achieve them.

b. Interoperability and equivalence of personnel, processes, and technology: Equivalence relates to backup procedures that are consistently used in the internal control biometrics system.

c. Individual factors, usability and exclusion: Research ought to be conducted as to the usability and the user-friendliness of the internal control biometrics system in real-life situations.

Table 3.3.   Behavioral Aspects of Internal Control Biometrics Systems

Clarity of purpose in relation to internal control biometrics system applications	The tool and processes introduced for one purpose will be extended to other purposes that were not discussed or agreed upon at the time of their implementation. That is, avoiding "function creep."
Interoperability and equivalence of performance and process	Backup for personnel, processes, and technology equivalence should be consistent in the system. This is extremely important as it impacts on the internal control biometrics system performance.
Individual factors, usability and exclusion	Individual factors such as age, ethnicity, gender, diseases or disabilities (including natural aging) should be examined on a case-by-case basis so as to lessen the possibility of exclusion of a small but significant part of employees, suppliers, customers etc.
Impact upon the trust model between the organization and outside stakeholders	Stakeholders may temporarily accept to allow an organization to penetrate through their privacy in exchange for a more safe and sound business transaction. But, trust may be diminished in the long term.

d. Impact upon the trust model between the organization and outside stakeholders: Customers, suppliers and others may for the interim accept to trade-in parts of their privacy in exchange for a more secure business transaction. However, when organizational control is perceived as excessive, disproportionate and/or 'too efficient' this may lead to an erosion of trust that will be in the interest of neither organization nor stakeholders.

CONCLUSION

There is currently a great deal of interest and pursuit associated with the use of internal control biometrics systems in many different areas due to the heightened performance of computers, the reduced cost of biometric technology, the Internet technology advances, and the elevated level of security awareness. These areas include agriculture, banking, transportation, forest, healthcare, education, public justice and safety, security, and government.

Controls and procedures must be in place in order to have a functioning and reliable system. For example, internal control biometrics systems must have segregation of duties. SOX formalized the legal requirements for corporations and for external auditors. Anyone who has access to the user name and password can simply perform the transaction. This disregards segregation of duties. Further, any vulnerabilities or security breach in these systems will either be very costly or disastrous. The challenge of SOX is making certain it is observed and that compliance can be demonstrated and correctly monitored and reported. The most common area of focus is the archiving of all communications and the formation of transparent and auditable internal control systems for recording transactions, dealings and any type of business correspondence.

It is imperative to bear in mind that an effective internal control biometric system cannot be achieved by relying on technology alone. Technology, processes and people must be integrated together as part of an overall internal control system that includes safeguarding assets and security. Weaknesses in any of these areas weaken the effectiveness of an internal control biometric system. The internal control system needs to account for limitations in biometric technology. For example, some individuals cannot enroll in a biometrics system since they lack the appropriate body part. In addition, errors sometimes occur during matching operations. Exception processing that is not as good as biometric-based primary processing could be exploited as a security hole. Further, non-technological processes for enrollment are critical to the success of an internal control biometrics system. Before an individual is granted a biometric credential, the issuing authority needs to assure itself that the individual is eligible to receive such a credential.

Safeguarding of assets/security concerns need to be balanced with practical cost and operational considerations as well as political and economic interests. To develop internal control biometrics systems, the high level goals of these systems need to be defined, and the concept of operations that will embody people, processes, and technologies required to accomplish these goals need to be developed. With these answers, the proper role of biometric technologies as part of an overall internal control system can be determined. One of the primary functions of any internal control biometric system is the control of people moving into or out of protected areas, such as physical buildings, information systems, and geographical boundaries. Tools described as biometrics can automate the identification/verification of individuals by one or more of their distinct physical or behavioral features.

An internal control biometrics system only needs the user to possess a minimum of required user knowledge and effort. An internal control biometrics system with the least user knowledge and effort would be very received to both the purchase and the end user. Alternative methods of authenticating an individual's identity are not only a good practice for making biometric systems accessible to people of different ability level. These tools will also serve as a viable alternative manner of handling authentication and enrollment errors.

Auditing processes and procedures on a normal basis during and after installation is an exceptional practice of ensuring that the internal control biometrics system is functioning within normal parameters. A well-executed biometric authentication internal control biometrics system should not only prevent and detect an impostor in instantaneous, but also should also keep a secure log of the transaction activities for prosecution of impostors. This is especially imperative, since a great deal of identity theft and fraud involves employees and a secure log of the transaction activities will provide the channel for prosecution or quick resolution of altercations.

Research will undoubtedly result in more sophisticated internal control biometric systems capable of monitoring inappropriate patterns of data usage. Whether discontented and naive employees or external terrorists are trying to modify or destroy data, advanced internal control biometrics systems and decision-making models will be needed.

Internal control biometrics systems can be applied to areas requiring logical access solutions, and it can be used to access applications, personal computers, networks, financial accounts, human resource records, the telephone system, and invoke customized profiles to enhance the mobility of the disabled. In a business-to-business scenario, the biometric authentication system can be connected to the business processes of an organization to amplify accountability of financial systems, vendors, and supplier transactions; the results can be extremely beneficial.

The global reach of the Internet has made the services and products of an organization available around the clock, provided the consumer or supplier has a user name and password to login. In many situations consumers and suppliers may have forgotten their user name, password, or both. The consumer or supplier must then take steps to retrieve or reset his/her lost or forgotten login information. By implementing an internal control biometrics system consumers and suppliers can opt to register their biometric trait or smart card with an organization's business-to-consumer e-commerce environment, which will allow a consumer to access their account and pay for goods and services (Rodgers, 2010). The advantage is that consumers and suppliers will never lose or forget their user name or password, and will be able to conduct business at their convenience. An internal control biometrics system can be advantageous to areas requiring physical access solutions, such as entry into a building, a room, a safe or it may be used to start a motorized vehicle. Moreover, an internal control biometrics system can easily be linked to a computer-based application used to monitor time and attendance of employees as they enter and leave company facilities. In short, internal control biometrics systems can and do lend themselves to individuals of all ability levels.

REFERENCES

Davis, K., & Stevenson, A. (2004). They've Got Your Numbers. *Kiplinger's Personal Finance* (January).

Davis, K. (2004). Targeting kids for identity theft. *Kiplinger's Personal Finance* (January 4).

Department of the Treasury. (2005). *The use of technology to combat identity theft. Report on the Study Conducted Pursuant to Section 157 of the Fair and Accurate Credit Transactions Act of 2003* (Feb.). http://www.scribd.com/doc/1193592/US-Treasury-biometrics-study.

Jain, A. K., Jain, R. B., & Pankanti, S. (1999). *Personal Identification in Networked Society*. New York, NY: Kluwer Academic Publisher.

Rodgers, W. (2010). *E-commerce and biometric issues addressed in a Throughput Model*. Hauppauge, NY: Nova Publication.

BIOMETRICS GLOSSARY

INTRODUCTION

This set of terms was developed by the National Science & Technology Council's (NSTC) Subcommittee on Biometrics with the full understanding that national (INCITS/M1) and international (ISO/IEC JTC1 SC37) standards bodies are working to develop standard references. The subcommittee will review this Glossary for consistency as standards are passed. The subcommittee recognizes the impact of ongoing challenge problems, technical evaluations, and technology advancements. The Glossary will be updated accordingly to reflect those changes. The statements herein are intended to further the understanding of a general audience and are not intended to replace or compete with sources that may be more technically descriptive/prescriptive.

GLOSSARY TERMS

Accuracy

A catch-all phrase for describing how well a biometric system performs. The actual statistic for performance will vary by task (verification, open-set identification (watchlist), and closed-set identification). See www.biometricscatalog.org/biometrics/biometrics_101.pdf for further explanation. See also d prime, detection error trade-off (DET), detect and identification rate, equal error rate, false acceptance rate (FAR), false alarm rate (FAR), false match rate, false non-match rate, false reject rate, identification rate, performance, verification rate.

Algorithm

A limited sequence of instructions or steps that tells a computer system how to solve a particular problem. A biometric system will have multiple algorithms, for example, image processing, template generation, comparisons, etc.

ANSI—American National Standards Institute

A private, nonprofit organization that administers and coordinates the U.S. voluntary standardization and conformity assessment system. The mission of ANSI is to enhance both the global competitiveness of U.S. business and the U.S. quality of life by promoting and facilitating voluntary consensus standards and conformity assessment systems, and safeguarding their integrity. For more information, visit www.ansi.org. *See also INCITS, ISO, NIST.*

Application Programming Interface (API)

Formatting instructions or tools used by an application developer to link and build hardware or software applications.

Arch

A fingerprint pattern in which the friction ridges enter from one side, make a rise in the center, and exit on the opposite side. The pattern will contain no true delta point. *See also delta point, loop, whorl.*

Attempt

The submission of a single set of biometric sample to a biometric system for identification or verification. Some biometric systems permit more than one attempt to identify or verify an individual. *See also biometric sample. Identification, verification.*

Authentication

1. The process of establishing confidence in the truth of some claim. The claim should be any declarative statement for example: "This individual's name is 'Joseph K.'" or "This child is more than 5 feet tall."
2. In biometrics, "authentication" is something used as a generic synonym for verification. *See also verification.*

Automated Biometric Identification Systems (ABIS)

1. Department of Defense (DOD) system implemented to improve the U.S. government's ability to track and identify national security threats. The system includes mandatory collection of 10 rolled fingerprints, a minimum of five mug shots from varying angles, and an oral swab to collect DNA.
2. Generic term sometimes used in the biometrics community to discuss a biometric system. *See also AFIS.*

Automated Fingerprint Identification System (AFIS)

A highly specialized biometric system that compares a submitted finger-print record (usually of multiple fingers) to a database of records, to determine the identity of an individual. AFIS is predominantly used for law enforcement, but is also being used for civil applications (e.g., background checks for soccer coaches, etc.). *See also IAFIS.*

Behavioral Biometric Characteristic

A biometric characteristic that is learned and acquired over time rather than one based primarily on biology. All biometric characteristics depend somewhat upon both behavioral and biological characteristic. Examples of biometric modalities for which behavioral characteristics may dominate include signature recognition and keystroke dynamics. See also biological biometric characteristic.

Benchmarking

The process of comparing measured performance against a standard, openly available, reference.

Bifurcation

The point in a fingerprint where a fingerprint ridge divides of splits to form two ridges as illustrated. *See also friction ridge, minutia(e) point, ridge ending.*

Binning

Process of parsing (examining) or classifying data in order to accelerate and/or improve biometric matching

BioAPI—Biometrics Application Programming Interface

Defines the application programming interface and service provider interface for a standard biometric technology interface. The bioAPI enables biometric devices to be easily installed, integrated or swapped within the overall system architecture.

Biological Biometric Characteristic

A biometric characteristic based primarily on an anatomical or physiological characteristic, rather than a learned behavior. All biometric characteristics depend somewhat upon both behavioral and biological characteristic.

Examples of biometric modalities for which biological characteristics may dominate include fingerprint and hand geometry. *See also behavioral biometric characteristic.*

Biometrics

A general term used alternatively to describe a characteristic or a process.

As a characteristic:
- A measurable biological (anatomical and physiological and behavioral characteristic that can be used for automated recognition.

As a process:
- Automated methods of recognizing an individual based on measurable biological (anatomical and physiological) and behavioral characteristics.

Biometric Consortium (BC)

An open forum to share information throughout government, industry, and academia. For more information, visit www.biometrics.org.

Biometric Data

A catch-all phrase for computer data created during a biometric process. It encompasses raw sensor observations, biometric samples, models, templates, and/or similarity scores. Biometric data is used to describe the information collected during an enrollment, verification, or identification process, but does not apply to end user information such as user name, demographic information and authorizations.

Biometric Sample

Information or computer data obtained from a biometric sensor device. Examples are images of a face or fingerprint.

Biometric System

Multiple individual components (such as sensor, matching algorithm, and result display) that combine to make a fully operational system. A biometric system is an automated system capable of:

1. Capturing a biometric sample from an end user.
2. Extracting and processing the biometric data from that sample.

3. Storing the extracted information in a database.
4. Comparing the biometric data with data contained in one or more references.
5. Deciding how well they match and indicating whether or not an identification or verification of identity has been achieved.

A biometric system may be a component of a larger system.

Capture

The process of collecting a biometric sample from an individual via a sensor. *See also submission*.

CBEFF—Common Biometric Exchange Formats Framework

A standard that provides the ability for a system to identify, and interface with, multiple biometric systems, and to exchange data between system components.

Challenge Response

A method used to confirm the presence of a person by eliciting direct responses from the individual. Responses can be either voluntary or involuntary. In a voluntary response, the end user will consciously react to something that the system presents. In an involuntary response, the end user's body automatically responds to a stimulus. A challenge response can be used to protect the system against attacks. *See also liveness detection*.

Claim of identify

A statement that a person is or is not the source of a reference in a database. Claims can be positive (I am in the database), negative (I am not in the database) or specific (I am end user 123 in the database).

Closed-set Identification

A biometric task where an unidentified individual is known to be in the database and the system attempts to determine his/her identity. Performance is measured by the frequency with which the individual appears in the system's top rank (or top 5, 10, etc.). *See also identification, open-set identification*.

Comparison

Process of comparing biometric reference with a previously stored reference or references in order to make an identification or verification decision. *See also match.*

Cooperative User

An individual willing provides his/her biometric to the biometric system for capture. Example: A worker submits his/her biometric to clock in and out of work. *See also indifferent user, noncooperative user, uncooperative user.*

Core Point

The "center(s)" of a fingerprint. In a whorl pattern, the core point is found in the middle of the spiral/circles. In a loop pattern, the core point is found in the top region of the innermost loop. More technically, a core point is defined as the topmost point on the innermost upwardly curving friction ridgeline. A fingerprint may have multiple cores or no cores. *See also arch, delta point, friction ridge, loop, whorl.*

Covert

An instance in which biometric samples are being collected at a location that is not known to bystanders. An example of a covert environment might involve an airport checkpoint where face images of passengers are captured and compared with a watchlist without their knowledge. *See also noncooperative user, overt.*

Crossover Error Rate (CER)

See equal error rate (EER).

Cumulative Match Characteristic (CMC)

A method of showing measured accuracy performance of a biometric system operating in the closed-set identification task. Templates are compared and ranked based on their similarity. The CMC shows how often the individual's template appears in the ranks (1, 5, 10, 100, etc.), based on the match rate. A CMC compares the rank (1, 5, 10, 100, etc.) versus identification rate as illustrated.

D-Prime (D′)

A statistical measure of how well a system can discriminate between a signal and a non-signal.

Database

A collection of one or more computer files. For biometric systems, these files could consist of biometric sensor readings, templates, match results, related end user information, etc. *See also gallery.*

Decision

The resultant action taken (either automated or manual) based on a comparison of similarity score (or similar measure) and the system's threshold. *See also comparison, similarity score, threshold.*

Degrees of Freedom

A statistical measure of how unique biometric data is. Technically, it is the number of statistically independent features (parameters) contained in biometric data.

Delta Point

Part of a fingerprint pattern that looks similar to the Greek letter delta (Δ), as illustrated. Technically, it is the point on a friction ridge at or nearest the point of divergence of two type lines, and located at or directly in front of the point of divergence. *See also core point, friction ridge.*

Detection and Identification Rate

The rate at which individuals, who are in a database are properly identified in an open-set identification (watchlist) application. *See also open-set identification, watchlist.*

Detection Error Trade-off (DET) Curve

A graphical plot of measured error rates, as illustrated. DET curves typically plot matching error rates (false nonmatch rate vs. false match rate) or decision error rates (false reject rate vs. false accept rate). *See also Receiver Operating Characteristics.*

Difference Score

A value returned by a biometric algorithm that indicates the degree of difference between a biometric sample and a reference. *See also hamming distance, similarity score.*

Eavesdropping

Surreptitiously obtaining data from an unknowing end user who is performing a legitimate function. An example involves having a hidden sensor co-located with the legitimate sensor. *See also skimming.*

EFTS—Electronic Fingerprint Transmission Specification

A document that specifies requirements to which agencies must adhere to communicate electronically with the Federal Bureau of Investigation's Integrated Automated Fingerprint Identification System (IAFIS). This specification facilitates information sharing and eliminates the delays associated with fingerprint cards. *See also Integrated Automated Fingerprinting Identification System (IAFIS).*

Encryption

The act of transferring data into an unintelligible form so that it cannot be read by unauthorized individuals. A key or password is used to decrypt (decode) the encrypted data.

End User

The individual who will interact with the system to enroll, to verify, or to identify. *See also cooperative user, indifferent user, noncooperative user, uncooperative user, user.*

Enrollment

The process of collecting a biometric sample from an end user, converting it into a biometric reference, and storing it in the biometric systems' database for later comparison.

Equal Error Rate (EER)

A statistic used to show biometric performance, typically when operating in the verification task. The EER is the location on a ROC or DET curve where the false accept rate and false reject rate (or one minus the verification rate {1-VR}) are equal, as illustrated. In general, the lower the equal error rate values, the higher the accuracy of the biometric system. Note, however that most operational systems are not set to operate at the "equal error rate" so the measure's true usefulness is limited to comparing biometric system performance. The EER is sometimes referred to as the "Crossover Error Rate." *See also Detection Error Trade-off (DET) curve, false accept rate, false reject rate, Receiver Operating Characteristics (ROC).*

Extraction

The process of converting a captured biometric sample into biometric data so that it can be compared with a reference. *See also biometric sample, feature, template.*

Face Recognition

A biometric modality that uses an image of the visible physical structure of an individual's face for recognition purposes.

Failure to Acquire (FTA)

Failure of a biometric system to capture and/or extract usable information from a biometric sample.

Failure to Enroll (FTE)

Failure of a biometric system to form a proper enrollment reference for an end user. Common failures include end users who are not properly trained to provide their biometrics, the sensor not capturing information correctly, or captured sensor data of insufficient quality to develop a template.

False Acceptance Rate (FAR)

A statistic used to measure biometric performance when operating in the verification task. The percentage of times a system produces a false accept, which occurs when an individual is incorrectly matched to another individual's existing biometric. Example: Frank claims to be John and the system verifies the claim. *See also false match rate, type II error.*

False Alarm Rate

A statistic used to measure biometric performance when operating in the open-set identification (sometimes referred to as watchlist) task. This is the percentage of times an alarm is incorrectly sounded on an individual who is not in the biometric system's database (the system alarms on Frank when Frank isn't in the database), or an alarm is sounded but the wrong person is identified (the system alarms on John when John is in the database, but the system thinks John is Steve).

False Match Rate

A statistic used to measure biometric performance when MISSING TEXT. Similar to the False Acceptance Rate (FAR).

False Nonmatch Rate

A statistic used to measure biometric performance. Similar to the False Reject Rate (FRR), except the FRR includes the Failure To Acquire error rate and the False NonMatch Rate does not.

False Rejection Rate (FRR)

A statistic used to measure biometric performance when operating in the verification task. The percentage of times the system produces a false reject. A false reject occurs when an individual is not matched to his/her own existing biometric template. Example: John claims to be John, but the system incorrectly denies the claim. *See also false nonmatch rate, type I error.*

Feature(s)

Distinctive mathematical characteristic(s) derived from a biometric sample; used to generate a reference. *See also extraction, template.*

Feature Extraction

See extraction.

FERET—Face Recognition Technology program

A face recognition development and evaluation program sponsored by the U.S. Government from 1993 through 1997. For more information, visit www.frvt.org/FERET/default.htm. *See also FRGC, FRVT.*

Fingerprint Recognition

A biometric modality that uses the physical structure of an individual's fingerprint for recognition purposes. Important features used in most fingerprint recognition systems are minutiae points that include bifurcations and ridge endings. *See also bifurcation, core point, delta point, minutia(e) point.*

FqVTE—Fingerprint Vendor Technology Evaluation (2003)

An independently administered technology evaluation of commercial fingerprint matching algorithms. For more information, visit fpvte.nist.gov.

FRGC—Face Recognition Grand Challenge

A face recognition development program sponsored by the U.S. Government from 2003–2005. For more information, visit www.frvt.org/FRGC. *See also FERET, FRVT.*

Friction Ridge

The ridges present on the skin of the fingers and toes, and on the palms and soles of feet, which make contact with an incident surface under normal touch. On the fingers, the distinctive patterns formed by the friction ridges that make up the fingerprints. *See also minutia(e) point.*

FRVT—Face Recognition Vendor Test

A series of larg-scale independent technology evaluations of face recognition systems. The evaluations have occurred in 2000, 2002, and 2005. For more information, visit www.frvt.org/FRVT2005/default.aspx. *See also FRGC, FERET.*

Gallery

The biometric system's database, or set of known individuals, for a specific implementation or evaluation experiment. *See also database, probe.*

Gait

An individual's manner of walking. This behavioral characteristic is in the research development stage of automation.

Hamming Distance

The number of noncorresponding digits in a string of binary digits; used to measure dissimilarity. Hamming distances are used in many Daugman iris recognition algorithms. *See also difference score, similarity score.*

Hand Geometry Recognition

A biometric modality that uses the physical structure of an individual's hand for recognition purposes.

ICE—Iris Challenge Evaluation

A large-scale development and independent technology evaluation activity for iris recognition systems sponsored by the U.S. Government in 2005. For more information, visit iris.nist.gov/ICE.

Identification

A task where the biometric system searches a database for a reference matching a submitted biometric sample, and if found, returns a corresponding identity. A biometric is collected and compared with all the references in a database. Identification is "closed-set" if the person is known to exist in the database. In "open-set" identification, sometimes referred to as a "watchlist," the person is not guaranteed to exist in the database. The system must determine whether the person is in the database, then return the identity. *See also closed-set identification, open-set identification, verification, watchlist.*

Identification Rate

The rate at which an individual in a database is correctly identified.

Identity Governance

The combination of policies and actions taken to ensure enterprise-wide consistency, privacy protection and appropriate interoperability between individual identity management systems.

Identity Management

The combination of systems, rules and procedures that defines an agreement between an individual and organization(s) regarding ownership, utilization and safeguard of personal identity information.

Impostor

A person who submits a biometric sample in either an intentional or inadvertent attempt to claim the identity of another person to a biometric system. *See also attempt.*

INCITS—International Committee for Information Technology Standards

Organization that promotes the effective use of information and communication technology through standardization in a way that balances the interests of all stakeholders and increases the global competitiveness of the member organizations. For more information, visit www.INCITS.org. *See also ANSI, ISO, NIST.*

Indifferent User

An individual who knows his/her biometric sample is being collected and does not attempt to help or hinder the collection of the sample. For example, an individual, aware that a camera is being used for face recognition, looks in the general direction of the sensor, neither avoiding nor directly looking at it. *See also cooperative user, non-cooperative user, uncooperative user.*

Infrared

Light that lies outside the human visible spectrum at its red (low frequency) end.

Integrated Automated Fingerprint Identification System (IAFIS)

The FBI's large-scale 10 fingerprint (open-set) identification system that is used for criminal history background checks and identification of latent prints discovered at crime scenes. This system provides automated and latent search capabilities, electronic image storage, and electronic exchange of fingerprints and responses. *See also AFIS.*

Iris Recognition

A biometric modality that uses an image of the physical structure of an individual's iris for recognition purposes, as illustrated below. The iris muscle is the colored portion of the eye surrounding the pupil.

IrisCode©

A biometric feature format used in the Daugman iris recognition system.

ISO—International Organization for Standardization

A nongovernment network of the national standards institutes from 151 countries. The ISO acts as bridging organization in which a consensus can be reached on solutions that meet both the requirements of business and the broader needs of society, such as the needs of stakeholder groups like consumers and users. For more information, visit www.iso.org. *See also ANSI, INCITS, NIST.*

Keystroke Dynamics

A biometric modality that uses the cadence of an individual's typing pattern for recognition.

Latent Fingerprint

A fingerprint "image" left on a surface that was touched by an individual. The transferred impression is left by the surface contact with the friction ridges, usually caused by the oily residue produced by the sweat glands in the finger. *See also friction ridge.*

Live Capture

Typically refers to a fingerprint capture device that electronically captures fingerprint images using a sensor (rather than scanning ink-based fingerprint images on a card or lifting a latent fingerprint from a surface). *See also sensor.*

Liveness Detection

A technique used to ensure that the biometric sample submitted is from an end user. A liveness detection method can help protect the system against some types of spoofing attacks. *See also challenge response, mimic, spoofing.*

Loop

A fingerpring pattern in which the friction ridges enter from either side, curve sharply and pass out near the same side they entered as illustrated. This pattern will contain one core and one delta. *See also arch, core point, delta point, friction ridge, whorl.*

Match

A decision that a biometric sample and a stored template comes from the same human source, based on their high level of similarity (difference or hammering distance). *See also false match rate, false nonmatch rate.*

Matching

The process of comparing a biometric sample against a previously stored template and scoring the level of similarity (difference or hamming distance). Systems then make decisions based on this score and its relationship (above or below) a predetermined threshold. *See also comparison, difference score, threshold.*

Mimic

The presentation of a live biometric measure in an attempt to fraudulently impersonate someone other than the submitter. *See also challenge response, liveness detection, spoofing.*

Minutia(e) Point

Friction ridge characteristics that are used to individualize a fingerprint image, see illustration below. Minutiae are the points where friction ridges begin, terminate, or split into two or more ridges. In many fingerprint systems, the minutiae (as opposed to the images) are compared for recognition purposes. *See also friction ridge, ridge ending.*

Modality

A type or class of biometric system. For example, face recognition, fingerprint recognition, iris recognition, etc.

Model

A representation used to characterize an individual. Behavioral-based biometric systems, because of the inherently dynamic characteristics, use models rather than static templates. *See also template.*

Mulitmodal Biometric System

A biometric system in which two or more of the modality components (biometric characteristic, sensor type or feature extraction algorithm) occurs in multiple.

Neural Net/Neural Network

A type of algorithm that learns from past experience to make decisions. *See also algorithm.*

NIST—National Institute of Standards and Technology

A nonregulatory federal agency within the U.S. Department of Commerce that develops and promotes measurement, standards, and technology to enhance productivity, facilitate trade, and improve the quality of life. NIST's measurement and standards work promotes the well-being of the nation and helps improve among many other things, the nation's homeland security. For more information visit www.nist.gov. *See also ANSI, INCITS, ISO.*

Noise

Unwanted components in a signal that degrade the quality of data or interfere with the desired signals processed by a system.

Noncooperative User

An individual who is not aware that his/her biometric sample is being collected. Example: A traveler passing through a security line at an airport is unaware that a camera is capturing his/her face image. *See also cooperative user, indifferent user, uncooperative user.*

One-to-many

A phrase used in the biometrics community to describe a system that compares one reference to many enrolled references to make a decision. The phrase typically refers to the identification or watchlist tasks.

One-to-one

A phrase used in the biometrics community to describe a system that compares one reference to one enrolled reference to make a decision. The phrase typically refers to the verification task (though not all verification tasks are truly one-to-one) and the identification task can be accomplished by a series of one-to-one comparisons.

Open-set Identification

Biometric task that more closely follows operational biometric system conditions to (1) determine if someone is in a database and (2) find the record of the individual in the database. This is sometimes referred to as the "watchlist" task to differentiate it from the more commonly referenced closed-set identification. *See also closed set identification, identification.*

Operational Evaluation

One of the three types of performance evaluations. The primary goal of an operational evaluation is to determine the workflow impact seen by the addition of a biometric system. *See also technology evaluation, scenario evaluation.*

Overt

Biometric sample collection where end users know they are being collected and at what location. An example of an overt environment is the US-VISIT program where non-U.S. citizens entering the United States submit their fingerprint data. *See also covert.*

Palm Print Recognition

A biometric modality that uses the physical structure of an individual's palm print for recognition purposes, as illustrated.

Performance

A catch-all phrase for describing a measurement of the characteristics, such as accuracy or speed, of a biometric algorithm or system. *See also accuracy, crossover error rate, cumulative match characteristics, d-prime, detection error trade-off, equal error rate, false accept rate, false alarm rate, false match rate, false reject rate, identification rate, operational evaluation, technology evaluation, true accept rate, true reject rate, verification rate.*

PIN Personal Identification Number

A security method used to show "what you know." Depending on the system, a PIN could be used to either claim or verify a claimed identity.

Pixel

A picture element. This is the smallest element of a display that can be assigned a color value. *See also pixels per inch (PPI), resolution.*

Pixels Per Inch (PPI)

A measure of the resolution of a digital image. The higher the PPI, the more information is included in the image, and the larger the file size. *See also pixel, resolution.*

Population

The set of potential end users for an application.

Probe

The biometric sample that is submitted to the biometric system to compare against one or more references in the gallery. *See also gallery.*

Radio Frequency Identification (RFID)

Technology that uses low-powered radio transmitters to read data stored in a transponder (tag). RFID tags can be used to track assets, manage inventory, authorize payments and serve as electronic keys. RFID is not a biometric.

Receiver Operating Characteristics (ROC)

A method of showing measured accuracy performance of a biometric system. A verification ROC compares false accept rate vs. verification rate. An open-set identification (watchlist) ROC compares false alarm rates vs. detection and identification rate.

Recognition

A generic term used in the description of biometric systems (e.g., face recognition or iris recognition) relating to their fundamental function. The term "recognition" does not inherently imply verification, closed-set identification or open-set identification (watchlist).

Record

The template and other information about the end user (e.g., name, access permissions).

Reference

The biometric data stored for an individual for use in future recognition. A reference can be one or more templates, models or raw images. *See also template.*

Resolution

The number of pixels per unit distance in the image. Describes the sharpness and clarity of an image. *See also pixel, pixels per inch (PPI).*

Ridge Ending

A minutiae point at the ending of a friction ridge, as illustrated. *See also bifurcation, friction ridge.*

Rolled Fingerprints

An image that includes fingerprint data from nail to nail, obtained by "rolling" the finger across a sensor as illustrated.

Scenario Evaluation

One of the three types of performance evaluations. The primary goal of a scenario evaluation is to measure performance of a biometric system operating in a specific application. *See also technology evaluation, operational evaluation.*

Segmentation

The process of parsing the biometric signal of interest from the entire acquired data system. For example, finding individual finger images from a slap impression, as illustrated.

Sensor

Hardware found on a biometric device that converts biometric input into a digital signal and conveys this information to the processing device.

Sensor Aging

The gradual degradation in performance of a sensor over time.

Signature Dynamics

A behavioral biometric modality that analyzes dynamic characteristics of an individual's signature, such as shape of signature, speed of signing, pen pressure when signing, and pen-in-air movements, for recognition.

Similarity Score

A value returned by a biometric algorithm that indicates the degree of similarity or correlation between a biometric sample and a reference. *See also difference score, hamming distance.*

Skimming

The act of obtaining data from an unknowing end user who is not willingly submitting the sample at that time. An example could be secretly reading data while in close proximity to a user on a bus. *See also eavesdropping*.

Slap Fingerprint

Fingerprints taken by simultaneously pressing the four fingers of one hand onto a scanner or fingerprint card, as illustrated. Slaps are known as four finger simultaneous plain impressions.

Speaker Recognition

A biometric modality that uses an individual's speech, a feature influenced by both the physical structure of an individual's vocal tract and the behavioral characteristics of the individual, for recognition purposes. Sometimes referred to as "voice recognition." "Speech recognition" recognizes the words being said, and is not a biometric technology. *See also speech recognition, voice recognition*.

Speaker Recognition Evaluations

An ongoing series of evaluations of speaker recognition systems. For more information, visit www.nist.gov/speech/tests/spk/index.htm.

Speech Recognition

A technology that enables a machine to recognize spoken words. Speech recognition is not a biometric technology. *See also speaker recognition, voice recognition*.

Spoofing

The ability to fool a biometric sensor into recognizing an illegitimate user as a legitimate user (verification) or into missing an identification of someone that is in the database. *See also liveness detection, mimic*.

Submission

The process whereby an end user provides a biometric sample to a biometric system. *See also capture*.

Technology Evaluation

One of three types of performance evaluations. The primary goal of a technology evaluation is to measure performance of biometric systems, typically only the recognition algorithm component, in general tasks. *See also operational evaluation, scenario evaluation.*

Template

A digital representation of an individual's distinct characteristics, representing information extracted from a biometric sample. Templates are used during biometric authentication as the basis for comparison. *See also extraction, feature, model.*

Threat

An intentional or unintentional potential event that could compromise the security and integrity of the system. *See also vulnerability.*

Threshold

A user setting for biometric systems operating in the verification or open-set identification (watchlist) tasks. The acceptance or rejection of biometric data is dependent on the match score falling above or below the threshold. The threshold is adjustable so that the biometric system can be more or less strict, depending on the requirements of any given biometric application. *See also comparison, match, matching.*

Thoroughput Rate

The number or biometric transactions that a biometric system processes within a stated time interval.

Token

A physical object that indicates the identity of its owner. For example, a smart card.

True Accept Rate

A statistic used to measure biometric performance when operating in the verification task. The percentage of times a system (correctly) verifies a true claim of identity. For example, Frank claims to be Frank and the system verifies the claim.

True Reject Rate

A statistic used to measure biometric performance when operating in the verification task. The percentage of times a system (correctly) rejects a false claim of identity. For example, Frank claims to be John and the system rejects the claim.

Type I Error

An error that occurs in a statistical test when a true claim is (incorrectly) rejected. For example, John claims to be John, but the system incorrectly denies the claim. *See also false reject rate (FRR)*

Type II Error

An error that occurs in a statistical test when a false claim is (incorrectly) not rejected. For example: Frank claims to be John and the system verifies the claim. *See also false accept rate (FAR).*

Uncooperative User

An individual who actively tries to deny the capture of his/her biometric data. Example: A detainee mutilates his/her finger upon capture to prevent the recognition of his/her identity via the fingerprint. *See also cooperative user, indifferent user, noncooperative user.*

User

A person such as an administrator, who interacts with or controls end user's interactions with a biometric system. *See also cooperative user, end user, indifferent user, noncooperative user, uncooperative user.*

US-VISIT—U.S. Visitor and Immigrant Status Indicator Technology

A continuum of security measures that begins overseas, at the Department of State's visa issuing posts, and continues through arrival and departure from the United States of America. Using biometric, such as digital, inkless finger-scans and digital photographs, the identity of visitors requiring a visa is now matched at each step to ensure that the person crossing the U.S. border is the same person who received the visa. For visa-waiver travelers, the capture of biometrics first occurs at the port of entry to the U.S. By checking the biometrics of a traveler against its databases, US-VISIT verifies whether the traveler has previously been determined inadmissible, is a known security risk (including having outstanding wants and warrants), or has previously overstayed the terms of a visa. These entry and exit procedures address the U.S. critical need for tighter security and ongoing commitment to facilitate travel for the millions of legitimate visitors welcomed each year to conduct business, learn, *see family, or tour the country*.

Verificaiton

A task where the biometric system attempts to confirm an individual's claimed identity by comparing a submitted sample to one or more previously enrolled templates. *See also identification, watchlist.*

Verification Rate

A statistic used to measure biometric performance when operating in the verification task. The rate at which legitimate end-users are correctly verified.

Voice Recognition

See speaker recognition.

Vulnerability

The potential for the function of a biometric system to be compromised by intent (fraudulent activity); design flaw (including usage error); accident; hardware failure; or external environmental condition. *See also threat.*

Watchlist

A term sometimes referred to as open-set identification that describes one of the three tasks that biometric systems perform. Answers the questions: Is this person in the database? If so, who are they? The biometric system determines if the individual's biometric template matches a biometric template of someone on the watchlist, as illustrated. The individual does not make an identify claim, and in some cases does not personally interact with the system whatsoever. *See also closed-set identification, identification, open-set identification, verification.*

Wavelet Scalar Quantization (WSQ)

An FBI-specified compression standard algorithm that is used for the exchange of fingerprints within the criminal justice community. It is used to reduce the data size of images.

Whorl

A fingerprint pattern in which the ridges are circular or nearly circular, as illustrated. The pattern will contain two or more deltas. *See also arch, delta point, loop, minutia(e) point.*

About the National Science and Technology Council

The National Science and Technology Council (NSTC) was established by Executive Order on November 23, 1993. This Cabinet-level Council is the principal means within the executive branch to coordinate science and technology policy across the diverse entities that make up the Federal research and development enterprise. Chaired by the President, the membership of the NSTC is made up of the Vice President, the Director of the Office of Science and Technology Policy, Cabinet Secretaries and Agency Heads with significant science and technology responsibilities, and other White House officials.

A primary objective of the NSTC is the establishment of clear national goals for Federal science and technology investments in a broad array of areas spanning virtually all the mission areas of the executive branch. The Council prepares research and development strategies that are coordinated across Federal agencies to form investment packages aimed at accomplishing multiple national goals. The work of the NSTC is organized under four primary committees; Science, Technology, Environment and Natural Resources, and Homeland and National Security. Each of these committees oversees a number of sub-committees and interagency working groups focused on different aspects of science and technology and working to coordinate the various agencies across the federal government. Additional information is available at www.ostp.gov/nstc.

About the Subcommittee on Biometrics

The NSTC Subcommittee on Biometrics serves as part of the internal deliberative process of the NSTC. Reporting to and directed by the Committee on Homeland & National Security and the Committee on Technology, the Subcommittee:

- Develops and implements multi-agency investment strategies that advance biometric sciences to meet public and private needs.
- Coordinates biometrics-related activities that are of interagency importance.
- Facilitates the inclusions of privacy-protecting principles in biometric system design.

- Ensures a consistent message about biometrics and government initiatives when agencies interact with Congress, the press and the public.
- Strengthen international and public sector partnerships to foster the advancement of biometric technologies.

Additional information on the Subcommittee is available at www.biometrics.gov

Subcommitte on Biometrics

Co-chair: Duane Blackburn (OSTP)
Co-chair: Chris Miles (DOJ)
Co-chair: Brad Wing (DHS)
Executive Secretary: Kim Shepard (FBI Contractor)

Department Leads

Mr Jon Atkins (DOS)
Mr Duane Blackburn (EOP)
Dr Joseph Guzman (DoD)
Ms Usha Karne (SSA)
Mr Chris Miles (DOJ)
Mr Brad Wing (DHS)

Dr Sankar Basu (NSF)
Ms Zaida Candelario (Treasury)
Dr Martin Herman (DOC)
Dr Michael King (IC)
Mr David Temoshok (GSA)
Mr Jim Zok (DOT)

Communications ICP Team

Champion: Kimberly Weissman (DHS US-VISIT)

Members & Support Staff:

Mr Richard Bailey (NSA Contractor)
Mr Duane Blackburn (OSTP)
Mr Jeffrey Dunn (NSA)
Ms Valerie Lively (DHS S&T)
Mr John Mayer-Splain (DHS US-VISIT Contractor)
Ms Susan Sexton (FAA)
Ms Kim Shepard (FBI Contractor)
Mr Scott Swann (FBI)
Mr Brad Wing (DHS US-VISIT)
Mr David Young (FAA)
Mr Jim Zok (DOT)

Special Acknowledgements

The Communications ICP Team wishes to thank the following external contributors for their assistance in developing this document:

- Kelly Smith, BRTRC, for performing background research and writing the first draft.
- Donald Reynolds, Hirotaka Nakasone, Jim Wayman, and the Standards ICP Team for reviewing the document and providing numerous helpful comments.

Document Source

This document, and others developed by the NSTC Subcommittee on Biometrics, can be found at www.biometrics.gov.

CHAPTER 4

THROUGHPUT MODELING FOR SUSTAINABILITY-RELATED ISSUES

Watch your thoughts; they become words. Watch your words; they become actions.
Watch your actions; they become habits. Watch your habits; they become character.
Watch your character; it becomes your destiny.

—Frank Outlaw

Ethics are pivotal in determining the success or failure of an organization. Ethics affect a company's reputation and help to define a business model that will thrive even in adversity. Organizations are increasingly becoming aware that managing ethical performance is going to become more central in its operations. Employees are in a position to add value to their organizations by contributing to managing ethical aspects of performance. Further, managing performance against ethical goals will become an increasing part of managers' roles pertaining to sustainability issues.

Sustainability has become a strategic success factor for organizations. More and more organizations have implemented sustainability as their business model, creating competitive advantages by integrating society, economy and environment factors in their strategy. In essence, sustainability concerns of individuals, societies and governments help form the world in which organizations have to operate.

Biometric and Auditing Issues Addressed in a Throughput Model, pp. 105–138
Copyright © 2012 by Information Age Publishing
All rights of reproduction in any form reserved.

Social factors echo the organization's impact on human and social capital. Human capital encapsulates the health, skills, knowledge and motivation of individuals. On the other hand, social capital is the value added by human relationships, partnerships and cooperation. *Economic factors* incorporate financial performance and indicate the organization's influence of the general economy as well as its own manufactured and financial capital. Manufactured capital depicts material goods and infrastructure implemented by the organization. Financial capital is critical to the continued existence of the organization and portrays the productive power and value of human and social capital. *Environmental factors* are related to natural capital (e.g., energy and matter sources) and processes utilized by an organization in delivering products and services.

Some organizations manage to take advantage of the opportunities and diminish the risks emerging from sustainability-driven trends. In their industry, these firms generate long-term shareholder value by participating in a pioneering role in sustainability. Sustain implies to keep in existence without diminishing and to nourish. Further, it entails operating in such a manner that a community does not diminish all its resources.

Many definitions of a sustainable community have been put forward; however, they all revolve around the interconnectedness of society, economy and environment. Sustainability measurements involves issues concerned with the environmental, social and economic domains, both individually and in various combinations) are still evolving: they include indicators, benchmarks, audits, indexes and accounting, as well as assessment, appraisal and other reporting systems (Dalal-Clayton & Sadler, 2009).

A widely held definition of sustainable development defines that sustainable development is a socioecological process characterized by the fulfillment of human needs while maintaining the quality of the natural environment indefinitely. The linkage between environment and development was globally recognized in 1980, when the International Union was presented by the Brundtland report in 1987. The report states that sustainable development is "development which meets the needs of the present without compromising the ability of future generations to meet their own needs" (WCED, 1987). This definition clearly implies that individuals and the natural environment have limited resources.

Our way of life is placing an escalating burden on the planet. The mounting strain we put on resources and environmental systems such as water, land and air cannot continue for perpetuity. In particular, as the world's population continues to increase and we already see a world where over a billion people live on less than a dollar a day. The goal of sustainable development is to enable all people throughout the world to satisfy their fundamental needs and benefit from an improved quality of life, without compromising the quality of life of future generations. Unless we start to make real progress toward reconciling these contradictions we face a future that is less certain and less secure.

WORLD COMMISSION ON ENVIRONMENT AND DEVELOPMENT

The primary objective of augmenting sustainability is to interconnect the essentials of economics, social, and environmental efficiency into a system that can be maintained in a healthy state. Efforts toward features of this aim are part of sustainability indicator identification. The sustainability magnitude can be calculated through a group of indicators including ecology, socioculture, history, politics, economics, technology, regulation, and natural resource. The magnitude of sustainability indicators can be divided into macro and micro levels, temporal (having to do with time, contrast with "spatial," which deals with space) and enduring effects, and high and low significance levels.

A useful methodology for sustainability is frequently referred to as the "triple bottom line" that takes into account environmental and social performance as well as economical performance. Conventional infrastructure development has mainly centered on maximizing economical performance attributable to budgetary constraints (constraints—a language for solving constraints using value inference (Mirza, 2006).

At the moment, sustainable development has spread out its boundaries to take into account constraints expressed from a range of interest groups and stakeholders. Their interests are primarily focused on social and environmental stewardship. The integration and application of environmental values into the military mission in order to sustain readiness, improve quality of life, strengthen civil relations, and preserve valuable natural resources.... for the duration of the development and life cycle. Augmenting the concept of sustainable development at a feasible level requires concurrently maximizing all three performance measures and minimizing negative influences from exceptionally complex relationships between sustainability issues. One chief problem is that many sustainability issues are complicated to quantify (quantify—a performance analysis tool from pure software) on a scale. Moreover, social and environmental issues tend to be subjective and qualitative, while economic issues can be transformed into a factor based on monetary values (Figure 4.1).

The Institute of Chartered Accountants in England and Wales (ICAEW, 2004) advanced eight different devices that are necessary for supporting information flows related to sustainability of organizations. These devices are

The Three Spheres of Sustainability

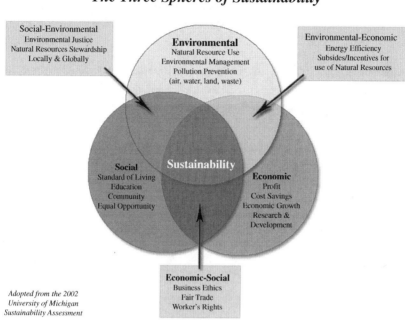

Figure 4.1. Path to sustainable development

1. corporate policies,
2. supply chain pressure,
3. stockholder engagement,
4. voluntary codes,
5. rating and benchmarking,
6. taxes and subsidies,
7. tradable permits, and
8. requirements and prohibitions (Figure 4.2).

Corporate policies relate to the expectation of societal influences on organization to adopt policies on sustainability as well as publishing information pertaining to the policies and their impact. *Supply chain* pressure conveys the expectation of societal influences on purchasers to put forward a preferred standard of sustainable performance and reporting among suppliers and

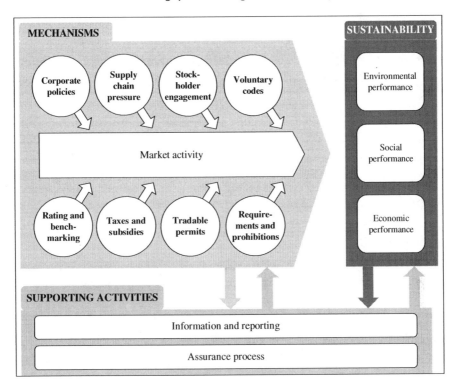

Figure 4.2. A market-based approach to sustainability
Source: Adopted from ICAEW, 2004.

others in the supply chain. *Stakeholder engagement* involves interested parties (e.g., customers, employees, shareholders, suppliers, community, etc.) dialogue and a process of feedback to organizations that is supported by information flows pertaining to sustainable performance. *Voluntary codes* transmit societal expectations and influences related to stakeholders' statement on compliance or an explanation of noncompliance. *Rating and benchmarking* relates to creditors, investors, regulatory and rating agencies grading of organizations by implementing benchmarks or ratings on the premise of sustainability policies and performance information. This process inevitably will influence the behavior of organizations and stakeholders. *Taxes and subsidies* provide an incentive for organizations to perform in a manner that contribute to sustainability as well as requiring information in the form of tax returns and credit claims. *Tradable permits* pertain to governments' ability to allocate/regulate scarce resources or undesirable influences whereby to improve

sustainability, which requires information about prices to support the operation of fair markets. *Requirements and prohibitions* refer to society consenting to
actions that improve sustainability as well as requiring relevant information
flows to enable enforcement agencies to monitor compliance.

Each of the aforementioned devices is dependent upon the support produced by reporting and assurance as well as the issues pertaining to the
overall progress towards sustainable development and the contributions of
organizations to sustainability (ICAEW, 2004). Information and reporting
assist the operation of devices to encourage sustainable development.
Assurance processes pertains to the fortification of the legitimacy of devices
to promote sustainable development. Finally, the Institute of Chartered
Accountants in England and Wales (ICAEW, 2004) asserted that the eight
devices and two supporting activities comprise an infrastructure for endors-
ing sustainability.

INTEGRATED GLOBAL SUSTAINABILITY PERSPECTIVE

Organizations' sustainability policies that are transparent are critical.
As long as stakeholders are provided with understandable and straightforward accessible information about these policies, the market will be able to
assign an appropriate risk premium to organizations. That is, organizations
attempting to bypass governance by having very few independent directors
or an overly aggressive compensation policy, or cutting the costs of capital
for companies that adhere to conservative accounting policies can result in
major long-term problems. Very few firms are indisputably transparent,
however, and this is an area where most organizations can and should do
much more. Corporate governance is a term that refers generally to the
processes, procedures, or laws by which firms are operated, regulated, and
controlled (Rodgers & Gago, 2001). This definition can be utilized to support sustainability factors described by the officers, stockholders or constitution of a firm, as well as to external forces such as consumer groups,
clients, and government regulations (see Figure 4.3).

Figure 4.3 suggests that the natural resource base offers the materials for
production by which jobs and shareholder profits are based upon. Employment affects the poverty rate and the poverty rate is associated with crime.
Air quality, water quality, and materials utilized for production have an
effect on health and perhaps a direct or indirect effect on shareholder profits. If a process necessitates clean water as a contribution, eliminating poor
quality water before processing is an additional expense that decreases
profits. Similarly, health problems attributable to common air quality problems or exposure to toxic materials have an effect on worker productivity
and play a part to the increasing costs of health insurance.

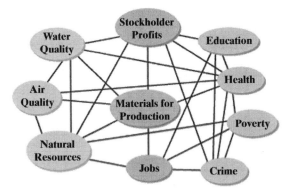

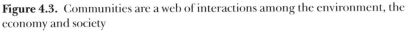

Figure 4.3. Communities are a web of interactions among the environment, the economy and society
Source: http://sustainablemeasures.com/Indicators/WhatIs.html.

Sustainability necessitates an integrated view of the world. It involves multidimensional factors that display the associations among a community's economy, environment, and society.

It is no longer adequate for organizations to meet minimum social and environmental constraints as a way of justifying their existence. They must also provide good reason for their continued existence in the future by building entirely new partnerships with stakeholders, including employees, customers and suppliers. These global megatrends will eventually lead to the emergence of new winners and losers in the different industries. The aim is to ascertain the most momentous sustainability-related challenges that will shape the future of each distinct sector.

BOARD INVOLVEMENT

There are many forms of corporate governance, which is predicated on distinct structures of ownership and impacted by vast variations on cultural and religious background, legal framework and political climate. The importance of board independence and the role of independent directors is an area of concern by stakeholders especially for widely held organizations. For example, an immediate concern involves the classic agency problem of how small and diverse shareholders attempt to make sure that managers are acting in the interest of shareholders (and other stakeholders at large) as opposed to their own self-interest.

Auditors ought to develop written guidelines on the use of risk assessment tools and risk factors and review these guidelines with the audit committee or the board of directors. Auditors should periodically assess the results of internal control processes and scrutinize financial or operational data for any impact on a risk assessment or scoring. Hence, operating management should be expected to update auditors on all major changes in departments or functions, such as the introduction of a new product, implementation of a new system, application conversions, or significant changes in organization or staff. From a theoretical perspective, independent directors and auditors serve as a partial recipe to this agency problem by providing checks and balances on sustainability issues.

This chapter highlights a *Throughput Model* that addresses sustainability issues by providing a structure that, at least in theory, works for the benefit of everyone (Rodgers, 1997). One of the primary sustainability issues addressed in this paper is the function of the independent auditors' report supporting board activities. Further, corporate governance and corporate responsibility factors were recognized as material to investment performance by 75% of investors (Ambachtsheer, 2006). The *Throughput Model* can capture ethical standards and sustainability practices as well as to formal laws. To that end, the *Throughput Model* may abate problems presenting confronting today's organizations.

A major challenge for auditors reporting to boards is to ensure that sustainability practices keep pace with changing risks that an entity faces in coming years. Unfortunately, dismissing or downplaying sustainability issues can compromise an auditor's opinion on the wellness of a firm. For example, auditors' independence issues have been tied to numerous financial scandals around the world, such as BCCI, Barings, Daiwa, Enron, Sumitomo, Credit Lyonnais, Bre-X, Lloyds, and WorldCom.

The *Throughput Model* suggests that a richer examination of corporate governance should include corporate financial performance (CFP) in relationship with corporate social performance (CSP) information that can enhance public trust with auditors. CSP is defined as a voluntary business action that produces social (third party) effects (Schuler and Cording, 2006). The interest in this reflection of moral and value system as drivers in firms along with CFP is viewed as more support and transparency for sustainability (Winnett & Lewis, 2000). For example, a 2002 DePaul University study (Timesizing News, 2004) indicated that overall financial performance of the 2001 *Business Ethics* Best Citizen firms was considerably better than that of the remaining firms in the S&P 500 Index, based on the *Business-Week* 2001 ranking of total financial performance. The ranking was established on eight statistical criteria, including total return, sales growth, and profit growth over the one-year and three-year periods, as well as net profit margins and return on equity. The Best Citizens scored 10 percentile points higher than the mean ranking of the remainder of the S&P 500 companies.

The next section deals with the decision-making model, followed by the importance of sustainability to CFP and CSP, and the independent auditor role. Lastly, conclusions and implications are drawn from this research paper.

BACKGROUND ON BOARD INVOLVEMENT

More and more boards are putting in place new structures and processes to enhance the efficacy of independent directors, such as lead independent directors, executive sessions, peer reviews, director training, and greater exposure to external appraisals from independent third parties (Dallas & Scott, 2006). For example, independent auditors' report can assist sustainability factors by addressing major issues confronting a firm's management. That is, the auditing standards typically require the auditor to obtain an understanding of the financial reporting internal control system, which may include internal control procedures designed to properly report in financial statements the consequences of compliance and material noncompliance with applicable laws and regulations, and report any detected material weaknesses to the suitable level within the firm. Together with other auditing standards, these procedures help increase sustainability practices occurring in a firm.

Even though directors may meet standards of independence in both thought and action, they may not be able to provide a complete solution to the agency problem of a self-interested management. This problem in part is due to the limited time that independent directors are able to devote to management oversight and control. Moreover, they may not develop an in-depth understanding of the firm and its sectors of activity. We suggest some possible independent auditing remedies to resolve some of these board issues.

With respect to institutional investors' ownership, even though these investors may have direct knowledge of a firm, they also have fiduciary responsibilities to their own investors, and therefore demand higher quality external monitoring in those firms in which they invest. Therefore, higher quality independent auditing demanded by institutional investors may be due to a larger investment at risk or a fiduciary responsibility to their own investors. On the contrary, firms with substantial family ownership are less likely to have information asymmetry problems since there is less division of ownership and control. Hence, these types of firms have less need for higher quality external auditors.

Institutional investors as a group are the most dominant investors in companies today (Rodgers & Gago, 2001). Institutional investors surveyed reported that 80% of them pursue a socially responsible approach that is driven by a desire to align investments with an underlying mission (Ambachtsheer, 2006). Institutional shareholders may be more concerned with global issues than are other shareholders. Johnson and Greening (1999) argued that institutional shareholders present diverse interests than other shareholders on corporate governance issues. In addition, they have different interest in those firms, and they are owners with large number of shares, hence influencing board matters (David et al., 1998). Bouma and Kamp-Roelands (2000) detected internal and external stakeholders' expectations regarding improving environmental performance, preventing environmental accidents, ensuring compliance with legislation, the provision of reliable information, and the control of waste handling in a global company. They found differences in the emphasis among internal and external stakeholders. Internal stakeholders demonstrated "more concern with the efficiency of generating information while external stakeholders were more concerned with the comparability of information" (2000, p. 140).

Westphal and Milton (2000) advocated that experience and network ties affect the influence of demographic minorities on corporate boards. They also commented, however "While the presence of demographic minorities on boards is typically viewed favorably by corporate stakeholders, the academic literature on organizational demography and social conformity is more pessimistic about the extent to which demographic minorities can successfully influence group decision making" (p. 367).

Most of the empirical evidence on the question of board independence is inconclusive in terms of causal links between board independence and firm performance (Dallas & Scott, 2006). The next section addresses this problem in the sense that we believe auditor independence portrayed in a theoretical model can influence board decisions on sustainability issues.

SUSTAINABILITY AND DECISION MAKING

Decision making can be quite complex when considering the adoption of a sustainability factors. Internal control biometrics technology has capabilities, features, and challenges that compound the complexity of interweaving the system with people, processes, and technology. For example, the supply chain encompasses those activities connected with the flow and transformation of goods from the raw material stage through to the end user including the related information flows (ICAEW, 2004). Supply chain management is the coordination of these activities in order to accomplish a competitive advantage. Figure 4.4 illustrates how it has advanced from an appeal to control product quality and price, as well as environmental and social impact. Hence, supply chain management functions have a vital role in contributing to the enhancement of sustainable consumption and production patterns.

The overall goal of this chapter is to provide decision makers with improved insight and knowledge into making often difficult and complex sustainability decision choices. Donaldson and Preston (1995) advocated that stakeholder theory focuses on managerial decision making. In addition, Jones and Wicks (1999) affirmed that although there is broad recognition for moral processes and outcomes based on the view that the claims of stakeholders have intrinsic value; however, there is a paucity of agreement on what those moral processes and outcomes should be, especially when influenced

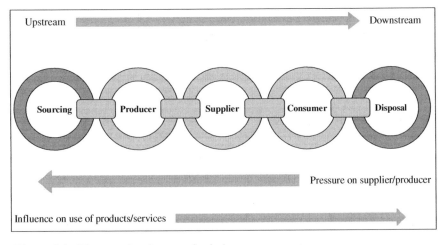

Figure 4.4. Diagram showing supply chain management
Source: Adopted from ICAEW, 2004.

by the "independence" of the auditor. The *Throughput Model* proposed here takes a distinctive approach to conceptualizing corporate governance issues by applying a decision making model to understanding this behavior within an organizational setting (Rodgers & Gago, 2001). The *Throughput Model* provides an expansive theoretical framework for examining interrelated processes that impact on decisions effecting organizations (Nutt, 1998). It incorporates the constructs of perception (framing), information, judgment (analysis of information/framing), and decision choice as it applies to firms (see Figure 4.5).

The *Throughput Model* emphasizes the six major elements that partners from the largest six accounting firms (PriceWaterhouseCoopers, KPMG, Deloitte, Ernst & Young, BDO and Grant Thornton) indicated that are important will be vital for capital market stability, efficiency and growth (DiPiazza et al., 2006, p. 1):

1. Investor needs for information (i.e., both CFP and CSP).
2. The roles of the various stakeholders (i.e., preparers, regulators, investors, standards setters and auditors) are aligned and supported with an effective communication link.
3. The auditing role provides a valuable link to stakeholders.
4. A model (e.g., *Throughput Model*) should be developed to deliver relevant and reliable information in a timely way.
5. Auditors provide an important service to the board of directors.
6. Information is reported and audited pursuant to globally consistent standards.

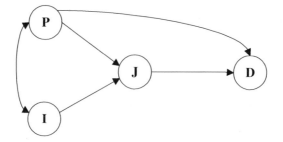

Figure 4.5. Diagram showing *Throughput Modeling* of individuals' decision processes. *P = perception, I = information, J = judgment, and D = decision choice*

The *Throughput Model* has shown to be useful in conceptualizing a number of different issues important to organizations (Culbertson & Rodgers, 1997; Rodgers, 1999; Rodgers & Housel, 2004). This *Throughput Model* is particularly relevant for it clarifies critical pathways influenced by ethical positions. Decision making in the *Throughput Model* is defined here as a multi-phase, information-processing function in which cognitive and social processes are used to generate a set of outcomes. There are differences of opinion about how many phases and subroutines within phases exist and the order in which the phases occur (Hogarth, 1987; Simon, 1957). The three phases in the *Throughput Model* proposed here appear with some consistency in the literature. These are (a) perception and information gathering, (b) analysis of information and processing (i.e., judgment), and (c) choice. This model represents a parsimonious way in capturing major concepts about organizations. Further, it provides a more interpretative cognitive schema. Finally, the *Throughput Model* conceptualizes an early warning system for organizations (Culbertson & Rodgers, 1997).

The *Throughput Model* of ethical considerations in Figure 4.5 can provide a useful analysis of sustainability issues that are prominent for firms. Arrows from one construct to another indicate the hypothesized causal relationships. Perception, in this model, is of a higher mental activity level that involves categorization and classification of information. Lower levels of perception include how people pick up or process information through their senses, such as vision, touch, hearing, etc. The lower level of perception normally involves automatic (and sometimes unconscious) reactions or responses to stimuli (information). The intensity of an ethical issue relates to the perceived importance of the issue by managers, auditors, employees, suppliers, and other stakeholders (Jones, 1991). Ethical issue intensity, then, can be defined as the perceived framing of an ethical issue by the independent auditor to the board of directors. Nutt added that "Studies of strategic decision making suggest that decisions are framed by stakeholders who call attention to seemingly developments by making a claim...The concerns and needs identified by stakeholders in the claim are examined by a decision maker who weighs the wisdom of taking action" (1998, p. 195). In the *Throughput Model*, the perceived framing of ethical issues has been found to have a strong impact on both ethical judgment and choice (Robin, Reidenbach & Forrest, 1996).

In addition, research has denoted that the perceptions of managers and professionals involved with technology are principal aspects in organizational decision making regarding the enrichment of internal control biometrics systems (Lease, 2005). These findings suggest that it is suitable to evaluate the managers' perceptions regarding internal control biometrics systems as well as their willingness to recommend or not to recommend biometrics as integral elements in the overall organizational technology adoption decision choice process. With regard to the evaluation of specific perceptions of technologies, Furthermore, many researchers have endorsed the justification for the decision choice to advocate a new biometric tool to perceptions of its cost-effectiveness, reliability, organizational need, and function-effectiveness (Lease, 2005).

The implications of internal control biometrics systems implementation relates to the enhancement of the quality of informed decision making. For example, significant changes in economic and business activity are continually having crucial inferences for the types of information investors' trust and need from financial reports channeled over the Internet in the future (DiPiazza et al., 2006). That is, the value of many firms resides in various "knowledge-based" assets (such as brand name, employee creativity and loyalty, and relationships with suppliers and customers). However, information to assess the value of these knowledge-based assets is not consistently reported (Rodgers, 2006). The utilization internal control biometrics systems may implicitly challenge the existing trust model between individuals and organizations since it influences the quality of information reported.

In the *Throughput Model*, perception and information are interdependent. That is, information can influence the way auditors frame a problem (perception) or their framing can influence the selection of information to be used in later analysis. The higher the coherence between perception and information generally indicates that the information set is more reliable and relevant. Further, this interdependence implies that perception can influence the kind of information selected for further processing. Likewise, information can influence and/or alter previous established perceptions. Information is later stored in memory (individual or corporate computer files) affects and contributes to auditors' analysis. Typically, before individuals, groups, or market participants can make a decision, they encode the information and develop a representation for the problem (Johnson-Laird, 1981). Finally, perception and judgment can affect decision choice.

Some authors, notably Kahneman and Tversky (1982), have suggested that automatic, perception-like heuristics and more deliberate information processing strategies (judgment) are involved in most decision choices. Errors, biases, and context-dependent heuristics may result from cognitive mechanisms of which decision makers (such as auditors, directors, and market participants) are largely unaware, and these may have a direct impact on decision choice (Rodgers, 1999). The strategies of judgment that influence decision choice are under decision makers' deliberate control. For example, there are also calls for boards of directors and auditors to consider the societal impacts of their firm's activities, given that those affected have the potential to appreciably impair or advance a firm's ability to generate wealth. In this fashion, the analysis of CFP and CSP include some of the broader elements of sustainability. In particular, this analysis can include corporate management deliberations in considering the effect of firm–society interactions on performance, to develop appropriate responses that minimize harmful social and environmental impacts and optimize opportunities, and to measure and disclose progress in this area.

The *Throughput Model* assists understanding the elements, such as auditors' reports, influence firms to act in a manner that may be ethical. Sustainability factors are a prerequisite for markets and society to function in an orderly manner. Investors purchasing stock from organizations that provide important contributions to society, such as education, medical care and child welfare encourages such initiatives taken by the corporations and promotes better social environment. Socially responsible investments' has shifted the profit-centric approaches of the business establishments to be more responsible organizations. Given the vastly increasing role of sustainability in the development of corporate strategy, it is clearly in the interest of business leaders to educate the financial markets on how these factors are linked to an organization's value.

The fund managers of major investment agencies implement different statistical methods and analysis to identify socially responsible stocks in the market. They grade the stocks based on the corporate ethics, values, and social service activities. Fund managers also scrutinize the sustainability indices of companies and rank them based on their carbon emissions (Rodgers, Choy, & Guiral, 2008).

Preeminent ethics policies address general employee conduct and encourage a sustainability factors in an organizational culture. A high-quality code of ethics should make available a small number of examples as needed to exhibit the application and solving of sustainability issues. It is not possible to produce a rule for every situation that may come up; hence an ethics policy should not be aimed at specifically defining each and every ethical dilemma that may occur.

The following general issues and topics should be addressed by an organization's code of conduct:

- General employee conduct while at work—What is expected in terms of ethical behavior and giving an employee's best efforts to the company?
- Conflicts of interest—Define conflicts of interest regarding sustainability issues and provide clear examples so that employees are sure of the types of things that fall under this guideline. Distinguish between acceptable conflicts of interest (those that are disclosed and monitored) as opposed to those that are unacceptable.
- Confidentiality—Address issues within the company (sharing information with other employees or departments) as well as sustainability issues connected with sharing information with people outside the company.
- Relationships with customers and suppliers—What types of professional and personal relationships are acceptable? Should they be disclosed? Will employees be reassigned in the event of such relationships?
- Gifts—Are employees allowed to receive gifts, and how large may the gifts be? Are there any types of gifts that are forbidden?
- Entertainment—Define the types of entertainment activities that are allowed, and how often they may occur.
- Unethical behavior—Define ethics in general and outline which behaviors are strictly prohibited, such as taking kickbacks or bribes, giving out confidential information, and falsifying employment documents.
- Using the organization's assets for personal activities—Are employees allowed to utilize any company resources for personal purposes? Consider things like Internet access, office supplies, copiers, and vehicles.
- Reporting fraud or unethical behavior—Encourage employees to report suspicions of fraud and outline the process followed when a complaint is received. Stress an open-door policy and the availability of the fraud hotline, the supervisors, and the managers going up the chain of command.

Additionally, antifraud training must include education on the ethics policy. The code of conduct must be explained and demonstrated, and employees should be given a chance to ask questions both publicly and in private.

It is perilous to take for granted that an employee can read the code of conduct and automatically comprehend all of its provisions. Probing the code of conduct during fraud awareness training is time well spent for an organization.

Employees should acknowledge their receipt and comprehension of the policy with an annual acknowledgment. It is a good idea to repeat the ethics policy training each year when these acknowledgments are due, to facilitate pointing out any changes or enhancements to the policy and to make employees aware of the new provisions.

Finally, the code of ethics must be obligatory in order for it to be a beneficial tool. Putting into operation and enforcing consistent and fair consequences for violations of the code is necessary.

ETHICAL CONSIDERATIONS IMPACT ON SUSTAINABILITY ISSUES

Ethical decision making is not always easy, and these guidelines do not explain the appropriate ethical behavior for every situation. As a guide to ethical decision making, the following questions can be put forward:

- Is it legal?
- Does it feel right?
- Will it reflect negatively on me?
- Would I be embarrassed if others knew about it?
- How would this look in the newspapers?
- Can I sleep at night?

Ethical guidelines should apply to organizational employees, officers, and members of the board of directors. Employees should make an obligation to uphold and carry out organizational commitment to lawful and ethical business conduct. This obligation includes, but it not limited to:

a. An understanding of and comply with organizational guidelines, as well as the legal requirements and other policies that apply to employees' work.

b. Seeking advice from either supervisor or human resources representative when there is a doubt about the best course of action in a particular situation or have questions regarding these guidelines.

c. Reporting promptly any organizational practice or other activity that an employee believes may be a possible violation of law or ethical guidelines.

d. Raising concerns through one of the other channels the organization makes available to employees if they believe the concern has not been satisfactorily addressed.

e. Cooperate fully in any organizational investigation related to possible violations of law or these guidelines and maintain the confidentiality of such investigation.

Leadership Responsibilities

Leaders, at every level, should serve their employees by internalizing the following values:

- Respect
- Integrity
- Personal courage
- Inspiration
- Knowledge
- Results
- Vision
- Change

In dealing with ethical issues, management should:

- Create and maintain a culture of integrity and sincerity by leading through example, ensuring compliance with ethical guidelines, and encouraging employees to raise integrity concerns.
- Prevent and uncover ethical violations by providing education and awareness to employees, monitoring activities in respective areas of responsibility, and putting into practice appropriate measures to detect violations.
- Respond to ethical concerns by promptly addressing issues and taking corrective action, augmenting internal controls as needed, and properly disclosing actions as required by law.

PENALTIES FOR VIOLATING THE WORKING WITH INTEGRITY GUIDELINES

Compliance with applicable laws and these guidelines should be meticulously enforced. If employees fail to comply with them, they should be subject to corrective action, up to and including termination of employment.

Following are examples of conduct that violate these guidelines and may result in discipline:

- Any action that violates an organization's policy or applicable law.
- Any request of another employee or third party to violate an organization's policy or applicable law.
- Failure to report a known or suspected ethics violation.
- Failure to cooperate in an investigation of a suspected ethics violation.
- Retaliation against an employee for reporting an ethics violation.

HOW TO RAISE INTEGRITY CONCERN OR POSSIBLE ETHICS VIOLATION

One of the most vital responsibilities for employees is the obligation to report possible workplace violations of law or ethical guidelines. Organizations should encourage employees to fulfill this responsibility and to seek advice when in doubt about the best course of action in a particular situation.

Organizations should offer several alternatives for achieving compliance advice and reporting possible violations of applicable law or ethical guidelines. Employees may contact their:

- supervisor or the next level of management above their supervisor,
- human resources department representative, or
- any member of the compliance (ethical) committee.

Employees may raise a concern either orally or in writing. Organizations may include a helpline and a Website established to provide employees channels to report possible violations confidentially and anonymously. When contacting the helpline or Website, employees may provide their name if they wish, but should not be required to do so. When employees contact the helpline or website, their report can be assigned to a tracking number that will enable them to receive an update on the reported matter or provide additional information.

The ethical program can be overseen by the organization's compliance committee. The compliance committee is responsible for ensuring that appropriate policies and procedures exist to help employees comply with organizational expectations of ethical conduct.

As part of the internal control system, an internal audit department can review reports of a possible violation of law or ethical guidelines on behalf of the compliance committee and refers the report to the appropriate department for investigation. The objective of the internal audit function is to independently inspect and evaluate the activities and assist the management in discharging their responsibilities, as a service to the Audit Committee. An internal audit department should furnish them with analysis, recommendations, advices and reports concerning the activities examined.

An internal audit department can report all complaints and concerns to the compliance committee. Complaints and concerns relating to an organization's accounting, internal accounting controls or auditing matters can be investigated by members of an internal audit department and reported to the audit committee of the organization's board of directors.

For example, audit committees are an important component of corporate governance. The audit committee independently reviews and watches over the general financial reporting process, the internal control system and the audit functions (internal and external). The committee, which reports to the board of directors, obtains advice and assistance from independent accounting, legal or other advisers as it deems necessary to carry out its duties.

Organizations must prohibit any employee from taking retaliatory action against anyone for making a good faith report of a possible violation or assisting in an investigation of a possible violation. If employees suspect that they have been retaliated against for reporting a possible violation or assisting in an investigation, they should contact their supervisor, human resources department, or a member of the compliance committee immediately.

Sustainability issues addressed in a *Throughput Model* may help explain how companies engaging in social responsibility activities may contribute to their current and future success by reducing potential risks and improving their performance (Cuesta-Gonzalez et al., 2006; Branco & Rodrigues, 2006). In addition to intangibles and the financial information, the sustainability issues in the *Throughput Model* depict the potential impact of CSP and auditors' opinion on firms' market value. The outside auditor can play a vital role in ensuring the integrity of a firm's CFP and CSP information. The auditor's position can be captured in the perception stage in the *Throughput Model* (see Figure 4.5). The reliability and relevance of CFP and CSP information is strategic to the management of the firm and to investor's decision making (McWilliams et al., 2006).

As investors use CFP and CSP information in deciding whether to invest in certain firms, they normally question how reliable the information is and whether the information is from a reliable source. Auditors' reports play a critical role in attesting to the reliability of CFP reported in a firm's annual report. Without the audit report, investors likely discount the value of CFP information reported in the annual report and the value of the firm's stock. Further, they are likely to conduct private search for further information in order to verify the accuracy and reliability of CFP information. The aggregate information search cost of the market can be significant and inefficient compared to the cost and benefit offered by the audit service. From the firm's point of view, engaging the auditor to provide the attestation service helps to reduce the cost of capital. And the benefits of the audit service should exceed its costs. Further, although the external audit function focuses apparently on the reliability of the financial information elaborated by the management, it is also indirectly providing an opinion regarding client's social responsibility performance. In this regard, independent auditors are responsible to evaluate and even, sometimes, disclose the impact of several kinds of uncertainties on clients' financial information. Most of those uncertainties are related to environment protection, the effects of potential lawsuits and litigations in progress, problems in terms of relationships with customers, suppliers, workers, government institutions, etc. Thus, a favorable audit opinion regarding the financial statements of a company is underlying a "tacit guarantee" that the firm is not involved in activities opposed to social responsibilities. Hence, audit services should improve the analysis of information and perceptual framing in the judgment stage of the sustainability issues in the *Throughput Model*.

Smart and Cohen (2010, p. 2) advocated the following recommendations for integrating ethics into strategy in order to enhance sustainable business models:

1. "Ethics must be embedded in business models, organization strategy and decision making processes.

2. Senior managers and business leaders must demonstrate an ethical approach by example. This will show that middle and junior managers will be rewarded for taking an ethical stance.

3. Nonexecutive directors should act as custodians of sustainability, with the particular duty of ensuring that their executive colleagues are building a sustainable business.

4. Managers must come to problems with "prepared minds," looking at ways in which an organization can benefit from an ethical approach rather than one that relies narrowly on cost cutting or compliance.

5. Finance professionals must play an active role as ethical champions by challenging the assumptions upon which business decisions are made. But they must do so while upholding their valued reputation for impartiality and independence.

6. Management accountants are encouraged to help ensure that their businesses are measuring performance on an appropriate timescale that will deliver sustained and sustainable success.

7. Business leaders should use the skills of the finance team to evaluate and quantify reputational and other ethical risks.

8. Finance professionals need to take social, environmental and ethical factors into account when allocating capital, so that sustainable innovation is encouraged."

Overall, the significant monitoring role played by auditors and others is supported by evidence documented in the various studies. This perspective is highlighted in the perception stage of the *Throughput Model*. Further, this monitoring role is not limited to U.S. but also is prevalent in other jurisdictions; it is not restricted to the common law jurisdiction but also in other jurisdictions; it is not limited to the developed economies but also in the developing economies.

CONCLUSIONS

Sustainability-driven organizations create threefold added value: environmental, sociocultural and economic. This capability to enhance effectiveness forms the basis for investments that will be successful in the longer term, generating attractive returns for investors while minimizing risk. As well as striving for economic competitiveness, sustainability-driven organizations elevate their strategy to draw on environmental and social growth potential, with the intention of generating substantial competitive advantage and greater shareholder value in the long term.

The greater environmental changes, the more essential it is for organizations to take both qualitative information and financial hard facts into account when making investment decisions. Hence, these organizations can boost their competitiveness by systematically exploiting changes in their business environment.

Organizations have recognized the importance of integrating sustainability performance data into their strategic planning, risk management and decision-making processes and are making significant progress in doing so. Furthermore, leading firms are exploring a range of types of audit and verification as a further means of increasing the credibility of their transparency and reporting efforts. Progressively more demands for enhanced transparency also embrace sustainability practices; stakeholders desire to know the manner in which firms use their ability to influence sustainability issues are consistent with stated social and environmental goals. As part of this move toward improved disclosure, many firms are placing ever more detailed information about their sustainability performance onto their publicly accessible websites.

Preeminent internal controls can be overridden by management. Quite a few of the organizational frauds which have come to light in the last few years were carried out when management circumvented controls. Committee members should gain an understanding of the degree of incentives and pressures faced by management; identify opportunities to override existing controls; and bring to bear an intensified amount of monitoring and attention over these areas. Management's adherence with the corporate code of conduct should be monitored and reviewed periodically. Any instances of inappropriate conduct by management should be dealt with fittingly to help avert and deter repetition.

Corporate governance, sustainability factors, human rights, and other global issues increasingly capture the attention of policy makers, the media, and other organizations. There are various reasons for firms becoming involved in social responsibility. Risk protection, market positioning, recruitment, and political–social relationships are a few reasons, each exhibiting an inverse relationship between short-term economic impact and long-term degree of commitment. For example, many firms may only engage in short-term socially responsible practice to protect against risks, reaping the short-term economic benefits, say, in environmentally required tasks. However, the real value is in long-term implementation tied to core value creation in the firm. The *Throughput Model* helps identify transparencies of CFP and CSP information sources impact on a firm's financial viability as depicted by the judgment stage in Figure 4.5. Further, the *Throughput Model* provides direct and indirect links of perceptual framing of the independent auditor role on market reaction to buying/selling firms' securities. In essence, the *Throughput Model* suggests that audit opinions can be more valuable for sustainability purposes.

Sustainability matters can be enhanced by an independent auditing mechanism that assesses an organization's all-embracing set of policies, practices and programs that are integrated into business operations, supply chains, and decision-making processes throughout the company. The issues that represent a firm's ethical behavior focus vary by business, by size, by sector and even by geographic region. The *Throughput Model* can relate to issues that include: business ethics, sustainability, environment, governance, human rights, marketplace and the workplace.

Institutional and other investors increasingly view sustainability issues as a strategic business concern. Numerous socially responsible investors are using the board of directors to pressure firms to change policies and increase disclosure on a wide range of corporate socially responsible issues, including environmental responsibility, workplace policies, community involvement, human rights practices, ethical decision-making and corporate governance. In addition, activist groups are also buying shares in targeted companies to give them access to annual meetings and the shareholder resolution process.

To truly embrace sustainability, changes must be made to the status quo of current infrastructure development practices and developing approaches for rewarding methods and materials employing sustainability principles should be adopted. Minimizing environmental impact, maximizing economical benefits, and minimizing sociocultural impacts should be quantified for application to infrastructure development.

In sum, the quest to standardize and have available sustainability metrics can, in part, aid auditors' reporting to the board of directors. Firms desire to verify what their sustainability initiatives have accomplished so that they can focus scarce resources most effectively. Hopefully, the *Throughput Model* can provide useful ways of approaching and structuring sustainability and corporate social responsibility issues in order to better serve society demands on firms.

REFERENCES

Ambachtsheer, J. (2006). *The Evolution of Responsible Investing.* http://www.northerntrust.com/pointofview/07_Jan/jan07_evolutioninvesting.html

Dalal-Clayton, B., & Sadler, B. (2009). *Sustainability appraisal. A sourcebook and reference guide to international experience.* London: Earthscan.

Institute of Chartered Accountants in England and Wales. (2004). *Sustainability: The role of accountants.* London: The Institute of Chartered Accountants in England and Wales.

Lease, D. R. (2005). *Factors influencing the adoption of biometric security technologies by decision making information technology and security managers* (Dissertation) Retrieved from http://etdindividuals.dlib.vt.edu:9090/305/1/David_Lease_UMI_Dissertation.pdf.

McWilliams, A. D., Siegel, P. M., & Wright, D. (2006). Guest editors' introduction. Corporate social responsibility: Strategic implications. *Journal of Management Studies, 43,* 1–18.

Mirza, S. (2006). Durability and sustainability of infrastructure—a state-of-the-art report. *Canadian Journal of Civil Engineering, 33,* 639–649.

Nutt, P. C. (1998). Framing strategic decisions. *Organization Science, 9,* 195–216.

Robin, D. P., Reidenbach, R. E., & Forrest, P. J. (1996). The perceived importance of an ethical issue as an influence on the ethical decision-making of ad managers. *Journal of Business Research, 35,* 17.

Rodgers, W. (1997). *Throughput modeling: Financial information used by decision makers.* Greenwich, CT: JAI Press.

Rodgers, W. (1999). The influences of conflicting information on novices' and loan officers' actions. *Journal of Economic Psychology, 20,* 123–145.

Rodgers, W. (2006). *Process thinking: Six pathways to successful decision making.* New York, NY: iUniverse.

Rodgers, W., Choy, H., & Guiral, A. (2008). The link between corporate social responsibility and corporate financial performance on the valuation of common stock. Collected abstracts of the 31st Annual Congress of the European Accounting Association, April.

Rodgers, W., & Gago, S. (2001). Cultural and ethical effects on managerial decisions: Examined in a *Throughput Model. Journal of Business Ethics, 31,* 355–367.

Rodgers, W., & Housel, T. (2004). The effects of environmental risk information on auditors' decisions about prospective financial statements. *European Accounting Review, 13,* 523–540.

Simon, H. A. (1957). *Models of man*. New York, NY: Wiley.

Smart, V., & Cohen, D. (2010). Incorporating ethics into strategy: Developing sustainable business models. Chartered Institute of Management Accountants (CIMA). www.cimaglobal.com/ethics.

Timesizing News. (2004). Purring beyond 'The Jungle' *Washington Times*, D. C., by Matt Daniels. http://www.timesizing.com/gts0411d.htm.

Westphal, J. D., & Milton, P. (2000). How experience and network ties affect the influence of demographic minorities on corporate boards. *Administrative Science Quarterly, 45*, 366–398.

Winnett, A., & Lewis, A. (2000). You'd have to be green to invest in this: Popular economic, financial journalism, and ethical investment. *Journal of Economic Psychology, 21*, 319–339.

WCED. (1987). *Our common future*. World Commission on Environmental and Development (WCED). Oxford, UK: Oxford University Press.

APPENDIX 4A

BUSINESS ETHICS TIMELINE

This appendix is taken from the Ethics Resource Center (ERC) (http://www.ethics.org/resource/business-ethics-timeline#60), which deals with the development of business ethics through five decades, examining:

- Ethical Climate
- Major Ethical Dilemmas
- Business Ethics Developments

1960S

Ethical Climate

Social unrest. Anti-war sentiment. Employees have an adversarial relationship with management. Values shift away from loyalty to an employer to loyalty to ideals. Old values are cast aside.

Major Ethical Dilemmas

- Environmental issues
- Increased employee -employer tension
- Civil rights issues dominate
- Honesty
- The work ethic changes
- Drug use escalates

Business Ethics Developments

- Companies begin establishing codes of conduct and values statements
- Birth of social responsibility movement
- Corporations address ethics issues through legal or personnel departments

1970S

Ethical Culture

Defense contractors and other major industries riddled by scandal. The economy suffers through recession. Unemployment escalates. There are heightened environmental concerns. The public pushes to make businesses accountable for ethical shortcomings.

Major Ethical Dilemmas

- Employee militancy (employee versus management mentality)
- Human rights issues surface (forced labor, sub-standard wages, unsafe practices)
- Some firms choose to cover rather than correct dilemmas

Business Ethics Developments

- ERC founded (1977)
- Compliance with laws high-lighted
- Federal Corrupt Practices Act passed in 1977
- Values movement begins to move ethics from compliance orientation to being "values centered"

1980S

Ethical Culture

The social contract between employers and employees is redefined. Defense contractors are required to conform to stringent rules. Corporations downsize and employees' attitudes about loyalty to the employer are eroded. Health care ethics emphasized.

Major Ethical Dilemmas

- Bribes and illegal contracting practices
- Influence peddling
- Deceptive advertising
- Financial fraud (savings and loan scandal)
- Transparency issues arise

Business Ethics Developments

- ERC develops the U.S. Code of Ethics for Government Service (1980)
- ERC forms first business ethics office at General Dynamics (1985)
- Defense Industry Initiative established (1986)
- Some companies create ombudsman positions in addition to ethics officer roles
- False Claims Act (government contracting)

1990S

Ethical Climate

Global expansion brings new ethical challenges. There are major concerns about child labor, facilitation payments (bribes), and environmental issues. The emergence of the Internet challenges cultural borders. What was forbidden becomes common.

Major Ethical Dilemmas

- Unsafe work practices in third world countries
- Increased corporate liability for personal damage (cigarette companies, Dow Chemical, etc.)
- Financial mismanagement and fraud

Business Ethics Developments

- Federal Sentencing Guidelines for Organizations (1991)
- Class action lawsuits
- Global Sullivan Principles (1999)
- In re Caremark (Delaware Chancery Court ruling re Board responsibility for ethics)
- IGs requiring voluntary disclosure
- ERC establishes international business ethics centers
- Royal Dutch Shell International begins issuing annual reports on their ethical performance

2000S

Ethical Culture

Unprecedented economic growth is followed by financial failures. Ethics issues destroy some high profile firms. Personal data is collected and sold openly. Hackers and data thieves plague businesses and government agencies. Acts of terror and aggression occur internationally.

Major Ethical Dilemmas

- Cyber crime
- Privacy issues (data mining)
- Financial mismanagement
- International corruption
- Loss of privacy—employees versus employers
- Intellectual property theft
- The role of business in promoting sustainable development

Business Ethics Developments

- Business regulations mandate stronger ethical safeguards (Federal Sentencing Guidelines for Organizations; Sarbanes-Oxley Act of 2002)
- Anticorruption efforts grow
- Stronger emphasis on Corporate Social Responsibility and Integrity Management
- OECD Convention on Bribery (1997–2000)
- UN Convention Against Corruption (2003); UN Global Compact adopts 10th principle against corruption (2004)
- Revised Federal Sentencing Guidelines for Organizations (2004)
- Increased emphasis on evaluating ethics program effectiveness

APPENDIX 4B

The following twelve principles, proposed by the *Ontario Round Table on Environment and Economy*, encompass the social, economic, environmental, and decision-making aspects of sustainable communities:

MODEL PRINCIPLES FOR SUSTAINABLE COMMUNITIES

Source: Ontario Round Table on Environment and Economy

A sustainable community is one which:

1. Recognizes that growth occurs within some limits and is ultimately limited by the carrying capacity of the environment
2. Values cultural diversity
3. Has respect for other life forms and supports biodiversity
4. Has shared values amongst the members of the community (promoted through sustainability education)
5. Employs ecological decision making (e.g., integration of environmental criteria into all municipal government, business and personal decision-making processes)
6. Makes decisions and plans in a balanced, open and flexible manner that includes the perspectives from the social, health, economic and environmental sectors of the community
7. Recognizes that growth occurs within some limits and is ultimately limited by the carrying capacity of the environment
8. Values cultural diversity
9. Has respect for other life forms and supports biodiversity
10. Has shared values amongst the members of the community (promoted through sustainability education)
11. Employs ecological decision making (e.g., integration of environmental criteria into all municipal government, business and personal decision-making processes)
12. Makes decisions and plans in a balanced, open and flexible manner that includes the perspectives from the social, health, economic and environmental sectors of the community
13. Makes best use of local efforts and resources (nurtures solutions at the local level)
14. Uses renewable and reliable sources of energy

15. Minimizes harm to the natural environment
16. Fosters activities which use materials in continuous cycles. *And, as a result, a sustainable community*
17. Does not compromise the sustainability of other communities (a geographic perspective)
18. Does not compromise the sustainability of future generations by its activities (a temporal perspective).

APPENDIX 4C

PRINCIPLES OF SUSTAINABLE DEVELOPMENT

This appendix sets out the shared United Kingdom (UK) principles of sustainable development in the UK. They apply to the UK Government, Scottish Executive, Welsh Assembly Government and the Northern Ireland Administration. For a policy to be sustainable, it must respect all five principles. We want to live within environmental limits and achieve a just society, and we will do so by means of sustainable economy, good governance, and sound science (http://www.defra.gov.uk/sustainable/government/what/principles.htm).

Living Within Environmental Limits

Respecting the limits of the planet's environment, resources and biodiversity - to improve our environment and ensure that the natural resources needed for life are unimpaired and remain so for future generations.

Ensuring a Strong, Healthy & Just Society

Meeting the diverse needs of all people in existing and future communities, promoting personal well-being, social cohesion and inclusion, and creating equal opportunity for all.

Achieving a Sustainable Economy

Building a strong, stable and sustainable economy which provides prosperity and opportunities for all, and in which environmental and social costs fall on those who impose them (Polluter Pays) and efficient resource use is incentivised.

Using Sound Science Responsibly

Ensuring policy is developed and implemented on the basis of strong scientific evidence, whilst taking into account scientific uncertainty (through the Precautionary Principle) as well as public attitudes and values.

Promoting Good Governance

Actively promoting effective, participative systems of governance in all levels of society - engaging people's creativity, energy, and diversity.

APPENDIX 4D

SUSTAINABILITY ASSESSMENT MODELS AND SYSTEMS

http://www.fsn.co.uk/channel_kpi_environment/sustainability_assessment_
models_and_systems

While environmental issues continue to rise up the organizational agenda, so does the importance of adopting financial analysis techniques for assessing sustainability issues. Models or framework are needed that enable valuations of corporate sustainability to be systematically and accurately made, and that also measure the impact of sustainability on an organization's financial performance.

ENVIRONMENTAL INTERNAL CONTROL SYSTEMS CYCLE

Internal control systems can be implemented to encapsulate and measure sustainability data such as the organization's core environmental impacts. Objectives and suitable actions can then be set for their reduction. Internal control systems can enable the inclusion of environmental performance measures into strategic management and operational monitoring. Such sustainability systems recognize that there may be no overall optimum solution to highly complex environmental and sustainability issues. Nonetheless, it is possible to assume a course of action that diminishes the influences to the environment, as well as to the organization's economic performance.

ANALYTICAL FRAMEWORKS FOR FINANCIAL EVALUATION OF ENVIRONMENTAL IMPACTS

Yachnin and Associates (Yachnin & Associates, Sustainable Investment Group Ltd & Corporate Knights, 2006) developed a framework entitled The sdEffect™, which encompasses seven steps of sustainable development into financial valuation measures. These steps are as follows:

1. identify the environmental metric to be analyzed;
2. establish the scope of the metric, including
   (a) operations that are to be reviewed
   (b) factors which are material
   (c) what is the timeline?
   (d) what can be measured and quantified?
   (e) what must be estimated?

3. gather data and quantify as many elements of the metric as possible;

4. consider valuation methodologies that are appropriate for the company's industry and apply these to the data;

5. convert the valuation impacts into per share impacts or another basis for communicating additive value in financial terms;

6. aggregate results for individual metrics to estimate the overall valuation impact of the environmental factors; and

7. communicate findings with relevant audiences.

A worked example of how this is translated is given below.

Appendix 4D Table 1.   Environmental Valuation Information for Solid Waste Diversion

Metric	*Valuation information*
Solid waste diversion	Identify volume of waste reduction/diversion
	Identify type of waste reduction/diversion
	Identify average cost/unit of waste reduction/diversion savings

Solid Waste Diversion

Performance:
Nonhazardous solid waste is diverted from municipal landfill at the Sudbury location

Translation:
Cost savings on landfill fees = $3.5 million per year

Valuation:
Example A—Discounted Cash Flow (DCF)
i) Estimate cost of capital

$$WACC = Rf + ß(Rm\text{-}Rf)$$

where;

$WACC$ = weighted average cost of capital
  Rf = risk free rate of return (10-year)
   $ß$ = stock beta
$(Rm\text{-}Rf)$ = equity risk premium
Therefore;

$WACC = 5.3\% = 1.4\ (7.5\%)$
$WACC = 15.8\%$

ii) Estimate value of cash flow assuming 6% annual growth in usage or avoided fees
DCF = incremental cash flow/(WACC-growth)
    = $3.5 million/(15.8%-6%)
Present value of savings = $36 million

iii) Convert to per share valuation
Shares outstanding = 200 million
Per share incremental value = $0.18 per share

Result
Waste diversion at INCO saves the company $3.5 million per year, which is equivalent to just over 1 cent earnings per share. These savings are worth $36 million in total shareholder value (using DCF).

Source: Yachnin & Associates, Sustainable Investment Group Ltd & Corporate Knights Inc. 2006.

Appendix 4D Table 1 above illustrates the translation of solid waste diversion to DCF, whereby at an estimated weighted average cost of capital of 15.8%, and an estimated value of cash flow assuming 6% annual growth in usage or avoided fees, this represents a present value of savings by waste diversion of approximately $36 million, and with 200 million shares outstanding, this converts to per share incremental value of this waste diversion of $0.18 per share.

INTEGRATED FRAMEWORK FOR FINANCIAL ANALYSIS OF SUSTAINABILITY

Appendix 4D Figure 1 below pinpoints six financial value drivers of sustainability; customer attraction, brand value and reputation, license to operate, human and intellectual capital, innovation and risk profile that have been integrated into a model of shareholder added value. This illustrates how the management of environmental matters can be linked to the organization's capability to produce value. From this cause and effect ratios can be developed.

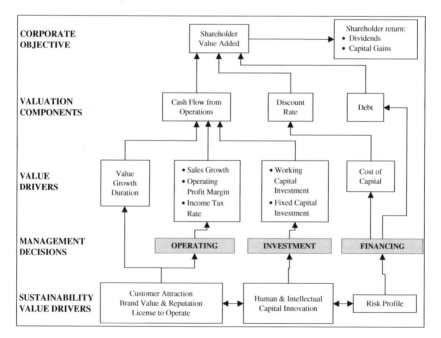

Appendix 4D Figure 1. Conceptual model of the financial analysis of sustainability

CHAPTER 5

ETHICAL ISSUES ADDRESSED IN BIOMETRICS MANAGEMENT

"Government and industry have a common challenge in today's global society to provide more robust identity management tools and identify governance principles on how to deploy these tools intelligently to meet national and international standards."

—National Science and Technology Council Subcommittee on
Biometrics and Identity Management, 2006

Biometric-based tools can provide for confidential financial transactions and personal data privacy. There are some signs that biometrics were implemented by the ancient Egyptians by measuring individuals for identification purposes. In ancient Babylon, fingerprints were impressed into clay tablets for commercial transactions. In ancient China, thumbprints were found on clay seals. In addition, there are also some early records of the utilization of biometrics by the fourteenth century Chinese, recording children's and footprints, again for identification purposes.

The requirement for biometrics can be located in federal, state and local governments, in the military, and in commercial applications. Biometric applications include workstation, network, and domain access, single sign-on, application logon, data protection, remote access to resources, transaction security and Web security. Trust in these electronic

Biometric and Auditing Issues Addressed in a Throughput Model, pp. 139–180
Copyright © 2012 by Information Age Publishing

transactions is essential to the vigorous growth of the global economy. Biometrics permeates nearly all aspects of the economy and our daily lives. Whether they are alone or combined with other technologies, biometrics such as smart cards, encryption keys and digital signatures are everywhere in our society.

The meaning of Biometrics is derived from the Greeks. The Greek hybrid of the word is *bio* meaning life and *metry* denoting to measure. The Webster's definition is the statistical measurement and analysis of biological observations and phenomena. In a more clear-cut sense, the word biometrics connotes using the body as a password. Biometrics is a general term utilized to depict a feature or process. As a feature, it is a measureable biological (physical or chemical) and behavioral tool implemented for recognition. As a process, it employs tools of recognizing a person based on measureable biological and behavioral characteristics. Consequently, biometrics is considered the discipline of determining the identity of a person founded on the physical, chemical or behavioral attributes of the individual (Jain, Flynn, & Ross, 2008).

For internal control systems, biometrics is utilized as a form of identity access management and access control. Furthermore, it is implemented to identify individuals in groups that are under surveillance. Vacca (2007) claimed "Biometrics technologies vary in complexity, capabilities, and performance, but all share several elements. Biometrics identification systems are essentially pattern recognition systems. They use acquisition devices such as cameras and scanning devices to capture images, recordings, or measurements of an individual's characteristics, and use computer hardware and software to extract, encode, store, and compare these characteristics." Hence, for internal control systems use, biometrics presents a technique that will continually impact on the way users interact with one another.

Enterprise-wide network security infrastructures, government IDs, passports, secure electronic banking, investing and other financial transactions, retail sales, law enforcement, and health and social services are now benefiting from these technologies. Among the biometric features measured are face, fingerprints, hand geometry, handwriting, iris, retinal, vein, and voice. There are a variety of ways in which biometrics is being used today. For instance, at Coca-Cola Co., hand-scanning machines recently replaced the time card for many employees. In New Jersey and six other states, fingerprint scanners are now implemented to eliminate people claiming welfare benefits listed in two different names. In Cook County, Illinois, a highly developed camera that analyzes the iris patterns of a person's eyeball is helping ensure that the right people are released from prison. At Purdue University in Indiana, the campus credit union inaugurated automated teller machines with a finger scanner that eliminates the need for plastic bankcards and personal identification numbers (http://www.geocities.com/ResearchTriangle/8028/biometrics.htm#V).

Other examples include MasterCard International Inc. and Visa USA Inc., the world's two biggest credit card companies; have begun to study the feasibility of using finger-scanning devices at the point of sale to verify that the card user is the actual card holder. The scanners will compare fingerprints with biometric information stored on a microchip embedded in the credit card. In addition, Walt Disney World in Orlando has begun to take hand scans of people who purchase yearly passes. These visitors now must pass through a scanner when entering the park thwarting them from lending their passes to other people.

The Immigration and Naturalization Service is allowing a limited group of travelers bypass lengthy lines at New York's John F. Kennedy International Airport and Newark international Airport by placing their bands and special cards the service has issued into an automated turnstile. International Business Machines Corp. is designing a project called FastGate to commercialize the service, possibly having airline frequent-flier programs and businesses pay for the program. Visitors to the United States are required to provide a full set of 10 fingerprints and a digital photograph at the port of entry. This information is checked against United States Government watch-lists of identified or suspected terrorists or criminals.

Biometric tools are becoming the bedrock of a wide-ranging assortment of highly secure identification and personal verification solutions. As the level of security breaches and transaction fraud increases, the necessity for highly secure identification and personal verification technologies is becoming apparent.

There are two different ways to recognize a person: identification and verification (or authentication). The *identification* process entails matching a biological or behavioral characteristic of an individual to an established and preconfirmed record of that characteristic (Jain, Hong, & Pankanti, 2000). For example, matching the image of my palm print to a palm print in a large number of palm prints in a database is considered an identification procedure. These "one-to-many" identification search tools are being extended to other entitlement programs such as healthcare, and to registration systems such as voting, driver's licenses and other applications. In all cases, your fingerprint pattern, or a derivative of that pattern, is stored in a database file.

On the other hand, *verification* is performed through the presentation of a "token" such as a PIN, a card, or a biometric whose validity is confirmed, and thereby substantiating one's eligibility to access a specific service. There is no searching and matching to a database, only the legitimacy of the token is determined, through a single one-to-one match. For example, if you are accessing money from a bank machine, the system has some form of control to serve as the gateway to let you in, and keep all the others out.

In this type of activity, the system is not searching a database to validate you. The system is authenticating your eligibility to access the bank machine. Employing biometrics for personal verification is becoming convenient and considerably more accurate than current methods (such as the utilization of passwords or PINs). This is because biometrics links the event to a particular individual (a password or token may be used by someone other than the authorized user), is expedient (nothing to carry or remember), precise (it provides for positive verification), can provide an audit trail and is becoming socially acceptable and cost-effective.

In sum, identification is a more challenging problem since it involves 1:N matching compared to 1:1 matching for verification. Verification (*Am I who I claim I am?*) entails substantiating or rebuffing an individual's *claimed identity* (Jain, Ross, & Prabhakar, 2004). Whereas, in identification, the system has to recognize an individual (*Who am I?*) from a list of N users in the template database (Table 5.1).

Biometric tools should be contemplated and evaluated in using the following characteristics:

1. *Universality*: Every man, woman, and child should have the characteristic. Individuals who are mute or without a fingerprint will need to be accommodated in some way.
2. *Uniqueness*: In general, no two people have the exact same characteristics. However, it may be challenging to distinguish between identical twins.
3. *Permanence*: The characteristics should not change throughout time. An individual's face, for example, may change with age.
4. *Collectability*: The characteristics must be simple to assemble and measure.
5. *Performance*: The technique must render accurate findings under dissimilar environmental circumstances.
6. *Acceptability*: The general public must be amenable to the sample gathering practices. Nonintrusive tools are more acceptable.
7. *Circumvention*: The technology should be very challenging to deceive.

Table 5.1.   Recognition: Identification vs. Verification

Identification	*Verification*
Who is this INDIVIDUAL?	Is this INDIVIDUAL who she says she is?
1:N	1:1
Data bank with linked personal information	No Data bank
Overt or Covert	Overt

Most biometric technology systems implement the same fundamental principles of operation. First, an individual must be registered, or enrolled, on the biometric system. This enrollment is achieved through the sampling and storehouse of unique biometric characteristics. The sampling is normally processed through a mathematical algorithm that exchanges the characteristics to a digital mathematical representation. This distinctive mathematical representation is referred to as a template or profile, and is implemented to as a basis of comparison when the registered individual needs to be authenticated. Biometric technology companies commonly consider these algorithms as proprietary, well-guarded secrets.

To be authenticated, an individual must provide a real-time biometric measurement. This measurement is then processed utilizing the same algorithm that was implemented at enrollment. The output of the live measurement is then match up to the stored template.

The system administrator can set the precision criteria the algorithm implements to contrast the live measurement and the template. The elevated the percentage of match required for a person, then the higher the degree of security. Authentication is approved on a match/no match basis.

Typically, there are three different techniques for confirming identity: (a) possessions, like cards, badges, keys; (b) knowledge, like user identification, password, Personal Identification Number (PIN); (c) biometrics like fingerprint, face, ear. Biometrics offer much higher accuracy than the more traditional ones. Possession can be lost, forgot or replicated easily. Knowledge can be erroneously reconstructed or forgotten. Both possessions and knowledge can be stolen or carved up with other people. In biometrics, these shortcomings exist only on an insignificant level.

With the increasing need for stronger internal control biometrics system, it is simpler than ever to obtain another individual's identifying information, and perpetrate identity fraud. To detect fraudulent or stolen identities and stem the increasing tide of losses due to identity fraud, organizations are employing biometric systems that enable them to stay one step ahead of potential frauds. Multifactor authentication consists of verifying and validating the authenticity of an identity using more than one validation mechanism.

Generally, this is accomplished by verifying:

1. Something you are, in the form of identifying information, or biometric identification, such as an iris scan or a fingerprint.

2. Something you have, for example a driver's license, or a security token.

3. Something you know, such as a password or pin number.

This is not a new notion in that it has been a foundation of cryptography for centuries. Today, multifactor authentication is used in numerous applications, from ATM cards that are secured by Personal Identification Numbers (PINs) to websites that are protected by digital certificates and passwords.

Evaluating the performance of a biometric identification system for internal control systems use is a challenging research topic. The overall performance of a biometric system is assessed in terms of its accuracy, speed, and storage. Several other factors, like cost and ease-of-use, also affect efficacy. Biometric systems are not perfect, and will now and then mistakenly accept an impostor as a valid person (a false match) or conversely, reject a valid person (a false nonmatch). The probability of committing these two types of errors is termed false nonmatch rate (FNR) and false match rate (FMR). The magnitudes of these errors depend upon how freely or conventionally the biometric system operates.

Information technology has changed what was once thought of as distance business transactions. Through computers, cable lines, satellites, and many other technologies, it is now possible to have a kind of face to face communication although the group of individuals may be many miles apart. Many issues will nevertheless be outstanding even with these advanced technologies. The following issues can be addressed: How do we effectively identify an individual or individuals during certification sessions, homework, and general correspondence? Who will we implement these technologies upon the user group? How cost effective will these technologies be? A variety of biometric technologies may be implemented into the distance learning business environment to ensure credibility.

A major issue the distance learning educational environment is confronted with is how to effectively identify a student whom the teacher cannot visibly see. A variety of biometric tools are proposed solutions to this predicament. A biometric tool available is a computer mouse which has a fingerprint scanning device built directly into it. The mouse with a finger-scanning device directly assembled into it is a substantial amount inexpensive than an attachable finger-scanning device. Many organizations implement an automated system to validate and verify users' identifying information. This is a highly effective means of mitigating fraud risk, but as fraudsters become more sophisticated, the following biometrics systems provide the means of detecting and preventing identity fraud.

EMPLOYMENT OF INTERNAL CONTROL BIOMETRICS SYSTEMS

In any internal control systems environment, it is essential to ensure that the biometric tool developed meets the needs of the organization, as well as the needs of the users. The business requirements help to specify what the organization wants to achieve (Rodgers, 2010). The following issues should be addressed:

1. Develop a system that will accurately and efficiently collect biometric samples.
2. Reduce the number of system errors.
3. Design an intuitive interface that will decrease the amount of assistance/help required to use the biometric device.

The internal control systems organizational requirements for management should include the following:

1. What is the purpose of the system?
2. What are the goals for the biometric tools?
3. How would you describe the system?
   (a) From an organization's standpoint?
   (b) From a user's standpoint?
4. What outcomes would management desire to achieve?
5. How would management define a successful system for the organization?

The next section introduces a review of physiological and behavioral biometrics (www.biometrics.gov) as well as how they would operate in security systems for government, society, and businesses (see Table 5.2).

Table 5.2.   Physiological and Behavioral Biometrics Classification

Physiological	Behavioral
Fingerprint	Speaker recognition
Palm print	Gait
Hand geometry	Dynamic signature
Vein patterns	Keystroke dynamics
DNA	
Retina scan	
Iris scan	
Face recognition	
Face thermography	
Ear recognition	
Body odor recognition	

PHYSIOLOGICAL BIOMETRICS (TABLE 5.3)

Fingerprint

A fingerprint is the depiction of the epidermis (the outer nonsensitive and nonvascular layer of the skin of a vertebrate that overlies the dermis) of a finger. It consists of a pattern of alternate layers of ridges and valleys (Diagram 5.1) (Ashbaugh, 1999). Fingerprint identification is one of the most recognized and implemented biometrics. Due to its uniqueness and consistency over time, fingerprints have been exploited for identification for well over a century. However, the utilization of biometric readers in this technology is fairly recent. Fingerprint technology is the most popular area of biometrics because it is simple to acquire, the numerous sources (10 fingers) available for collection. In addition, there is a wide storage database within law enforcement agencies. Biometric readers for fingerprints calculate the ridge endings and the splits in the ridge paths of the high part of the fingerprint. The configuration of the fingerprint is also matched. The large database of stored fingerprints permits for rapid identification. Fingerprint recognition tools are found to be highly reliable with very few errors. Biometric readers capable of reading fingerprints are now making their way into the commercial arena such as laptop computers since their reliability is quite high.

Table 5.3.   Biometrics Types

Biometrics type	Strength	Weakness	Cost	Countermeasures	Convenience
Physiological					
Fingerprint	Easy, inexpensive	Easily spoofed	Low	Guards present to observe the process	Good
Palm print	Able to deal with minor variations	Cost, large scanner	Medium	Guards present	Good
Hand geometry	Simple acquisition	Cost, injury to hand may be rejected	Medium	Implement with compatible biometrics to increase accuracy	Excellent
Vein pattern	Accurate, proof of life	Expensive, not yet mature	Medium to high	Not needed	Excellent
DNA	Deterministic, accurate	Requires a long time to process	High	Not needed	Poor

Biometrics type	Strength	Weakness	Cost	Countermeasures	Convenience
Retinal scan	Accurate	Expensive, difficult to train users, rare	High	Guards needed to oversee the process	Poor
Iris scan	Very accurate	Not many vendors	Medium	Guards need to oversee the process	Excellent
Face recognition	Simple to acquire from a distance	Facial image may be hard to obtain	Low to medium	Implement with compatible biometrics to increase accuracy	Excellent
Face thermography	Not vulnerable to disguises	View dependent, depends on emotional state	Medium	Implement with compatible biometrics to increase accuracy	Excellent
Ear recognition	Accurate	Not mature yet	Low to medium	Implement with compatible biometrics to increase accuracy	Excellent
Odor	Unique	Verification may be unpleasant	High	Not needed	Excellent
Behavioral					
Speaker recognition	Simple acquisition	Easily spoofed unless countermeasures are implemented	Low	Use with speech recognition whereby recordings do not work	Excellent
Gait	Simple to acquire from a distance	Not very accurate	Medium	Implement with compatible biometrics to increase accuracy	Excellent
Dynamic signature	Relates a person to documents	Not very accurate	Low	n/a	Excellent
Keystroke dynamics	No new sensors needed	Requires software on the devices	Low	Secure the transmission path to prevent replay attacks	Excellent

Diagram 5.1. Fingerprint image
http://education.vetmed.vt.edu/curriculum/vm8054/labs/Lab14/IMAGES/
FINGERPRINT.jpg

Palm Print

Palm print is concerned with the inner surface of a hand (Diagram 5.2).
Palm print recognition intrinsically implement many of the same matching
characteristics that enable fingerprint recognition to be one of the most
familiar and best publicized biometrics (Jing & Zhang, 2004). That is, a
palm is covered with the same skin type as the fingertips and it is larger
than a fingertip in size. Both palm and finger biometrics are embodied by
the information portrayed in a friction ridge impression. This information
unites ridge flow, ridge characteristics, and ridge structure of the raised
segment of the epidermis. Each palm print is distinctive to the person and
the mathematical formulas are fairly simple to store in a large database
(Jing & Zhang, 2004). Since fingerprints and palms have both uniqueness
and permanence, these tools have been implemented well over a century as
a reliable mode of identification. These biometric readers are currently
very appealing to law enforcement because many times forensics can only
find a palm print as a clue. Nevertheless, palm print recognition has been
slower in becoming automated due to some limitations in computing capabilities and live scan technologies.

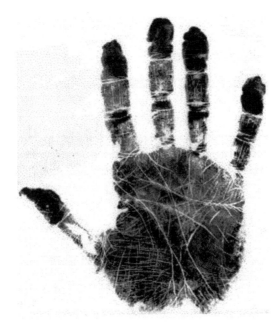

Diagram 5.2. Palm print image
http://www.akribis.org/images/hand_print_3_small.gif

Hand Geometry

The physical dimensions of a human hand contain information that is capable of verifying the identity of a person (Diagram 5.3). This information has been readily known as hand geometry for ages. For example, the ancient Egyptians used body measurements to classify and identify people. Hand geometry is a verification technology, which is one of the longest implemented biometric types. Today's hand geometry scanners use infrared optics and microprocessor technology to swiftly and precisely record and compare hand proportions dimensions. The systems are in widely used for their simplicity, public acceptance, and integration capabilities (Zunkel, 1999).

At birth, people hands are almost symmetrical. As the body ages, the hands change as a result of natural and environmental changes. Most people turn out to be either right or left handed, triggering one hand to be somewhat larger than the other. The "favored" hand is inclined to have a greater tendency to injury from sports or work activities. Young individuals' hands change quickly as they mature. Older individuals' hands change with the natural aging process or the inception of arthritis. These issues compel that practical hand geometry scanners "learn" minor hand shape

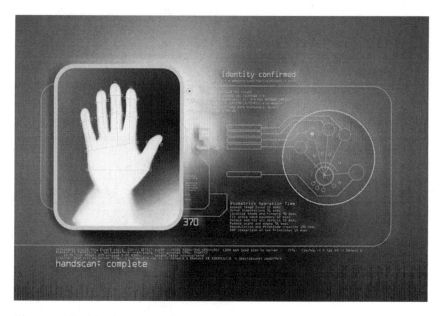

Diagram 5.3. Hand geometry image
Hand Geometry—Website
Website: http://www.biometricvisions.com/technology/technology.htm
Image = http://www.biometricvisions.com/images/hand_geometry_2.jpg

changes and frequently update templates as users are verified by the system. This procedure is acknowledged as template averaging. Template averaging updates the mathematical portrayal of the user's hand. It occurs when the discrepancies between user's hand and the template stored during enrollment reach a predetermined limit. One of the limitations of the hand geometry characteristic is that it is not highly distinctive, which limits the use of the hand geometry system to verification tasks only. Hand geometry based verification systems are widely used in a variety of access control, time and attendance, and point-of-sale applications (Zunkel, 1999).

Vascular Pattern Recognition (Vein Patterns)

Vascular pattern recognition (hand vein recognition) uses near-infrared light, reflected or transmitted images of blood vessels of a hand or finger derived and used for personal recognition (Diagram 5.4). Hand vascular technology is exceptional in the usability measure and has many benefits since it uses biometric features inside the human body rather than on the surface. This results in a very stable verification performance during long

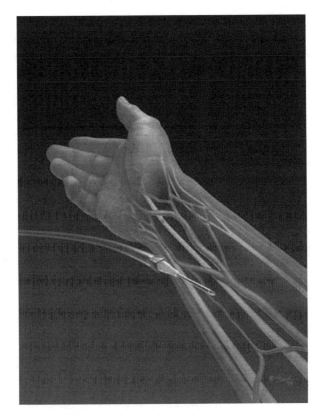

Diagram 5.4. Vein patterns image
http://s3.images.com/huge.56.284299.JPG

periods of time. Different vendors utilize different segments of the hand, palms, or fingers; however, rely on a similar methodology. Researchers have determined that the vascular pattern of the human body is distinct to a specific person and does not change over time as people age (Roberts, 2006).

Vascular pattern recognition technology originated from a conventional vein pattern recognition system, which verifies or recognizes individuals by utilizing a recognition algorithm based on unique veins and capillaries found on the back of the human hand or finger.

Vascular pattern recognition technology has been developed to minimize the disadvantages of commercially available biometric systems. This technology can provide users the most effective tool as a biometric system by providing incomparable security, usability, reliability, accuracy, and user convenience. Vascular pattern recognition technology uses near-infrared light generated from a bank of LEDs projected through an person's skin to enable a high-contrast matching of vein patterns (e.g., vein branching points, vein thickness, and branching angles). Vascular pattern recognition systems scan the de-oxygenated veins, extract key pattern features via contactless, near-infrared optical sensor systems, digitize the extracted pattern recognition, and then match the transaction templates to the respective preestablished enrollment template. By measuring the veins under the skin, it is very challenging for unauthorized people to observe or capture this pattern (Roberts, 2006).

Too new to have much data, vascular pattern recognition technology does seem to have a few advantages over its counterparts. Advantages include the great difficulty in emulating another person's vein structure, and not having to worry about rain, glasses, or external injuries. The problem with conventional hand vascular technology is that the vascular pattern is extracted without considering the directional characteristics of the vascular patterns. As a result, there is some loss of connectivity of vascular patterns and verification performance degradation.

Although vascular pattern recognition technology is minimally used at the present, vascular pattern recognition scanners can be found at major military installations, some multioutlet retailers, and currently as a means of gun control. The scanner is built into the guns handle whereby when an authorized person grasp the handle the firing mechanism is automatically unlocked enabling them to shoot (Roberts, 2006).

DNA (Diagram 5.5)

Deoxyribonucleic acid (DNA) biometrics could be the most precise way of identifying any particular individual. DNA is a chain of nucleotides contained in the nucleus of our cells. Further, it can be implemented as a biometric device to catalog and guide the identification of unknown individuals or biological samples left by them. Every individual has his or her own personal map for every cell made, and this map or blueprint can be found in every body cell. Since DNA is the structure that defines who we are physically and intellectually, it is highly improbable that any other person will have the same exact set of genes.

The analysis of the DNA molecule in forensic discipline is referred to as forensic DNA profiling. DNA encompasses in its coding elements the genetic instructions providing the encoding of distinctive biological functions. Approximately, 32,000 genes are the component of an individual DNA (Butler, 2005).

DNA can be collected from any number of sources: blood, hair, finger nails, mouth swabs, blood stains, saliva, straws, and any number of other sources that has been attached to the body at some time. People have 23 pairs of chromosomes containing their DNA blueprint. One member of

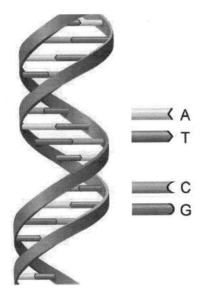

Diagram 5.5. DNA image
http://www.biotechnologyonline.gov.au/images/contentpages/helix.jpg

each chromosomal pair comes from their mother; the other comes from their father (Baird, 2002). Every cell in a human body contains a copy of this DNA. The majority of DNA does not differ from individual to individual, but 0.10% of a person's entire genome would be unique to each person. This represents 3 million base pairs of DNA. Genes make up 5% of the human genome. The other 95% are noncoding chains. In noncoding regions there are matching duplicate sequences of DNA, which can be repeated anywhere from one to 30 times in a row. These sections are described as variable number tandem repeats (VNTRs). The number of tandem repeats at exact places (called loci) on chromosomes differs among people. For any given VNTR loci in a person's DNA, there will be a certain number of repeats. The higher number of loci is examined, the smaller the probability to find two unrelated people with the same DNA profile (Baird, 2002).

DNA profiling ascertains the number of VNTR repeats at a number of distinctive loci, and implements it to generate a particular individual's DNA profile. The most essential procedures to create a DNA profile are: (1) isolate the DNA (from a sample such as blood, saliva, hair, semen, or tissue), (2) slice the DNA up into shorter fragments containing known VNTR areas, type the DNA fragments by size, and (3) compare the DNA leftovers in separate samples (Baird, 2002; Butler, 2005).

DNA matching has become an established use in criminal trials, especially in proving rape cases. The primary difficulties surrounding DNA biometrics is that it is a slow process to identify someone by their DNA. The process is also a very expensive one. DNA biometrics is not a fool proof method of identification. If forensic scientists are unable to conduct a DNA test properly, a person's identification code can be imprecise. Another obstacle is matching prior DNA samples to new samples. This is a bigger problem in DNA fingerprinting. The information looks like a bar code, and if not carefully inspected an incorrect match could be made.

Retina Scan

The retina is the neural part of the eye accountable for vision and the pattern of blood vessels serving the retina is as unique as a fingerprint (Diagram 5.6). The tool that scans the retina is identified as retinal scanning. The chief objective for the scan is the capillary pattern in the retina. The process relies on producing images of the retina using a low-intensity light source (Samples & Hill, 1984).

Retinal scans are built on the presence of the threadlike network of capillaries supplying the retina with oxygen and nutrients. These vessels absorb light and can be easily visualized with appropriate lighting. Retinal scans necessitate close connection of user and scanner, a precise configuration of the eye with a scanner, and no movement of the eye. The examiner is required to keep the person's eye within half an inch of the retina scanner. The person must focus on a ray of light (to properly align the eye) and avoid blinking. A low-intensity consistent light is then transmitted through

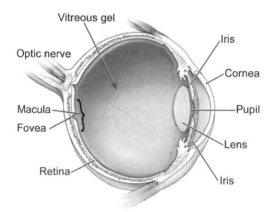

Diagram 5.6.   Retina scan image
http://www.westtexasretina.com/images/normaleye_150.jpg

the eye and the reflected image of the retinal capillary design is recorded by the computer (Samples & Hill, 1984).

Retinal scanners are generally implemented for authentication and identification purposes. These scanners have been used by government agencies have become more viable commercially. Retinal scans have also been utilized in prisons, for ATM identity verification and the prevention of welfare fraud.

Iris Recognition (Diagrams 5.7 and 5.8)

Iris recognition is the process of distinguishing an individual by analyzing the random pattern of the iris. The iris is a muscle within the eye that regulates the size of the pupil, while controlling the amount of light that enters the eye. The iris is located behind the cornea of the eye, and behind the aqueous humor (a transparent fluid occupying the space between the crystalline lens and the cornea of the eye), but in front of the lens. Iris scanning gauges the iris pattern in the colored part of the eye, although the iris color has nothing to do with the biometric. Iris patterns are formed randomly. As a result, the iris patterns in a person's left and right eyes are different, and therefore are the iris patterns of identical twins. Iris scanning can be implemented quickly for both identification and verification applications since the iris are highly distinctive and robust. Even though the coloration and structure of the iris is genetically linked, the details of the patterns are not. The iris matures during prenatal growth through a process of tight forming and folding to the tissue membrane. Before a person's birth, degeneration occurs, resulting in the pupil opening and the random, unique patterns of the iris.

The iris is a distinctive organ that is composed of pigmented vessels and ligaments forming unique linear marks, slight ridges, grooves, furrows, vasculature, and other similar features and marks (Daugman, 2003a). Each iris is specialized by very narrow lines, rakes, and vessels in different individuals. The precision of identification by the use of iris is increased by using more and more details. That is, comparing more features of the iris increases the likelihood of uniqueness. Since more features are being measured, it is less probable for two irises to match. It has been proven that iris patterns are never changed nearly from the time the child is 1 year old through out all her or his life.

The process of iris recognition is complex. It begins by scanning an individual's iris. The person stares into a camera for at least a second permitting the camera to scan her or his iris. An algorithm processes the digital image employed by the camera to locate the iris. Once the iris has been positioned, another algorithm encodes the iris into a phase code that is the

Diagram 5.7.   Iris recognition image

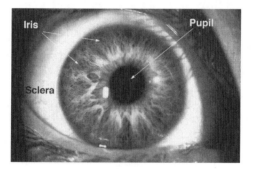

Diagram 5.8.   Iris, pupil, and sclera image
http://webvision.med.utah.edu/imageswv/pupil.jpeg

2048-bit binary representation of an iris (Daugman, 2003b). The phase code is then evaluated with a database of phase codes searching for a match.

Iris recognition has been shown to be a very effective and versatile security measure.

It is a speedy and accurate way of identifying a person with no room for human error. Iris recognition is extensively implemented in the transportation industry and can have many uses in other fields where security is necessary. Its application has been successful with little to no exception, and iris recognition will more than likely be implemented as a security measure in the future.

Face Recognition

People often use faces to recognize individuals and advancements in computing capability over the past several decades have enable similar

Diagram 5.9. Facial recognition image

recognitions automatically (Diagram 5.9). Facial recognition is a concept in biometric readers. Technology in facial recognition has progressed from a simple geometric recognition pattern to matching complex points on the face. Facial recognition analyzes the characteristics of an individual's face images input through a digital video camera (Jing & Zhang, 2004). This biometric tool measures the overall facial structure, including distances between eyes, nose, mouth, and jaw edges. The user typically faces the camera, standing about two feet from it. The system will detect the user's face and perform matches against the claimed identity or the facial database. These measurements are kept in a database and implemented as a comparison when a user stands before the camera.

Facial recognition is currently gaining support as a potential technique for preventing terrorist crimes. This tool is already in use in many law enforcement areas. Software has also been developed for computer networks and automated bank tellers that use facial recognition for user verification purposes. Facial recognition is used most widely in passport identification, missing people identification (Jing & Zhang, 2004).

Facial recognition provides several advantages. One of the potent positive aspects of facial recognition is that it is nonintrusive. Identification and verification can be achieved from two feet away or more, and without requiring the user to wait for extended periods of time or do anything more than look at the camera. The system captures faces of individuals in public areas, which reduces legal concerns. In addition, since faces can be captured from some distance away, facial recognition can be done without any physical contact. This feature also gives facial recognition a covert capability.

Facial recognition also provides a surveillance capability desire to locate specific individuals namely, criminals, terrorists, and missing children. Additional advantages of facial recognition surveillance includes: uses faces that are public, uses legacy databases, and can integrate with existing surveillance systems.

The nonintrusiveness of facial recognition is also one of its drawbacks when it comes to public opinion. Since a person's face can be captured by a camera from some distance away, facial recognition has a clandestine or covert capability (i.e., the subject does not necessarily know she or he has been observed). For this reason, facial recognition has been used in projects to identify card counters or other undesirables in casinos, shoplifters in stores, criminals and terrorists in urban areas.

Many individuals have conveyed concern over the possible use of facial recognition cameras placed inconspicuously around cities that would endeavor to identify passers-by without their knowledge or consent. Nevertheless, the inbuilt impediments in making a positive identification (lighting requirements, facial position, etc.) are greater than most people realize. Apparently, it seems to make this biometric a better choice for verification systems, rather than identification. It has been argued that 3D images biometric recognition should employ measurements that are purely subject-intrinsic, avoiding incorporation of other contaminating inputs and the effects of imaging system transformations as much as possible (Jing & Zhang, 2004).

Face Thermography (Thermo Imaging Recognition)

Using thermal imaging recognition technology can process infrared patterns in the face by measuring the thermal energy emitted (Diagram 5.10). Each thermal signature is unique, like a fingerprint. Thermal provides the ability to 'read' below the surface, detecting different patterns of heat based on blood vessels, muscles and fat deposits. Another benefit of this technology is that the thermal signature produced cannot be manipulated, copied or stolen. Collecting a distinguishing biometric thermal signature can be implemented to combat identity fraud, identify authorized personnel and enhance overall security (Maldague, Jones, Kaplan, Marinetti, & Prystay, 2001).

Diagram 5.10. Thermo Imaging recognition image
http://biometrics.pbworks.com/f/facial%20thermography.png

The underlying vascular system in an individual face produces a unique facial signature when heat passes through the facial tissue and is emitted from the skin. Such facial signatures can be portrayed using an infrared camera, resulting in an image called a "face thermogram." A face thermogram is unique to each person and is not vulnerable to disguises. Even plastic surgery, which does not reroute the flow of blood through the veins, is believed to have no effect on the formation of the face thermogram. Face thermogram is a nonintrusive biometric technique which can confirm an identity without contact. The claimed superiority of face thermogram-based recognition over visual face recognition using infrared cameras is based on the following observations. First, an infrared camera can capture the face thermogram in very low ambient light or in the absence of any light at all. Second, the vascular structure may be more plentiful in information and remains invariant to intentional or unintentional variations in visual facial appearance (Maldague, Jones, Kaplan, Marinetti, & Prystay, 2001).

Although it may be true that face thermograms are distinctive to each individual, it has not been proven that face thermograms are sufficiently discriminative. Face thermograms may depend a great deal on a number of aspects such as the emotional state of the subjects, or body temperature, and like face recognition, face thermogram recognition is view-dependent.

Ear Recognition

The human ear is a new feature in biometrics that has several merits over face, fingerprint and iris biometrics (Diagram 5.11). Ears have gained attention in biometrics due to the robustness of the ear shape. The shape does not change due to emotion as the face does. Unlike the fingerprint and iris, it can be easily captured from a distance without a fully cooperative subject; however, sometimes it may be hidden with hair, scarf and jewellery. In addition, unlike a face, the ear is a relatively stable structure that does not change much with the age and facial expressions.

Ears also have other several advantages over complete faces: reduced spatial resolution, a more uniform distribution of color, and less variability with expressions and orientation of the face. In face recognition there can be problems with for example, changing lightning, and different head positions of the person. These are same kinds of problems with the ear; however, the image of the ear is smaller than the image of the face, which can be an advantage (Chang, Bowyer, Sarkar, & Victor, 2003).

In practice, ear biometrics are not used very often. There are only some cases in the crime investigation area where the earmarks are used as evidence in court. However, it is still inconclusive if the ears of all people are unique.

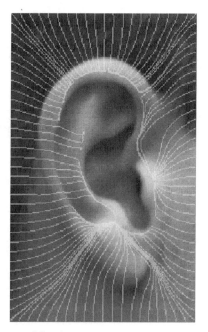

Diagram 5.11. Ear recognition image
http://www.isis.ecs.soton.ac.uk/images/newear.gif

There are at least three methods for ear identification: (1) taking a photograph of an ear, (2) taking "earmarks" by pushing ear against a flat glass, and (3) taking thermogram pictures of the ear. The most interesting parts of the ear are the outer ear and ear lope; however, the whole ear structure and shape is used (Chang et al., 2003).

Taking photograph of the ear is the most commonly used method in research. The photograph is taken and it is combined with the photographs taken previously for identifying a person. The earmarks are used mainly in crime solving. Even though some judgments are made based on the earmarks, currently they are not accepted in courts. The thermogram pictures could be one solution for solving the problem with for example, disquising the ear with hair or a hat (Chang et al., 2003).

Body Odor (scent) Recognition (Diagram 5.12)

No two humans have the exact same scent and that dogs can smell the difference. It is well known that animals can tell things about each other by odor. They can also sniff out a body under a building and there is evidence that they can scent disease (Freeman, 1991). Humans have lost this ability to sniff out each other's scents so accurately; however, we can use technology to do it for us. There appears to be evidence of an individual fingerprint. Every individual has a unique body odor, like their fingerprints, that could be used as an 'odor print' to identify them. Olfaction has an extremely high importance in the human being. It is one of the five main senses: sight, smell, taste, hearing, and touch. Philosophers and scientists have been trying to comprehend the sense of the smell for over millieums of time. It is a difficult task, as individuals often have problem with finding words even to describe their smell sensations. However, odorants influence deeply our life, mood. Reactions like discomfort, attraction, and etc. sensation are difficult to extinguish since neurons of the nose are connected straight to a part of the brain, so-called olfactory bulb, and the olfaction apparatus is still relatively unknown (Freeman, 1991).

The main difficulty associated with odor perception is there is no physical range as sound frequency in hearing or Newton's circle in color vision. The main rationale in human odor recognition is to build an electronic system that is very sensitive. Such an electronic system is understood to be fashioned on the human olfactory model. This technology would use an odor-sensing instrument (an electronic "nose") to encapsulate the volatile chemicals that skin pores all over the body emit to make up an individual's smell. Although distinguishing one individual from another by odor may eventually be feasible, the fact that personal habits such as the use of deodorants and perfumes, diet, and medication influence

Diagram 5.12. Scent image
http://static.htowstuffworks.com/gif/istock_000002439257medium.jpg

human body odor renders the development of this technology quite complex. Therefore, to create this device the human olfactory model must be comprehend entirely (Freeman, 1991).

A scent is made up of traces of chemicals that evaporate off the body in what scientists call the "thermal plume." These chemicals can be left behind in sweat and other bodily fluids. Anything that has an odor constantly evaporates tiny quantities of molecules that produce the smell, so-called odorants. A sensor that is capable of detecting these molecules is called a chemical sensor. In this way, a person's nose is a chemical sensor and the smell is a chemical sense. An individual's ability to smell is not so precise in comparison with animals. Despite human smelling frailties, a person has about 40 million olfactory nerves (Mamlouk, 2002). This permits detecting even slight traces of some chemical components. Some odorants can be detected even if the concentration in the air is only one part per trillion. Odor information processing in human model is tremendously complicated task.

The olfaction starts with *sniffing* that combines the odorants into a uniform concentration and delivers these mixtures to the mucus layer in the upper part of nasal cavity. Next these molecules are dissolved in this layer and carried to the cilia of the olfactory receptor neurons (Mamlouk, 2002). *Reception* process includes connecting these odorant molecules to the olfactory receptors. Odorant molecules are connected temporarily to proteins that transport molecules across the receptor membrane with simultaneous stimulation of the receptors. During this stimulation the chemical reaction manufactures an electrical stimulus. These electrical signals from the receptor neurons are transported to the olfactory bulb (Mamlouk, 2002). From the olfactory bulb the receptor response information is advanced to the olfactory cortex (*detection*).

Odor *recognition* part takes place specifically in the olfactory cortex. Then the information is passed on to the cerebral cortex. *Cleansing* completes the olfaction process. For this end, the breathing fresh air removing of odorant molecules from the olfactory receptors are required (Mamlouk, 2002).

Some researchers cautioned that some individuals appear to have less distinctive odors than others. More importantly, some individuals' odors change over time. These challenges are likely to be significant, and they will multiply if odor recognition techniques are deployed in the field. A European research project to improve airline security has also been looking at the use of an electronic nose to detect dangerous chemicals and explosives that passengers take on to planes (http://www.telegraph.co.uk/news/uknews/1540110/Scientists-learn-what-every-dog-knows---that-we-all-have-a-unique-smell.html).

In studies funded by the U.S. Army Research Office, scientists found they could identify people by looking at the differing combinations of 44 chemical compounds secreted by the body. They examined body odor samples of about 200 adults from Carinthia, a village in the Austrian Alps, chosen because no one from outside had settled there for many generations and the residents were primarily members of large families and genetically similar. Despite this, analysis showed that each person had a distinct scent signature. Scent may allow us to learn about a person's gender, their lifestyle, if they smoke, what they had for dinner the previous night, and whether they are stressed. Scientists hope scent technology will be useful in criminal court cases (http://www.telegraph.co.uk/news/uknews/1540110/Scientists-learn-what-every-dog-knows---that-we-all-have-a-unique-smell.html).

BEHAVIORAL BIOMETRICS (TABLE 5.3)

Speaker Recognition

Recent information on mobile telephones users' worldwide, telephone landlines in operation number, and recent voice over Internet Protocol (IP) networks deployments, corroborates that voice is the most accessible biometric trait as no extra acquisition device or transmission system is required. IP is a protocol used for communicating data across a packet switched network. Speaker (voice) recognition (Diagrams 5.13 and 5.14) uses vocal characteristics to identify people using a pass-phrase (Baumann, 2009). This technique is the process of automatically recognizing who is speaking on the basis of individual information included in speech waves. Speaker recognition biometric readers are used to recognize a particular speaker's voice.

Speaker recognition can be classified as identification or verification technique. A telephone or microphone can operate as a sensor that makes it a relatively inexpensive and easily deployable tool. However, speaker recognition can be affected by environmental factors such as background noise. That is, voice trait is not only related with personal characteristics, but also with many environmental and sociolinguistic variables. This technology has been the focus of substantial efforts on the part of the telecommunications industry and the U.S. government's intelligence community, which continue to work on improving reliability. Another important application of speaker recognition technology is for forensic purposes (Baumann, 2009).

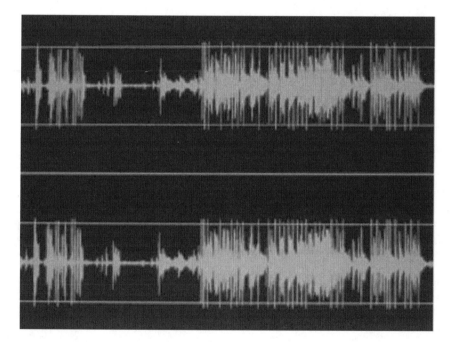

Diagram 5.13. Voice recognition image
Speaker recognition Website: http://www.poegles.com/tag/science-daily/

Diagram 5.14. Speaker recognition image

Speaker recognition makes it possible to use the speaker's voice to verify her or his identity and control access to services such as voice dialing, banking by telephone, telephone shopping, database access services, information services, voice mail, security control for confidential information areas, and remote access to computers. AT&T and Texas Instruments (with Sprint) have begun field tests and actual application of speaker recognition technology. Sprint's Voice Phone Card is currently used by many customers.

Speaker recognition technology can also be divided into text-dependent and text-independent methods. The former necessitate the user to say key words or sentences having the same text for both training and recognition trials, whereas the latter do not rely on a specific text being spoken. Both text-dependent and independent techniques share a dilemma however. These techniques can be easily misled since someone who plays back the recorded voice of a registered speaker saying the key words or sentences can be accepted as the registered speaker. To cope with this drawback, there are methods in which a small set of words, such as digits, are used as key words and each person is prompted to utter a given sequence of key words that is randomly chosen every time the system is used. However, this method is not completely reliable, since it can be deceived with advanced electronic recording equipment that can reproduce key words in a requested order. Therefore, a text-prompted (machine-driven-text-dependent) speaker recognition method has recently been proposed by researchers working on this problem.

Speaker recognition and speech recognition are not to be mistaken with one another. Speaker recognition relies on the physical structure of a person's vocal tract and their personality. Speech recognition merely recognizes certain words. Speaker recognition can be used, as a way of identifying an individual while speech recognition cannot. There are at least two major limitations in speaker recognition technology (Baumann, 2009). First, it is dependent on a scripted text. Second, the biometric readers can be deceived by a recording of the voice or may not recognize the voice of a person with a cold. Research is currently being performed to strengthen these two areas of the technology. In this manner, speaker recognition technology is expected to create new services that will make people lives more convenient.

Generally, individuals are willing to accept a speech-based biometric system. However, speech-based features are susceptible to a number of features such as background noise as well as the emotional and physical state of the speaker. Speech-based authentication is currently restricted to low-security applications due to its high variability in an person's voice and poor accuracy.

Gait Recognition

One of the newest biometrics is gait recognition which is a behavioral biometric. This tool is a combination of genetics and the way a person has learned to walk. The goal of gait recognition is to identify individuals at a distance of up to 500 feet away with no invasive testing. Gait recognition allows individuals to be identified without the use of a database that is required for other biometrics. Gait recognition can also be used when other identification techniques such as facial recognition are obscured and cannot be used. Since gait recognition is not always a uniquely distinguishing feature of a person, many researchers believe that gait recognition may only be a filtering tool for finding suspicious individuals as they walk in a crowd, private property, or if people are walking on an airport tarmac.

People recognition is a vital assignment in a variety of applications, such as access control, surveillance, etc. To differentiate different individuals by the style they walk is a normal task people perform everyday. Psychological studies (Johansson, 1973; Stevenage, Nixon & Vince, 1999) have demonstrated that gait signatures acquired from video can be implemented as a reliable signal to identify people. These findings inspired other researchers in computer vision to obtain potential gait signatures from images to detect people.

The gait of an individual is determined by their underlying musculoskeletal structure. Therefore, it is possible that it has some ability to differentiate between individuals. The gait of an individual is a periodic activity with each gait cycle covering two strides. The left foot forward and right foot forward strides. Gait recognition is determined to be the coordinated, cyclic combination of movements that result in human locomotion. The movements are synchronized in the sense that they must take place with a certain temporal pattern for the gait to occur. The movements in a gait repeat as a person cycles between steps with alternating feet (Diagrams 5.15 and 5.16). It is both the coordinated and cyclic nature of the motion that makes gait a unique spectacle.

Diagram 5.15. Movements in a gait repeat as a person cycles between steps

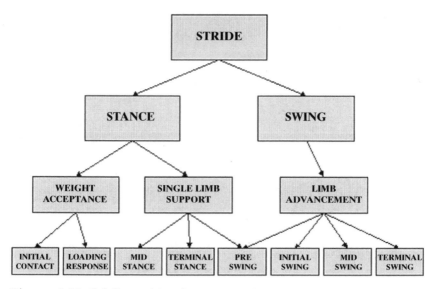

Diagram 5.16. Gait Recognition chart
http://sprojects.mmi.mcgill.ca/gait/normal/chart.gif

Gait biometrics would be particularly beneficial in identifying criminal suspects. Police could scan a large crowd for a suspect without them knowing they were on to them. Gait biometrics may also be used to identify shoplifters particularly pregnant women. That is, women pretending to be pregnant will walk differently than women who are actually pregnant. This may be a significant advance in technology if introduced to department stores.

There are also several confounding properties of gait as a biometric. Unlike fingerprints, it is yet unknown regarding the extent to which an individual's gait is only one of its kinds. In addition, there are several factors, other than the person, that cause variations in gait, including footwear, terrain, fatigue, and injury. Notwithstanding, researchers are making progress and understanding more about gait with each new development and how it can be used for commercial and noncommercial use.

Dynamic Signature

Dynamic signature is a biometric tool that implements, for recognition functions behavioral characteristics that a person shows when signing her or his name (Diagram 5.17). World history is replete in regards to a written signature as a way to recognize a person's identity (Jain, Griess, & Connell, 2002). Dynamic signature is a useful tool due to the social and legal

Diagram 5.17. Dynamic signature image
Website:http://spie.org/x2434.xml?parentid=x2410&parentname=Electronic%20
Imaging%20&%20Signal%20Processing&highlight=x2410

acceptance and prevalent use of the handwritten signature as a personal authentication method. Dynamic signature verification is an automated method of measuring a person's signature. This tool scrutinizes such dynamics as speed, direction, and pressure of writing; the time that the instrument used for writing or marking (stylus) is in and out of contact with the "paper," and the total time taken to make the signature. Also this tool measures where the stylus is raised from and lowered onto the "paper." Dynamic signature tools should not be mistaken for electronic signature capture systems that are implemented to portray a graphic image of the signature and are widespread in locations where merchants are capturing signatures for transaction authorizations.

Data such as the dynamically captured direction, stroke, pressure, and shape of a person's signature can enable handwriting to be a reliable gauge of a person's identity. That is, measurements of the encapsulated data, when contrasted to those of matching samples, are a reliable biometric for writer identification. Further, the sophistication of attacks focusing on Internet banking is continuously increasing. These attacks are becoming more accurate with respect to choosing the most profitable target. Therefore, banking institutions have responded to this development. By introducing a more complex signing procedure for high-risk transactions only, banks can guarantee secure payments with the same procedure as the customer is used to when making payments at the bank office. In this regard, dynamic signatures better reflect the customer's act of will. Dynamic signatures are risk based and enable the bank to control the risk in each and every transaction.

Despite the advantages of the dynamic signatures modality, the practical deployment of this tool is very sluggish. One of the main reasons has to do with forgeries. Imposters may know some information about the client that degrades signature verification performance when it is exploited (e.g., signature shape). Other problems of signature biometrics include that not everyone may be able to sign, and low permanence relating to the handwritten signature tending to vary along time (Jain, Griess, & Connell, 2002).

Keystroke Dynamics

Biometrics has long been one of the solutions make known by internal control systems security vendors to meet multifactor authentication objectives. However, user acceptance and cost issues often thwart companies' from adopting biometrics as a solution. This is not to say that other multifactor solutions are any less cost prohibitive. The capital expenditure and on-going maintenance costs of token-based systems are often higher than those for biometrics. Solutions based on keystroke dynamics might help meet these organizational challenges.

Keystroke dynamics is a mechanized method of examining a person's keystrokes on a keyboard (Diagram 5.18). This tool assesses such dynamics as speed and pressure, the total time taken to type particular words, and the time elapsed between hitting certain keys. This tool's algorithms are still being built on to improve robustness and distinctiveness. One potentially useful application that may emerge is an internal control systems base organization access, where this biometric could be implemented to confirm the computer user's identity continuously.

Keystroke dynamics usually measure both of the following (Obaidat & Sadoun, 1997):

1. Dwell time—how long a key is pressed;
2. Flight time—how long it takes to move from one key to another.

As an individual types, the keystroke dynamics tool accumulate the time each key is pressed down and the cycle time between one key-down and the next (Diagram 5.19). For verification purposes, a known verification string is characteristically typed (i.e., account identification and password). Once the verification string is entered, it is processed through an algorithm that matches the user's typing behavior to a sample collected in a previous session. The output of the assessment is a score. If this is the first time, the keystroke dynamics system has seen this user, the algorithm is applied to enroll her or him instead of confirming her or his identity.

Diagram 5.18.   Keystroke dynamics image
Website: http://blogs.technet.com/steve_lamb/archive/2006/03/13/421925.aspx

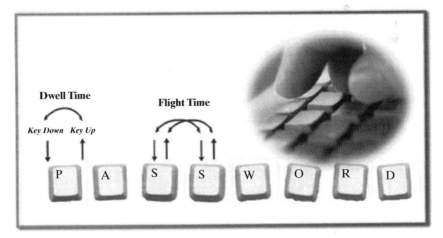

Diagram 5.19.   Dwell Time and Flight Time
Website: http://articles.techrepublic.com.com/5100-10878_11-6150761.html

If the score falls within a range defined by the organization as acceptable, and the password entered is precise, the user is authenticated and verified. Then, access to the network is granted. If the score is not satisfactory, organizational rules can be defined to ascertain how to proceed (Obaidat & Sadoun, 1997).

Keystroke Dynamics as an identity verification solution is rapidly transpiring as a feasible, low cost, nonintrusive alternative to traditional biometric technologies. As with all technology, keystroke dynamics is not without its problems. Higher error rates and potential troubles with physical and logical access control convergence require a review of how keystroke dynamics is suited for an internal control systems organizational strategy. For many organizations, however, keystroke dynamics tools can be a low impact answer for multifactor authentication internal control systems requirements.

DECISION MAKING PATHWAYS

An individual brings innate qualities and experiences to the interactions that affect performance. Without a careful consideration of individual qualities, internal control biometrics system designers and evaluators grapple to make noteworthy enhancements, which advances in biometrics technology alone cannot accomplish. To date, many internal control biometric systems have focused solely on the limitations and capabilities of a technology, without fully understanding the impact a person's features, experience levels and abilities will have on an internal control biometrics system.

Biometrics usability is the evaluation of an internal control system including the requirements definition, design, development and evaluation phases of a biometric tool in order to produce a system which is measurably easier to use, learn and remember. Too often ethical considerations are not considered when an internal control systems biometric system has been designed and developed. When ethical considerations are conducted at the end of a project lifecycle, recommendations and improvements are much more costly to make. By including ethical considerations early on in the design lifecycle, it is possible to integrate ethical pathway positions into the initial designs and draft prototypes, when it is much easier and less costly to make changes. The importance of including ethical positions early on in the development process cannot be emphasized enough. Successful internal control systems involve ethical considerations in the early stages of the design in order to continually evolve and refine the design in an iterative process.

This section views six dominant ethical pathways that provide guidance in the employment of biometric tools in an organization. *Throughput*

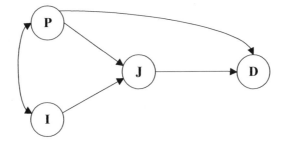

Figure 5.1. *Throughput Modeling* pathways. *P = perception, I = information, J = judgment,* and *D = decision choice*

Modeling depicts the most influential ethical pathways using biometrics in arriving at a decision (Figure 5.1). Our *perception* helps frame our environment and it can in turn influence our judgment and decision choice. Our *judgment* processes information sources dealing with the use of biometrics and analyzes what is acceptable as useful information. This judgment stage also analyzes our perception, and is appropriate to answer questions about a particular part of the biometric system that is influenced by what we hold as valuable. Decision making in the use of biometrics for the *Throughput Model* is defined here as a multistage, information-processing function in which cognitive, economic, political, and social processes are used to generate a set of outcomes.

Based on Figure 5.1, we can establish six ethical pathways

1	**P → D**	Ethical egoism
2.	**P → J → D**	Deontology
3.	**I → J → D**	Utilitarianism
4.	**I → P → D**	Relativism
5.	**P → I → J → D**	Virtue ethics
6.	**I → P → J → D**	Virtue ethics

In-line table showing ethical pathways.

The *ethical egoism position* (**P → D** pathway) emphasizes that individuals are always motivated to act in their perceived self-interest. This position holds that the moral worth of an action or practice is determined solely by the consequences of the action or practice (consequential oriented). For example, a home security system that installs a motion detection system that alert attack dogs that could cause the intruder serious bodily harm is an example of the ethical egoism position. That is, the homeowners' wants and desires are more important than the intruders' condition after being attacked by the dogs.

$P \rightarrow J \rightarrow D$ depicts the *deontology position* call attention to the rights of individuals. This viewpoint examines perceptual effect (or framing of the issues) on the judgment stage en route to a decision choice. A basic premise to this position is that equal respect must be given to all individuals, thus this process is nonconsequential. That is, $P \rightarrow J \rightarrow D$ implies that information from I is disregarded, and a decision choice is reached by the use of judgment. Therefore, the judgment stage implement decision rules that help guide individuals to a decision. Deontologists also regard the nature of moral principles as permanent and stable, and that compliance with these principles defines ethicalness. A community or city that installs cameras (facial recognition) at major intersections in order to punish those drivers passing through a red light is an example of a biometric approach emphasizing the deontology position. Regardless of the circumstances for driver (e.g., late for work, rushing to the hospital, etc.), he or she will receive a ticket for running a red light (i.e., nonconsequential approach).

$I \rightarrow J \rightarrow D$ pathway exhibits the *utilitarian position*, which is similar to *ethical egoism position* in that it is concerned with consequences, but differs from this approach in that it emphasizes the greatest good for the greatest number of people. Further, this position advocates that society should always produce the greatest possible balance of positive value or the minimum balance of disvalue for all people affected. Therefore, the utilitarian position assumes that quantities of benefits produced by an action can be measured and added and the quantities of harm can be measured and subtracted. This will establish which action produces the greatest total benefits or the lowest total costs. For example, an airport implementing an iris-scanning security procedure to screen airline passengers before they board flights are invading their privacy in order to protect the greatest number of passengers from harm. Since iris scans are very reliable, each passenger must subject him or herself to be scanned in order to locate known terrorists or violent criminals. The procedure is an inconvenience for most passengers; however, it provides maximum safety for everyone.

$I \rightarrow P \rightarrow D$ highlights the *relativist position* that assumes that individuals use themselves or the people around them as their basis for defining ethical standards. They observe the actions of members of some relevant group and endeavor to determine the group consensus on a given behavior. Relativism acknowledges that people live in a society in which they have varied views and positions from which to give good reason for decisions as right or wrong. Therefore, ethical relativists uphold that all ethical beliefs and values are relative to one's own culture, feelings, or religion. For example, a high security manufacturer of telecommunication parts implements a gait recognition tool in order to permit individuals into its headquarters. If a person who is not in the system (i.e., manner of walking) walks into the building lobby, then no action is taken against them except for a guard providing assistance. That is, the guard assumes that this person has business to take care of in the building and simply got lost along the way or he or she requested information. On the other hand, if individuals, who are not in the system, somehow get through to the high security area, then an assumption is automatically made that they have a hostile intent, thereby sending armed security personnel to apprehend them.

$P \rightarrow I \rightarrow J \rightarrow D$ highlights the *virtue ethics position* that represents the cultivation of virtuous traits of character, which is viewed as morality's primary function. This pathway conveys that an individual's perceptions or framing of the problem will influence the selection and type of information to be implemented in judgment before a decision choice is made. For example, receiving information from individuals using keystroke dynamics may provide a method of determining whether they are providing truthful statements.

$I \rightarrow P \rightarrow J \rightarrow D$ represents the *ethics of care position* that centers on a array of character traits that are deeply valued in close personal relationships, such as sympathy, compassion, fidelity, love, friendship, and the like. In this sequence, an individual studies the given information, frames the problem, and then proceeds to analyze (judgment) the problem before rendering a decision choice. For example, body odor (scent) recognition can be implemented at public locations where illegal drugs are identified and confiscated without causing inconvenience to individuals (i.e., not subjecting people to personal searches).

By designing with these aforementioned ethical pathways in mind, developers of biometric systems can produce a system that is more effective and efficient. With a focus on users and the usability of biometric systems, design teams have the opportunity to improve image captures, increase throughput, and reduce errors.

Based on a review of the context of implementation, ethical requirements should be developed to address the attributes and characteristics of the physical location where the system will be located. These requirements may include determining the optimal height of a biometric device, defining interaction styles based on noise and lighting levels, and/or specifying space and furniture requirements.

While these requirements primarily depend on an evaluation of the physical surroundings, it is also important to review how ethical considerations impact on the environmental factors and adjust the physical design of a biometric system based on users' characteristics. For instance, the optimal height of a biometric tool should be based upon a thorough evaluation of the physical environment where the device will be located, but also should take into consideration common attributes, such as the average the height of organization user population. Moreover, these decisions should also be augmented by observation of users in internal control systems settings to evaluate users' posture, as well as how users of differing heights use the system. Based on an analysis of these factors, a suitable height should be defined and included in the requirements documentation.

Furthermore, it may be essential to build on a distinctive set of ethical requirements for each physical location in which a biometric system will be located. For example, a noisy environment may require dissimilar requirements than a quiet location, just as a biometric system located under low light may have dissimilar requirements than a system which is in direct sunlight.

Below are some example requirements for different kinds of ethical considerations:

1. *Noisy environment* could bring about a system that relies on visual and other types of nonauditory feedback, as users may not be able to hear audio feedback in a noisy location.

2. *Low light* requirement may specify that interaction screens, visual cues and colored displays are bright enough to be seen in locations with poor lighting. Or the requirement could necessitate that supplemental lighting be offered to sufficiently light the system.

3. *Natural light* requirement may specify that in outdoor settings, it is best to rely on audio and other types of sensory feedback as the direct sunlight might produce a glare, making it hard to see visual feedback. Or the requirement could involve developing screens that do not reflect light and reduce the amount of glare. Another requirement could be to use screen filters as a way to lessen the potential problems of glare.

4. *Temperature and humidity* requirement might state that the system is capable to maintain extreme temperatures and high levels of humidity. Or the requirement may state that the system must function within a range of temperatures and humidity.

Since biometrics devices may be used under a variety of conditions and in a plethora of locations, it is essential to review the physical attributes of each location and define ethical considerations to address the differing needs.

Other ethical considerations for an biometric system that are not specifically tied to a feature or function may include the following:

1. Graphic design requirements (or look and feel)—*The design of the system should reflect the ethical position of the organization.*

2. Usability requirements—*The vast majority of users will be productive when using the system without assistance or help.*

3. User Experience—*The biometric system will provide users with a reliable interface, interactions and affordances.*

4. Performance requirements—*The biometric system will accurately collect a very high percentage of samples for the users on the first attempt.*

5. Social requirements—*The ethical position established by the organization should mitigate users' perceived health risks of biometric devices.*

6. Legal requirements—*The ethical position implemented by the organization should protect the privacy of the end users who submit samples.*

In developing a biometric system, it is also essential to document the hardware and software systems upon which the product will be based. The requirements should identify any issues or constraints regarding the ethical considerations and should also specify system requirements for the security and maintenance of the device.

CONCLUSION

While biometric systems, particularly automatic fingerprint identification systems, has been extensively used in forensics for criminal identification, recent innovations in biometric sensors and matching algorithms have led to the application of biometric authentication in a significant number of business, civilian and government applications. Biometrics is being implemented for physical access control, computer log-in, welfare disbursement, international border crossing and national identification cards. It can be administered to verify a customer during transactions conducted via telephone and Internet (electronic commerce and electronic banking). In automobiles, biometrics has been adopted to replace keys for keyless entry and keyless ignition. As a result to increased security threats, the ICAO (International Civil Aviation Organization) has approved the use of e-passports (passports with an embedded chip containing the holder's facial image and other traits).

With the use of biometrics increasing everyday and the need to stop fraud and improve information systems, it appears that the future will display more social, government, and internal control systems use of this technology. Will there be a central database to include the digital templates from everyone eyes, finger or voices? Will smartcards escort us into the need for the centralized database? Will there be an owner of the database and who will it be? How will the data be kept from the commercial market, the government, and the black market or from criminals?

While actual affordance is a key component of any particular internal control biometrics system, it is also imperative for designers to consider perceived ethical considerations implemented in this system. For example, do users expect an action to take place when in reality ethical considerations do not exist? Understanding how users anticipate ethical considerations to be part of an internal control system is just as essential as understanding how users interact with the intended affordances. Vital questions to consider are as follows:

1.   Do users comprehend what ethical considerations are involved when they encounter a biometric device or system?
2.   What ethical pathways do users perceive are available?
3.   What information does the biometric system provide to users to communicate the ethical positions that users should take?

An important issue to contemplate is providing users with knowledge concerning the ethical considerations involved for fingerprint readers, iris/retina scanning, voice recognition, etc.

1.   How can biometric designers create systems that will be usable for individuals who are visually impaired and may have difficulty using posted instructional guides or feedback provided through a graphical interface?
2.   What other types of tools can be provided for this user population? What about hearing-impaired users who may have difficulty distinguishing or understanding audio cues?
3.   How can biometric systems be designed to accommodate users in wheelchairs, including the height of a system and allow ample area around the tool for users to access the system?
4.   What other types of needs should be considered? How can designers develop a biometric system that is universally accessible and usable to all audiences?

By taking into consideration an individuals' ethical characteristics, as well as instructional guides and feedback, anthropometrics, affordance, and accessibility, biometric developers have a much greater chance of producing a truly usable, user-friendly system.

REFERENCES

Ashbaugh, D. R. (1999). *Quantitative-qualitative friction ridge analysis: An introduction to basic and advanced ridgeology.* Boca Raton, FL: CRC Press.

Baird, S. L. (2002). Biometrics: Security technology. *The Technology Teacher, 61*(5), 18–22.

Baumann, J. (2009). Voice recognition, human interface technology laboratory, University of Washington. www.hitl.washington.edu/scivw/EVE.

Butler, J. M. (2005). *Forensic DNA typing.* Burlington, MA: Elsevier Academic Press.

Chang, K., Bowyer, K. W., Sarkar, S., Victor, B. (2003). Comparison and combination of ear and face images in appearance-based biometrics. *IEEE Transactions on Pattern Analysis and Machine Intelligence, 25,* 1160–1165.

Daugman, J. (2003a). Demodulation by complex-valued wavelets for stochastic pattern recognition. *International Journal of Wavelets, Multi-resolution and Information Processing, 1,* 1–17.

Daugman, J. (2003b). The importance of being random: Statistical principles of iris recognition. *Pattern Recognition, 36,* 279–291.

Freeman, W. (1991). *The physiology of perception. Scientific American, 264,* 78–85.

Jain, A. K., Flynn, P., & Ross, A. (2008). *Handbook of biometrics.* New York, NY: Springer.

Jain, A. K., Griess, F. D., & Connell, S. D. (2002). *Online Signature Verification, 35,* 1–3.

Jain, A. K., Hong, L., & Pankanti, S. (2000). Biometric identification. *Communication of the ACM, 43,* 90–98.

Jain, A. K, Ross, A., & Prabhakar, S. (2004). An introduction to biometric recognition. *IEEE Transactions on Circuits and Systems for Video Technology, 14,* 4–20.

Jing, X. Y., & Zhang, D. (2004). A face and palmprint recognition approach based on discriminant DCT feature extraction. *IEEE Transactions on Systems, Man, and Cybernetics—part B: Cybernetics, 34,* 2405–2415.

Johansson, G. (1973). Visual perception of biological motion and a model for its analysis. *Perception and Psychophysics, 14,* 201–211.

Maldague, X. P. V., Jones, T. S., Kaplan, H., Marinetti, S., & Prystay, M. (2001). Chapter 2: Fundamentals of infrared and thermal testing: Part 1. Principles of infrared and thermal testing. In X. P. V. Maldague (Technical ed.,) & P. O. Moore (Ed.), *Nondestructive Handbook, Infrared and Thermal Testing: Vol. 3.* Columbus, OH: ASNT Press.

Mamlouk, A. (2002). *Quantifying olfactory perception* (Master of Science Thesis). University of Lubeck, Germany.

Obaidat, M. S., & Sadoun, B. (1997). Verification of computer users using keystroke dynamics. *IEEE Transactions on Systems, Man and Cybernetics, 27,* 261–269.

Roberts, C. (2006). Biometric technologies—palm and hand. Retrieved from http://www.ccip.govt.nz/newsroom/information-notes/2006/biometrics-technologies-palmhand.pdf.

Rodgers, W. (2010). *E-commerce and biometric issues addressed in a Throughput Model.* Hauppauge, NY: Nova Publication.

Samples, J. R, & Hill, R. V. (1984). Use of infrared fundus reflection for an identification device. *American Journal of Ophthalmology, 98*, 636–640.

Stevenage, S. V., Nixon, M. S., & Vince, K. (1999). Visual analysis of gait as a cue to identity. *Applied Cognitive Psychology, 13*, 513–526.

Vacca, J. R. (2007). *Biometric technologies and verification systems*. New York, NY: Elsevier.

Zunkel, R. (1999). *Biometrics: Personal identification in networked society*, chapter Hand Geometry Based Authentication. New York, NY: Kluwer Academic Publishers.

CHAPTER 6

BIOMETRICS LEGAL AND ETHICAL ISSUES

"What I may see or hear in the course of the treatment or even outside of the treatment in regard to the life of men, which on no account must spread abroad, I will keep to myself, holding such things to be shameful to be spoken about."

—Excerpt from the Hippocratic Oath

"Cowardice asks the question, Is it safe?
Expediency asks the question, Is it politic?
Vanity asks the question, Is it popular?
But conscience asks the question, Is it right?
And there comes a time when one must take a position...
because his conscience tells him it is right."

—Martin Luther, monk

In this age of digital impersonation, biometric tools are being used increasingly as a guard against identity theft. The premise is that a biometric is a measurable physical characteristic or behavioral trait. In addition, for internal control systems data storage/retrieval and dissemination, biometrics is a more reliable indicator of identity than legacy systems such as passwords and PINs. Internal control systems data storage/retrieval and dissemination involves the capability to store or link to data in a manner that it can be brought forward for utilization in other processes. An identity management system for improved deterrence of illegal entry should include the capability

Biometric and Auditing Issues Addressed in a Throughput Model, pp. 181–217

to store or link data in a manner that can be transmit to, and utilized by the organizations system designers and monitoring unit. Data storage/retrieval and dissemination addresses two aspects deficient in previous response to incidents of unauthorized entry into a system. The first deficit involves the matter of the training credential. The second part includes "the set of ethical considerations" by which an individual is recognizable as an authorized user of the internal control systems services. Providing this information is a function of a comprehensive identity management system.

Informational privacy relates to the right of an individual to maintain her or his personal information private and out of the reach of the government. A key element of such right is the sensitivity of such information and whether an important government need overrides the individual's interest to keep sensitive information private. In spite of the perceived privacy uneasiness of the average individual, in the law privacy concerns generally arise when biometrics are used to make available access to other information about a person, or are used in a manner that violates upon a person's rights. For example, a disturbing feature regarding the 2001 Super Bowl event was not necessarily the video cameras that captured the faces of the football fans, but rather the fact that those images were then match up to images in a law enforcement database.

People of many countries, including the United States, value their privacy and autonomy above all else, passionately protecting their rights as individuals. These rights such as life, liberty, and the pursuit of happiness are the very concepts many nations champion and were founded upon including the United States. Privacy issues in our society are challenged due to technological breakthrough as well as an increase need for security against acts of fraud and terrorism. A major question that is continuing being addressed is how much of our privacy will we forfeit or relaxed for security and the advantages of technological progress (National Biometric Security Project, 2006)?

An important element in using privacy law to biometrics recognition is the distinction between: (1) identification and (2) verification (authentication). Identification biometric systems are used to determine who a person is and can occur without the individual's knowledge or consent. Ethical issues may arise since identification systems require a databank that may contain personal information without the subject's knowledge or consent. On the other hand, verification systems are used in a voluntary and nonsecret manner, similar to PIN's or passwords. Verification biometric systems make sure you are who you claim to be. Typically, this type of system requires two informational sources: (1) a representation of your identity (e.g., user name to retrieve your biometric template embedded in it), and (2) your biometric information, such as your hand to create your hand geometry template (Rodgers, 2010).

Biometric verification systems are presently implemented for many reasons, such as controlling right of entry to specified secured locations. Verification of identity is legally mandatory for many functions, such as driving, border crossing, and obtaining government assistance. The simple act of verification to confirm ethical behavior (i.e., to confirm an individual is who she or he purports to be) by using information the individual has voluntarily given (such as a photograph or other biometric) does not raise any privacy issues.

The Privacy Act of 1974 (U.S. Code, 1974) is the first and predominant comprehensive statutory law enacted to address privacy concerns in the United States. The Privacy Act regulates the collection, maintenance, use, and dissemination of personal information of United States citizens and legal resident aliens by the federal government (it does not apply to state and local governments and it does not apply to private individuals or private entities). The Act requires all federal agencies to adopt and publish minimum standards with respect to the collection, maintenance, use, and dissemination of personal information and it restricts such agencies from disclosing personally identifiable records.

However, despite the growing use of biometric technology, very few laws currently are in existence that even mentions biometrics, let alone the use of biometrics with respect to privacy. However, as the use of biometrics becomes more pervasive, especially in the wake of the September 11, 2001 attacks, we can anticipate that in the near future, a significant portion of the public will become increasingly concerned over its implications with respect to privacy. Envisaging that the government's use of biometric recognition technology will eventually lead to an Orwellian "Big Brother" America, some people are already up in arms, warning that such "function creep" is to be anticipated (National Biometric Security Project, 2006). The proper use of biometrics is not only invaluable to an organization's security for its system, but also as a formidable protector of privacy.

Ethics is a multidimensional construct. Research has shown that ethical decision making is affected by individual difference characteristics, the issue itself, and the organizational context (Rodgers, Guiral, & Gonzalo, 2009). Validation of the information is based upon ethical considerations supporting trust. Ethics inspires trust and is essential to the reputation of people and institutions.

Validation of the information is based upon ethical considerations supporting trust. Ethics inspires trust and is essential to the reputation of people and institutions. The heart of identity management lies in the establishment of ethical behavior in order for the creation and maintenance of trust. Trust allows for users to have a defined level of certainty in the authenticity of a credential based on the process by which it was issued and the security of a system. Ethical systems underlying trust provides a level of certainty to users to answer the question, "Who is this?" Certainty and trust are measured through encountering an internal control system that allow for the purchase of products and/or services.

In order to provide certainty and trust in an identity credential, it must be sound in both product and process. The process must provide assurances that a user has been scrutinized through an identity proofing process. The process should include common conditions and assurances prior to enrollment and issuance. The more stringent the criteria and assurances are, the higher the level of certainty and trust. Strong conditions may include elements such as background investigations, collection and verification of biometric information, and requirements for presentation of certain identity documents prior to issuance.

In relationship to privacy concerns and identity management issues, The First Amendment to the U.S. Constitution states:

> "Congress shall make no law ... prohibiting the
> free exercise [of religion]; or abridging the
> freedom of speech, or of the press; or the
> right of the people peaceably to assemble ...."

The First Amendment has been interpreted to grant a fundamental right of privacy, protecting individuals from having to disclose their political leanings or religious beliefs. It has been described by the Supreme Court as imposing limitations on the government's capbility to abridge one's "freedom to associate and privacy in one's associations." (e.g., NAACP v. State of Alabama, 1958). Therefore, violations of the First Amendment could be asserted if the use of biometric recognition technology were to become widespread and were used to identify people. For example, this amendment could be violated if biometric recognition technology devices were used at voting booths or to enter a church or a building where a particular organization assembles (National Biometric Security Project, 2006).

A suitably structured and effective identity management system would provide real time usable information to managers and others concerning the number, location, and qualifications of assets at his/her disposal. Although, verification systems can be connected to databanks, from an ethical point of view, the need for the subject's consent and the lack of a databank greatly reduces the privacy concerns. This chapter will explore how six dominant ethical positions handle issues of identification and verification biometric systems, as well as legal issues. These six ethical positions are as follows:

> Ethical egoism, deontology, utilitarianism, relativism, virtue ethics, and ethics of care.

Each of these ethical positions will be tied to a Throughput Decision-Making Model that depicts how individuals' decisions are motivated by information or their perceptions (framing of the problem). Perception, information, judgment, and decision choice are the main features of the Throughput Decision-Making Model (Rodgers, 1997, 2006, 2009; Rodgers & Gago, 2001, 2003, 2004). This theoretical model attempts to clarify the multiple ways in which ethical positions can influence students' behavior. The model captures several different pathways and stages that can influence a decision at the individual or organizational level. Further, depending upon individuals or organizations' viewpoint, certain pathways may be weighted heavier than or dominate other pathways. From this depiction, only six dominant decision-making pathways to a decision choice can be made.

The outline of this chapter will be:

1. Description of the Throughput Decision-Making Model
2. How Ethical Positions are tied to a six pathways of perception, information, judgment and decision choice
3. Discussion of the Six Dominant Ethical Positions
4. Strengths and Weaknesses of the six ethical positions as they relate to privacy issues
5. Cases for Ethical egoism, deontology, utilitarianism, relativism, virtue ethics, and ethics of care positions as they relate to identification and verification biometrics systems (overt and covert)
6. Conclusion

DESCRIPTION OF THE THROUGHPUT
DECISION-MAKING MODEL

Ethical and social responsibility is no new phenomenon; social changes in society due to considerations of applied ethics can be traced over time for thousands of years. The assumption is that ethical, social, and environmental responsibility will have a more probable influence on individuals' and organizations' ethical behavior than what governments' regulations will have. These beliefs tend to be held by those who argue that ethical and social responsibility behaviors are effective regarding privacy rights in some sense that goes beyond individual conscience salving.

Privacy rights are typically subject to matching the privacy interests of people against the interests of society, such as national security and law enforcement. There is a persistent stress between privacy and civil liberties in general, and these societal concerns. Especially this is the case during times of relative peace and stability in society.

The model proposed here takes a unique approach to conceptualizing six ethical philosophical positions by applying a decision making model to understanding this behavior within an organizational setting. This *Throughput Model* provides a broad conceptual framework for examining interrelated processes that impact on decisions effecting individuals and organizations. It incorporates the use of information as well as constructs of perceptual processing (information framing), judgmental processing (analysis of information/experiences), and decision choice as it applies to individuals and organizations. This model is particularly relevant for it clarifies critical pathways influenced by ethical positions. Decision making in this model is defined here as a multiphase, information-processing function in which cognitive and social processes are used to generate a set of outcomes. There are differences of opinion about how many phases and subroutines within phases exist and the order in which the phases occur. The three phases in the model proposed here appear with some consistency in the literature. These are (a) perception and information gathering, (b) analysis of information and processing (i.e., judgment), and (c) choice. This model represents a parsimonious way in capturing major concepts about organizations. Further, it provides a more interpretative cognitive schema. Finally, this model conceptualizes an early warning system.

Ethical guidelines in combination with regulated educational requirements can be viewed as more effective at securing the competence of individuals more so than securing the commitments of individuals. However, when trust is present, communication and problem solving are relatively easy for people to make ethical commitments. That is, trust can lead to superior information sharing and lower transaction cost, thus providing organizations with a source of reasonable benefits. Trust as a basis for organizations operating with responsibility, accountability, fairness, and transparency has many implications for effective ethical consideration policies and frameworks. Ethical considerations are defined as a set of moral principles or values that that binds a society together. This module enhances that trust is a basis of information exchange and framing of problems in promoting organizations to follow ethical consideration policies in creating wealth, providing employment, paying taxes and generating investment returns.

The conceptual model of ethical considerations is presented in Figure 6.1. Arrows from one construct to another indicate the hypothesized causal relationships. Perception, in this model, is of a higher mental activity level that involves categorization and classification of information. Lower levels of perception include how people pick up or process information through their

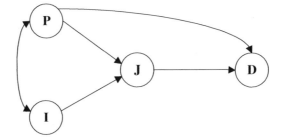

Figure 6.1. Individuals' decision processes diagram. *P = perception, I = information, J = judgment,* and *D = decision choice*

senses, such as vision, touch, hearing, etc. The lower level of perception normally involves automatic (and sometimes unconscious) reactions or responses to stimuli (information). The intensity of an ethical issue relates to the perceived importance of the issue to the decision-maker. Ethical issue intensity, then can be defined as the perceived relevance or importance of an ethical issue to the individual or group. In our model, the perceived importance of "ethical issue intensity" has been found to have a strong impact on both ethical judgment and choice.

In the model, perception and information are interdependent. That is, information can influence the way a decision-maker frames a problem (perception) or their framing can influence the selection of information to be used in later analysis. The higher the coherence between perception and information generally indicates that the information set is more reliable and relevant. Further, this interdependence implies that perception can influence the type of information selected for further processing. Likewise, information can influence and/or alter previous established perceptions. Information is later stored in memory affects and contributes to decision-makers' analysis. Typically, before an individual can make a decision, that individual encodes the information and develops a representation for the problem. Finally, perception and judgment can affect decision choice. Errors, biases, and context-dependent heuristics may result from cognitive mechanisms of which decision-makers are largely unaware, and these may have a direct impact on decision choice. The strategies of judgment that influence decision choice are under an individual's deliberate control. Our model helps us understand what causes individuals to act in a manner that we decide are unethical. Ethical behavior is a prerequisite for a society to function in an orderly way.

The decision-making processes of individuals can be represented in an organized manner. In order to study the methods of these decision processes it is important to break up all the paths marked with arrows in Figure 6.1 into sets of individual pathways. These fragments can then be independently analyzed for their contributing properties to individuals' decision processes. Further, it is common for decision-makers to differ in their moral philosophical values. Even if two individuals agree on the ethical principles that determine ethical behavior, it is unlikely that they will agree on the relative importance of each principle. These differences are highlighted in Figure 6.1, depicting several pathways toward making a decision.

HOW ETHICAL POSITIONS ARE TIED TO SIX PATHWAYS OF PERCEPTION, INFORMATION, JUDGMENT AND DECISION CHOICE

Based on Figure 6.1, six general pathways are established:
In-line table showing six general pathways.

(1)	$P \rightarrow D$	ethical egoism
(2)	$P \rightarrow J \rightarrow D$	deontology
(3)	$I \rightarrow J \rightarrow D$	utilitarianism
(4)	$I \rightarrow P \rightarrow D$	relativist
(5)	$P \rightarrow I \rightarrow J \rightarrow D$	virtue ethics
(6)	$I \rightarrow P \rightarrow J \rightarrow D$	ethics of care

There are many philosophies which are complex in nature. We discuss six prominent approaches depicted in the *Throughput Model* six general pathways. **(1) P → D** represents *ethical egoism position*, which stresses that individuals are always motivated to act in their perceived self-interest. **(2) P → J → D** depicts the *deontology position*, which emphasizes the rights of individuals and on the judgments associated with a particular decision process rather than on its choices. **(3) I → J → D** reflects the *utilitarian position* which is concerned with consequences, as well as the greatest good for the greatest number of people. **(4) I → P → D** highlights the *relativist position*, which assumes that decision-makers use themselves or the people around them as their basis for defining ethical standards. **(5) P → I → J → D** underscores the *virtue ethics position*, which is the classical Hellenistic tradition represented by Plato and Aristotle, whereby the cultivation of virtuous traits of character is viewed as morality's primary function. **(6) I → P → J → D** represents the *ethics of care position*, which focuses on a set of character traits that are deeply valued in close personal relationships, such as sympathy, compassion, fidelity, love, friendship, and the like.

These six pathways are viewed as the most dominant and influential for decision making dominated by particular moral perspectives. Although, it is important to note that other pathways in the *Throughput Model* also contributes to the above philosophical positions. Our argument is that the corresponding pathway to each particular philosophical view is the most dominant.

DISCUSSION OF THE SIX DOMINANT ETHICAL POSITIONS

Ethical egoism ($P \rightarrow D$) stresses that individuals are always motivated to act in their perceived self-interest. Ethical decisions need to be in line with long-term goals. Utility theory (game theory), which supports this position, is the study of the ways in which strategic interactions among rational players produce outcomes with respect to the preferences (or utilities) of those players, none of which might have been intended by any of them.

For example, The Ninth Amendment of the U.S. Constitution states:

> "The enumeration in the Constitution, of certain rights, shall not be construed to deny or disparage others retained by the people."

Even though little attention has been paid to this amendment in comparison to, for example, the First Amendment, it is perhaps the broadest of all of the amendments. The Ninth Amendment prescribes that the absence of a mention of a right (e.g., the right to privacy) does not indicate that such a right does not exist. The failure, however, to state a right to privacy does leave open for debate (and judicial elucidation) the extent and scope of such right for an individual. Thus, this Amendment could be used to make a case that individuals have a fundamental right to privacy with respect to their biometric and other personal information.

The ethical egoism pathway of decision making is made in a particular way that downplays nonsupporting information or analysis. A circumstance is perceived and the decision is taken by downplaying previous judgment or information. Prevailing market and other social forces supported the idea that short run profit maximization was the solo raison d'etre of the firm. Hence, ethical egoism in its purest form is the manifestation of maximizing shareholder wealth. In economics, the neoclassical marginal analysis regards the firm as a profit-maximizing unit. The main point of this position is that shareholders differ from other constituencies since they are residual risk-bearers and they have unique problems of contracting that are best met by having control. The tenets of this position rest with the rational choice perspective in that the behaviors of individuals are causally depicted as outcomes determined by the maximization of individual objective functions.

The *deontology position* or obligation-based approaches to ethics ($P \rightarrow J \rightarrow D$), and emphasizes the rights of individuals. Deontological philosophy usually contains or implies the words "should," "ought," or "it is (or was) right or wrong to…". The function of deontology moral judgments such as "You should help me," and "You owe me," is to persuade recipients to behave in accordance with the prescriptions they contain. The function of more abstract deontology judgments such as "Honesty is the best policy," "People should obey the law" is to induce recipients to adopt strategies that uphold social systems from which senders benefit. It is a relatively short step from making deontology moral judgments buttressed by reasons to espousing more formal systems of rules and laws.

Kant argued that moral actions are based on a "supreme principle of morality" which is objective, rational, and freely chosen: the categorical imperative. That is, this decision-making position emphasizes that one's perception (P) is oriented by conditioning judgment (J) of the rules and laws before rendering a decision (D). In other words, the decision is induced by a judgment based on a perception of a circumstance. Further, deontology underscores the property rights perspective which answers puzzling business questions that occurs in corporate law. This corporate form of business organization is justified on the grounds that it represents an extension of the property rights and the right of contract enjoyed by everyone. Ethical considerations come into play in difficult cases where the rules are unclear or in conflict. However, generalized rules of ethics may be unhelpful in counseling students. That is, students who know the rules of law and individual rights, but have no mature personal beliefs about their own duty to obey them, have not been fully educated in ethical considerations. Pertaining to individual rights, The Fourteenth Amendment states:

" … No State shall … deprive any person of life, liberty, or property, without due process of law…."

Besides the Bill of Rights, the Fourteenth Amendment is probably the most quoted and well-known constitutional amendment. It is also one of the extended and most wide-ranging topically, spanning from requirements pertaining to equal protection of all citizens under the law, to how people of each State are counted for purposes of electing representatives, to who can be a Congressman, to the legitimacy of public debt. The above-cited language is from what is acknowledged as the "due process clause" of the Fourteenth Amendment.

It is the Fourteenth Amendment's due process clause that the Supreme Court in 1973 in Roe v. Wade interpreted as giving a woman a restricted right to terminate her pregnancy (Roe v. Wade, 1973). Due to its historically far-reaching interpretation, it is expected that the due process clause would be essential in any constitutional objection to of the use of biometric identification as a violation of an individual's right of privacy.

From a deontology perspective, privacy law can be broken down into two main categories. The first category of laws applies to the government

Table 6.1.   Sources of Privacy Law

Public sector	*Private sector*
U.S. Constitution	--------
State constitutions	--------
Federal law	Federal law
State law	State law
Common law	Common law

(the public sector) and second category applies to everyone else (the private sector). Constitutional law and statutory laws govern the public sector. Statutory laws govern the private sector. Both the public sector and private sector are subject to common law tort privacy rights (Table 6.1).

Within these two sets of laws, the United States legal system recognizes different types of privacy rights, including informational privacy, physical privacy, decisional privacy, and communications privacy (Table 6.2). Regarding biometrics, informational privacy and physical privacy are the two most significant areas. Informational privacy allows individuals to control their own personal data. Even though it may be arguable whether a biometric is personal data, biometrics is often linked to other information that is personal data. Consequently, biometrics are classified under the informational privacy category. Physical privacy includes the right to control access to one's body and personal space, which would arguably include the right to control access to one's biometric information. The two other forms of privacy rights recognized by the courts, decisional privacy and communications privacy, could also impact the use of biometrics, but to a much lesser degree.

The *utilitarian position* $(\mathbf{I} \to \mathbf{J} \to \mathbf{D})$ is concerned with consequences, as well as "the greatest good for the greatest number of people." Utilitarianism is based on collective "economic egoism." The judgment is based on information and the information conditions the decision. Utilitarianism is an expansion of ethical egoism in that it is committed to the maximization of the good and the minimization of harm and evil to a society.

A utilitarian test can be applied to the use of biometric identification by authorities for security purposes (Table 6.3). While the U.S. concern about national security, mainly in air travel, have increased the call for biometric technology since September 11, 2001, there is still an intense concern about privacy and civil liberties and a perception that biometrics is somehow privacy invasive. Therefore, in applying biometric recognition technology for security purposes, even if the technology will only be used for verification purposes without a databank, the government can be prepared to demonstrate that the maximization of the good (e.g., protection of lives, or even property, such as buildings, bridges, railways, parks, and monuments) is a

Table 6.2.   Recognized Privacy Rights

Privacy type	Definition
Informational privacy	The right to have a hold over one's own personal data (e.g., criminal, financial, and medical records).
Physical privacy	The right to be in charge of access to one's body and personal space, e.g. search and seizures, Peeping Toms, blood tests, DNA swabs.
Decisional privacy	The right to make self-governing decisions about one's personal life (e.g., abortions, sexual preference).
Communications privacy	The right to communicate to another person without being heard by others (e.g., intrusive hi-tech hearing devices).

"special need" and that the interest of national security is furthered by the use of biometric identification. The government could endeavor to utilize the least intrusive, least offensive method possible without compromising the security goals (National Biometric Security Project, 2006). In addition, it can also implement measures to safeguard any information collected to protect against unauthorized uses and disclosures (i.e., the minimization of harm and evil to society).

Utilitarianism is based on collective "economic egoism." The judgment (J) is based on information (I) and the information conditions the decision (D). The central theme is what is good for the company is good for the country or community. Utilitarianism is an expansion of psychological egoism in that it is committed to the maximization of the good and the minimization of harm and evil to a society. Utilitarianism can be traced to the English political philosopher Jeremy Bentham, who designed a calculus in weighing criminal behavior and corresponding punishment. This calculus was extended to value judgments by the principle of maximizing happiness and minimizing pain. This calculus formed the basis of later utility calculations (i.e., cost-benefit analysis) in act-utilitarianism. John Mill is associated with the new version of utilitarianism (i.e., rule-utilitarianism) that accommodates the moral values of rights of duties. In this method, utility-maximizing principle is not directly applied to the action itself, but is only applied to an abstract rule that is to govern moral judgments as follows:

1. An action is moral if it follows morally correct rules, and
2. A rule is considered morally correct if the net utility produced when everyone acts on that rule is greater than the net utility produced when everyone acts on any other alternative rule.

Table 6.3.   Biometrics Used for Security Purposes

Factors Used in the Utilitarian Test

Public interest (maximization of the good of society)	*Individual privacy interest (ethical egoism and individual's rights)*
Public interest	**Reasonable expectation of privacy**
Courts look to whether the public interest is important enough to justify the action.	Courts look to society's views on what is reasonable
(1) What is the purpose of the action? e.g. criminal investigation, crime prevention, health and safety, national security.	(1) Where is the intrusion? There is a diminished expectation of privacy in certain places and situations, such as prisons, schools, and airports.
(2) Is the public interest furthered by the action?	(2) What is the level of intrusion? e.g. what is the extent of the risk, trauma, pain, an indignity of the intrusion?
(3) Does the situation rise to the level of a special need permitting the action without a warrant based on probable cause?	(3) What technology (e.g. sensory-enhancing) is being used? How commonplace is the technology? (e.g. metal detectors)
Safeguard measures	**Sensitivity of information**
What are the measures used to safeguard the information?	How sensitive is the information? Courts have found certain information to be more sensitive, such as health information, while other information, such as Social Security numbers, less so.
The more sensitive the information, the stronger the safeguards need to be. Strong safeguards can tip the scale in favor of the public interest even if the information is highly sensitive	

A utilitarian prospective can be viewed during times of relative peace and stability, that Americans are generally more concerned about civil liberties. During times of war or instability, "the greatest good for the greatest number of people," Americans are generally more willing to forego some degree of liberty in exchange for increased security.

The *relativist position* ($\mathbf{I} \rightarrow \mathbf{P} \rightarrow \mathbf{D}$) assumes that people uses themselves or the people around them as their basis for defining ethical standards. A clash of values and interests, and tensions between what is and what some groups believe can prevent accommodations with other interested parties. Ethical relativism is the position that maintains that morality is relative to the norms of one's culture. An action that is right or wrong rests upon the moral norms of the society in which it is practiced. The same action may be morally right in one society but be morally wrong in another. For the ethical relativist, there are no universal moral standards since standards that can be universally applied to all peoples at all times. The only moral standards against which an organization or society's practices can be judged are its own.

Relativism is a function of a company operating differently due to the rules or laws (or lack thereof) governing another state, country, or region. The present information influences the perception and the immediate decision without a previous judgment. The information helps shape a company's perception to act in a particular manner. Therefore, information is examined, the perception is framed and the decision is adopted.

What constitutes a "record" and what constitutes a "system of records" is critical to understanding whether an individual's biometric information would be subject to the Privacy Act (U.S. Code, 1974). The Office of Management and Budget (OMB, 1987) Guidelines instruct that a record can be "any item of information about an individual that includes an individual identifier" and "can include as little as one descriptive item about an individual." In addition, the The Privacy Act (U.S. Code, 1974) defines "record" as:

> " ... any item, collection, or grouping of information about an individual that is maintained by an agency, including, but not limited to, his education, financial transactions, medical history, and criminal or employment history and that contains his name, or the identifying number, symbol, or other identifying particular assigned to the individual, such as a finger or voice print or photograph."

The use of the terms "finger or voice print or photograph" leaves little doubt that biometrics presumably fall within the parameters of the Privacy Act. However, to what degree biometrics are records is not completely obvious. A particular relativist ethical position might consider a narrow interpretation of the definition. That is, a biometric must be linked to something else about that individual, such as his or her "education, financial transactions, medical history, and criminal or employment history" to be considered a record. Based upon the circumstances, a relativist position might entail a broader interpretation of the definition. That is, as long as that biometric is linked to anything about that individual, including his or her name or Social Security number or anything else that can be traced back to that individual, it is a record. Finally, a relativist position under the broadest reading of the definition, may assume a biometric in and of itself is a record even if it is not linked to any other information about the person (Table 6.4).

Table 6.4.   Interpretations of the Term "Record"

Narrow	Broad	Very broad
Biometric must be linked to information "about" the individual, such as medical history	Biometric can be linked to any other part of information, such as name or SSN	Biometric need not be linked to anything else for the reason that it is a record in and of itself

A relativist ethical position may adjust the meaning of record based upon the situation that the information system is operating. Such differing interpretations are imperative to a relativist ethical position to how broadly biometrics will be construed as a record. For example, the relativist position can shift based on a biometric that is linked to a individual's name and/or Social Security number. Or it can be based on such information about the individual's education, financial transactions, medical history, and criminal or employment history. Or maybe a biometric itself is a record.

The *virtue ethics position* ($P \rightarrow I \rightarrow J \rightarrow D$), which is the classical Hellenistic tradition represented by Plato (427 BC–347 BC) and Aristotle (384 BC–322 BC), whereby the cultivation of virtuous traits of character is viewed as morality's primary function. Aristotle was quite explicit when he stated that a wicked person is responsible for his or her character. That is, not because he or she could now alter it but because he or she could have and should have acted differently early on and established very dissimilar habits and states of character. That is, the notion of an individual (citizen) as an entity in principle is capable of recognizing, knowing about, acting appropriately in respect of rights and duties. In the virtue ethics position, a circumstance is perceived (P). A conscious look for information (I) is initiated. Based on the information a judgment (J) is made, which will support a decision (D). Virtue ethics position began to rise during the 1960s prompted by television and other mediums of advertising. The corporate image began to change to assume a disposition to act fairly but also a morally appropriate desire to do so. Popular social celebrities endorsed products and the corporate leaders appeared to have the traits of a virtuous character. However, shareholders still occupied center stage as the only stakeholder as opposed to employees, suppliers, customers, and the community.

The increased investment in identity-related technology can translate into value for individuals. The challenge for an identity management system is to create a framework that leverages existing investments to increase individuals' value. An improved identity management system that provides benefits and improves processes may result in greater efficiency in the delivery of public services.

The cornerstone to identity management acceptance can be viewed from the perspective of individual's value that is created through more efficient systems. In addition to the obvious benefits to terrorism protection, prevention, and response missions, the capabilities of smart cards represent an opportunity for a revolution in government administration.

Courts have stated that its holding was reached on the facts of the case, and that the integrity and values of a is a cherished value of our society. For example, the Fifth Amendment states:

"No person ... shall be compelled in any criminal case to be a witness against himself, nor be deprived of life, liberty, or property, without due process of law; nor shall private property be taken for public use, without just compensation."

The Supreme Court has described the Fifth Amendment as depicting "the Constitution's concern for" one's right to "a private enclave where [one] may lead a private life." The Fifth Amendment prohibits the government from forcing an individual to disclose incriminating information about oneself. The Fifth Amendment has been examined in the context of compulsory blood sampling and fingerprinting, which have been found to not violate the Fifth Amendment's protection against being forced to be a witness against oneself. It is, therefore, likely that the same analysis could be applied to other forms of compulsory biometric identification in organization's systems that can demonstrate it adds values to individuals associated with the information system (National Biometric Security Project, 2006).

Finally, the *ethics of care position* ($I \rightarrow P \rightarrow J \rightarrow D$), which is a set of character traits that echo ingrain values in close personal relationships, such as honesty, sympathy, compassion, fidelity, love, friendship, and the like. The *ethics of care position* (stakeholders perspective), which focuses on a willingness to listen to distinct and previously unacknowledged perspectives. In other words, an organization must build solidarity among employees, suppliers, customers, shareholders, and the community. The ethics of care position recognizes the moral priority of caring for the particular others for whom we are responsible. This stakeholder position focuses on responsiveness to need, empathetic understanding, and the interrelatedness of people, rather than on individual rationality or universal moral rules. It emphasizes relations between people rather than the preferences or dispositions of individuals; it is thoughtful relations that are thought to have primary value. This position suggests:

1. Sensitivity to situations or dimensions of situations that involve abandonment, detachment, hurt, pain, or violations of intimacy;

2. Need to balance the needs of all parties, make them feel attached, and accept people for all their subtle distinctiveness;

3. Resolve conflicts by emphasizing procedures, consensus, wisdom, the logic of affect, and sensitivity to context; and

4. Commitment to nonviolence, moral values, and the welfare of generations (Gilligan, 1993).

The ethics of care position can be implemented in order to address use of biometric recognition technology as follows:

1. Only essential and relevant information is maintained,

2. Information is unidentifiable to fullest degree possible,

3. A person is notified and has access to information and ability to correct,

4. Appropriate controls, procedures, and oversights are in place,
5. Adequate penalties and redress for violations of controls and procedures are enforced,
6. Used for verification purposes with individual's knowledge, and
7. Identification and/or covert employment necessitate stringent controls and restricted use and circumstances.

Ethics of care position states that existing important information (I) influences one's perception (P) of a circumstance. The influenced perceptions are judged (J) before rendering a decision (D). Also, ethics of care viewpoint emphasizes that not only shareholders have property rights but also employees, suppliers, customers, and the community. This presumptive equality among these groups is assumed to be enforceable in, their interactions and communications with each other.

The increased investment in biometrics technology in terms of the ethics of care position is that it must translate into stakeholders' value. The challenge in biometrics management for organizational use is to create a framework that leverages existing investments to increase stakeholders value (i.e., customers, suppliers, employees, shareholders, and the community). An implemented biometrics management system that provides benefits, not only to stakeholders, but improves processes and results in greater efficiency in the delivery of public services is a necessary justification for such a system.

The cornerstone to organizational acceptance for biometrics use will be the stakeholders' value that is created through more efficient management. In addition to the obvious benefits to the company, that is prevention and security measures, the capabilities of biometrics represent an opportunity for a revolution in how companies perform and operate.

CONCLUSION

Appropriate biometrics ethics governance program helps organizations confidently address critical business issues such as internal control biometrics systems as well as assure the security, reliability and integrity of their strategic information. Implementing a biometric ethics governance program also helps an organization protect its investment in biometrics and ensure appropriate management of information assets, many of which are vital to the survival and growth of the organization itself.

The challenge in identity management for enhanced incident response is to fashion a framework that leverages existing investments to increase public value. An enhanced identity management system that provides advantages and improves processes that results in greater efficiency in the delivery of public services is a necessary.

The common denominator in a great deal of privacy cases is to weigh the individual's privacy interest against a particular public (i.e., government) interest. One of the major factors to consider in the public's favor is the importance of the public interest and the precautions taken to safeguard the information. On the person's side, is whether there is a reasonable expectation of privacy and the level of the intrusion on the person.

Ethic considerations are fundamental to establishing trust. Anytime there is a lack of trust, there will be missed opportunities. Trust can be built up over time through the consistent application of ethical process thinking. Trust is constituted by perception and judgment of the motivation and ability of others that would make them more or less trustworthy in particular contexts.

Even though technology will not modify ethical considerations, new laws and policies could restrict or expand the application of biometrics and the extent biometric recognition technology can be used to unlock ethical considerations.

Practices of data collectors can threaten or harm your privacy and way of life. Further, an individual can be confronted with ID theft, and profile as a deadbeat or a security risk. Worse, there's no way to find out what they are telling others about you. To this end, we were interested in finding out whether six major ethical philosophical positions (Rodgers & Gago, 2001), namely ethical egoism, deontology, utilitarianism, relativist, virtue ethics, and ethics of care and social responsibility can better guide us into the area of privacy management and biometrics.

Even though technology will not modify ethical considerations, new laws and policies could restrict or expand the application of biometrics and the extent biometric recognition technology can be used to unlock ethical considerations.

Biometric recognition technology is not a panacea. Identification of a person through biometrics and matching identity to information in a central database can help identify terrorists and prevent future attacks. Such use arguably rises to the level of an important government and ethical considerations. Verification of an individual's identity through biometrics provides authorities with no more information about an individual than it had before. Biometric recognition technology helps thwart falsifying identification. The use and understanding of six dominant ethical positions may assure the public that biometric use will not be abused, that personal information will be safeguarded, and that privacy and civil liberties will not be jeopardized.

CASES

Based on Figure 6.1, six general pathways highlight the ethical egoism, deontology, utilitarianism, relativism, virtue ethics, and ethics of care positions.

In each of the cases please indicate which (1) ethical position underlines the actions taken by organizations; (2) ethical position you suggest to improve the case situation. Finally, note whether the case situation should be classified as "identification" (covert or overt) or verification.

Case 1: Selling Your Information

Data brokers provide individual background searches for organizations and others. They also receive large revenues from dividing your information with data-mining software to create targeted lists to appeal to marketers. For instance, your colorful bits of detail data regarding your ailments, vacations, and hobbies supplied on warranty cards can be data-mined. That is, in the data industry, this type of information can be combined with other informational sources such as public records and credit transactions to provide a "three-dimensional view." For example, Focus USA's, a data broker, database covers over 105 million U.S. households, with labels such as "Christian Donors," who give twice the portion of their incomes that nonreligious households give to politicians and causes, and a group it calls "Hooked on Plastic," consisting of 4.2 million American families for who "using credit cards doesn't feel like they're spending money."

Some data brokers are not above selling people most private information. For example, InfoUSA, a database marketer with over $400 million in sales, promises on its Web site to "find people who suffer from health conditions such as diabetes" or "search for people taking a certain medication." For instance, clients can order a mailing list of Prozac users or refine the list to include only those with incomes over $100,000 a year. However, InfoUSA's senior management claims that only legitimate organizations that are primarily large pharmaceutical manufacturers are permitted to buy the lists.

Case 1 Suggested Answer

Organization ethical decision making: Ethical egoism or relativist positions.

Suggested ethical position: Deontology, utilitarian or ethics of care position.

The ability to access and correct personal information, while generally regarded as a central aspect of privacy protection, is not an absolute right. This notion includes specific conditions for what would be considered reasonable in the provision of access, including conditions related to timing, fees, and the manner and form in which access would be provided. What is to be considered reasonable in each of these areas will vary from one situation to another depending on circumstances, such as the nature of the information-processing activity. Access will also be conditioned by security requirements that preclude the provision of direct access to information and will require sufficient proof of identity prior to provision of access. Access must be provided in a reasonable manner and form. A reasonable manner should include the normal methods of interaction between organizations and individuals.

Case 2: Organizations Need Counterintelligence

The FBI is asking more companies to join its Counterintelligence Domain Program so that together, they can proactively fight against hacks and data theft.

Certain foreign entities have denied involvement in a series of hacks carried out against internal control systems at the Pentagon; however, the threat of technology driven espionage has forced the FBI to encourage businesses and academic institutions to better prepare for such attacks.

Scan evidence exists that indicates foreign governments and companies have backed or planned to launch attempts to steal intellectual property from U.S. corporations and researchers. Nonetheless, officials with the FBI claim that the problem is real and that American organizations must begin policing their operations more aggressively today to prevent valuable data from being stolen tomorrow.

The FBI's Counterintelligence Domain Program aims to foster cooperation between the agency and private entities to order to assist them in the identification and protection of potential intelligence risks. The program has made significant steps in helping to close the gap between businesses and law enforcement to defend intellectual property from being left vulnerable to potential theft, FBI officials maintain.

First and foremost, the Domain project has materialized in the form of relationships built between the FBI's agency and the leading corporate entities and research groups that control data that criminals and governments could try to get their hands on.

The program is targeting companies that are developing cutting edge technologies and other products that are considered to give the U.S. a technological or business-related advantage. In addition, training seminars held by the FBI in the name of expanding Domain, are aimed at identifying any research, information, or technologies that might be targeted by U.S. adversaries. It also establishes an ongoing information exchange among the program's members to improve protections and reduce opportunities for theft.

Two of the most significant trends feeding the need for corporate counterintelligence are offshore outsourcing and the heavy flow of foreign engineering talent into U.S. corporations and research institutions.

Traditional spies are no longer the norm, but the engineer, student, or business partner could be the threat. Hence, this could allow access to corporate secrets, intellectual property, and prepatent research information at universities.

Case 2 Suggested Answer

Organization ethical decision making: Deontology or utilitarian position. Suggested ethical position: Virtue ethics or ethics of care position.

Claims for access are repetitious or vexatious by nature; cases where providing the information would constitute a violation of laws or would compromise security; or, incidences where it would be necessary in order to protect commercial confidential information that an organization has taken steps to protect from disclosure, where disclosure would benefit a competitor in the marketplace, such as a particular computer or modeling program. "Confidential commercial information" is information that an organization has taken steps to protect from disclosure, where such disclosure would facilitate a competitor in the market to use or exploit the information against the business interest of the organization causing significant financial loss. The particular computer program or business process an organization uses, such as a modeling program, or the details of that program or business process may be confidential commercial information.

Where confidential commercial information can be readily separated from other information subject to an access request, the organization should redact the confidential commercial information and make available the nonconfidential information, to the extent that such information constitutes personal information of the individual concerned.

Case 3: Data Security in a Global Market

A good number of intelligence experts trained in the art of finding holders of sensitive corporate and national defense information may be attempting to liberate the data. Further, many may be employed in efforts to steal whatever plans they can sell to others for a profit today.

It is not about spying so much as being able to identify business risk and what is occurring with competitors in the global environment. Organizations are creating separate entities from traditional security or internal control biometrics system security to provide management to identify people internally who might have access to high-level information or might be targeted by competitors or foreign entities.

One of the most difficult areas to track is data formats. Techniques such as gloss marks and infrared stamps are implemented to create a trail of evidence as to who might have accessed, printed and walked off with sensitive data when copies of any stolen documents are recovered.

Companies cannot rely on the government alone to watch out for their interests overseas. That is, when a company enters into a new country a risk assessment must be conducted. Every country has its own IP protections and concepts.

Case 3 Suggested Answer

Organization ethical decision making: Deontology or utilitarian position.

Suggested ethical position: Virtue ethics or ethics of care position.

Providing information that could constitute a violation of laws or would compromise security could pose ethical dilemmas for an organization. Organizations should provide the necessary and reasonable constraints in order to protect its commercial confidential information. Further, an organization should take steps to protect from disclosure, where disclosure would benefit a competitor in the marketplace, such as a particular computer, hostile country, or modeling program. "Confidential commercial information" is information that an organization has taken steps to protect from disclosure, where such disclosure would facilitate a competitor in the market to use or exploit the information against the business interest of the organization causing significant financial loss. The particular computer program or business process an organization uses, such as a modeling program, or the details of that program or business process may be confidential commercial information. Where confidential commercial information can be readily separated from other information subject to an access request, the organization should redact the confidential commercial information and make available the nonconfidential information, to the extent that such information constitutes personal information of the individual concerned. Organizations may deny or limit access to the extent that it is not practicable to separate the personal information from the confidential commercial information and where granting access would reveal the organization's own confidential commercial information as defined above, or where it would reveal the confidential commercial information of another organization that is subject to an obligation of confidentiality.

Case 4: Ethical Issues: Privacy and the Workplace Just Don't Mix

The bigger the organization, the more likely it monitors employees' e-mail, instant messaging (IM), or website surfing.

According to a 2005 survey by the American Management Association and The ePolicy Institute (http://www.amanet.org/press/amanews/ems05.htm), three out of four companies monitor where their employees go on the website, and more than half scan their e-mail. One out of four organizations report having terminated employees for e-mail abuse, and another 25% have dismissed employees for inappropriate website surfing. In addition, 2% of companies have fired workers over offensive blog entries, according to the 2006 version of the survey.

The report also indicates that there's background checks (80% of businesses conduct them, according to Spherion), drug tests (50%), surveillance cameras, and that GPS transponder are placed in the company car.

However, companies do have to be concerned about trade secrets leaking out via e-mail, employee misrepresentation, harassment suits stemming from inappropriate e-mail or website surfing, and employees simply not working on the company time.

One of the leading problems is that increased surveillance inevitably collects nonwork-related information about employees and offers employers more opportunity to make employment decisions pertaining to hiring, firing, promotion, etc. The criteria implemented could be established on factors other than qualifications and job performance.

Case 4 Suggested Answer

Organization ethical decision making: Deontology or utilitarian position. Suggested ethical position: Virtue ethics or ethics of care position.

When an organization denies, terminates, or censors an employee, the reasons should be specified. That is, an organization should provide the individual with an explanation as to why it has made that determination and information on how to challenge that denial. An organization would not be expected to provide an explanation, however, in cases where such disclosure would violate a law or judicial order.

Case 5: Conflicting Laws—U.S., EU Passenger Data Accord

The long-running dispute over the handling of personal data for airline travelers has been resolved. The European Union has reached an agreement in the long-running dispute over the handling of personal data and flying to the U.S.

U.S. authorities have been trying to use the renewal of a transatlantic agreement permitting the transfer of European air passengers' data, known as passenger name records (PNRs), to increase their powers of surveillance of foreigners entering the U.S.

Sharing the data violates strict European data protection laws; however, the European Commission and national governments in the E.U. negotiated an exemption from the rules in order to allow the U.S. to better protect itself from potential terrorist attacks. The agreement was deemed illegal by the European Court of Justice. Consequently, this court decision exposed European airlines to massive fines and the possible loss of landing slots in the U.S. if they had continued to hand over the data.

Case 5 Suggested Answer

Organization ethical decision making: Deontology or utilitarian position. Suggested ethical position: Virtue ethics or ethics of care position.

Organizations may deny or limit access to the extent that it is not practicable to separate the personal information from the confidential commercial information and where granting access would reveal the organization's own confidential commercial information as defined above, or where it would reveal the confidential commercial information of another organization that is subject to an obligation of confidentiality. When an organization denies a request for access, for the reasons specified above, such an organization should provide the individual with an explanation as to why it has made that determination and information on how to challenge that denial. An organization would not be expected to provide an explanation, however, in cases where such disclosure would violate a law or judicial order.

Case 6: Texas State Website Leaks Sensitive Information

State and local governments are struggling to remove personal information online so it cannot be misused by criminals. Certain individuals are not happy about the State of Texas providing their addresses and social security numbers on the Internet.

Sensitive information of thousands of people are available on the Texas Secretary of State's SOSDirect website. As government pushes more and more documents online, Texas is one of many state and local governments across the United States that is now plagued to remove sensitive information so that it cannot be misused by criminals.

Certain information are stated such as social security numbers on tax liens and on loan agreement notifications filed with the state, called Uniform Commercial Code (UCC) financing statements. Texas has been automatically removing sensitive information from all documents filed with SOSDirect since June 2005. Further, the state is now in the process of redacting this information from earlier filings.

Although, users must submit a credit card number in order to search the Texas database, the lax security makes that barrier meaningless to most hackers. Criminals may be able to obtain information from the website using phony credit card numbers. That is, a name and social security number is all that criminals need to set up a phony credit card application.

Some states like California and Colorado have shut down access to their UCC databases due to privacy advocates notifying them that they could be misused by identity thieves.

Case 6 Suggested Answer

Organization ethical decision making: Relativist position.

Suggested ethical position: Deontology or utilitarian position.

Organizations may halt the availability of personal information from the commercial information. An organization should provide an explanation, however, in cases where such disclosure would violate a law or judicial order.

Individuals should be able to:

a. obtain from the personal information controller confirmation of whether or not the personal information controller holds personal information about them;

b. have communicated to them, after having provided sufficient proof of their identity, personal information about them;

    1. within a reasonable time;
    2. at a charge, if any, that is not excessive;
    3. in a reasonable manner;
    4. in a form that is generally understandable; and,

c. challenge the accuracy of information relating to them and, if possible and as appropriate, have the information rectified, completed, amended or deleted.

REFERENCES

Gilligan, C. (1993). *In a different voice: Psychological theory and women's development.* Boston: Harvard University Press.

Landahl, M. R. (2006). *First responder identity management: Policy options for improved terrorism incident response* (Thesis). Naval Postgraduate School, Monterey California.

NAACP v. State of Alabama, 357 U.S. 449, at 462 (1958).

National Biometric Security Project. (2006). *Report on United States Federal Laws Regarding Privacy and Personal Data and Applications to Biometrics.* Website: www.nationalbiometric.org.

Rodgers, W. (1997). *Throughput modeling: Financial information used by decision makers.* Greenwich, CT: JAI Press.

Rodgers, W. (2006). *Process thinking: Six pathways to successful decision making*. New York, NY: iUniverse.

Rodgers, W. (2009). *Ethical beginnings: preferences, rules and principles*. New York, NY: iUniverse.

Rodgers, W. (2010). *E-commerce and biometric issues addressed in a Throughput Model*. Hauppauge, NY: Nova Publication.

Rodgers, W., & Gago, S. (2001). Cultural and ethical effects on managerial decisions: Examined in a Throughput Model. *Journal of Business Ethics, 31*, 355–367.

Rodgers, W., & Gago, S. (2003). A model capturing ethics and executive compensation. *Journal of Business Ethics, 48*, 189–202.

Rodgers, W., & Gago, S. (2004). Stakeholder influence on corporate strategies over time. *Journal of Business Ethics, 52*, 349–363.

Rodgers, W., Guiral, A., & Gonzalo, J. A. (2009). Different pathways that suggest whether auditors' going concern opinions are ethically based. *Journal of Business Ethics, 86*, 347–361.

Roe v. Wade, *410 U.S. 113* (1973).

U.S. Code. *Privacy Act of 1974*, 5 U.S.C. § 552(a)(1) & (b) (1974).

APPENDIX 6A

NBSP Publication 0205

March 2006
Report on International Data Privacy Laws and Application to the Use of
Biometrics in the United States

PART ONE: REPORT ON THE STATE OF INTERNATIONAL PRIVACY LAWS AND APPLICATION TO BIOMETRICS AND THEIR IMPACT ON THE UNITED STATES

In 2004, the National Biometric Security Project (the NBSP) prepared a
report on the state of federal privacy law in the United States and the
impact of those laws on the use of biometrics in the United States to identify or verify the identity of individuals, particularly with respect to national
security That report on federal privacy law, which was completed in August
of 2004, demonstrated how to use biometric recognition technology as part
of the United States' efforts to increase security and protect itself against
future terrorist attacks without being at odds with United States privacy
laws. That report discussed how, under the current legal system and law in
the United States, biometrics can legally be used as a system to verify a person's identity in most overt and consensual situations and, under certain
circumstances, to positively identify individuals through the use of databases. The report concluded with a recommendation of seven measures to
employ as part of any biometric recognition technology system to protect
the privacy of individuals who are part of any such system.

The course of privacy protections and the use of biometrics at the international level are taking a direction that the United States and its citizens
must recognize will unfold, whether or not the United States actively par-
ticipates in guiding its course. Biometrics are viewed globally as personal
data deserving of the highest level of privacy protection. We know from our
last report that it is legal to use biometrics in any context where the use of
personal data is legal. Biometric recognition technology is being used
around the globe in ever increasing applications. The technology is now on
the cusp of being used for the most universally accepted form of identification, the passport.

The use of biometric recognition technology on an international level
will occur regardless of the opinions of individual opponents to such technology or the official position of the United States government. Simply
stated, if one wishes to travel outside of the United States, biometrics has
been accepted by the international community as the most reliable method

of positive identification of travelers. Methods of reliable positive identification are crucial when it comes to supporting national security and countering threats of harm to people or the destruction of property and infrastructure.

For nations to have access and effectively exploit biometric information, the international community is establishing guidelines as to how a traveler's biometric data can be used by the traveler's country of origin and the traveler's country of destination.

In order to participate in the global community it is necessary that each country focus on these guidelines in establishing that country's data privacy protection laws. Ultimately, a fully participatory system of sharing biometrics or other personal data will require all countries to establish and agree to be governed in this matter by a common set of ground rules. It can be reasonably anticipated that once the international travel systems are in place to identify individuals through biometric information, those same types of systems will become ubiquitous and shall be employed in other transactions and situations besides international travel and border control.

After the events of 9/11, the government of the United States increased its participation in the development of governing rules, including data privacy protection principles, for the use of biometrics in international travel. One course used by the U.S. government to affect international policies and standards is to participate and appoint representatives to such organizations as the International Civil Aviation Organization ("ICAO"), a proponent of biometrics in international travel. Advocacy and compliance with new rules that effectively impose the mandatory use of biometric recognition technology also results in an impact on U.S. citizens. In other words, policies and standards are being imposed on United States citizens that may not otherwise have been enacted in the United States through the normal legislative process. Such "policy laundering" is frowned upon by privacy advocates, but may be an inevitable consequence of cooperation in creating a more secure infrastructure for international travel. On the other hand, the government has also appointed representatives to the Organization for Economic Cooperation and Development ("OECD"), which has been the leader in setting the standards for data privacy, which standards are far higher than any standards ever adopted by the United States in legislation.

This report examines the privacy laws in the European Union and four other leading industrialized nations. In particular, the report focuses on data privacy, since it has come to be universally accepted that biometrics are considered personal data, and because it is the transfer of personal data, including biometrics, across international borders that makes privacy and biometrics a global concern. It would be impossible to understand international privacy law without examining the privacy policies of the OECD. Therefore, in Part Two of this report, before reporting on the EU and the four other countries selected, we shall review the 1980 OECD

Guidelines on the Protection of Privacy and Transborder Flows of Personal Data[1] (hereinafter referred to as the "OECD Guidelines").

This report will demonstrate how the European Union has emerged as a leader and a trendsetter in personal data privacy protection law. The EU prides itself in its view that it has the most comprehensive approach to protecting personal data and has been publicly urging other countries, in particular the United States, to follow its approach.[2]

Admittedly, the EU's system for data privacy controls has been criticized for its lack of uniformity among EU member countries and the failure of many member countries to fully comply with the EU's data protection laws. Nevertheless, nations around the world are looking to the EU in formulating their own data privacy laws.

Three of the countries examined in this report, Canada, Australia, and New Zealand, along with many of countries of the EU, have a federal/central government Privacy Commissioner (or an equivalent position) whose role it is to ensure that privacy protection laws are enforced and to recommend changes. There is no federal Privacy Commissioner or equivalent role in the United States. However, the position of Chief Privacy Officer is gaining prominence within some key government organizations. This trend has been met with approval from other countries. For example, Canada's current Privacy Commissioner saw the 2003 appointment of Nuala O'Connor Kelly as Chief Privacy Officer for the White House's Department of Homeland Security as a "positive development."[3] The Intelligence Reform Act of 2004, which President Bush signed into law in December 2004, creates a Privacy and Civil Liberties Board, which will review regulations and policies related to the war on terrorism.[4]

Each of the countries examined has adopted standards for protecting the privacy of data in both the public and private sectors that are directly based on the OECD Guidelines. Even Japan, who, until the 1960s, did not have a word for the concept of privacy, has enacted data privacy laws that embrace the full spirit of the OECD Guidelines.[5] The United States however, itself an OECD member, has not yet adopted a uniform standard. Instead, United States data privacy law, and United States privacy law in general, has been built on a miscellany of statutes and Constitutional principles. The closest the United States comes to having data protection privacy standards that resemble the standards set forth in the OECD Guidelines are set forth in various laws impacting select segments of the public and private sectors.

In the public sector, The Department of Health and Human Services Regulations for the Protection of Human Subjects,[6] which has certain similarities to the principles of the OECD Guidelines, only applies to government agencies engaged in studies involving human subjects. Executive Order 12333,[7] dated December 4, 1981 (approximately one year after the OECD Guidelines were published) only applies to certain government agencies, and does little to set forth standards, other than to place the responsibility of developing standards into the hands of the individual agencies to which the Order applies, with little guidance as to the parameters. The Privacy Act of 1974,[8] discussed below, only applies to government agencies and is also limited in scope.

In the private sector, there are only laws directed at certain industries; there is no uniform standard for privacy protection in the private sector. However, in order to do business with the EU, hundreds of U.S. companies have voluntarily agreed to take measures to satisfy the EU that they will adequately protect data transferred to them from EU countries, either by undergoing an adequacy determination by the transferring country's government or by self-certifying to the US Department of Commerce that they will adhere to a set of "Safe Harbor Privacy Principles."[9] In this respect, the private sector has demonstrated a capacity and willingness to comply with international data privacy standards. This is in part due to the fact that commerce is at a global level and in order to effectively participate in a global economy, the private sector is recognizing the need to comply with global privacy standards.

The Privacy Act of 1974 regulates the collection, maintenance, use, and dissemination of personal information of United States citizens and legal resident aliens by the federal government.[10] It does not protect nonresident aliens, such as foreigners traveling to the U.S or otherwise transacting business in or with the U.S. Further, it does not regulate state and local governments, private individuals, or private commercial enterprises. The Privacy Act of 1974 requires all federal agencies to adopt and publish minimum standards with respect to the collection, maintenance, use, and dissemination of personal information, and it restricts such agencies from disclosing personally identifiable records.[11] Much like Executive Order 12333, any such standards would be applicable only to the particular agency responsible for self-imposing them. A preliminary review has not uncovered any adopted or published agency privacy standards.

The Privacy Act of 1974 focuses on four basic policy objectives: (1) to restrict *disclosure* of personally identifiable records maintained by agencies; (2) to grant individuals increased rights of *access* to agency records maintained on themselves; (3) To grant individuals the right to seek *amendment* of agency records maintained on themselves upon a showing that the records are not accurate, relevant, timely or complete; and (4) to establish a code of "*fair information practices*" that requires agencies to comply with statutory norms for collection, maintenance, and dissemination of records.[12]

Although these four objectives have some obvious similarities to some of the privacy principles of the subsequently published OECD Guidelines, they do not encompass the full scope of those principles and, in any event, have limited application. As an OECD member country, the United States has an implicit obligation to carefully consider following the OECD's recommended guidelines. As of this writing however, it does not appear that the U.S. government has initiated any formal action for adoption of the OECD Guidelines. This ambivalence may be increasingly difficult to sustain if it results in conflict in the sharing of personal data with other OECD member countries. At a minimum, the U.S. government should, as Japan did in 1999, appoint a committee to engage in a thorough review of the OECD Guidelines and make recommendations as to uniform data privacy standards suitable for adoption by the U.S.[13]

The wariness of other nations, in particular the EU, to the transfer of personal data to the United States because of what they perceive as a lack of adequate protection for such data, may create a serious obstacle to progress. Such perceptions, accurate or not, may translate into resistance to cooperate. Inevitably, such resistance on cooperation will affect the utility on the use of biometrics, which can only be fully exploited if applied in an international practice. Less than complete Reexaminations of U.S. policy on this issue, or piecemeal applications on a program by program basis will not, we believe, lead to a comprehensive solution for international cooperation. Failure to reach an agreement on international application of privacy rules will almost certainly mean failure to fully and effectively exploit biometric technology. The convergence of the need for privacy rules that are shared on an international basis with the application of biometrics in the same universal environment provide an opportunity for the U.S. to act as a trendsetter by developing and establishing standards for the use of biometrics with regard to privacy. Such biometric data privacy principles should take into consideration the privacy principles set forth in the OECD Guidelines, as well as the privacy principles found in the laws and policies of other countries and organizations. For example, the principles proposed by the Biometric Institute in Australia, discussed in this report, were developed to comply with Australia's privacy laws and integrate many of the emerging global privacy standards. By developing and implementing such biometric privacy principles, the U.S. can have a significant impact on the issue and scope of biometric data privacy principles and standards. Failure to exercise this initiative will, at best, risk better progress on this issue, and even lead to further conflict.

Resistance to both U.S. and foreign biometric privacy legislation has come from both sides of the fence. Some proponents of biometric recognition technology are concerned that any legislation will restrict the currently legal uses of biometrics. Opponents of biometric recognition technology (on the basis of its perceived threat to privacy) are concerned that legislation will condone the use of such technology on a broad or unrestricted scale. The NBSP concludes that the best compromise is implementation of data privacy policy and/or legislation that takes into consideration: (a) the fact that most overt and consensual uses of biometric recognition technology are legal and nonintrusive; (b) that public concerns over misuses (such as could occur with databases or unrestricted data-mining) should be competently addressed; and (c) participation in global privacy standards will enhance proper and effective use of the technology.

The purpose of this report is to understand the international privacy law and its impact on the use of biometric recognition technology on both the United States in isolation and as well as on a global scale. Biometric recognition technology is here to stay, and resistance to its general use is futile. The focus of the government and concerned citizens should not be on *preventing* the use of the technology, but instead on controlling that aspect of its use that directly merges with personal data and privacy considerations.

Our previous report concluded that there are no legal impediments to the public sector (i.e., the federal government) using biometrics in the United States, so long as such uses comply with current privacy laws. Such laws mainly act as a control (rather than a prohibition) for government uses of biometrics for surveillance purposes or for other uses that do not require the consensual participation of the subject individual or where data is stored in a government database. However, the report also demonstrated that one of the biggest challenges biometrics face is public acceptance. At least some of the resistance to acceptance is based on a lack of understanding of how the various biometric systems operate. Educating the public, as we suggested in our first report, is essential. This is no less true on the international level than it is in the U.S. A key way to gain public approval is through the successful implementation of biometrics that clearly benefits the public (in any country) while including adequate provision for protection against abuse. Conversely, a poor choice of technology, or a decision to use that technology in an environment where abuse of data associated with the technology is not restricted will only set back biometric use by decreasing public confidence and confirming people's fears. For this reason, the type of technology selected for use in international infrastructure applications, should be carefully matched with protective laws, policies, guidelines, or protocols that are appropriate to the characteristics of that technology in its operational environment. Stated differently, if one form of biometric technology is believed to be more intrusive from a privacy perspective than another, but its overall security value argues for its use nonetheless, than it should be employed under more stringent privacy protective measures to retain public confidence and acceptance.

Biometrics can and should be part of the United States' national security program, as the 9/11 Commission Report recommends.[14] The 9/11 Commission Report recommends that a comprehensive biometric screening system be designed and integrated into a larger network of screening points, which includes transportation and vital facilities.[15] The 9/11 Commission Report further recommends biometric passports and asserts that linking biometric passports to sound data systems is essential to detecting terrorists and deterring future attacks.[16] To comply with these recommendations, the U.S. will require access to biometric and other data of individuals from other nations. The ability to gain this access will be enhanced by developing a set of privacy principles based on the OECD Guidelines that also includes principles aimed at addressing the particular concerns of biometrics. If the United States successfully implements such principles, the United States can emerge as a leader in setting the standards for biometric privacy protection.

NOTES

1. Organization for Economic Co-operation and Development, Council Recommendation Concerning Guidelines Governing the Protection of Privacy and Transborder Flows of Personal Data, Oct. 1, 1980, 20 I.L.M. 422 [*hereinafter* OECD Guidelines].

2. Albert J. Marcella, Jr & Carol Stucki, Privacy Handbook: Guidelines, Exposures, Policy Implementation, and International Issues 77 (2003) [*hereinafter* PRIVACY HANDBOOK].

3. Jennifer Stoddart, Public Safety and Privacy: An Inevitable Conflict? Address at the Reboot Communications Public Safety Conference Strategies for Public Safety Technology and Counter-Terrorism: Prevention, Protection and Pursuit (April 27, 2004) (transcript available at the Office of the Privacy Commissioner of Canada, http://www.privcom.gc.ca/speech/2004/sp-d_040401_e.asp) (last visited December 14, 2004).

4. Walter Pincus, *President Gets to Fill Ranks of New Intelligence Superstructure*, WASH. POST, December 16, 2004, at A35.

5. *See* the discussion of Japan, *infra* pp. 103–119.

6. Department of Health and Human Services Regulations for the Protection of Human Subjects, 45 C.F.R. 46 (1991).

7. Exec. Order No. 12333, 46 Fed. Reg. 59,941, 87 Stat. 555 (1981).

8. 5 U.S.C. § 552a *et seq.*

9. *See infra* III.D.1 for a discussion of "Safe Harbor" at 58–59.

10. § 552a.

11. § 552a(e).

12. § 552a.

13. *See infra* VII.B.3(b) for a discussion of Japan's review of various privacy laws during the creation of a personal information privacy act at 111–112.

14. National Commission on Terrorist Attack, The 9/11 Commission Report: Final Report of the National Commission on Terrorist Attacks upon the United States 387 (2004) [*hereinafter* 9/11 COMMISSION REPORT].

15. *Id.*

16. *Id.* at 389.

BIBLIOGRAPHY

Books, Pamphlets, and Non-Periodicals

Borchardt, Klaus-Dieter, *The ABC of Community Law*. (5th ed. 2000), *available at* http://www.nefmi.gov.hu/letolt/nemzet/law_abc.pdf

Data Protection in the European Union, *available at* http://ec.europa.eu/justice/policies/privacy/index_en.htm

Electronic Privacy Information Center. *Privacy & Human Rights: An International Survey of Privacy Laws and Developments. The European Union. A Guide for Americans* (2003), *available at* http://gilc.org/privacy/survey/intro.html

Hata, Hiroyuki & Go Nakagawa. *Constitutional Law of Japan* (1997). *Japanese Constitutional Law* (Percy R. Luney, Jr. & Kazuyuki Takahashi eds., 1993).

Korff, Douwe. *EC Study on Implementation of Data Protective Directive: Comparative Study of National Laws*. (Sep. 2002), *available at* http://www.garanteprivacy.it/garante/document?ID=455584

The Law Commission. Protecting Personal Information from Disclosure. (2002), *available at* http://www.lawcom.govt.nz/.

Marcella, Jr. Albert J. & Carol Stucki. *Privacy Handbook: Guidelines, Exposures, Policy Implementation, and International Issues* (2003).

Ministry of Justice. *The New Zealand Legal System: A Guide to the Constitution, Government, and Legislature of New Zealand* (2001), *available at* http://cabinetmanual.cabinetoffice.govt.nz/node/68

National Commission on Terrorist Attack. *The 9/11 Commission Report: Final Report of the National Commission on Terrorist Attacks Upon the United States*. (2004). Oda, Hiroshi. Japanese Law (2nd ed. 1999).

Registrar of the European Court of Human Rights. *The European Court of Human Rights: Historical Background, Organization and Procedure*. (Sep. 2003), *available at* http://www.echr.coe.int/echr/

"Special Issue on Consumer Privacy in Japan and the New National Privacy Law," *Privacy & American Business*. 10(8) (Nov. 2003).

Woodward, John et al. *Biometrics: Identity Assurance in the Information Age* (2003).

MEDIA ARTICLES

"An Area of Security? Fights against Terrorism and criminality-Predominantly still on National Level." *Prima: A Privacy and Information Magazine* (Germany). (July 30, 2004).

"Belgian e-ID card enters deployment phase." *e-Government News*. (Sep. 24, 2004), *available at* http://europa.eu/documentation/index_en.htm

Biometrics Institute. "Biometrics Institute Privacy Code submitted to the Federal Privacy Commissioner's Office." (May 6, 2004).

Bronskill, Jim. "Canada to Introduce Biometric Passports." (July 18, 2004), *available at* Globe and Mail.

Canada Border Services Agency. "CANPASS-Air launched at Vancouver International Airport." (July 17, 2003), *available at* http://www.thefreelibrary.com/Vancouver+International+Airport+Deploys+Iris+Recognition+from+Iridian...-a0105519919

Closa Montero,Carlos. "Ratification of the Constitution of the EU: A Minefield." *Real Instituto Elcano de Estudios Internacionales y Estratégicos* (Spain). (July 7, 2004).

"Dutch biometric passport trials taking shape." *e-Government News*. (June 9, 2004).

Griffin, Peter. "Biometrics Code Needed to Keep Big Brother Honest." The New Zealand Herald. (Oct. 11, 2004).

"Japan, Europe Forge Biometric Union." Agence France-Presse. (Jan. 09, 2004), *available at* http://www.findbiometrics.com/viewnews.php?id=736.

McBride, Tim. "Recent New Zealand Case Law on Privacy: Part I: Privacy Act and the Bill of Rights Act." *Privacy Law & Reporter*. (Jan. 2000).

Pincus, Walter. "President Gets to Fill Ranks of New Intelligence Superstructure." *Washington Post*. (Dec. 16, 2004).

STATUTORY AND LEGISLATIVE MATERIAL

5 U.S.C. §552a *et seq.*

49 U.S.C. 44909(c)(3).

Act for the Protection of Computer-Processed Personal Data Held by Administrative Organizations, Act No. 95, 1988 (Japan).

Agreement Between the European Community and the United States of America on the Processing and Transfer of PNR Data by Air Carriers to the United States Department of Homeland Security, Bureau of Customs and Border Protection (May 28, 2004).

An Act to Make Provision to Protect the Privacy of Individuals, and for Related Purposes, 1988 (Austl.).

Bill of Rights Act, 1990 (N.Z.). Biometric Institute, Biometrics Institute Draft Privacy Code (2004) (Austl.). Available at http://www.biometricsinstitute.org/bi/Documents/Biometrics%20Institute%20Privacy%20Code%20(submitted%20Version).doc.

Canadian Charter of Rights and Freedoms, 1982. Commission Communication to the European Parliament and the Council, Development of the Schengen Information System II, COM (01) 720 final.

Commission Decision, 2004 (C1914). Commission Decision of 26 July 2000 pursuant to Directive 95/46/EC of the European Parliament and of the Council on the adequacy of the protection provided by the safe harbor privacy principles and related frequently asked questions issued by the U.S. Department of Commerce 2000 O.J. (L 215) 1 (E.U.).

Communication from the Commission to the Council and the European Parliament-Development of the Schengen Information System II and possible synergies with a future Visa Information System (VIS), COM(03) 0771 final.

Community Institutions and Bodies and on the Free Movement of Such Data, 2001 O.J. (L 008) 1-22 (E.U.).

Convention determining the State responsible for examining applications for asylum lodged in one of the Member States of the European Communities-Dublin Convention, 1997 O.J. (C 254) 1. (E.U.).

Council Conclusions on the development of the Visa Information System (VIS) (Feb. 19, 2004) (6253/04 VISA 28 COMIX 93) (E.U.).

Council Decision of 8 June 2004 establishing the Visa Information System (VIS) (2004/512/EC), 2004 O.J. (L 213) 5 (E.U.).

Council Directive 2004/82/EC (on the obligation of carriers to communicate passenger date).

Council of the European Union, Presidency Conclusions (Nov. 5, 2004) (14292/04).

Council of the European Union, Draft Council Regulation on Standards for Security Features and Biometrics in Passports and Travel Documents Issues by Member States, Brussels (Oct. 19, 2004) 13490/04.

Council Regulation (EC) No 334/2002 of 18 February 2002 amending Regulation (EC) No 1683/95 laying down a uniform format for visas 2002 O.J. (L 053) 7 (E.U.).

Council Regulation (EC) No 2424/2001 of December 6, 2001 on the development of the second generation Schengen Information System (SIS II) 2001O.J. (L 328) 4 (E.U.).

Council Regulation (EC) No 2725/2000 of 11 December 2000 concerning the establishment of "Eurodac" for the comparison of fingerprints for the effective application of the Dublin Convention, 2000 O.J. (L 316) 1 (E.U.).

Council Regulation (EC) No 1030/2002 of 13 June 2002 laying down a uniform format for residence permits for third-country nationals 2002 O.J. (L 157) 1 (E.U.).

Council Regulation (EC) No 45/2001 of the European Parliament and of the Council of 18 December 2000 on the Protection of Individuals with Regard to the Processing of Personal Data by the Community Institutions and Bodies and on the Free Movement of Such Data, 2001 O.J. (L 008) 1-22 (E.U.).

Department of Health and Human Services Regulations for the Protection of Human Subjects, 45 CFR 46 (1991).

Directive 95/46/EC of the European Parliament and of the Council of 24 October 1995 on the Protection of Individuals with Regard to the Processing of Personal Data and on the Free Movement of Such Data, 1995 O.J. (L 281) 31-50 (E.U.)

Directive 97/66/EC of the European Parliament and of the Council of 15 December 1997 concerning the processing of personal data and the protection of privacy in the telecommunications sector, 1997 O.J. (L 024) 1 (E.U.). 126.

Directive 2002/58/EC of the European Parliament and of the Council of 12 July 2002 concerning the processing of personal data and the protection of privacy in the electronic communications sector, 2002 O.J. (L 201) 37 (E.U.).

Directive 2000/31/EC of the European Parliament and of the Council of 8 June 2000 on certain legal aspects of information society services, in particular electronic commerce, in the Internal Market (Directive on electronic commerce), 2000 O.J. (L 178) 1 (E.U.).

European Parliament Draft Report on the proposal for a Council Regulation on standards for security features and biometrics in EU citizens' passports, Committee on Civil Liberties, Justice and Home Affairs, Provisional 2004/0039(CNS) (Sep. 30, 2004) (E.U.).

Helllenic Republic Authority for the Protection of Personal Data, Biometric data in International Athens Airport, Decision 52/2003 (May 11, 2003) (Greece).

Helllenic Republic Authority for the Protection of Personal Data, Biometric technology in Athens Metro high-risk installations, Decision No 9/2003 (March 31, 2003) (Greece).

Human Rights Act, 1993 (N.Z.).

Information Privacy Principles, Privacy Act, §II(6), (N.Z.). Law Concerning Access to Information Held by Administrative Organizations, Law No. 42 of 1999 (Japan).

Minpō [Japanese Civil Code], Law No. 89 of 1896, art. 1.

Model Contracts for the transfer of personal data to third countries, http://europa. eu.int/comm/internal_market/privacy/modelcontracts_en.htm (E.U.).

Personal Information Protection Act, 2003 (Japan). Personal Information Protection and Electronic Documents Act, R.S.C., ch.5 (2000) (Can.).

Privacy Act 1988 sched. 3, Privacy Amendment (Private Sector) Act 2000, 2000 (Austl.).

Privacy Act, 1993 (N.Z.).

Privacy Act, R.S.C., ch. P-21 (1985) (Can.).

Proposal for A Comprehensive Plan to Combat Illegal Immigration and Trafficking of Human Beings in the European Union, 2002 O.J. (C 142) 23 (E.U.).

Proposal for a Council Regulation amending Regulation (EC) 1683/95 laying down a uniform format for visas and Proposal for a Council Regulation amending Regulation (EC) 1030/2002 laying down a uniform format for residence permits for third-country nationals, COM(03) 0558 final (E.U.).

Proposal for a Council Decision establishing the Visa Information System (VIS), COM(04) 0099 final (E.U.).

Proposal for a Council Regulation on standards for security features and biometrics in EU citizens' passports, COM(04) 0116 final (E.U.).

Proposal for a Council Regulation amending Regulation (EC) 1030/2002 laying down a uniform format for residence permits for third-country nationals, COM(03) 0558 final-CNS 218 (E.U.).

CHAPTER 7

AUDITING SECURED BIOMETRIC TRANSACTIONS: TRUST ISSUES

"Give Me Liberty Or Give Me Death"

—Patrick Henry, March 23, 1775

"Who steals my purse, steals trash; 'tis something, nothing
T'was mine, tis his, and has been slave to thousands
But he that filches from me my good name
Robs me of that which not enriches him
And makes me poor indeed"

—Shakespeare, Othello, Act III Scene ii

An important question in shielding personal privacy by means of biometric transactions is: Could, would and should personal information assembled for one purpose be used for another purpose?

These are at least four audit areas of privacy protection that a person should have control over (Prosser, 1960):

1. seclusion, solitude and private affairs,
2. embarrassing public revelations pertaining to private facts,
3. publicity that puts a person in an unfavorable light, and
4. appropriation of an individual's name or likeness for someone else's advantage

Biometric and Auditing Issues Addressed in a Throughput Model, pp. 219–259
Copyright © 2012 by Information Age Publishing
All rights of reproduction in any form reserved.

As information technology in internal control biometrics system facilitates more information to be gathered, sorted, stored and shared, how will audit controls in the four areas listed above be affected? Trust issues loom large in terms of users' uncertainty regarding the employment of biometrics tools in their transactions. Such uncertainty may lead to distrust and less cooperation as well as a degree of defensiveness to participate in internal control biometrics system transactions. Therefore, this chapter will explore biometric systems, privacy issues as depicted by the amendments of the U.S. constitution followed by a section of trust issues.

BIOMETRICS SYSTEMS

Biometrics can be part of an internal control systems of recognizing an individual centered on physiological or behavioral characteristics. Biometric technologies are becoming the bedrock of a widespread collection of very well developed secure identification and personal verification systems. The capability of a biometric enhanced internal control system is its capacity to isolate attackers as measured by the false accept rate (FAR). Attackers may obtain some else finger prints or abrade and cut their fingerprints in order to avoid being recognized (see Figure 7.1 for example of security system).

Figure 7.1. Using fingerprint recognition for physical access
Source: National Coordination Office for Information Technology Research and Development (GAO, 2003).

The following are utilized as performance metrics for biometric systems (Jain, Flynn, & Ross, 2008):

1. **The false accept rate or false match rate (FAR or FMR).** It is the probability that the internal control biometrics system incorrectly affirms a successful match between the input pattern and a non-matching configuration in the database. It gauges the percent of unacceptable matches. These types of internal control biometrics systems are significant since they are commonly used to forbid certain actions by disallowed people.

2. **The false reject rate or false non-match rate (FRR or FNMR).** It is the probability that the internal control biometrics system incorrectly affirms failure of match between the input pattern and the matching template in the database. It gauges the percent of valid inputs being rejected.

3. **The receiver operating characteristic or relative operating characteristic (ROC).** It is when the matching algorithm performs a decision choice implementing some parameters (e.g., a threshold). In internal control biometrics systems the FAR and FRR can generally be traded off against each other by varying those parameters. The ROC plot is acquired by graphing the values of FAR and FRR, changing the variables implicitly. A common variation is the *detection error trade-off (DET)*, which is acquired implementing normal deviate scales on both axes. This linear graph sheds light on the variations for higher performances (rarer errors).

4. **The equal error rate or crossover error rate (EER or CER).** It is the rate whereby both accept and reject errors are equal. ROC or DET plotting is implemented because how FAR and FRR can be changed. When immediate contrast of the two systems is required, the EER is typically utilized. By obtained from the ROC plot the point where FAR and FRR have the same value. The lower the EER, the more precise the internal control biometrics system is considered to be.

5. **The failure to enroll rate (FTE or FER).** It is the percentage of data input that is deemed invalid and fails to input into the internal control biometrics system. Failure to enroll occurs when the data attained by the sensor are considered invalid or of poor quality.

6. **The failure to capture rate (FTC).** It is within an internal control biometrics system when the probability that the system fails to detect a biometric characteristic when it is presented correctly.

7. **The template capacity.** It is the maximum number of sets of data that can be entered into the system.

As the sensitivity of biometric tools increases, it decreases the FAR but increases the FRR.

Another method of judging an internal control biometrics system is by EER. That is, there are two particular values of FAR and FRR to illustrate how one parameter can change as a result of the other parameter value.

The implementation of biometrics has a number of benefits, which includes decreased cost of internal control biometrics system support, convenience for the user and improved security for users and system owners.

Typical applications that are in use or under trial include:

1. User authentication at Automated Teller Machines (ATM's),
2. Passports,
3. Border control,
4. Automated group surveillance,
5. Examining time and attendance,
6. Identification cards,
7. Physical access control,
8. Internal control biometrics system user surveillance, and
9. Fraud prevention.

Biometri-based security methods can offer confidential financial transactions and personal data privacy. The need for biometrics can be found in federal, state and local governments, as well as in the military, and in commercial applications. Organizations network security infrastructures, government IDs, secure electronic banking, investing and other financial transactions, retail sales, law enforcement, and health and social services are benefits from these tools.

For the most part security systems such as automatic fingerprint identification systems have been commonly used in forensics for criminal identification. However, progress in biometric sensors and matching algorithms have led to the deployment of biometric authentication in a significant number of civilian and government uses. Biometrics is being used for physical access control, computer log-in, welfare disbursement, international border crossing and national ID cards. In addition, biometrics can be implemented to verify a customer during transactions conducted by means of telephone and Internet (electronic commerce and electronic banking). In automobiles, biometrics is being embraced to replace keys for keyless entry and keyless ignition. As a result of increased security threats, the International Civil Aviation Organization (ICAO webpage: http://www2.icao.int/en/home/default.aspx) has approved the use of e-passports (passports with an embedded chip containing an individual's facial image and other traits).

Biometric provides one of the most secure and convenient authentication tools for internal control biometrics system transactions. It can not be borrowed, stolen, or forgotten and forging one is practically impossible. Biometrics forging, stealing or borrowing can be made very difficult to capture individuals' unique physical or behavioral characteristics in order to recognize or authenticate their identity. As discussed in the previous chapter, common physical biometrics includes fingerprints, ear, hand or palm geometry, retina, iris, DNA, and facial characteristics. Whereas, behavioral characteristics comprise signature, voice, keystroke pattern, and gait technologies. Of this technology category of biometrics, technologies for signature and voice are the most developed.

Biometric technology, implemented effectively, is an area in Internal control biometrics system that can not be disregarded. Biometric tools provide security advantages in a wide range, from information technology vendors to end users, and from security system developers to security system users. For many years, many highly secure environments have used biometric technology for entry entrance. In many of its applications, physical security control access to secure locations (rooms or buildings) remains the most dominant purpose. Biometric tools allow unmanned access control. In general, biometric devices such as hand geometry readers are in office buildings, hospitals, casinos, health clubs and lodges. Biometric tools are quite useful for high-volume access control.

There are several promising prototype biometric applications. For example, EyeTicket, associates a passenger's frequent-flyer number to an iris scan (http://www.m-cam.com/patentlyobvious/20010702_eyeticket.pdf). After the passenger enrolls in the system, an unmanned kiosk executes ticketing and the check-in procedure without luggage. Quite a few United States airports implement a type of hand geometry biometric technology for attaining citizen-verification functions. A person's iris is unique that captures a pattern of flecks and speckles and freckles described as crips (ph) and furrows. These patterns can be calculated to make up a password that is unique to each person. For example, a person looks into an iris-scanning device. And then on the monitor to your right, you can see that her iris there, shown in black and white, and the patterns in it are showing up. The picture itself is not going to be saved, but the patterns within the person's iris will be converted into a password that's made up of letters and numbers that is 512 characters long.

Virtual access with the use of biometric applications may provide the critical mass to move biometrics for network and computer access. In general, physical lock-downs can guard and defend hardware, and passwords are currently the most popular way to protect data on a network. Biometrics on the other hand can increase an organization's capability to safeguard its sensitive data by implementing a more secure key than a password. In addition, the implementation of biometrics provides a hierarchical structure of data protection, allowing the data more increase security. Finally, biometric tools expand improve security levels of access to network data.

SECURITY AND PRIVACY ISSUES

For internal control biometrics system transactions, biometric tools can have pervasive application and provide numerous functions where dated technologies may not evolve with privacy norms. Typically, biometrics is seen as a way for reducing the cost and risk of internal control biometrics system transactions and creating more convenience and trust. For example, biometrics may be implemented to identify and verify a company's buyers or sellers, or using biometrics to discourage fraudulent credit card usage and identity theft. However, these issues may present challenges concerning privacy and data security. The notion of risk (privacy threat and data security) and reward (protection of identity and stronger verification tools) should be taken into consideration in every application of biometric tools, particularly within the extent of law.

In sum, three of the most typically used reasons for the implementation of biometrics are as follows:

1. to enhance better security;
2. to improve convenience; and
3. to reduce expenses or increase a return on investment.

In terms of security, Sec. 403(c) of the USA PATRIOT Act (2001) specifically necessitate the federal government to "develop and certify a technology standard that can be used to verify the identity of persons" requesting for or looking for entry into the United States on a U.S. visa "for the purposes of conducting background checks, confirming identity, and ensuring that a person has not received a visa under a different name."

In addition, the Enhanced Border Security and Visa Entry Reform Act (2002), Sec. 303 (b)(1), requires that only "machine-readable, tamper-resistant visas and other travel and entry documents that use biometric identifiers" shall be issued to aliens by October 26, 2004. The Immigration and Naturalization Service (INS) and the State Department currently are evaluating biometrics for use in U.S. border control as a result to this act.

Some biometric experts have maintained that the "irreversibility of the biometric templates stored in some systems should be considered a privacy enhancement rather than detriment" (Langenderder & Linnhoff, 2005). That is, biometric templates are implemented for matching rather than reproduction. Hence, it is nearly impossible to reconstruct an individual's biometrics from the template. Although, a person is able to access the template, there is relatively little fraud that can be committed, unlike that of a stolen credit card or Social Security number.

Some of the key issues to be taken into account before selecting a biometric tool for internal control biometrics system use are:

1. *Ease of use*: some biometric tools are challenging to handle unless there is proper training.
2. *Error incidence*: Time and environmental conditions may affect the exactness of biometric data. For example, biometrics may change as an individual aged. Environmental conditions may either modify the biometric directly (if a finger is cut and scarred) or impede with the data collection (background noise when using a voice biometric).
3. *Accuracy*: Organizations may put into practice two different tools to rate biometric accuracy: false-acceptance rate (FAR) or false-rejection rate (FRR). These tools focus on the system's capability to permit restricted entry to authorized users. However, these measures can vary considerably depending on how an individual adjust the sensitivity of the instrument that matches the biometric. There may be instances where FAR decreases and FRR increases. Therefore, understandability is necessary regarding the biometrics that organizations arrive at quoted values of FAR and FRR. Since FAR and FRR are interdependent, a plot can be constructed, which can facilitate to determine the crossover error rate (CER). The lower the CER implies a more precise information system.

Other key components to be analyzed for internal control biometrics system utilization are:

1. *Cost*: biometrics tools and related systems, such as installation, connection, user system integration, research and test of the biometric system, system maintenance, etc.
2. *User acceptance*: some user groups reject biometric tools on several grounds due to of privacy concerns.

Some function-specific requirements such as security level may be low, moderate or high. These decisions will to a great extent influence the types of biometric tools are most appropriate for this type of functions.

As a final point, organizations should take into account biometrics' stability including maturity of the technology, degree of standardization, level of vendor and governmental support, market share and other support factors. Mature and standardized biometric tools typically have more durable stability.

There are a variety of biometric tools available for internal control biometrics system adoption. It is very essential to select the one which is accommodating to user profiles, privacy concerns, the need to interface with other systems or databases, environmental conditions, and a host of other application-specific parameters. However, biometric opponents have sensible fears of "mission creep," where a specific tool or project designed for one purpose gradually becomes an instrument to various applications (Michael & Michael, 2006). Mission creep enables sufficient opportunity for the misuse of biometric information.

For example, in January 2008, *The Independent* newspaper gave details regarding the United Kingdom's plans to implant select prisoners with under-the-skin microchips as part of an electronic tagging system plan to provide more space in British jails. These microchips, known as radio frequency identification (RFID) tags, will replace more normally worn electronic ankle monitor bracelets. The RFIDs are about the length of two grains of rice and can carry scan-related personal information. This information comprises of an individual's address, identity, and criminal record (Brady, 2008). Opponents of biometrics tools could argue that the RFID technology may carryover to the general population under the appearance of national security or as a presage for protecting privacy. In a globalized economy, what happens in one nation has a profound, swelling effect on what happens in another.

The rights to privacy, to due process and preventing unreasonable search and seizure are depicted in the following U.S. Constitutional Amendments.

First Amendment

"Congress shall make no law ... prohibiting the free exercise [of religion]; or abridging the freedom of speech, or of the press; or the right of the people peaceably to assemble ...."

If an internal control biometrics system were widely adopted, say palm printing, the many databases enclosing the digitized versions of the prints could be amalgamated. While such a system is most likely to be cultivated by the internal control biometrics sector for use in financial transactions, government and law enforcement authorities could likely want to take advantage of these massive databases for other purposes. Typically, government agencies and law enforcement are the topmost subscribers to the many databases amassed by private sector information brokers.

Of the many biometrics technologies that are being developed, facial recognition biometrics is one of the most threatening since it can be arranged clandestinely, and can be invisible to those inspected. In addition, tests have found that the error rates for facial biometrics tools are high. Overall, innocent people can be wrongly identified as criminals (false-positives), and known criminals and suspected terrorists can fall short to be detected (false-negatives).

Unless law enforcement and other government users institute guidelines and stringent oversight of internal control biometrics systems, many innocent people are likely to be apprehended. Limits should be placed on the types of uses that can be made of biometrics tools by government and law enforcement authorities, as well as clear-cut and expeditious procedures to handle cases of erroneous identification.

Third Amendment

"No Soldier shall, in time of peace be quartered in any house, without the consent of the Owner, nor in time of war, but in a manner to be prescribed by law."

This prohibition against quartering soldiers in one's home acknowledges a right to privacy that exists with respect to one's home. Even though this amendment is exceedingly limited in scope and has no application to biometrics, it reveals the sensitive expectation of privacy with respect to the home, as opposed to invasions of privacy outside the home, where there is a lesser expectation of privacy (e.g., at an airport). A person's expectation of privacy is used by the courts in balancing the interests of the public (i.e., the government) and the individual.

Fourth Amendment

The right of the people to be secure in their persons, houses, papers, and effects, against unreasonable searches and seizures, shall not be violated; and no warrants shall issue, but upon probable cause, supported by oath or affirmation, and particularly describing the place to be searched and the persons or things to be seized.

The Fourth Amendment protect against government intrusions of the sanctity of a person's home. In *Katz v. United States*, the Supreme Court make clear that the fourth amendment protects people, not places (Friedman, 1978). As a result, wherever people have a reasonable anticipation of privacy they are entitled to be uninhibited from unreasonable government intrusion. Nonetheless, there are examples of the government reasonably offsetting individuals' fourth amendment rights when it is in the interest of public safety from a utilitarian perspective. Therefore, does the taking of a bio-metric reading constitute a search? Most courts will answer, yes, as they have done for other physiologically based information gathering, like fin-gerprinting or drug testing.

In addition, the legitimacy of administrative searches was upheld in *United States v. $124,570* (1989). The Ninth Court of Appeals stated that:

"Americans submit to metal detectors and x-ray devices without a sec-ond thought. The intrusion into our privacy—and an intrusion it surely is—is accepted by most travelers with equanimity. The unavoidable conse-quence of [security checks] is that security personnel will become aware of many personal items that do not pose a danger to air safety.... When pack-ages are opened, or when pockets are emptied, [airport security] agents will see many items that are considered private."

Thus, the government has a powerful interest in encouraging the use of biometrics as a means of protecting its citizens, as well as preventing any harm. Although the use of biometrics is reasonable, it is essential that such use "serve a narrow but compelling administrative objective and that the intrusion be as limited as is consistent with satisfaction of the administra-tive need that justifies it" (*United States v. $124,570*, 1989). Consequently, an internal control biometrics system must be carefully put into operation whereby that no Fourth Amendment violation is committed.

Fifth Amendment

Any person shall be held to answer for a capital, or otherwise infamous, crime, unless on a presentment or indictment of a grand jury, except in cases arising in the land or naval forces, or in the militia, when in actual service, in time of war, or pub-lic danger; nor shall any person be subject, for the same offense to be twice put in jeopardy of life or limb; **nor shall any person be compelled , in any criminal case, to be a witness against himself, nor be deprived of life, liberty or prop-erty, without due process of law;** *nor shall private property be taken for public use, without just compensation.*

The Fifth Amendment protects against government intrusions of the privacies of life. The Fifth Amendment protection from self-incrimination has been expanded to include both criminal proceedings and non-criminal procedures that might result in criminal prosecution. The actual tools used to assemble biometric data may be controversial, particularly if they are so intrusive that they upset or traumatize our existence. In *Rochin v. California* (Warden, 1952). The consequences of an obligatory stomach pumping was concluded unacceptable in court since this procedure of self-incrimination was very intrusive and traumatizing. However, what the courts deliberated as non-intrusive is a case of a blood sample taken from an unconscious suspect engaged in a deadly car in *Breithraupt v. Abram* (1957). The court ruled that this evidence was admissible since blood samples, like finger-printing and urine samples are ordinary, relatively nonintrusive, and agreeable to society. In addition, *Schmerber v. California* (1966) reiterated the same message in that forced writing, speaking, fingerprinting, and walking or gesturing could be used for identification in court.

Given the aforementioned, biometric measures may be dealt with in the same manner, since many of the biometric tools use commonplace and socially acceptable actions. Submitting a fingerprint or handwriting sample are examples of acceptable ways of gathering information. Hence, a chief consideration for the utilization, development, and enhancement of biometrics for internal control biometrics system use is the level of intrusiveness.

Ninth Amendment

"The enumeration in the Constitution, of certain rights, shall not be construed to deny or disparage others retained by the people."

The ninth Amendment creates zones of privacy for individuals. That is, the Ninth Amendment conveys that we have an untold number of rights that are not enumerated in the Constitution. The question is not whether we have a right to anonymity, but whether government has the power to take it away especially in the case of internal control biometrics system use of biometrics. To be sure, the right to anonymity is not absolute.

The Ninth Amendment has binding authority, and it can be implemented to protect implicit internal control biometrics system transactions rights hinted at but not explicated elsewhere in the Constitution. Implicit rights include both the right to privacy outlined in *Griswold v. Connecticut* (1965).

Fourteenth Amendment

Section 1. All persons born or naturalized in the United States, and subject to the jurisdiction thereof, are citizens of the United States and of the State wherein they reside. No State shall make or enforce any law which shall abridge the privileges or immunities of citizens of the United States; **nor shall any State deprive any person of life, liberty, or property, without due process of law,** *nor deny any person within its jurisdiction the equal protection of the laws.*

The Fourteenth Amendment finds support pertaining to the right to privacy. **The due process clause of the Fourteenth Amendment protects certain fundamental** "personal decisions relating to internal control biometrics system transactions. The concept of due process necessitates the United States government to execute its obligations in an acceptable manner. If a government agency is going to consider a person not entitled it must have sound reason and it must also provide a timely appeal process. The tool implemented for appealing non entitlement is the pre-termination or pre-determination hearing. This is a hearing proceeding to the actual suspension of privileges.

However, there have been occurrences when the government has refuted rights without offering a hearing and, since it was defensible as in the interests of public safety, it was ruled that due process had not been violated. For example, cases take account of the confiscating of mislabeled vitamins and spoiled food and preventing employment of certain individuals in a defense contractor's plant.

Along with a timely hearing, the issue of information accuracy in internal control biometrics system applications should be taken into account with biometrics use. Case law exemplifies that government decisions recognized on inaccurate data or flawed procedures are unconstitutional. The accuracy of a biometric tool should be considered as well as the implementation procedures. If poor execution or an error in the device itself results in an individual's rights, a court may conclude that due process has been violated.

These are major issues for internal control biometrics system organizations using biometric technology. The constructive use of biometric tools by internal control biometrics system-based organizations weights heavily on the training of their personnel to use such device(s) for accuracy.

TRUST ISSUES IN INTERNAL CONTROL BIOMETRICS SYSTEM

The proliferation of the potential uses for biometrics complicates the job of preventing internal control biometrics system transaction exploitations. The enticement to use these technologies in unethical and mistrust manners for economic gain may be greatest in the internal control biometrics system area. A bank using online transactions, for example, could use biometric information from a smart card tied to its insurance subsidiary to deny a person loans, having determined them to be too great of a risk. Companies could use keystroke dynamics for monitoring productivity. In addition, companies could boost productivity by threatening an employee with termination centered on keystroke data.

In internal control biometrics system transactions for commercial use, individuals will have fewer protections than in the public sector as they will not be able to rely on the common law, constitutional rights, and statutory provisions that are used in the public sector. Employees and consumers must rely on labor management and consumer protection agreements, and laws that clarify these relationships to represent them.

Just as government can state its measures are essential to enhance the interests of common good of the people, internal control biometrics system organizations should assert that their actions are essential to further the normal course of business for its shareholders. Could smart identification cards, with a small microcomputer that permits the employer to trace the location of an employee, be implemented for more than internal control biometrics system operation? With this novel tool, every person's movement can be scrutinized, including how frequently and time-consuming one remains in a restroom, taking coffee breaks, or visiting fellow workers away from a workspace. When does the service of biometric tools go outside the ordinary course of business and into the deliberate cause of distrust issues?

Across the internal control biometrics system domain, consumers are presented with product and service information in order to assist in their decisions. While information serves as an important element for consumers' decisions, their trust positions can strongly influence their purchasing behavior. That is, consumers are reluctant to purchase unless they believe they can trust a company's web site. Globalization and the universal adoption of new biometric tools have dramatically changed the internal control biometrics system companies operate and interact with consumers and suppliers. As identity and security breaches continue to increase, achieving consumer and supplier's 'trust' is a goal ever more highly sought by companies and governments across the globe.

In expanding access to internal control biometrics system solutions, organizations increase their risk of exposing important corporate information to external parties. For example, this vulnerability is highlighted when a computer virus spreads rapidly. Such viruses and hacker tools are available around the world virtually instantaneously by means of the Web. Viral detection software can locate and eliminate computer viruses. However, even though a problem is addressed, companies cannot get too comfortable, since safe today does not mean safe tomorrow.

Creating an infrastructure to protect a company, its suppliers, and its customers is essential if organizations are to realize the full potential of internal control biometrics system transactions. Nevertheless, finding the proper balance between the propaganda and reality of security issues continues to be a challenge for many organizations. Biometric technologies may lead to enhanced security in internal control biometrics system transactions, thereby reinforcing online trust positions. However, can you trust someone that you have never met? You could meet them in person or rely on the word of someone you know who trust them, or someone who they trust in turn. Hence, it is the person that decides to trust and how much. Internal control biometrics system trust transactions mirror human relations and interactions in social, political, and economic settings. To this end, the next section covers trust definitions that cover internal control biometrics system transactions.

Almost all definitions presented in the literature seem to be based, at least in part, upon an underlying assumption of a moral duty with a strong ethical component owed by the trusted person to the trusting individuals. Perhaps, it is the presence of this implied moral duty that has made a precise definition of the concept of "trust" very difficult (Hosmer 1995, p. 381). Related to the moral duty aspect is the important question posed by Baier (1986, p. 234): "What is the difference between trusting others and merely relying upon them?" To rely upon their good will as distinct from their regular habits is a duty principle. In other words, trust is reliance upon another's good will. According to Hosmer (1995, p. 389) "good will is the most precisely defined concept in normative or moral philosophy." Butler (1991, p. 647) believed that it would be more instrumental to investigate the conditions or determinants of trust rather than spend time on further refining its definition of what he called the global "attitude" of the concept. Current literature has yet to develop a consensus on a definition of trust, as well as the vital question of how it is established and maintained in reciprocal relationships (Gambetta, 2000, Serva et al., 2005). Nevertheless, Gambetta (2000, p. 51) proposed a formal definition of trust as follows:

> The word 'trust' is used in the sense of correct expectations about the actions of other people that have a bearing on one's own choice of action when that action must be chosen before one can monitor the actions of those others.

Based on this formal definition and consistent with Rousseau et al. (1998, p. 395) we use a lose definition as it has been conceptualized and studied across numerous disciplines: trust is "a psychological state comprising the intention to accept vulnerability based upon positive expectations of the intentions or behavior of another." By defining an individual's trust in another person as willingness to be vulnerable to that person, trust is differentiated from both perceptions of the other person's trustworthiness and from risk-taking behaviors. This may occur for reasons other than trust. It is important to note that if trustworthiness perceptions of the other party change, a party's willingness to be vulnerable, which means that trust, may be immediately affected. Notwithstanding, it takes time for a change in trust to manifest itself in a different level of risk-taking behavior.

An assumption is made between the trust process and the risk-taking process (Mayer et al., 1995). Trust is the decision to rely on another party under a condition of risk perception (Slovic, 1993). That is, trust has two principal components: reliance and risk. Risk refers to the possibility that the trusting party will experience costs or damage if the other party proves untrustworthy. Risk, therefore, creates an opportunity for trust. Reliance involves one's fate being determined by another's actions. Further, it is possible that a decision not to take action can signify trust (e.g., a decision not to maintain updated information on a new product/service).

That is, trust is viewed in this chapter as a (1) set of beliefs or expectations, and (2) willingness to act on those beliefs (Doney et al., 1998; Moorman et al., 1993). These beliefs or expectations have grown up due to often long-lived relationships, intense in nature when there may be a great depth to the relationships between the parties, or where there are frequent interactions between them; the parties may also be reciprocally interdependent, and bounded whether by law or contract, such that the parties have incentives to maintain their relationship (Kleinman & Palmon 2000).

At a very broad level, trust is something that individuals may exhibit to brands, services, stores, product categories (e.g., automobiles) and activities (e.g., golf). Six dominant trust positions taken from Kramer (1999) are put forward to decrease uncertainty and simplifying complexity by providing specific assumptions regarding individuals' decision-making pathways. In this respect, an examination of dominant determinants of six trust positions (a rational choice, rule-based trust, category-based trust, third parties as conduits of trust, role-based trust, and history-based trust/dispositional-based trust) can highlight how different trust perspectives may be used to describe the internal control biometrics system consumers' decision-making processes.

Trust as a rational choice entails that people are always motivated to act in their perceived self-interest (Adam Smith's doctrine: the good man or woman should act for his or her short-term self-gain, but that those individual actions would lead, through the invisible hand of market forces, toward an ultimate net benefit for society [Hosmer, 1995, p. 395]). Decision choices regarding trust are assumed to be similar to other forms of risky choice in that individuals are presumed to be motivated to make rational and efficient choices. That is, in harmony to traditional economic models individuals are assumed to act to maximize expected gains or minimize expected losses from their transactions. This viewpoint consists of two significant elements (Hardin, 1991). First, the knowledge that enables an individual to trust another is considered. Second, it relates to the incentives of the person who is trusted to honor that trust. This type of trust is predicated on a complete awareness with the other party's desires and intentions. Therefore, this type of trust permits one to act as an "agent" for the other and substitute the other in interpersonal transactions (Whitener et al., 1998). Hardin (1991, p. 189) stated "You can more confidently trust me if you know that my interest will induce me to live up to your expectations. Your trust then encapsulates my interests."

An expectation entails a prediction regarding whether another person will behave in a trustworthy or untrustworthy manner. We typically contemplate about an expectation in terms of a probability, such as an "80% chance of trustworthiness," and we make approximate judgments about whether it is likely or unlikely that another person will behave in a trustworthy manner. There are three principal criteria used in forming expectations. First, does the individual have benevolent intentions? In other words, does the individual aim to assist us and guard our interests, even at his or her personal cost? People who are sensitive, empathetic, and unselfish are generally viewed as having benevolent intentions. We tend to have faith that these individuals will act in a trustworthy manner, and so we are predisposed to rely on them. Nevertheless, we recognize those who are selfishly oriented and have agendas that may put their interests before ours. Hence, our doubts that the other person might put his or her interests ahead of ours, may lead us to believe that the individual is likely to be untrustworthy. As a result, we decline to trust.

In economic transactions, other dynamics may influence the perceptions of an individual's intentions. Financial incentives, for example, may be an influential element between parties. In a relationship, parties may have little interest in empathy or sensitivity. Rather, they may be more interested in gauging information as trustworthy or not and whether this maximizes the alignment of client's actions. If the parties are convinced that information focuses them on maximizing economic benefit then it is likely that a more trustworthy relationship will exist.

A second consideration influencing an individual's expectations is whether the individual has technical competence (i.e., the technical knowledge and interpersonal skill) in order to provide accurate and relevant information. For instance, if internal control biometrics system buyers do not believe that sellers possess solid knowledge of their products or services, they will not rely upon their information.

A third consideration impacting expectations is whether a person is committed to protecting our interests. Commitment to be trustworthy refers to whether a person is sufficiently motivated to protect our interests. Individuals may have benevolent intentions and be technically competent; however, if we believe that they are unwilling to expend sufficient effort to guard our interests, we will lack confidence that they will behave in a trustworthy manner.

TRUST VIEWED IN THE THROUGHPUT MODEL

Throughput modeling begins with individuals stating their views of what should be noticed out of available information. The advantage of this approach is that it helps others understand why individuals have selected some information, which supports their position, and have ignored other information, which does not support their position. This approach helps uncover the values that individuals rely upon when taking positions on issues. Also, the model is useful in depicting latter stages of processes, such as judgment, that are implemented in supporting individuals' positions.

The modeling shows how an individual thinks and places importance on *perceived* trust issues. Therefore, perception is interdependent with information in Figure 7.2. In the context of business, a trust issue has consequences for others inside the organization and/or external to the organization in terms of valuing corporate knowledge assets. The intensity of a trust issue relates to the perceived importance of the issue to the individual (Jones, 1991). Hence, perception can influence the type of information selected for later processing in the model or information can influence or change the way individuals' perceive the problem (Rodgers, 1997).

In the *perception stage*, perceived trust is a critical cognitive predictor of trust (Mayer et al., 1995). In addition, researchers from diverse areas agree that trust develops through repeated social interactions about others' trust (McAllister, 1995; Sheppard & Sherman, 1998).

A higher level of trust in a work partner increases the likelihood that one will take a risk with a partner (e.g., cooperate, share information) and/or increases the amount of risk that is assumed (Dirks & Ferrin, 2002, p. 452). These ideas apply for studies that utilize trust as a predictor for future behavior (Dirks & Ferrin, 2002, p. 452).

The *judgment* stage contains the process individuals' implement to analyze incoming information as well as the influences from the perception stage. From these sources, rules are implemented to weight, sort, and classify knowledge and information for problem solving or decision-making purposes.

Since this judgment stage attempts to provide structure on trust, it can be referred to as "rationalist" mode of trust (Zucker, 1986). In the *Throughput Model*, information (circle I in Figure 7.2) affects judgment. For example, information stored in memory affects decision makers' evaluations of perceived trust issues. Typically, before an individual can make a decision, that individual encodes the information into short-term memory and

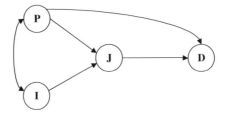

Figure 7.2. Individuals' trust decision processes diagram. *P = perception, I = information, J = judgment, and D = decision choice*

develops a mental representation, that is, a "mental model," for the problem (Johnson-Laird, 1981).

Finally, as shown in Figure 7.2, perception and judgment can affect decision choice. Some researchers, notably Kahneman and Tversky (1982), have suggested that both automatic, perception-like heuristics ($P \rightarrow D$) and more deliberate information processing strategies (judgment, $P \rightarrow J \rightarrow D$) are involved in most decision choices. Errors, biases, and context-dependent heuristics may result from cognitive mechanisms of which decision-makers are largely unaware, and these may have a direct impact on decision choice ($P \rightarrow D$) (Kahneman & Tversky, 1982; Rodgers, 1992). However, the strategies of judgment that influence decision choice are under individual's deliberate control.

The decision-making outcome processes of individuals can be represented in an organized, verbally stated manner. In order to study the moods of these decision processes it is important to break up all the paths marked with arrows in Figure 7.2 into sets of individual pathways. These individual pathways can then be independently analyzed for their contributing properties to individuals' decision processes (Rodgers, 1997).

Further, it is common for decision-makers to differ in their trust values. Even if two individuals agree on the trust principles that determine a certain trustworthy behavior, it is unlikely that they will agree on the relative importance of each trust principle. These differences are highlighted in Figure 7.2, depicting several pathways toward making a decision.

Although, different trust positions may be present, emphasis is placed on the most dominant trust position associated with each pathway. The model proposed here takes a unique approach to conceptualizing six trust positions related to the above six decision-making pathways in understanding behavior (Rodgers, 2010). The six trust positions are: trust as (1) a rational choice, (2) rule-based trust, (3) category-based trust, (4) third parties as conduits of trust, (5) role-based trust, and (6) history-based trust/dispositional-based trust (Figure 7.3). These six pathways are viewed as the most dominant and influential for decision making dominated by particular trust positions (Rodgers, 2010).

Rule-based trust put emphasis on the rules, norms or laws established for a particular environment. Reputable rules provide guidance or incentives to behave in a particular way in decision-making situations. In robust rule-based situations, outcomes dependent entirely on trust is expected to decline. Referring to Kant's "Groundwork for the Metaphysics of Morals" (Kant, 1964, p. 1) and his universal law and the first formulation of the "Categorical Imperative" states that "if it was right for one person to take a given action then it must be right for all others to be encouraged to take that same action."

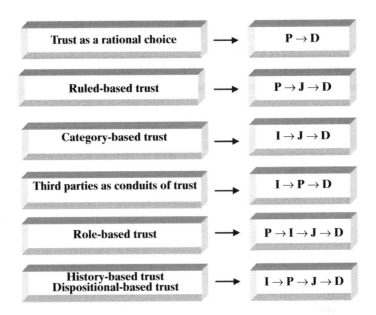

Figure 7.3. Trust's influence in decision making

When circumstances are less rule-based, a higher level of trust will have the chance to result in positive outcomes (Dirks & Ferrin, 2002). In mid-range situations, where signals are neither weak nor strong in directing a person toward an outcome, trust helps to "tip the scales," as it helps a person to appraise the future behavior of another party and/or decipher past behavior (Dirks & Ferrin, 2001, p. 461). The structural and interpersonal workings of rules are likely to influence perceived trust (Brockner & Siegel, 1996) since they are learnt and used in a variety of tasks. Hummels and Roosendaal (2001) asserted that one way to deal with complexity is to put together an extensive contract that stipulates the rights and obligations of the contract partners and to decide on the penalties when one of the parties is unsuccessful to meet the obligations.

Risk-taking behavior (Mayer et al., 1995) is often the consequence of individual motives (e.g., propensity to risk), goals, or incentives. Trust may become the gauge for engaging in risk-taking behavior. For example, a person who considers another to be dependable may find it relatively easy to work toward a goal with him or her. That is, one does not have to be anxious or concerned about the partner's potential behavior. In this example, trust functions not in a causal role, but as a moderator that influences the strength of the relationship between a motivator (the goal) and a person's behavior. This concept may also explain people's behavior in response to other signals that encourage people's behavior.

To the extent that employees trust their managers, they are likely to be able to devote their resources (e.g., attention, effort) to norm conformance, rule compliance, and/or managers' requests. That is, they may be confident to receive appropriate rewards and not be undeservedly penalized for their actions. Conversely, if employees are concerned about a manager's response, they might find it worrisome to behave as expected or requested. Under this scenario, the role, norm, rule, or managerial request is likely to exert a much weaker effect on the person's behavior, as the individual reroute resources for self-protection. Therefore, trust functions by not causing a person to operate in a particular behavior; but, as a moderating construct that influences the strength of the relationship between a situation and the individual's behavior.

Category-based trust is predicated on norms of obligation and cooperation rooted in social similarity. That is, it is the expectation that an individual can or cannot be trusted because of age, ethnicity, family background, financial position, religion, social reasons or status, and so forth. The base of this information is the social relations between individuals with respect to dependence, trade, competition, collaboration, and so on. The relations and the role or roles an individual plays in society influence his/her behavior and the interaction with the others.

Category-based trust may be extended broadly within a society and may be reinforced by ritual and symbolic behaviors (Dore, 1987) that emphasize common group membership and familiarity (Good, 1988). Competitive or cooperative interdependence that exists between two people influences their beliefs about each other's trustworthiness. However, cooperation can exist without trust relationships (Mayer et al., 1995). Trust can also promulgate cooperation in circumstances where other means of producing cooperation (e.g., the use of coercion) are not possible or are likely to be unsuccessful.

Common characteristics of a person may offer an impetus to trust and may provide a positive, self-reinforcing process of interaction with others. Due to the cognitive consequences of categorization into in-groups, people are apt to attribute positive features such as honesty, cooperativeness, and trust to other in-group members (Brewer, 1996). Nonetheless, in situations where co-dependent individuals have varied motives can provide an untrusting atmosphere which is the case when challenged with a social dilemma (e.g., the prisoners' dilemma game; Hardin, 1991).

The Prisoner Dilemma Game is widely utilized to examine how cooperation between interdependent but unfamiliar people may develop. In this game, each player can either "cooperate" (invest in a common good) or "defect" (exploit the other's investment). Trust helps smooth the progress of cooperative behavior, since, under high trust; the individual believes that a partner is willing to cooperate. Under high levels of trust, the individual will be more likely to attend to the cooperative motives; while under low levels of trust, the individual will be more likely to attend to the competitive motives. This prediction builds on the idea that since trust affects the person's appraisal of the partner's future action, it helps people gauge the viability of cooperative behavior. For example, people with low trust, their partner is likely to perceive that cooperative behavior is unlikely to result in personal gains, as they believe a partner will take benefit of their actions.

The *third parties as conduits of trust* assume that decision-makers use themselves or the people around them as their basis for delineating ethical standards in unruly settings. For example, witness information (also referred to as word-of-mouth or indirect information) is the information that is obtained from other individuals. Ferrin, Dirks, and Shah (2006, forthcoming) advocated that there are three ways that a trustor and trustee may be connected to each other by way of third parties. First, network closure (linked via social interactions with third parties); second, trust conveyance (linked by trusted third parties); and third, structural likeness (linked by the similarity of their trust relationships).

Since a trust decision often involves personal consequences, it is for the most part a solitary decision. Yet, under certain conditions, decision choices to trust also may be influenced by what others do or urge us to do. Indeed, it is common for us to be swayed to trust someone by what others tell us about him or her. Furthermore, although trust is an evidentiary decision, we may use the experience of others as a proxy for our own decision. Since trust decisions are often made in the context of incomplete information, we may even seek out procedures and/or guidelines as a replacement to our available information.

Third-party information serves to strengthen existing relations, making one's perception more certain of another's trustworthiness (or untrustworthiness). Thus, trust depends on the direct connection between two individuals versus their indirect connections through third parties and the conditions in which the strong indirect connections that augment trust reverse their effect to create distrust. The certainty may also be a false impression of whether or not the person is trustworthy or not. Labianca, Brass, and Gray's (1998) study showed that third parties can be drawn into negative interpersonal interactions. Further, Blau (1964, p.112, 113) advocates that trust develops because social exchange involves unspecified obligations for which no binding contract can be written. Hence, trust is consigned to a social exchange without one knowing how the other individual will reciprocate. In accordance with Aryee, Budhwar, and Chen (2002, p. 267), social exchange between two parties is viewed as a "long-term exchange of favors that precludes accounting and is based on a diffuse obligation to reciprocate."

If concrete proof of untrustworthiness emerges from third parties, trust is destroyed quickly and distrust emerges. The velocity with which trust can be obliterated depends on the magnitude of damage from untrustworthiness, as well as the perceived intentionality of the untrustworthiness. In cases when the loss is acutely high, trust can dissolve almost immediately. If untrustworthiness is viewed as intentional, the destruction of trust is chiefly severe, since intentional untrustworthiness reveals malevolent intentions, which are highly probable of predicting future untrustworthiness. Whereas, technical mistakes or untrustworthiness due to deficiency of commitment may be less damaging to trust as they can be more easily rationalized and do not reveal malevolent intent. Once distrust is produced, it demands even more compelling evidence of trustworthiness, contrast with the evidence required during the primary trust-creating stage.

The apparent frequency with which trust has been broken suggests a need for its repair. One problem pointed out by Kim et al. (2004) is that information about the violation may remain particular salient, reinforcing the low trust level despite efforts by the mistrusted party to demonstrate trustworthiness (Slovic, 1993). The result by Kim, Dirks, Cooper, and Ferrin (2006, p. 60), when focusing on newly formed trust relationships rather than longer term relationships, show that when one has committed an integrity-based trust violation, an apology that transmits an internal attribution repairs trust less effectively than efforts to alleviate this blame, with either an external attribution or, as Kim et al. (2004) have observed, a denial. Thus, decision-makers should do everything possible to avoid such integrity-based trust violations from the beginning. Many violations of trust may be ambiguous enough to be framed in multiple ways.

Role-based trust is joined to formal societal structures, depending on individual or institution-specific elements. This process implies that a person's perceptions or framing of the problem will influence the selection and type of information to be employed in judgment. That is, an individual is motivated to take action appropriately (perceptual behavior) that influences the information set implemented to be analyzed (judgment behavior) before a trust decision is made. This viewpoint suggests that a morally bounded individual with good motivations is more likely to understand what task should be performed than a morally lacking individual would do. Beauchamp and Bowie (1997, p. 39) advocated, "A person who simply follows rules of obligation and who otherwise exhibits no special moral character may not be trustworthy."

Simon (1947, p. 125) put forward that the readiness to agree to an authority's decision choices can occur through consideration to the authorities' organizational role and can be made "independently of judgments of the correctness or acceptability of the premise (of their decisions)." Further, Tyler and Degoey (1996) declared that individuals' evaluations of organizational authority trust shaped their willingness to accept the decisions of authorities as well as influencing feelings of obligation to follow organizational rules and laws. Additionally, Fisher, Gunz, and McCutheon (2001) advocated that individuals are bounded together by professional roles within society. The importance of what that profession does places it in a special trust relationship with society and its market actors, and has the potential both to help and harm the users of the services. This leads to proposition five:

The *history-based trust* and/or *dispositional trust* arises either through the personal experience of recurring exchanges, such as gathering previous years credit payment history on an organization, or determining its capability to attain a lower interest rate based on its reputation. This is comparable to the view that trust is a generalized response based on the reinforcement history inherent in prior social exchange interactions (Rotter, 1967, 1971, 1980).

The historical-based/dispositional trust position takes into account the probability of others likely actions predicated on past and present information. In a long-term relationship, reciprocity is at the heart of this process. Through this process, economic business transactions become part of the social exchange context where psychological factors intertwine with economic considerations in arriving at a trust decision (Bradach & Eccles, 1989). In fact, the security and stability of recurring reciprocal social exchanges enable learning (Hedelin & Allwood, 2001), and is a useful predictor of the other party's behavior in the future. This perspective represents the last possible way for individuals' decision-making based on perception and information processing. In this process, an individual studies the given information, frames the problem, and then proceeds to scrutinize the problem before rendering a decision leading to some level of trust or distrust.

CONCLUSION

A biometric security system is basically a pattern recognition system that acknowledges a person by establishing the authenticity of a certain anatomical or behavioral characteristic possessed by the person. Several vital concerns should be considered in designing a functional biometric system. First, individuals must be enrolled in the security system whereby their biometric templates or reference can be captured. This template is securely located in a central database or a smart card issued to the person. The template is used for matching when a person must be identified. Depending on the context, a biometric security system may operate either in verification (authentication) or an identification style.

The cases brought before the legislatures and courts will guide the biometric applications. To reduce the problems and make the execution of biometrics beneficial and rewarding, it is important to take into account the wide-ranging societal and legal implications as plans are developed. Careful considerations in the employment of biometrics tools can accomplish an acceptable balance between privacy and security, safety and individual Internal control biometrics system developers are exploring the use of biometrics and smart cards to more accurately verify a trading party's identity. Banks are bound to use this combination to better authenticate customers and ensure nonrepudiation of online banking, trading and purchasing transactions. Point-of-sales (POS) system vendors are working on the cardholder verification method that would enlist smart cards and biometrics to replace signature verification. Biometrics can help to obtain secure services over the telephone through voice authentication. For applications of covert surveillance, using facial and body recognition technologies, organizations may be able to implement biometrics to automatically identify known suspects entering buildings or traversing crowded security areas such as airports.

Biometric-based security applications include workstation, network, and domain access, single sign-on, application logon, data protection, remote access to resources, transaction security and Web security. Ethical use of this technology for transactions is paramount for a vibrant global economy. Implemented alone or integrated with other tools such as smart cards, encryption keys and digital signatures, biometric security is set to pervade nearly all aspects of our daily lives and the economy. For example, biometrics for individual authentication is becoming convenient and considerably more precise than methods such as the use of passwords or PINs. Reasons for this advantage are that biometrics links the event to a particular person, is convenient, accurate, socially acceptable, cost-effective, and can provide an audit trail. On the other hand, a password or token may be exploited by someone other than the authorized user, is convenient, may be difficult to remember, and may not provide for a positive identification.

The purpose of this chapter is to formalize the implications of perception, information, judgment, and decision choice with relevant trust positions. The performance of an internal control biometrics system market price can be in part related to buyers' overall perception of the sellers' information.

We each have a set of values, although we may or may not have considered them explicitly. Normative philosophers, religious institutions, and others have defined in many instances ideal sets of moral principles or values. Examples of prescribed sets of moral principles or values at the implementation level include laws and regulations, church doctrine, codes of trust for professional groups such as auditors, and a code of conduct within distinct institutions. Uniformly applied rules by auditors enable individuals to trust and collaborate with others because they expect others to operate under these known rules. The need for "trust" is such an important factor that many commonly held trust values are assimilated into auditing rules. However, many trust issues cannot be assimilated into rules due to the judgmental nature of certain values. For example, it is impractical to have written rules that deal with auditors' feelings, values, and beliefs. This does not imply that these principles are less important for orderly markets. They may be considered as a group of unwritten laws.

Legal inquiries related to due process may not be as frequent as those related to issues of privacy. Questions raised surrounding issues of privacy take into account the following:

1. Does the taking of a biometric measurement is tantamount to a search?
2. Does it represent a reasonable search?
3. Can biometric information be used in criminal, noncriminal searches and trust related ("suspicion-less search") searches?
4. Could information assembled for one concern be used for another concern?
5. Which tools of congregating information are reasonable and which tools assault an individual's personal privacy?

As more applications for biometric tools become available, the privacy rights entrenched in the fourth, fifth, and fourteenth amendments that protect an individual from unreasonable search and seizure, from self-incrimination, and which preserve an individual's control over personal information will undoubtedly come up for future debates.

REFERENCES

Aryee, S., Budhwar, P. S., & Chen, Z. X. (2002). Trust as a mediator of the relationship between organizational justice and work outcomes: Test of a social exchange model. *Journal of Organizational Behavior, 23*(3), 267–285.

Baier, A. C. (1986). Trust and antitrust. *Ethics, 96,* 231–260.

Beauchamp, T. L., & Bowie, N. E. (Eds.) (1997). *Ethical theory and business.* Upper Saddle River, NJ: Prentice Hall.

Blau, P. M. (1964). *Exchange and power in social life.* New York, NY: Wiley.

Bradach, J. L., & Eccles, R. G. (1989). Price, authority, and trust: From ideal types to plural forms. *Annual Review of Sociology, 15,* 97–118.

Brady, B. (2008). Prisoners 'to be chipped like dogs,' *The Independent*, January 13, 2008, http://www.independent.co.uk/news/uk/politics/prisoners-to-be-chipped-like-dogs-769977.html.

Breithaupt v. Abram, 352 U.S. 432. U.S. Supreme Court (1957). http://supreme.vlex.com/vid/breithaupt-v-abram-20013253.

Brockner, J., & Siegel, P. (1996). Understanding the interaction between procedural and distributive justice. In R. M. Kramer, & T. R. Tyler (Eds.), *Trust in organizations* (pp. 16–38). Thousand Oaks, CA: Sage.

Butler, J. K. (1991). Toward understanding and measuring conditions of trust: Evolution of a condition of trust inventory. *Journal of Management, 17,* 643–663.

Dirks, K. T., & Ferrin, D. L. (2002). Trust in leadership: Meta-analytic findings and implications for organizational research. *Journal of Applied Psychology, 87,* 611–628.

Doney, P. M., Cannon, J. P., & Mullen, M. R. (1998). Understanding the influence of national culture on the development of trust. *Academy of Management Review, 23,* 601–620.

Dore, R. (1987). *Taking Japan seriously.* Stanford, CA: Stanford University Press.

Enhanced Border Security and Visa Entry Reform Act, ALDAC No. 1, United States. Department of State, § 303 b(1) (2002).

Ferrin, D. L., Dirks, K. T., & Shah, P. P. (2006). Direct and indirect effects of third-party relationships on interpersonal trust. *Journal of Applied Psychology, 91,* 870–883.

Fisher, J., Gunz, S., & McCutheon, J. (2001). Private/public interest and the enforcement of a code of professional conduct. *Journal of Business Ethics, 34,* 191–207.

Friedman, L. (1978). *The Justices of the United States Supreme Court: Their Lives and Major Opinions* (Vol. V, p. 292). New York, NY: Chelsea House Publishers.

Gambetta, D. (2000). Can we trust trust? In D. Gambetta (Ed.), *Trust: Making and breaking cooperative relations.* Oxford: Basil Blackwell.

GAO. (2003). United States General Accounting Office. *Information Security Challenges in Using Biometrics.* www.gao.gov/cgi-bin/getrpt? GAO-03-1137T.

Good, D. (1988). Individuals, interpersonal relations, and trust. In D. Gambetta (Ed.), *Trust: Making and breaking cooperative relations* (pp. 31–48). Oxford: Basil Bernstein.

Griswold v. Connecticut, 381 U. S. 479 (1965). http://supreme.justia.com/us/381/479/case.html.

Hardin, R. (1991). Trusting persons, trusting institutions. In R. J. Zechhauser (Ed.), *Strategy and Choice* (pp. 185–209). Cambridge, MA: MIT Press.

Hedelin, L., & Allwood, C. M. (2001). Managers' strategic decision processes in large organizations. In C. M. Allwood, & M. Selart (Eds.), *Decision making: Social and creative dimensions* (pp. 259–280). Dordrecht, The Netherlands: Kluwer Academic Press.

Hosmer, L. T. (1995). Trust: The connecting link between organizational theory and philosophical ethics. *The Academy of Management Review, 20,* 379–403.

Hummels, H., & Roosendaal, H. E. (2001). Trust in scientific publishing. *Journal of Business Ethics, 34,* 87–100.

Jain, A. K., Flynn, P., & Ross, A. (2008). *Handbook of biometrics*. New York, NY: Springer.

Johnson-Laird, P. N. (1981). Mental models in cognitive science. In D. A. Norman (Ed.), *Perspectives on cognitive science* (pp. 147–191). Hillsdale, NJ: Erlbaum.

Jones, T. M. (1991). Ethical decision making by individuals in organizations: An issue-contingent model. *Academy of Management Review, 16*, 366–395.

Kahneman, D., & Tversky, A. (1982). On the study of statistical intuitions. *Cognition, 11*(2), 123–141.

Kant, I. (1964). Groundwork for the metaphysics of morals. New York, NY: Harper & Row.

Kim, P. H., Ferrin, D. L., Cooper, C. D., & Dirks, K. T. (2004). Removing the shadow of suspicion: The effects of apology versus denial for repairing competence-versus integrity-based trust violation. *Journal of Applied Psychology, 89,* 104–118.

Kim, P. H., Dirks, K. T., Cooper, C. D., & Ferrin, D. L. (2006). When more blame is better than less: The implications of internal vs. external attributions for the repair of trust after a competence- vs. integrity-based trust violation. *Organizational Behavior and Human Decision Processes*, 99, 49–65.

Kleinman, G., & Palmon, D. (2000). A negotiation-oriented model of auditor-client relationships. *Group Decision and Negotiation, 9*, 17–45.

Labianca, G., Brass, D. J., & Gray, B. (1998). Social networks and perceptions of intergroup conflict: The role of negative relationships and third parties. *Academy of Management Journal, 41*, 55–67.

Langenderder, J., & Linnhoff, S. (2005). The emergence of biometrics and its effect on consumers. *The Journal of Consumer Affairs, 39*, 325.

Mayer, R. C., Davis, J. H. & Schoorman, F. D. (1995). An integrative model of organizational trust. *Academy Management Review, 20*(3), 709–734.

McAllister, D. J. (1995). Affect- and cognition-based trust as foundations for interpersonal cooperation in organizations. *Academy of Management Journal, 38*(1), 24–59.

Michael, K., & Michael, M. G. (2006). Historical lessons on ID technology and the consequences of an unchecked trajectory. *Prometheus, 24*, 365.

Moorman, C., Deshpande, R., & Zaltman, G. (1993). Factors affecting trust in market research relationships. *Journal of Marketing 57*, 81–101.

Prosser, W. L. (1960). Privacy. *California Law Review, 48*, 383.

Rodgers, W. (1992). The effects of accounting information on individuals' perceptual processes. *Journal of Accounting, Auditing and Finance* (Winter), 67–96.

Rodgers, W. (1997). *Throughput modeling: Financial information used by decision makers*. Greenwich, CT: JAI Press.

Rodgers, W. (2010). Three primary trust pathways underlying ethical considerations. *Journal of Business Ethics, 91*, 83–93.

Rotter, J. B. (1967). A new scale for the measurement of interpersonal trust. *Journal of Personality, 35*, 651–665.

Rotter, J. B. (1971). *Generalized expectancies for interpersonal trust. American Psychologist, 26*, 443–452.

Rotter, J. B. (1980). Interpersonal trust, trustworthiness, and gullibility. *American Psychologist, 35*, 1–7.

Rousseau, D. E., Sitkin, S. B., Burt, R. S., & Camerer, C. (1998). Not so different after all: A cross-discipline view of trust. *Academy of Management Review, 23,* 387–392.

Schmerber v. California, 384 U.S. 757. U.S, Supreme Court (1966). http://supreme.justia.com/us/384/757/

Serva, M. A., Fuller, M. A., & Mayer, R. C. (2005). The reciprocal nature of trust: A longitudinal study of interacting teams. *Journal of Organizational Behavior, 26,* 625–648.

Sheppard, B. H., & Sherman, D. M. (1998). The grammars of trust: A model and general implications. *Academy of Management Review, 23*(3), 422–437.

Simon, H. A. (1947). *Administrative behavior.* New York, NY: Macmillan.

Slovic, P. (1993). Perceived risk, trust, and democracy. *Risk Analysis,13,* 675–682.

Tyler, T. R., & Degoey, P. (1996). Trust in organizational authorities: The influence of motive attributions on willingness to accept decisions. In R. M. Kramer, & T. R. Tyler (Eds.), *Trust in organizations: Frontiers of theory and research* (pp. 331–357). Thousand Oaks, CA: Sage.

United States v. $124,570 U.S. Currency, 873 F.2d 1240, 1243, 1244 (9th Cir. Court, 1989). http://www.michbar.org/computer/pdfs/Vol23_6.pdf.

USA PATRIOT Act. *Uniting and Strengthening America by Providing Appropriate Tools Required to Intercept and Obstruct Terrorism Act of 2001.* Pub. L. 107–56, title IV, subtitle A, § 403 (2001).

Warden, L. M. (1952). Constitutional law: Due process under the fourteenth amendment: Protection against physical mistreatment: Admissibility of evidence. *California Law Review, 40* (2), 311–317.

Whitener, E. M., Brodt, S. E., Korsgaard, M. A., & Werner, J. M. (1998). Managers as initiators of trust: An exchange relationship framework for understanding managerial trustworthy behavior. *Academy of Management Review, 23*(3), 513–530.

APPENDIX 7A

THE PREAMBLE TO THE BILL OF RIGHTS

Congress of the United States begun and held at the City of New York, on Wednesday the fourth of March, one thousand seven hundred and eighty nine.

THE Conventions of a number of the States, having at the time of their adopting the Constitution, expressed a desire, in order to prevent misconstruction or abuse of its powers, that further declaratory and restrictive clauses should be added: And as extending the ground of public confidence in the Government, will best ensure the beneficent ends of its institution.

RESOLVED by the Senate and House of Representatives of the United States of America, in Congress assembled, two thirds of both Houses concurring, that the following Articles be proposed to the Legislatures of the several States, as amendments to the Constitution of the United States, all, or any of which Articles, when ratified by three fourths of the said Legislatures, to be valid to all intents and purposes, as part of the said Constitution; viz.

ARTICLES in addition to, and Amendment of the Constitution of the United States of America, proposed by Congress, and ratified by the Legislatures of the several States, pursuant to the fifth Article of the original Constitution.

CONSTITUTIONAL AMENDMENTS 1–10 MAKE UP WHAT IS KNOWN AS THE BILL OF RIGHTS

AMENDMENT I

Congress shall make no law respecting an establishment of religion, or prohibiting the free exercise thereof; or abridging the freedom of speech, or of the press; or the right of the people peaceably to assemble, and to petition the Government for a redress of grievances.

AMENDMENT II

A well regulated Militia, being necessary to the security of a free State, the right of the people to keep and bear Arms, shall not be infringed.

AMENDMENT III

No Soldier shall, in time of peace be quartered in any house, without the consent of the Owner, nor in time of war, but in a manner to be prescribed by law.

AMENDMENT IV

The right of the people to be secure in their persons, houses, papers, and effects, against unreasonable searches and seizures, shall not be violated, and no Warrants shall issue, but upon probable cause, supported by Oath or affirmation, and particularly describing the place to be searched, and the persons or things to be seized.

AMENDMENT V

No person shall be held to answer for a capital, or otherwise infamous crime, unless on a presentment or indictment of a Grand Jury, except in cases arising in the land or naval forces, or in the Militia, when in actual service in time of War or public danger; nor shall any person be subject for the same offence to be twice put in jeopardy of life or limb; nor shall be compelled in any criminal case to be a witness against himself, nor be deprived of life, liberty, or property, without due process of law; nor shall private property be taken for public use, without just compensation.

AMENDMENT VI

In all criminal prosecutions, the accused shall enjoy the right to a speedy and public trial, by an impartial jury of the State and district wherein the crime shall have been committed, which district shall have been previously ascertained by law, and to be informed of the nature and cause of the accusation; to be confronted with the witnesses against him; to have compulsory process for obtaining witnesses in his favor, and to have the Assistance of Counsel for his defence.

AMENDMENT VII

In Suits at common law, where the value in controversy shall exceed twenty dollars, the right of trial by jury shall be preserved, and no fact tried by a jury, shall be otherwise re-examined in any Court of the United States, than according to the rules of the common law.

AMENDMENT VIII

Excessive bail shall not be required, nor excessive fines imposed, nor cruel and unusual punishments inflicted.

AMENDMENT IX

The enumeration in the Constitution, of certain rights, shall not be construed to deny or disparage others retained by the people.

AMENDMENT X

The powers not delegated to the United States by the Constitution, nor prohibited by it to the States, are reserved to the States respectively, or to the people.

THE CONSTITUTION: AMENDMENTS 11-27

AMENDMENT XI

Passed by Congress March 4, 1794. Ratified February 7, 1795.
   Note: Article III, section 2, of the Constitution was modified by amendment 11.
   The Judicial power of the United States shall not be construed to extend to any suit in law or equity, commenced or prosecuted against one of the United States by Citizens of another State, or by Citizens or Subjects of any Foreign State.

AMENDMENT XII

Passed by Congress December 9, 1803. Ratified June 15, 1804.
   Note: A portion of Article II, section 1 of the Constitution was superseded by the 12th amendment.
   The Electors shall meet in their respective states and vote by ballot for President and Vice-President, one of whom, at least, shall not be an inhabitant

of the same state with themselves; they shall name in their ballots the person voted for as President, and in distinct ballots the person voted for as Vice-President, and they shall make distinct lists of all persons voted for as President, and of all persons voted for as Vice-President, and of the number of votes for each, which lists they shall sign and certify, and transmit sealed to the seat of the government of the United States, directed to the President of the Senate; —the President of the Senate shall, in the presence of the Senate and House of Representatives, open all the certificates and the votes shall then be counted; —The person having the greatest number of votes for President, shall be the President, if such number be a majority of the whole number of Electors appointed; and if no person have such majority, then from the persons having the highest numbers not exceeding three on the list of those voted for as President, the House of Representatives shall choose immediately, by ballot, the President. But in choosing the President, the votes shall be taken by states, the representation from each state having one vote; a quorum for this purpose shall consist of a member or member from two -thirds of the states, and a majority of all the states shall be necessary to a choice. [And if the House of Representatives shall not choose a President whenever the right of choice shall devolve upon them, before the fourth day of March next following, then the Vice-President shall act as President, as in case of the death or other constitutional disability of the President.—]* The person having the greatest number of votes as Vice-President, shall be the Vice-President, if such number be a majority of the whole number of Electors appointed, and if no person have a majority, then from the two highest numbers on the list, the Senate shall choose the Vice-President; a quorum for the purpose shall consst of two-thirds of the whole number of Senators, and a majority of the whole number shall be necessary to a choice. But no person constitutionally ineligible to the office of President shall be eligible to that of Vice-President of the United States.

*Superseded by section 3 of the 20th amendment.

AMENDMENT XIII

Passed by Congress January 31, 1865. Ratified December 6, 1865.

Note: A portion of Article IV, section 2, of the Constitution was superseded by the 13th amendment.

Section 1

Neither slavery nor involuntary servitude, except as a punishment for crime where of the party shall have been duly convicted, shall exist within the United States, or any place subject to their jurisdiction.

Section 2

Congress shall have power to enforce this article by appropriate legislation.

AMENDMENT XIV

Passed by Congress June 13, 1866. Ratified July 9, 1868.
   Note: Article I, section 2, of the Constitution was modified by section 2 of the 14th amendment.

Section 1

All persons born or naturalized in the United States, and subject to the jurisdiction thereof, are citizens of the United States and of the State wherein they reside. No State shall make or enforce any law which shall abridge the privileges or immunities of citizens of the United States; nor shall any State deprive any person of life, liberty, or property, without due process of law; nor deny to any person within its jurisdiction the equal protection of the laws.

Section 2

Representatives shall be apportioned among the several States according to their respective numbers, counting the whole number of persons in each State, excluding Indians not taxed. But when the right to vote at any election for the choice of electors for President and Vice-President of the United States, Representatives in Congress, the Executive and Judicial officers of a State, or the members of the Legislature thereof, is denied to any of the male inhabitants of such State, being twenty-one years of age,* and citizens of the United States, or in any way abridged, except for participation in rebellion, or other crime, the basis of representation therein shall be reduced in the proportion which the number of such male citizens shall bear to the whole number of male citizens twenty-one years of age in such State.

Section 3

No person shall be a Senator or Representative in Congress, or elector of President and Vice-President, or hold any office, civil or military, under the United States, or under any State, who, having previously taken an oath, as a member of Congress, or as an officer of the United States, or as a member of any State legislature, or as an executive or judicial officer of any State, to support the Constitution of the United States, shall have engaged in insurrection or rebellion against the same, or given aid or comfort to the enemies thereof. But Congress mayby a vote of two -thirds of each House, remove such disability.

Section 4

The validity of the public debt of the United States, authorized by law, including debts incurred for payment of pensions and bounties for services in suppressing insurrection or rebellion, shall not be questioned. But neither the United States nor any State shall assume or pay any debt or obligation incurred in aid of insurrection or rebellion against the United States, or any claim for the loss or emancipation of any slave; but all such debts, obligations and claims shall be held illegal and void.

Section 5

The Congress shall have the power to enforce, by appropriate legislation, the provisions of this article.
Changed by section 1 *of the 26th amendment.*

AMENDMENT XV

Passed by Congress February 26, 1869. Ratified February 3, 1870.

Section 1

The right of citizens of the United States to vote shall not be denied or abridged by the United States or by any State on account of race, color, or previous ndition of servitude—

Section 2

The Congress shall have the power to enforce this article by appropriate legislation.

AMENDMENT XVI

Passed by Congress July 2, 1909. Ratified February 3, 1913.

Note: Article I, section 9, of the Constitution was modified by amendment 16.

The Congress shall have power to lay and collect taxes on incomes, from whatever source derived, without apportionment among the several States, and without regard to any census or enumeration.

AMENDMENT XVII

Passed by Congress May 13, 1912. Ratified April 8, 1913.

Note: Article I, section 3, of the Constitution was modified by the 17th amendment.

The Senate of the United States shall be composed of two Senators from each State, elected by the people thereof, for six years; and each Senator shall have one vote. The electors in each State shall have the qualifications requisite for electors of the most numerous branch of the State legislatures.

When vacancies happen in the representation of any State in the Senate, the executive authority of such State shall issue writs of election to fill such vacancies: *Provided*, That the legislature of any State may empower the executive thereof to make temporary appointments until the people fill the vacancies by election as the legislature may direct.

This amendment shall not be so construed as to affect the election or term of any Senator chosen before it becomes valid as part of the Constitution.

AMENDMENT XVIII

Passed by Congress December 18, 1917. Ratified January 16, 1919. Repealed by amendment 21.

Section 1

After one year from the ratification of this article the manufacture, sale, or transportation of intoxicating liquors within, the importation thereof into, or the exportation thereof from the United States and all territory subject to the jurisdiction thereof for beverage purposes is hereby prohibited.

Section 2

The Congress and the several States shall have concurrent power to enforce this article by appropriate legislation.

Section 3

This article shall be inoperative unless it shall have been ratified as an amendment to the Constitution by the legislatures of the several States, as provided in the Constitution, within seven years from the date of the submission hereof to the States by the Congress.

AMENDMENT XIX

Passed by Congress June 4, 1919. Ratified August 18, 1920.
   The right of citizens of the United States to vote shall not be denied or abridged by the United States or by any State on account of sex.
   Congress shall have power to enforce this article by appropriate legislation.

AMENDMENT XX

Passed by Congress March 2, 1932. Ratified January 23, 1933.
   Note: Article I, section 4, of the Constitution was modified by section 2 of this amendment. In addition, a portion of the 12th amendment was superseded by section 3.

Section 1

The termsof the President and the Vice-President shall end at noon on the 20th day of January, and the terms of Senators and Representatives at noon on the 3rd day of January, of the years in which such terms would have ended if this article had not been ratified; and the terms of their successors shall then begin.

Section 2

The Congress shall assemble at least once in every year, and such meeting shall begin at noon on the 3rd day of January, unless they shall by law appoint a different day.

Section 3

If, at the time fixed for the beginning of the term of the President, the President elect shall have died, the Vice President elect shall become President. If a President shall not have been chosen before the time fixed for the beginning of his term, or if the President elect shall have failed to qualify, then the Vice-President elect shall act as President until a President shall have qualified; and the Congress may by law provide for the case wherein neither a President elect nor a Vice President shall have qualified, declaring who shall then act as President, or the manner in which one who is to act shall be selected, and such person shall act accordingly until a President or Vice-President shall have qualified.

Section 4

The Congress may by law provide for the case of the death of any of the persons from whom the House of Representatives may choose a President whenever the right of choice shall have devolved upon them, and for the case of the death of any of the persons from whom the Senate may choose a Vice President whenever the right of choice shall have devolved upon them.

Section 5

Sections 1 and 2 shall take effect on the 15th day of October following the ratification of this article.

Section 6

This article shall be inoperative unless it shall have been ratified as an amendment to the Constitution by the legislatures of thee fourths of the several States within seven years from the date of its submission.

AMENDMENT XXI

Passed by Congress February 20, 1933. Ratified December 5, 1933.

Section 1

The eighteenth article of amendment to the Constitution of the United States is hereby repealed.

Section 2

The transportation or importation into any State, Territory, or Possession of the United States for delivery or use therein of intoxicating liquors, in violation of the laws thereof, is hereby prohibited.

Section 3

This article shall be inoperative unless it shall have been ratified as an amendment to the Constitution by conventions in the several States, as provided in the Constitution, within seven years from the date of the submission hereof to the States by the Congress.

AMENDMENT XXII

Passed by Congress March 21, 1947. Ratified February 27, 1951.

Section 1

No person shall be elected to the office of the President more than twice, and no person who has held the office of President, or acted as President, for more than two years of a term to which some other person was elected President shall be elected to the office of President more than once. But this Article shall not apply to any person holding the office of President when this Article was proposed by Congress, and shall not prevent any person who may be holding the office of President, or acting as President, during the term within which this Article becomes operative from holding the office of President or acting as President during the remainder of such term.

Section 2

This article shall be inoperative unless it shall have been ratified as an amendment to the Constitution by the legislature of three -fourths of the several States within seven years from the date of its submission to the States by the Congress.

AMENDMENT XXIII

Passed by Congress June 16, 1960. Ratified March 29, 1961.

Section 1

The District constituting the seat of Government of the United States shall appoint in such manner as Congress may direct:

A number of electors of Presidnt and Vice-President equal to the whole number of Senators and Representatives in Congress to which the District would be entitled if it were a State, but in no event more than the least populous State; they shall be in addition to those appointed by the States, but they shall be considered, for the purposes of the election of Presidnt and Vice-President, to be electors appointed by a State; and they shall meet in the District and perform such duties as provided by the twelfth article of amendment.

Section 2

The Congress shall have power to enforce this article by appropriate legislation.

AMENDMENT XXIV

Passed by Congress August 27, 1962. Ratified January 23, 1964.

Section 1

The right of citizens of the United States to vote in any primary or other election for Prsident or Vice-President, for electors for Prsident or Vice-President, or for Senator or Representative in Congress, shall not be denied or abridged by the United States or any State by reason of failure to pay poll tax or other tax.

Section 2

The Congress shall have power to enforce this article by appropriate legislation.

AMENDMENT XXV

Passed by Congress July 6, 1965. Ratified February 10, 1967.
   Note: Article II, section 1, of the Constitution was affected by the 25th amendment.

Section 1

In case of the removal of the President from office or of his death or resignation, the Vice President shall become President.

Section 2

Whenever there is a vacancy in the office of the Vice-President, the President shall nominate a Vice-President who shall take office upon confirmation by a majority vote of both Houses of Congress.

Section 3

Whenever the President transmits to the President pro tempore of the Senate and the Speaker of the House of Representatives his written declaration that he is unable to discharge the powers and duties of his office, and until he transmits to them a written declaration to the contrary, such powers and duties shall be dicharged by the Vice-President as Acting President.

Section 4

Whenever the Vice-President and a majority of either the principal officers of the executive departments or of such other body as Congress may by law provide, transmit to the President pro tempore of the Senate and the Speaker of the House of Representatives their written declaration that the President is unable to discharge the powers and duties of his office, the Vice-President shall immediately assume the powers and duties of the office as Acting President.

Thereafter, when the President transmits to the President pro tempore of the Senate and the Speaker of the House of Representatives his written declaration that no inability exists, he shall resume the powers and duties of his ofice unless the Vice-President and a majority of either the principal officers of the executive department or of such other body as Congress may by law provide, transmit within four days to the President pro tempore of the Senate and the Speaker of the House of Representatives their written declaration that the President is unable to discharge the powers and duties of his office. Thereupon Congress shall decide the issue, assembling within forty-eight hours for that purpose if not in session. If the Congress, within twenty-one days after receipt of the latter written declaration, or, if Congress is not in session, within twenty-one days after Congress is required to assemble, determines by two-thirds vote of both Houses that the President is unable to discharge the powers and duties ofhis office, the Vice-President shall continue to discharge the same as Acting President; otherwise, the President shall resume the powers and duties of his office.

AMENDMENT XXVI

Passed by Congress March 23, 1971. Ratified July 1, 1971.
Note: Amendment 14, section 2, of the Constitution was modified by section 1 of the 26th amendment.

Section 1

The right of citizens of the United States, who are eighteen years of age or older, to vote shall not be denied or abridged by the United States or by any State on account of age.

Section 2

The Congress shall have power to enforce this article by appropriate legislation.

AMENDMENT XXVII

Originally proposed Sept. 25, 1789. Ratified May 7, 1992.
No law, varying the compensation for the services of the Senators and Representatives, shall take effect, until an election of representatives shall have intervened.

CHAPTER 8

FRAUD AND INTERNAL CONTROL

"Reputation, reputation, reputation! Oh, I have lost my reputation! I have lost the immortal part of myself, and what remains is bestial."

—William Shakespeare, *Othello. Act ii. Sc. 3.*

Eliminating fraud typically starts with identifying organization greatest risk factors. Top offenders typically include the failure to divide key duties among several employees; inefficient physical and procedural safeguards over cash, other assets and transactions; inadequate supervision of employees; and lack of mandatory vacations for employees with financial responsibilities. Unfortunately, the risks to organizations from frauds are greater than ever. Although organizational complexity is increasing, organizations historically pay modest attention to fraud, under-staff internal audit functions and put up with some fraudulent activity as the cost of doing business. The appropriate procedures and technology such as involved board of directors, management and internal control biometrics systems; however, can facilitate in preventing many workplace crimes.

To what extent has an organization identified and had approved by the board of directors its tolerance for different types of fraud risks? For instance, some fraud risks may constitute a tolerable cost of doing business, while others may pose a catastrophic risk of financial or reputational damage to the entity. The organization will likely have a dissimilar tolerance for these risks.

For example, phishing for logins is a major fraud risk problem for individuals and organizations. Phishing is the act of sending an e-mail to a user deceitfully claiming to be a reputable legitimate enterprise in an attempt to cheat the user into surrendering private information to be utilized for identity theft. Furthermore, corporate fraud, credit card skimming, insider theft, and counterfeiting of digital information and ID "trafficking" are also on the rise. All of these kinds of fraud are costly for individuals and organizations engrossed both financially and often in terms of the time needed to clear their name when illegal use has been made of their personal details.

Many firms are concerned with the aforementioned problems that have affected financial markets and organizations worldwide. Investor and creditors' confidence is easily shaken, but difficult to reinstate. Along with these fraudulent crimes and corporate scandals; regulators, issuers, investors and independent auditors have all had vital functions in working to win back that trust. These business scandals as well as legislation have focused attention on the role of strong internal controls in discouraging fraud in organizations. The potential for internal fraud is still a fact of life for organizations today. However, there are many mechanisms a decision-maker have at their disposal to make it arduous for employees to perpetrate fraud.

Fraud is an intentional deception that brings about to its victim an economic loss and/or the person responsible to realize a gain. The legal definition of fraud is similar regardless if the offense is criminal or civil. The difference is that criminal cases must meet a superior burden of proof.

Fraud includes the following four fundamentals:

1. A material false report,
2. Awareness that the report was false when it was spoken,
3. Reliance on the false report by the victim, and
4. Damages ensuing from the victim's reliance on the false report.

Force, trickery, and larceny are the three techniques to relieve a victim of money illegally. Fraud includes those offences that make use of trickery. The legal designation for stealing is larceny. This term is defined as "felonious stealing, taking and carrying, leading, riding, or driving away with another's personal property, with the intent to convert it or to deprive the owner thereof" (Black, 1979: 792). The following four elements are necessary in order to prove that an individual has committed larceny:

1. There was a seizing or carting off
2. of the money or property of another
3. without the approval of the owner, and
4. with the intention to deprive the owner of its use or possession (Kranacher, Riley, & Wells, 2011).

Fraud is a wide-ranging area of crime encompassing everything from forging a signature on a check to filing a false insurance claim. For example, identity theft occurs when someone uses your personal information such as your name, Social Security number or credit card number without your permission to commit fraud or other crimes. Identity theft and other types of fraud are an increasing concern to consumers who interact with online businesses routinely.

Examples of fraud include:

a. Forgery or modification of a check, bank draft, or any other financial document.
b. Theft of a check or other change of a taxpayer payment.
c. Embezzlement of funds, securities, supplies, or other assets.
d. Irregularity in the handling or reporting of money or financial transactions.
e. Profiteering as a consequence of insider knowledge of agency operations.
f. An employee with access to confidential taxpayer information who sells this information or uses it in the conduct of an outside organization activity.
g. Disclosing to others the securities activities connected in or contemplated by the agency.

Internal control biometrics systems are designed to provide reasonable assurance that organizations achieve their objectives. Implementing a comprehensive system of internal control biometrics system is a good start. This type of system assists in providing checks and balances that can prevent fraud, limit financial losses, and reduce errors or oversights by employees. The most basic internal control concept requires that different employees handle different financial and accounting tasks. This process portrayed as "separation of duties" can decidedly limit the probability of loss. Some guidelines for a basic system can include:

1. One person opening the mail and list all the checks on the deposit slip while another enters cash receipts in your financial records by using keystroke dynamics.
2. Putting someone who does not handle the checkbook or purchasing in charge of payments to suppliers or vendors.
3. Bank reconciliation performed by someone who does not have access to daily checkbook transactions.
4. Checking all orders to make sure they are accurate and of the quantity intended; and
5. Before signing each check, review the invoice, delivery receipt, and purchase order.

Every effort must be made to prevent any instances of fraud, waste, and abuse in organizations. When organizations' top executives put into place a biometrics system designed to promote efficiency, assure implementation of a policy, safeguard assets, and/or avoid fraud and error, this set of procedures is considered a measure of internal control.

While the definition of "internal control" has been a major province of the accounting profession, it has evolved over time. The U.S. Securities and Exchange Commission (SEC) has acknowledged that having proper internal controls is indispensable in the prevention and detection of fraud. That makes it a strategic component in an auditor's examination of a business or government entity, and a significant component to both the Foreign Corrupt Practices Act of 1977 and the Sarbanes-Oxley Act of 2002, which required that improvements be made to internal controls within U.S. publicly traded corporations.

The Committee of Sponsoring Organizations of the Treadway Commission (COSO, 1992), created in 1985 by five professional accounting associations and institutes, sponsored the National Commission on Fraudulent Financial Reporting. The organization primary responsibility was to establish internal controls for publicly traded companies and their auditors. Additionally, it also developed recommendations for the SEC, other regulators, and for educational institutions. The objective was to assist identifying the factors that cause fraudulent financial reporting and to make recommendations to diminish its occurrence. In the process, it managed to help institute what is deemed today as the common definition of internal control. According to COSO, everyone in an organization is accountable in one way or another for internal control. It starts with the tone at the top whereby an organization's president or CEO ultimately "assumes 'ownership' of the system."

WHAT IS FRAUD?

Fraud deals with an assortment of irregularities and illegal acts portrayed by intentional deception. It can be perpetrated for the benefit of or to the detriment of the organization and by individuals outside as well as inside the organization. In addition, fraud can be depicted as varied means utilized by resourceful individuals to get an advantage over another by blocking out the truth, trickery, misinformation, false suggestions, cunning, deceit, and other techniques by which to deceive.

Fraud is a very critical issue as it not only affects people and organizations alike, it also causes damage to a government and trade relations in the more serious cases. As many individuals already know fraud is not merely defined as lying about money that you shouldn't have, fraud actually includes a wide range of possible issues.

The risk of fraud exists in every organization including all industries, entity types, functional departments, and geographic areas. Internal control with its system of policies and procedures that operate within an organization can strengthen an organization against malfeasance. That, is strong internal controls can shield an organization from fraud and abuse.

Fraud is a purposeful act (or failure to act) with the intention of acquiring an unauthorized benefit, either for oneself or for the institution, by using deception or false suggestions or inhibiting of truth or other unethical means that are believed and relied upon by others. Depriving another individual or the organization of a benefit to which he/she/it is entitled by implementing any of the means described above also is tantamount to fraud.

Examples of fraudulent acts comprise of, but are not limited to the following:

1. Embezzlement
2. Forgery or alteration of documents
3. Unauthorized alteration or manipulation of computer files
4. Fraudulent financial reporting
5. Misappropriation or misuse of organization's resources (e.g., tangible assets, intangible assets such as, patents, equipment, services, inventory, or other assets)
6. Authorization or receipt of payment for goods not received or services not performed
7. Authorization or receipt of unearned wages or benefits
8. Conflict of interest, ethics violations

CHARACTERISTICS FOR FRAUD

There are typically three requirements for fraud to occur: pressure (motivation), opportunity and rationalization (personal characteristics). Motivation is generally situational pressures in the form of a need for money, personal satisfaction, or to an anxiety of failure. Opportunity is access to a situation where fraud can be carried out, such as weaknesses in internal controls, necessities of an operating environment, management styles and corporate culture. Rationalization represents personal characteristics that include a willingness to commit fraud. Personal integrity and moral standards need to be "bendable" enough to validate the fraud, perhaps prompted by the need to feed their children or pay for a family illness. It is difficult to have an effect on a person's motivation for fraud. Personal features can occasionally be changed through training and awareness programs. Opportunity is the simplest and most effective requirement to address to reduce the probability of fraud. By developing effective systems of internal control, you can remove opportunities to commit fraud.

What is a Fraud Triangle?

Employees who commit fraud generally are able to do so because there is pressure, opportunity, and rationalization. Figure 8.1 depicts what is known as the fraud triangle. In order for fraud to occur, all three elements have to be present. An organization can takes steps to influence all three elements. Organizational employees should be cognizant of pressures and how they relate to its overall fraud risk. Rationalizations can be reduced by promoting a strong sense of ethical behavior amongst employees and creating a positive work environment. By implementing strong internal controls, an organization can remove much of the opportunity for fraud to take place and can amplify the chances of detecting it. Next, each of the areas of pressure, opportunity, and rationalization will be discussed in detail.

Pressure

Pressure is what causes a person to commit fraud. Pressure can include almost anything including medical bills, expensive tastes, addiction problems, etc. Most of the time, pressure comes from a significant financial need/problem. Often this need/problem is nonsharable in the eyes of the fraudster. That is, the person believes, for whatever reason, that their problem must be solved in secret. However, some frauds are committed simply out of greed alone.

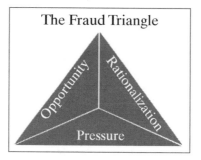

Figure 8.1. Three essential components of fraud

Pressure (or motive) can be imposed due to

- Personal financial problems; unforeseen expenses.
- Personal vices/addictions such as gambling, drugs, shopping, etc.
- Unrealistic deadlines and performance goals.

Opportunity

Opportunity is the ability to commit fraud. Because fraudsters don't wish to be caught, they must also believe that their activities will not be detected. Opportunity is created by weak internal controls, poor management oversight, and/or through the use of one's position and authority. Failure to establish adequate procedures to detect fraudulent activity also increases the opportunities for fraud to occur. Of the three elements, opportunity is the leg that organizations have the most control over. It is essential that organizations build processes, procedures and controls that don't needlessly put employees in a position to commit fraud and that effectively detect fraudulent activity if it occurs.

Opportunity is generally provided through weaknesses in the internal controls.

Some examples include inadequate or no

- Supervision and review
- Separation of duties
- Management approval
- System controls

Rationalization

Rationalization is a crucial component in most frauds. Rationalization involves a person reconciling his/her behavior (stealing) with the commonly accepted notions of decency and trust. Some common rationalizations for committing fraud are:

a. The person believes committing fraud is justified to save a family member or loved one.
b. The person believes they will lose everything—family, home, car, etc. if they don't take the money.
c. The person believes that no help is available from outside.
d. The person labels the theft as "borrowing," and fully intends to pay the stolen money back at some point.

e. The person, because of job dissatisfaction (salaries, job environment, treatment by managers, etc.), believes that something is owed to him/her.

f. The person is unable to understand or does not care about the consequence of their actions or of accepted notions of decency and trust.

Rationalization occurs when the individual develops a justification for their fraudulent activities. The rationalization varies by case and individual.
Some examples include the following:

a. "I really need this money and I'll pay it back when I get my paycheck."

b. "Other people are doing it."

c. "I didn't get a raise. The Company owes me."

Breaking the Fraud Triangle is the key to fraud deterrence. Breaking the Fraud Triangle entails removing one of the elements in the fraud triangle in order to reduce the likelihood of fraudulent activities. "Of the three elements, removal of Opportunity is most directly affected by the system of internal controls and generally provides the most actionable route to deterrence of fraud" (Cendrowski, Martin, Petro, The Handbook of Fraud Deterrence).

Conditions that may bring about fraud includes an unhealthy organizational culture, domineering management, management abusing or overriding internal controls, low staff morale and weak management. Collectively they reflect the culture of the organization. Until there is a healthy culture and strong management in all branches and departments of an organization, endeavors to discourage fraud will not be very successful. Only when prospective fraudsters think fraud will be detected and when whistle-blowers believe they will be protected will there be an effective deterrence of fraud. Some of the most effective ways of detecting fraud have been found to be:

1. Internal controls
2. Internal audit
3. Management review
4. Whistle-blowers
5. Change of management
6. Anonymous tip-offs
7. Outside information
8. Use of Biometrics
9. External audit
10. Accident
11. Access/exit controls

Perhaps, the most important concept in achieving internal control is an appropriate subdivision or separation of duties. Responsibilities should be assigned so that no one person or department handles a transaction completely from beginning to end.

When duties are divided in this manner, the work of one employee serves to verify that of another and any errors which occur tend to be detected promptly. To illustrate this concept, let us review the typical procedures followed by a wholesaler in processing a credit sale. The sales department of the company is responsible for securing the order from the customer; the credit department must approve the customer's credit before the order is filled; the stock room assembles the goods ordered; the shipping department packs and ships the goods; the billing department prepares the sales invoice; and the accounting department records the transaction.

Each department receives written evidence of the action by the other departments and reviews the documents describing the transaction to see that the actions taken correspond in all details. The shipping department, for instance, does not release the merchandise until after the credit department has approved the customer as a credit risk.

The accounting department does not record the sale until it has received documentary evidence that (1) an order was received from a customer, (2) the extension of credit was approved, (3) the merchandise was shipped to the customer, and (4) a sales invoice was prepared and mailed to the customer.

DEVELOPING STRONG INTERNAL CONTROLS

To what extent has the organization implemented measures to eliminate or reduce through an internal control biometrics system each of the significant fraud risks identified in its risk assessment? Basic controls comprise segregation of duties relating to authorization, custody of assets and recording or reporting of transactions. In some cases, it may be more cost-effective to change practices and processes in order to reduce fraud risks rather than layer on additional controls over existing processes. For example, some fraud risks relating to receipt of funds can be done away with or greatly diminished by centralizing that function or outsourcing it to a bank's lockbox processing facility, where stronger controls can be more affordable (see Appendix 8A).

To what degree has the organization employed measures at the process level designed to prevent, deter and detect each of the significant fraud risks identified in its risk assessment? For example, the risk of sales representatives fabricating sales to earn sales commissions can be decreased through effective scrutinizing by their sales manager, with approval necessitated for sales above a certain threshold.

To what extent has the organization identified and had approved by the board of directors a policy on how the entity will manage its fraud risks? Such a policy should identify the risk owner responsible for managing fraud risks, what risks will be rejected (e.g., by declining certain business opportunities), what risks will be transferred to others through insurance or by contract, and what procedures will be taken to manage the fraud risks that are retained.

A satisfactory manner of instilling a healthy culture and managing risk in the organization is to provide every employee a copy of the organization's ethics policy as part of their contract of employment or company handbook. This ensures that every employee knows what is expected of them by the organization. The ethics policy should:

1. Define and give examples of fraud.
2. Explain what external interests may give rise to a conflict of interests.
3. Define the organization's policy on receiving gifts from external parties.
4. Explain why it is essential to keep certain information about the organization confidential.
5. Require employees to report alleged fraud to a named individual.
6. State that breach of the policy will be handled as a disciplinary offense.
7. Provide particulars of the fraud contingency plan.

What are the Red Flags for Fraud (see Appendix 8B)?

Managers and employees responsible for stewardship of an organization's resources should be aware of the red flags for fraud. These are warning signs that may indicate that fraud risk is higher. They are not evidence that fraud is actually occurring. The existence of one or two flags is not something to be overly concerned about. However, if multiple flags are present and accounting irregularities or weak controls are identified, then the Internal Audit department should be contacted.

Examples of red flags include, but are not limited to the following:

Employee Red Flags

a. Employee way of life changes: expensive cars, jewelry, homes, clothes
b. Major personal debt and credit problems
c. Behavioral changes—These may be a signal for drugs, alcohol, gambling, or just anxiety of losing the job

d. High employee turnover, particularly in those areas which are more susceptible to fraud
e. Declining to take vacation or sick leave
f. Lack of segregation of duties in a susceptible area

Management Red Flags

a. Management repeatedly overrides internal controls.
b. Management decisions are dictated by an individual or small group.
c. Managers display considerable disregard for regulatory bodies.
d. Policies and procedures are not documented or enforced.
e. Weak internal control environment.
f. Accounting personnel are negligent or inexperienced in their duties.
g. Decentralization without sufficient monitoring.
h. Excessive number of checking accounts; recurrent changes in banking accounts.
i. Excessive number of year end transactions; needless complicated transactions.
j. Elevated employee turnover rate; depressed employee morale.
k. Reject to the use of serial numbered documents (receipts).
l. Compensation program that is out of proportion.
m. Photocopied or missing documents.
n. Unwillingness to provide information to, or engage in repeated disputes with, auditors.

Any employee who presumes that dishonest, unethical, or fraudulent activity is taking place should not endeavor to personally contact the suspected person in an effort to determine facts, conduct investigations or interviews/interrogations. Care must be taken to avoid mistaken accusations or alerting suspected individuals that an investigation may be under way. In addition, an organization should have a fraud policy and a procedure established to make available means to report behaviors that may be fraudulent or unethical. The policy should provide recommendations in order to determine the appropriate action for the situation. The identity of the reporting individual should be kept confidential or anonymous (AICPA, 2010).

KEY ACTORS IN MAINTAINING STRONG INTERNAL CONTROLS

Board of Directors, audit committees, management, employees, anti-fraud specialists, internal and independent auditors each play an important role in the reduction or elimination of fraud. Organizational policies should form a multifaceted approach in emphasizing and maintaining a strong and viable internal control system. The following discuss important issues pertaining to each of the aforementioned participants that are necessary in maintaining a strong internal control system.

To what extent has the organization instituted a process for oversight of fraud risks by the board of directors or others charged with governance (e.g., an audit committee)? The audit committee (or the board of directors where no audit committee is in existence) should assess management's identification of fraud risks, implementation of anti-fraud measures, and creation of the suitable "tone at the top." A committed and functioning supervision by the audit committee can facilitate reinforcing management's commitment to generating a culture with "zero tolerance" for fraud. An organization's audit committee also should make certain that senior management put into operation suitable fraud deterrence and prevention measures to better safeguard investors, employees, and other stakeholders. The audit committee's appraisal and oversight not only helps make certain that senior management fulfills its responsibility, but also can serve as a deterrent to senior management engaging in fraudulent activity (i.e., by ensuring an environment is fashioned whereby any attempt by senior management to include employees in committing or concealing fraud would lead quickly to reports from such employees to appropriate individuals, including the audit committee).

To what extent has the organization created "ownership" of fraud risks by pinpointing a member of senior management as having duty for managing all fraud risks within the organization? Management is responsible for assessing the risk of fraud and implementing appropriate anti-fraud programs and controls to reduce that risk to an acceptable level. Executives also play an important role in determining the ethical tone of the company by setting the proper example. Employees have a right to expect that their leaders set high standards. In the absence of management integrity, fraud can permeate the company.

To what degree has the organization implemented a process to promote ethical behavior, deter wrongdoing and facilitate two-way communication on difficult issues? Such a process generally includes involving a senior member of management who is responsible for the organization's processes to promote ethical behavior, deter wrongdoing and communicate appropriately on difficult issues. Management should also provide a mechanism for employees to report concerns about unethical behavior, actual or suspected fraud, or violations of the entity's code of conduct or ethics policy.

A code of conduct for employees at all levels, based on the organization's core values should provide clear direction on what behavior and actions are permitted and which ones are banned. Further, training should be provided for all personnel upon hiring and regularly thereafter concerning the code of conduct, seeking advice and communicating potential wrongdoing.

Additionally, communication systems ought to be available to enable employees to seek advice where necessary prior to making difficult ethical decisions and to express concern about known or potential wrongdoing affecting the entity.

Every organization should have an ethics policy and a fraud policy that should be communicated to employees upon hiring and periodically thereafter. Employees should be trained as to the kinds of fraud that can occur and what they should do when they presume fraud exist.

It is essential that employees be constantly encouraged to provide an account of irregularities. Often an employee can surmise when something does not appear to be acceptable. For example, a manager is adamant regarding handling a specific account himself and becomes annoyed when anyone else gets concerned. The employee has no evidence that fraud is taking place; however, he knows that something is suspicious. Employees should be encouraged to provide an account of this type of conduct.

This is why an anonymous reporting mechanism is so important. The Association of Certified Fraud Examiners' Report to the Nation on Occupational Fraud and Abuse reported that the most common method for detecting occupational fraud was a tip from an employee, customer, vendor, or anonymous source (Kranacher, Riley & Wells, 2011). An anonymous employee hotline is one of the most valuable reporting mechanism.

Anti-fraud specialists, such as certified fraud examiners, may assist the board of directors and audit committee with aspects of the oversight process either directly or as part of a team of internal or independent auditors. They can support the audit committee and board of directors in evaluating the fraud risk assessment and fraud prevention measures implemented by management. Certified fraud examiners also conduct examinations to settle allegations or fraud suspicions, reporting either to a suitable management level or to the board of directors or audit committee, contingent upon the nature of the issue and the level of personnel involved.

An effective internal audit team can be enormously useful in performing characteristics of the oversight function. Their knowledge about the organization may enable them to identify indicators that suggest fraud has been committed.

Both detection and deterrence measures can be an integral part of internal audits. Internal auditors can assist in the deterrence of fraud by scrutinizing and appraising the sufficiency and the effectiveness of the system of internal control. In addition, the internal control system should be commensurate with the extent of the potential exposure or risk in the various segments of the organization's operations.

Internal auditors may carry out proactive auditing in order to search for corruption, misappropriation of assets, and financial statement fraud. This may include the utilization of computer-assisted and analytical procedures to isolate anomalies and performing detailed reviews of high-risk accounts and transactions to identify possible financial statement fraud. The internal auditors should have an independent reporting line directly to the audit committee. This can enable them to express any concerns about management's commitment to suitable internal controls or to report suspicions or allegations of fraud involving senior management.

Independent auditors can aid management and the board of directors (or audit committee) by providing an appraisal of the organization's process for identifying, assessing, and responding to fraud risks. The board of directors (or audit committee) should have a receptive and forthright discourse with the independent auditors pertaining to management's risk assessment process and the internal control system. Such a dialogue should embrace a discussion of the susceptibility of the organization to fraudulent financial reporting and exposure to misappropriation of assets (see Appendix 8C).

In sum, the following actions aid an organization internal control system against potential fraud:

1. An ethical tone at the top will help discourage misconduct and unethical behavior.

2. A strong Internet usage policy will help thwart abusive Internet usage and increase employee productivity.

3. Biometrics technology effectively and efficiently utilized that does not violate individuals' rights or slow down productivity.

4. An organization's policies and procedures should specifically designate the proper use of time, and specifically forbid an employee's use of position and other organizational resources for personal gain.

5. Hiring practices should be impartial; personal motives for hiring job candidates should always be circumvented.

6. Developing a communication methodology (such as a fraud hotline) whereby employees can report misconduct without fear of retribution.

"Prevention" and "detection" are the two primary approaches to assist in reducing white-collar crime. These two approaches can help thwart illegal and inappropriate acts from taking place in an organizational setting. Employees are responsible for ensuring that tangible and intangible assets are safeguarded from loss. One critical underlying concept that should be accepted is the reality that a fraud is possible in any organization. If certain mechanisms are not in place, then it will be very difficult to identify a fraudulent act even if it is abundantly evident. Often times, fraud symptoms are viewed as administrative errors since people cannot conceive of the existence of fraud particularly in organizations where there is a long-time affiliation with coworkers. The following measures ought to be instituted to assist the elimination of impropriety in organizations:

a. *Identify tangible and intangible assets of the organization*: Examples include department expenditures, supplies, computers, software, petty cash, copyrights, patents, etc.
b. *Identify the risks associated with safeguarding these assets*: How can these assets be misused or improperly utilized? If assets are misappropriated, how will responsible persons know? What controls exist to prevent or detect inappropriate use or loss of assets? What additional controls are necessary to make sure that assets are properly protected from loss? Is the cost of extra controls sensible in relation to the risk involved?
c. *Establish a positive control environment*: It is essential to make obvious control awareness. An authentic interest and concern for controls should be conveyed to all employees.
d. Make certain that an adequate internal control biometrics system exists. The major tenets of a control system include: separation of duties, physical safeguards over assets, proper documentation, proper approvals, adequate supervision, physical inventories, and independent validation of transaction accuracy.
e. Make certain that all employees are familiar with the professional and business conduct policies: Copies of the policies should be issued to employees and questions should be addressed by management.

CONCLUSIONS

Every organization should indicate clearly the persons of responsible for such functions as sales, purchasing, receiving incoming shipments, paying bills, and maintaining accounting records. The lines of authority and responsibility can be shown in an organization chart. The organization chart should be supported by written job descriptions and by procedures manuals that explain in detail the authority and responsibilities of each person or department appearing in the chart.

If management is to direct the activities of an organization according to plan, every transaction should go through four separate steps; it should be authorized, approved, executed, and recorded. For example, consider the sales of merchandise on credit. Management has the authority and responsibility to approve credit sales to categories of customers who meet certain standards. The credit department is responsible for approving a credit sale of a given dollar amount to a particular customer. The transaction is executed by the shipping department which ships or delivers the merchandise to the customer. Finally, the transaction is recorded in the accounting department by an entry debiting Accounts Receivable and crediting Sales.

An organization should implement proactive fraud detection tests that are purposely designed to detect the significant potential frauds identified in the organization's fraud risk assessment. Other measures can include audit "hooks" embedded in the organization's transaction processing systems that can flag suspicious transactions for investigation and/or approval prior to completion of processing. Leading edge fraud detection techniques include computerized e-mail monitoring (where legally permitted) to identify use of certain phrases that might indicate planned or ongoing wrongdoing.

The capabilities supplied by forensic accounting consultants for preventing and detecting fraud can complement the work of the internal and external auditors. Forensic accounting consultants can serve a proactive role in assessing risks where vulnerability to fraud exists. Moreover, where fraud is assumed, the audit committee should hire forensic consultants to conduct an investigation.

A proactive fraud prevention program includes a process for promptly investigating where appropriate and resolving expressions of concern regarding known or potential wrongdoing, then communicating the resolution to those who expressed the concern. Moreover, a strong fraud prevention system includes monitoring of compliance with the code of conduct and participation in the related training. A fraud system should provide for regular measurement of the extent to which the organization's ethics, compliance and fraud prevention goals are being achieved. Finally, an organization's incorporation of ethics, compliance and fraud prevention goals should be part of the performance measures against which managers are evaluated and which are implemented to determine performance related compensation.

Fraud is an expensive drain on an entity's financial resources. In today's globally competitive environment, no one can afford to throw away a percentage of revenues that represents the largely hidden cost of fraud. Those organizations that have identified their most significant fraud costs (such as insurance and credit card companies) have made great strides in attacking and reducing those costs. If an organization is not identifying and tackling its fraud costs, they are in a weaker position to competitors who lower their costs by doing so.

REFERENCES

American Institute of Certified Public Accountants. (2010). Fraud Prevention. http://www.aicpa.org/InterestAreas/ForensicAndValuation/Resources/Fraud-PreventionDetectionResponse/InterviewingSkillsandGuidelines/Pages/FraudPrevention.aspx.

Black, H. C. (1979). *Black's law dictionary* (5th ed.). St. Paul, MN: West Publishing Company.

Committee of Sponsoring Organizations (COSO). (1992). *The committee of sponsoring organizations of the treadway commission.* Retrieved from http://www.coso.org/ (accessed August 9, 2010).

Kranacher, M. J., Riley, R. A., & Wells, J. T. (2011). *Forensic accounting and fraud examination.* New York, NY: Wiley.

APPENDIX 8A

TOP TEN INTERNAL CONTROLS TO PREVENT AND DETECT FRAUD!

A recent "KPMG Fraud Survey" found that organizations are reporting more experiences of fraud than in prior years and that three out of four organizations have uncovered fraud. The New York State Office of Mental Health's Bureau of Audit has provided the following list of internal controls to assist you in preventing and detecting fraud at your agency (http://www. omh.state.ny.us/omhweb/resources/internal_control_top_ten.html).

1. **Use a system of checks and balances to ensure no one person has control over all parts of a financial transaction.**
   - Require purchases, payroll, and disbursements to be authorized by a designated person.
   - Separate handling (receipt and deposit) functions from record keeping functions (recording transactions and reconciling accounts).
   - Separate purchasing functions from payables functions.
   - Ensure that the same person is not authorized to write and sign a check.
   - When opening mail, endorse or stamp checks "For Deposit Only" and list checks on a log before turning them over to the person responsible for depositing receipts. Periodically reconcile the incoming check log against deposits.
   - Require supervisors to approve employees' time sheets before payroll is prepared.
   - Require paychecks to be distributed by a person other than the one authorizing or recording payroll transactions or preparing payroll checks.
   - If the agency is so small that you cannot separate duties, require an independent check of work being done, for example, by a board member.
   - Require accounting department employees to take vacations.
2. **Reconcile agency bank accounts every month**
   - Require the reconciliation to be completed by an independent person who does not have bookkeeping responsibilities or check signing responsibilities or require supervisory review of the reconciliation.
   - Examine canceled checks to make sure vendors are recognized, expenditures are related to agency business, signatures are by authorized signers, and endorsements are appropriate.

- Examine bank statements and cancelled checks to make sure checks are not issued out of sequence.
- Initial and date the bank statements or reconciliation report to document that a review and reconciliation was performed and file the bank statements and reconciliations.

3. **Restrict use of agency credit cards and verify all charges made to credit cards or accounts to ensure they were business-related**
   - Limit the number of agency credit cards and users.
   - Establish a policy that credit cards are for business use only; prohibit use of cards for personal purposes with subsequent reimbursement.
   - Set account limits with credit card companies or vendors.
   - Inform employees of appropriate use of the cards and purchases that are not allowed.
   - Require employees to submit itemized, original receipts for all purchases.
   - Examine credit card statements and corresponding receipts each month, independently, to determine whether charges are appropriate and related to agency business.

4. **Provide Board of Directors oversight of agency operations and management**
   - Monitor the agency's financial activity on a regular basis, comparing actual to budgeted revenues and expenses.
   - Require an explanation of any significant variations from budgeted amounts.
   - Periodically review the check register or general ledger to determine whether payroll taxes are paid promptly.
   - Document approval of financial procedures and policies and major expenditures in the board meeting minutes.
   - Require independent auditors to present and explain the annual financial statements to the Board of Directors and to provide management letters to the Board.
   - Evaluate the Executive Director's performance annually against a written job description.
   - Participate in the hiring/approval to hire consultants including the independent auditors.

5. **Prepare all fiscal policies and procedures in writing and obtain Board of Directors approval. Include policies and/or procedures for the following:**
   - cash disbursements
   - attendance and leave
   - expense and travel reimbursements
   - use of agency assets

- purchasing guidelines
- petty cash
- conflicts of interest

6. **Ensure that agency assets such as vehicles, cell phones, equipment, and other agency resources are used only for official business**
   - Examine expense reports, credit card charges, and telephone bills periodically to determine whether charges are appropriate and related to agency business.
   - Maintain vehicle logs, listing the dates, times, mileage or odometer readings, purpose of the trip, and name of the employee using the vehicle.
   - Periodically review the logs to determine whether usage is appropriate and related to agency business.
   - Maintain an equipment list and periodically complete an equipment inventory.

7. **Protect petty cash funds and other cash funds**
   - Limit access to petty cash funds. Keep funds in a locked box or drawer and restrict the number of employees who have access to the key.
   - Require receipts for all petty cash disbursements with the date, amount received, purpose or use for the funds, and name of the employee receiving the funds listed on the receipt.
   - Reconcile the petty cash fund before replenishing it.
   - Limit the petty cash replenishment amount to a total that will require replenishment at least monthly.
   - Keep patient funds separate from petty cash funds.

8. **Protect checks against fraudulent use**
   - Prohibit writing checks payable to cash.
   - Deface and retain voided checks.
   - Store blank checks in a locked drawer or cabinet, and limit access to the checks.
   - Require that checks are to be signed only when all required information is entered on them and the documents to support them (invoices, approval) are attached.
   - Require two signatures on checks above a specified limit. Require board member signature for the second signature above a higher specified limit. (Ensure that blank checks are not presigned.)
   - Mark invoices "Paid" with the check number when checks are issued.
   - Enable hidden flags or audit trails on accounting software.

9. **Protect cash and check collections**
   - Ensure that all cash and checks received are promptly recorded and deposited in the form originally received.
   - Issue receipts for cash, using a prenumbered receipt book.
   - Conduct unannounced cash counts.
   - Reconcile cash receipts daily with appropriate documentation (cash reports, receipt books, mail tabulations, etc.)
   - Centralize cash receipts whenever possible.
10. **Avoid or discourage related party transactions**
    - Require that a written conflict of interest and code of ethics policy is in place and that it is updated annually.
    - Require that related party transactions be disclosed and be approved by the Board.
    - Require competitive bidding for major purchases and contracts.
    - Discourage the hiring of relatives and business transactions with Board members and employees.

APPENDIX 8B

FEDERAL BUREAU OF INVESTIGATION

Listed below are tips to protect yourself and your family from various forms of fraud schemes (http://www.fbi.gov/scams-safety/fraud/fraud).

INTERNET FRAUD

Avoiding Internet Auction Fraud

Understand as much as possible about how the auction works, what your obligations are as a buyer, and what the seller's obligations are before you bid.

Find out what actions the web site/company takes if a problem occurs and consider insuring the transaction and shipment.

Learn as much as possible about the seller, especially if the only information you have is an e-mail address. If it is a business, check the Better Business Bureau where the seller/business is located.

Examine the feedback on the seller.

Determine what method of payment the seller is asking from the buyer and where he/she is asking to send payment.

If a problem occurs with the auction transaction, it could be much more difficult if the seller is located outside the US because of the difference in laws.

Ask the seller about when delivery can be expected and if there is a problem with the merchandise is it covered by a warranty or can you exchange it.

Find out if shipping and delivery are included in the auction price or are additional costs so there are no unexpected costs.

There should be no reason to give out your social security number or drivers license number to the seller.

Avoiding Non-Delivery of Merchandise

Make sure you are purchasing merchandise from a reputable source.

Do your homework on the individual or company to ensure that they are legitimate.

Try to obtain a physical address rather than merely a post office box and a phone number, call the seller to see if the number is correct and working.

Send them e-mail to see if they have an active e-mail address and be wary of sellers who use free e-mail services where a credit card was not required to open the account.

Consider not purchasing from sellers who won't provide you with this type of information.

Check with the Better Business Bureau from the seller's area.

Check out other web sites regarding this person/company.

Do not judge a person/company by their web site.

Be cautious when responding to special offers (especially through unsolicited e-mail).

Be cautious when dealing with individuals/companies from outside your own country.

Inquire about returns and warranties.

The safest way to purchase items via the Internet is by credit card because you can often dispute the charges if something is wrong.

Make sure the transaction is secure when you electronically send your credit card numbers.

Consider utilizing an escrow or alternate payment service.

Avoiding Credit Card Fraud

Do not give out your credit card number(s) online unless the site is a secure and reputable site. Sometimes a tiny icon of a padlock appears to symbolize a higher level of security to transmit data. This icon is not a guarantee of a secure site, but might provide you some assurance.

Do not trust a site just because it claims to be secure.

Before using the site, check out the security/encryption software it uses.

Make sure you are purchasing merchandise from a reputable source.

Do your homework on the individual or company to ensure that they are legitimate.

Try to obtain a physical address rather than merely a post office box and a phone number, call the seller to see if the number is correct and working.

Send them e-mail to see if they have an active e-mail address and be wary of sellers who use free e-mail services where a credit card was not required to open the account.

Consider not purchasing from sellers who won't provide you with this type of information.

Check with the Better Business Bureau from the seller's area.

Check out other web sites regarding this person/company.

Do not judge a person/company by their web site.

Be cautious when responding to special offers (especially through unsolicited e-mail).

Be cautious when dealing with individuals/companies from outside your own country.

The safest way to purchase items via the Internet is by credit card because you can often dispute the charges if something is wrong.

Make sure the transaction is secure when you electronically send your credit card numbers.

You should also keep a list of all your credit cards and account information along with the card issuer's contact information. If anything looks suspicious or you lose your credit card(s) you should contact the card issuer immediately.

Avoiding Investment Fraud

Do not invest in anything based on appearances. Just because an individual or company has a flashy web site does not mean it is legitimate. Web sites can be created in just a few days. After a short period of taking money, a site can vanish without a trace.

Do not invest in anything you are not absolutely sure about. Do your homework on the investment to ensure that it is legitimate.

Do your homework on the individual or company to ensure that they are legitimate.

Check out other web sites regarding this person/company.

Do not judge a person/company by their web site.

Be cautious when responding to special investment offers (especially through unsolicited e-mail).

Be cautious when dealing with individuals/companies from outside your own country.

Inquire about all the terms and conditions.

If it sounds too good to be true it probably is.

Avoiding Business Fraud

Purchase merchandise from reputable dealers or establishments.

Try to obtain a physical address rather than merely a post office box and a phone number, call the seller to see if the number is correct and working.

Send them e-mail to see if they have an active e-mail address and be wary of those that utilize free e-mail services where a credit card was not required to open the account.

Consider not purchasing from sellers who won't provide you with this type of information.

Purchase merchandise directly from the individual/company that holds the trademark, copyright, or patent.

Beware when responding to e-mail that may not have been sent by a reputable company.

Avoiding the Nigerian Letter Scam

Be skeptical of individuals representing themselves as Nigerian or foreign government officials asking for your help in placing large sums of money in overseas bank accounts.

Do not believe the promise of large sums of money for your cooperation. Guard your account information carefully.

The *Nigerian Letter Scam* is described on the Common Fraud Schemes webpage.

AUCTION FRAUD

Auction fraud involves fraud attributable to the misrepresentation of a product advertised for sale through an Internet auction site or the nondelivery of products purchased through an Internet auction site.

Consumers are strongly cautioned against entering into Internet transactions with subjects exhibiting the following behavior:

- The seller posts the auction as if he resides in the United States, then responds to victims with a congratulatory email stating he is outside the United States for business reasons, family emergency, etc. Similarly, beware of sellers who post the auction under one name, and ask for the funds to be transferred to another individual.

- The subject requests funds to be wired directly to him/her via Western Union, MoneyGram, or bank-to-bank wire transfer. By using these services, the money is virtually unrecoverable with no recourse for the victim.

- Sellers acting as authorized dealers or factory representatives in countries where there would be no such dealers should be avoided.

- Buyers who ask for the purchase to be shipped using a certain method to avoid customs or taxes inside another country should be avoided.

- Be suspect of any credit card purchases where the address of the card holder does not match the shipping address. Always receive the card holder's authorization before shipping any products.

Auction Fraud—Romania

Auction fraud is the most prevalent of Internet crimes associated with Romania. The subjects have saturated the Internet auctions and offer almost every in-demand product. The subjects have also become more flexible, allowing victims to send half the funds now, and the other half when the item arrives.

The auctions are often posted as if the seller is a United States citizen, then the subject advises the victim to send the money to a business partner, associate, sick relative, a family member, etc., usually in a European country. The money is usually transferred via MoneyGram or Western Union wire transfer. The Internet Crime Complaint Center has verified in order to receive funds via Western Union, the receiver must provide the complete information of the sender and the receiver's full name and address. The funds can be picked up anywhere in the world using this information. There is no need to provide the money transfer control number (MTCN) or the answer to any secret question, as many subjects have purported to the victims. Money sent via wire transfer leaves little recourse for the victim.

The most recent trend is a large increase in bank-to-bank wire transfers. Most significantly, these wire transfers go through large United States banks and are then routed to Bucharest, Romania or Riga, Latvia.

Similarly, the sellers also occasionally direct the victims to pay using phony escrow services. Sometimes actual escrow websites are compromised and other sites resembling them are created by the subjects. Once the funds are wire transferred to the escrow website, the seller discontinues contact.

In addition, visit eBay and PayPal for additional security alerts and fraud prevention tips.

Counterfeit Cashier's Check

The counterfeit cashier's check scheme targets individuals that use Internet classified advertisements to sell merchandise. Typically, an interested party located outside the United States contacts a seller. The seller is told that the buyer has an associate in the United States that owes him money. As such, he will have the associate send the seller a cashier's check for the amount owed to the buyer.

The amount of the cashier's check will be thousands of dollars more than the price of the merchandise and the seller is told the excess amount will be used to pay the shipping costs associated with getting the merchandise to his location. The seller is instructed to deposit the check, and as soon as it clears, to wire the excess funds back to the buyer or to another associate identified as a shipping agent. In most instances, the money is sent to locations in West Africa (Nigeria).

Because a cashier's check is used, a bank will typically release the funds immediately, or after a one or two day hold. Falsely believing the check has cleared, the seller wires the money as instructed.

In some cases, the buyer is able to convince the seller that some circumstance has arisen that necessitates the cancellation of the sale, and is successful in conning the victim into sending the remainder of the money. Shortly thereafter, the victim's bank notifies him that the check was fraudulent, and the bank is holding the victim responsible for the full amount of the check.

Credit Card Fraud

The Internet Crime Complaint Center has received multiple reports alleging foreign subjects are using fraudulent credit cards. The unauthorized use of a credit/debit card, or card number, to fraudulently obtain money or property is considered credit card fraud. Credit/debit card numbers can be stolen from unsecured websites, or can be obtained in an identity theft scheme.

Visit any of the three credit bureaus, *Equifax*, *Experian*, or *TransUnion*, for more information or to place a fraud alert on your credit report.

DEBT ELIMINATION

Debt elimination schemes generally involve websites advertising a legal way to dispose of mortgage loans and credit card debts. Most often, all that is required of the participant is to send $1,500–$2,000 to the subject, along with all the particulars of the participant's loan information and a special power of attorney authorizing the subject to enter into transactions regarding the title of the participant's homes on their behalf. The subject then issues bonds and promissory notes to the lenders that purport to legally satisfy the debts of the participant. In exchange, the participant is then required to pay a certain percentage of the value of the satisfied debts to the subject. The potential risk of identity theft related crimes associated with the debt elimination scheme is extremely high because the participants provide all of their personal information to the subject.

PARCEL COURIER EMAIL SCHEME

The Parcel Courier Email Scheme involves the supposed use of various National and International level parcel providers such as DHL, UPS,

FedEx and the USPS Often, the victim is directly emailed by the subject(s) following online bidding on auction sites. Most of the scams follow a general pattern which includes the following elements:

- The subject instructs the buyer to provide shipping information such as name and address.
- The subject informs the buyer that the item will be available at the selected parcel provider in the buyer's name and address, thereby, identifying the intended receiver.
- The selected parcel provider checks the item and purchase documents to guarantee everything is in order.
- The selected parcel provider sends the buyer delivery notification verifying their receipt of the item.
- The buyer is instructed by the subject to go to an electronic funds transfer medium, such as Western Union, and make a funds transfer in the subject's name and in the amount of the purchase price.
- After the funds transfer, the buyer is instructed by the subject to forward the selected parcel provider the funds transfer identification number, as well as their name and address associated with the transaction.
- The subject informs the buyer the parcel provider will verify payment information and complete the delivery process.
- Upon completion of delivery and inspection of the item(s) by the receiver, the buyer provides the parcel provider funds transfer information, thus, allowing the seller to receive his funds.

EMPLOYMENT/BUSINESS OPPORTUNITIES

Employment/business opportunity schemes have surfaced wherein bogus foreign-based companies are recruiting citizens in the United States on several employment-search websites for work-at-home employment opportunities. These positions often involve reselling or reshipping merchandise to destinations outside the United States.

Prospective employees are required to provide personal information, as well as copies of their identification, such as a driver's license, birth certificate, or social security card. Those employees that are "hired" by these companies are then told that their salary will be paid by check from a United States company reported to be a creditor of the employer. This is done under the pretense that the employer does not have any banking set up in the United States.

The amount of the check is significantly more than the employee is owed for salary and expenses, and the employee is instructed to deposit the check into their own account, and then wire the overpayment back to the employer's bank, usually located in Eastern Europe. The checks are later found to be fraudulent, often after the wire transfer has taken place.

In a similar scam, some web-based international companies are advertising for affiliate opportunities, offering individuals the chance to sell high-end electronic items, such as plasma television sets and home theater systems, at significantly reduced prices.

The affiliates are instructed to offer the merchandise on well-known Internet auction sites. The affiliates will accept the payments, and pay the company, typically by means of wire transfer. The company is then supposed to drop-ship the merchandise directly to the buyer, thus eliminating the need for the affiliate to stock or warehouse merchandise. The merchandise never ships, which often prompts the buyers to take legal action against the affiliates, who in essence are victims themselves.

ESCROW SERVICES FRAUD

In an effort to persuade a wary Internet auction participant, the perpetrator will propose the use of a third-party escrow service to facilitate the exchange of money and merchandise. The victim is unaware the perpetrator has actually compromised a true escrow site and, in actuality, created one that closely resembles a legitimate escrow service. The victim sends payment to the phony escrow and receives nothing in return. Or, the victim sends merchandise to the subject and waits for his/her payment through the escrow site which is never received because it is not a legitimate service.

In addition, visit *Escrow.com* for security alerts and fraud prevention tips.

IDENTITY THEFT

Identity theft occurs when someone appropriates another's personal information without their knowledge to commit theft or fraud. Identity theft is a vehicle for perpetrating other types of fraud schemes. Typically, the victim is led to believe they are divulging sensitive personal information to a legitimate business, sometimes as a response to an email solicitation to update billing or membership information, or as an application to a fraudulent Internet job posting.

In addition, visit the *Federal Trade Commission* for additional information on security and fraud prevention tips.

INTERNET EXTORTION

Internet extortion involves hacking into and controlling various industry databases, promising to release control back to the company if funds are received, or the subjects are given web administrator jobs. Similarly, the subject will threaten to compromise information about consumers in the industry database unless funds are received.

INVESTMENT FRAUD

Investment fraud is an offer using false or fraudulent claims to solicit investments or loans, or providing for the purchase, use, or trade of forged or counterfeit securities.

LOTTERIES

The lottery scheme deals with persons randomly contacting email addresses advising them they have been selected as the winner of an International lottery. The Internet Crime Complaint Center has identified numerous lottery names being used in this scheme.

The email message usually reads similar to the following:

> "This is to inform you of the release of money winnings to you. Your email was randomly selected as the winner and therefore you have been approved for a lump sum payout of $500,000.00. To begin your lottery claim, please contact the processing company selected to process your winnings."

An agency name follows this body of text with a point of contact, phone number, fax number, and an email address. An initial fee ranging from $1,000 to $5,000 is often requested to initiate the process and additional fee requests follow after the process has begun. These emails may also list a United States point of contact and address while also indicating the point of contact at a foreign address.

COMMON FRAUD SCHEMES

Telemarketing Fraud

When you send money to people you do not know personally or give personal or financial information to unknown callers, you increase your chances of becoming a victim of telemarketing fraud.

Warning signs—what a caller may tell you:

"You must act 'now' or the offer won't be good."

"You've won a "free' gift, vacation, or prize." But you have to pay for "postage and handling" or other charges.

"You must send money, give a credit card or bank account number, or have a check picked up by courier." You may hear this before you have had a chance to consider the offer carefully.

"You don't need to check out the company with anyone." The callers say you do not need to speak to anyone including your family, lawyer, accountant, local Better Business Bureau, or consumer protection agency.

"You don't need any written information about their company or their references."

"You can't afford to miss this 'high-profit, no-risk' offer."

If you hear these—or similar—"lines" from a telephone salesperson, just say "no thank you," and hang up the phone.

Some Tips to Avoid Telemarketing Fraud

It's very difficult to get your money back if you've been cheated over the phone. Before you buy anything by telephone, remember:

Don't buy from an unfamiliar company. Legitimate businesses understand that you want more information about their company and are happy to comply.

Always ask for and wait until you receive written material about any offer or charity. If you get brochures about costly investments, ask someone whose financial advice you trust to review them. But, unfortunately, beware—not everything written down is true.

Always check out unfamiliar companies with your local consumer protection agency, Better Business Bureau, state Attorney General, the National Fraud Information Center, or other watchdog groups. Unfortunately, not all bad businesses can be identified through these organizations.

Obtain a salesperson's name, business identity, telephone number, street address, mailing address, and business license number before you transact business. Some con-artists give out false names, telephone numbers, addresses, and business license numbers. Verify the accuracy of these items.

Before you give money to a charity or make an investment, find out what percentage of the money is paid in commissions and what percentage actually goes to the charity or investment.

Before you send money, ask yourself a simple question. "What guarantee do I really have that this solicitor will use my money in the manner we agreed upon?"

You must not be asked to pay in advance for services. Pay services only after they are delivered.

Some con-artists will send a messenger to your home to pick up money, claiming it is part of their service to you. In reality, they are taking your money without leaving any trace of who they are or where they can be reached.

Always take your time making a decision. Legitimate companies won't pressure you to make a snap decision.

Don't pay for a "free prize." If a caller tells you the payment is for taxes, he or she is violating federal law.

Before you receive your next sales pitch, decide what your limits are—the kinds of financial information you will and won't give out on the telephone.

It's never rude to wait and think about an offer. Be sure to talk over big investments offered by telephone salespeople with a trusted friend, family member, or financial advisor.

Never respond to an offer you don't understand thoroughly.

Never send money or give out personal information such as credit card numbers and expiration dates, bank account numbers, dates of birth, or social security numbers to unfamiliar companies or unknown persons.

Your personal information is often brokered to telemarketers through third parties.

If you have information about a fraud report it to state, local, or federal law enforcement agencies.

Nigerian Letter or "419"

Named for the violation of Section 419 of the Nigerian Criminal Code, the 419 scam combines the threat of impersonation fraud with a variation of an advance fee scheme in which a letter, email, or fax is received by the potential victim. The communication from individuals representing themselves as Nigerian or foreign government officials offers the recipient the "opportunity" to share in a percentage of millions of dollars, soliciting for help in placing large sums of money in overseas bank accounts. Payment of taxes, bribes to government officials, and legal fees are often described in great detail with the promise that all expenses will be reimbursed as soon as the funds are out of the country. The recipient is encouraged to send information to the author, such as blank letterhead stationery, bank name and account numbers, and other identifying information using a facsimile number provided in the letter. The scheme relies on convincing a willing victim to send money to the author of the letter in several installments of increasing amounts for a variety of reasons.

Visit the *Economic and Financial Crimes Commission* to learn more about combating financial and economic crimes in Nigeria.

Some Tips to Avoid Nigerian Letter or "419" Fraud

> If you receive a letter from Nigeria asking you to send personal or banking information, do not reply in any manner. Send the letter to the U.S. Secret Service, your local FBI office, or the U.S. Postal Inspection Service. You can also register a complaint with the Federal Trade Commission's Consumer Sentinel.
>
> If you know someone who is corresponding in one of these schemes, encourage that person to contact the FBI or the U.S. Secret Service as soon as possible.
>
> Be skeptical of individuals representing themselves as Nigerian or foreign government officials asking for your help in placing large sums of money in overseas bank accounts.
>
> Do not believe the promise of large sums of money for your cooperation. Guard your account information carefully.

Impersonation/Identity Fraud

Impersonation fraud occurs when someone assumes your identity to perform a fraud or other criminal act. Criminals can get the information they need to assume your identity from a variety of sources, such as the theft of your wallet, your trash, or from credit or bank information. They may approach you in person, by telephone, or on the Internet and ask you for the information.

The sources of information about you are so numerous that you cannot prevent the theft of your identity. But you can minimize your risk of loss by following a few simple hints.

Some Tips to Avoid Impersonation/Identity Fraud

> Never throw away ATM receipts, credit statements, credit cards, or bank statements in a usable form.
>
> Never give your credit card number over the telephone unless you make the call.
>
> Reconcile your bank account monthly and notify your bank of discrepancies immediately.

Keep a list of telephone numbers to call to report the loss or theft of your
wallet, credit cards, etc.

Report unauthorized financial transactions to your bank, credit card
company, and the police as soon as you detect them.

Review a copy of your credit report at least once each year. Notify the
credit bureau in writing of any questionable entries and follow
through until they are explained or removed.

If your identity has been assumed, ask the credit bureau to print a statement to that effect in your credit report.

If you know of anyone who receives mail from credit card companies or
banks in the names of others, report it to local or federal law enforcement authorities.

Advance Fee Scheme

An advance fee scheme occurs when the victim pays money to someone in
anticipation of receiving something of greater value, such as a loan, contract, investment, or gift, and then receives little or nothing in return.

The variety of advance fee schemes is limited only by the imagination of
the con-artists who offer them. They may involve the sale of products or
services, the offering of investments, lottery winnings, "found money," or
many other "opportunities." Clever con-artists will offer to find financing
arrangements for their clients who pay a "finder's fee" in advance. They
require their clients to sign contracts in which they agree to pay the fee
when they are introduced to the financing source. Victims often learn that
they are ineligible for financing only after they have paid the "finder"
according to the contract. Such agreements may be legal unless it can be
shown that the "finder" never had the intention or the ability to provide
financing for the victims.

Some Tips to Avoid the Advanced Fee Schemes

If the offer of an "opportunity" appears too good to be true, it probably
is. Follow common business practice. For example, legitimate business is rarely conducted in cash on a street corner.

Know who you are dealing with. If you have not heard of a person or company that you intend to do business with, learn more about them.
Depending on the amount of money that you intend to spend, you
may want to visit the business location, check with the Better Business Bureau, or consult with your bank, an attorney, or the police.

Make sure you fully understand any business agreement that you enter
into. If the terms are complex, have them reviewed by a competent
attorney.

Be wary of businesses that operate out of post office boxes or mail drops and do not have a street address, or of dealing with persons who do not have a direct telephone line, who are never "in" when you call, but always return your call later.

Be wary of business deals that require you to sign nondisclosure or non-circumvention agreements that are designed to prevent you from independently verifying the bona fides of the people with whom you intend to do business. Con-artists often use noncircumvention agreements to threaten their victims with civil suit if they report their losses to law enforcement.

Common Health Insurance Frauds

Medical Equipment Fraud:

Equipment manufacturers offer "free" products to individuals. Insurers are then charged for products that were not needed and/or may not have been delivered.

"Rolling Lab" Schemes:

Unnecessary and sometimes fake tests are given to individuals at health clubs, retirement homes, or shopping malls and billed to insurance companies or Medicare.

Services Not Performed:

Customers or providers bill insurers for services never rendered by changing bills or submitting fake ones.

Medicare Fraud:

Medicare fraud can take the form of any of the health insurance frauds described above. Senior citizens are frequent targets of Medicare schemes, especially by medical equipment manufacturers who offer seniors free medical products in exchange for their Medicare numbers. Because a physician has to sign a form certifying that equipment or testing is needed before Medicare pays for it, con-artists fake signatures or bribe corrupt doctors to sign the forms. Once a signature is in place, the manufacturers bill Medicare for merchandise or service that was not needed or was not ordered.

Some Tips to Avoid the Health Insurance Fraud:

Never sign blank insurance claim forms.

Never give blanket authorization to a medical provider to bill for services rendered.

Ask your medical providers what they will charge and what you will be expected to pay out-of-pocket.

Carefully review your insurer's explanation of the benefits statement. Call your insurer and provider if you have questions.

Do not do business with door-to-door or telephone salespeople who tell you that services of medical equipment are free.

Give your insurance/Medicare identification only to those who have provided you with medical services.

Keep accurate records of all health care appointments.

Know if your physician ordered equipment for you.

Redemption/Strawman/Bond Fraud

Proponents of this scheme will claim that the U.S. Government or the Treasury Department controls bank accounts—often referred to as "U.S. Treasury Direct Accounts"—for all U.S. citizens that can be accessed by submitting paperwork with state and federal authorities. Individuals promoting this scam frequently cite various discredited legal theories and may refer to the scheme as "Redemption," "Strawman," or "Acceptance for Value." Trainers and websites will often charge large fees for "kits" that teach individuals how to perpetrate this scheme. They will often imply that others have had great success in discharging debt and purchasing merchandise such as cars and homes. Failures to implement the scheme successfully are attributed to individuals not following instructions in a specific order or not filing paperwork at correct times.

This scheme predominately uses fraudulent financial documents that appear to be legitimate. These documents are frequently referred to as "Bills of Exchange," "Promissory Bonds," "Indemnity Bonds," "Offset Bonds," "Sight Drafts," or "Comptrollers Warrants." In addition, other official documents are used outside of their intended purpose, like IRS forms 1099, 1099-OID, and 8300. This scheme frequently intermingle legal and pseudo legal terminology in order to appear lawful. Notaries may be used in an attempt to make the fraud appear legitimate. Often, victims of the scheme are instructed to address their paperwork to the U.S. Secretary of the Treasury.

Some Tips to Avoid Redemption/Strawman/Bond Fraud

Be wary of individuals or groups selling kits that they claim will inform you on to access secret bank accounts.

Be wary of individuals or groups proclaiming that paying federal and/or state income tax is not necessary.

Do not believe that the U.S. Treasury controls bank accounts for all citizens.

Be skeptical of individuals advocating that speeding tickets, summons, bills, tax notifications, or similar documents can be resolved by writing "acceptance for value" on them.

If you know of anyone advocating the use of property liens to coerce acceptance of this scheme, contact your local FBI office.

INVESTMENT RELATED SCAMS

Letter of Credit Fraud

Legitimate letters of credit are never sold or offered as investments.

Legitimate letters of credit are issued by banks to ensure payment for goods shipped in connection with international trade. Payment on a letter of credit generally requires that the paying bank receive documentation certifying that the goods ordered have been shipped and are en route to their intended destination.

Letters of credit frauds are often attempted against banks by providing false documentation to show that goods were shipped when, in fact, no goods or inferior goods were shipped.

Other letter of credit frauds occur when con-artists offer a "letter of credit" or "bank guarantee" as an investment wherein the investor is promised huge interest rates on the order of 100–300% annually. Such investment "opportunities" simply do not exist. (See Prime Bank Notes for additional information.)

Some Tips to Avoid Letter of Credit Fraud

If an "opportunity" appears too good to be true, it probably is.

Do not invest in anything unless you understand the deal. Con-artists rely on complex transactions and faulty logic to "explain" fraudulent investment schemes.

Do not invest or attempt to "purchase" a "Letter of Credit." Such investments simply do not exist.

Be wary of any investment that offers the promise of extremely high yields.

Independently verify the terms of any investment that you intend to make, including the parties involved and the nature of the investment.

Prime Bank Note

International fraud artists have invented an investment scheme that offers extremely high yields in a relatively short period of time. In this scheme, they purport to have access to "bank guarantees" which they can buy at a discount and sell at a premium. By reselling the "bank guarantees" several times, they claim to be able to produce exceptional returns on investment. For example, if $10 million worth of "bank guarantees" can be sold at a 2% profit on ten separate occasions, or "traunches," the seller would receive a 20% profit. Such a scheme is often referred to as a "roll program." To make their schemes more enticing, con-artists often refer to the "guarantees" as being issued by the world's "Prime Banks," hence the term "Prime Bank Guarantees." Other official sounding terms are also used such as "Prime Bank Notes" and "Prime Bank Debentures." Legal documents associated with such schemes often require the victim to enter into nondisclosure and noncircumvention agreements, offer returns on investment in "a year and a day," and claim to use forms required by the International Chamber of Commerce (ICC). In fact, the ICC has issued a warning to all potential investors that no such investments exist.

The purpose of these frauds is generally to encourage the victim to send money to a foreign bank where it is eventually transferred to an off-shore account that is in the control of the con-artist. From there, the victim's money is used for the perpetrator's personal expenses or is laundered in an effort to make it disappear.

While foreign banks use instruments called "bank guarantees" in the same manner that U.S. banks use letters of credit to insure payment for goods in international trade, such bank guarantees are never traded or sold on any kind of market.

Some Tips to Avoid Prime Bank Note Related Fraud

Think before you invest in anything. Be wary of an investment in any scheme, referred to as a "roll program," that offers unusually high yields by buying and selling anything issued by "Prime Banks."

As with any investment perform due diligence. Independently verify the identity of the people involved, the veracity of the deal, and the existence of the security in which you plan to invest.

Be wary of business deals that require nondisclosure or noncircumvention agreements that are designed to prevent you from independently verifying information about the investment.

What is a "Ponzi" Scheme?

A Ponzi scheme is essentially an investment fraud wherein the operator promises high financial returns or dividends that are not available through traditional investments. Instead of investing victims' funds, the operator pays "dividends" to initial investors using the principle amounts "invested" by subsequent investors. The scheme generally falls apart when the operator flees with all of the proceeds, or when a sufficient number of new investors cannot be found to allow the continued payment of "dividends."

This type of scheme is named after Charles Ponzi of Boston, Massachusetts, who operated an extremely attractive investment scheme in which he guaranteed investors a 50% return on their investment in postal coupons. Although he was able to pay his initial investors, the scheme dissolved when he was unable to pay investors who entered the scheme later.

Some Tips to Avoid Ponzi Schemes

As with all investments, exercise due diligence in selecting investments and the people with whom you invest.

Make sure you fully understand the investment before you invest your money.

Pyramid Scheme

Pyramid schemes, also referred to as franchise fraud, or chain referral schemes, are marketing and investment frauds in which an individual is offered a distributorship or franchise to market a particular product. The real profit is earned, not by the sale of the product, but by the sale of new distributorships. Emphasis on selling franchises rather than the product eventually leads to a point where the supply of potential investors is exhausted and the pyramid collapses. At the heart of each pyramid scheme there is typically a representation that new participants can recoup their original investments by inducing two or more prospects to make the same investment. Promoters fail to tell prospective participants that this is mathematically impossible for everyone to do, since some participants drop out, while others recoup their original investments and then drop out.

Some Tips to Avoid Pyramid Schemes

Be wary of "opportunities" to invest your money in franchises or investments that require you to bring in subsequent investors to increase your profit or recoup your initial investment.

Independently verify the legitimacy of any franchise or investment before you invest.

Related Links

LooksTooGoodToBeTrue website
Consumer Action website
Federal Trade Commission Consumer Information

Phishing/Spoofing

Phishing and spoofing are somewhat synonymous in that they refer to forged or faked electronic documents. Spoofing generally refers to the dissemination of email which is forged to appear as though it was sent by someone other than the actual source. Phishing, often utilized in conjunction with a spoofed email, is the act of sending an email falsely claiming to be an established legitimate business in an attempt to dupe the unsuspecting recipient into divulging personal, sensitive information such as passwords, credit card numbers, and bank account information after directing the user to visit a specified website. The website, however, is not genuine and was set up only as an attempt to steal the user's information.

Ponzi/Pyramid

Ponzi or pyramid schemes are investment scams in which investors are promised abnormally high profits on their investments. No investment is actually made. Early investors are paid returns with the investment money received from the later investors. The system usually collapses. The later investors do not receive dividends and lose their initial investment.

Reshipping

The "reshipping" scheme requires individuals in the United States, who sometimes are coconspirators and other times are unwitting accomplices, to receive packages at their residence and subsequently repackage the merchandise for shipment, usually abroad.

"Reshippers" are being recruited in various ways but the most prevalent are through employment offers and conversing, and later befriending, unsuspecting victims through Internet Relay Chat Rooms.

Unknown subjects post help-wanted advertisements at popular Internet job search sites and respondents quickly reply to the online advertisement. As part of the application process, the prospective employee is required to complete an employment application, wherein he/she divulges sensitive personal information, such as their date of birth and social security number which, unbeknownst to the victim employee, will be used to obtain credit in his/her name.

The applicant is informed he/she has been hired and will be responsible for forwarding, or "reshipping," merchandise purchased in the United States to the company's overseas home office. The packages quickly begin to arrive and, as instructed, the employee dutifully forwards the packages to their overseas destination. Unbeknownst to the "reshipper," the recently received merchandise was purchased with fraudulent credit cards.

The second means of recruitment involves the victim conversing with the unknown individual in various Internet Relay Chat Rooms. After establishing this new online "friendship" or "love" relationship, the unknown subject explains for various legal reasons his/her country will not allow direct business shipments into his/her country from the United States. He/she then asks for permission to send recently purchased items to the victim's United States address for subsequent shipment abroad for which the unknown subject explains he/she will cover all shipping expenses.

After the United States citizen agrees, the packages start to arrive at great speed. This fraudulent scheme lasts several weeks until the "reshipper" is contacted. The victimized merchants explain to the "reshipper" the recent shipments were purchased with fraudulent credit cards. Shortly thereafter, the strings of attachment are untangled and the boyfriend/girlfriend realizes their Cyber relationship was nothing more than an Internet scam to help facilitate the transfer of goods purchased online by fraudulent means.

Visit the *Economic and Financial Crimes Commission* to learn more about combating financial and economic crimes in Nigeria.

Spam

With improved technology and world-wide Internet access, spam, or unsolicited bulk email, is now a widely used medium for committing traditional white collar crimes including financial institution fraud, credit card fraud, and identity theft, among others. It is usually considered unsolicited because the recipients have not opted to receive the email. Generally, this bulk email refers to multiple identical messages sent simultaneously. Those sending this spam are violating the Controlling the Assault of Non-Solicited Pornography and Marketing (CAN-SPAM) Act, Title 18, U.S. Code, Section 1037.

Spam can also act as the vehicle for accessing computers and servers without authorization and transmitting viruses and botnets. The subjects masterminding this Spam often provide hosting services and sell open proxy information, credit card information, and email lists illegally.

THIRD PARTY RECEIVER OF FUNDS

A general trend has been noted by the Internet Crime Complaint Center regarding work-at-home schemes on websites. In several instances, the subjects, usually foreign, post work-at-home job offers on popular Internet employment sites, soliciting for assistance from United States citizens. The subjects allegedly are posting Internet auctions, but cannot receive the proceeds from these auctions directly because his/her location outside the United States makes receiving these funds difficult. The seller asks the United States citizen to act as a third party receiver of funds from victims who have purchased products from the subject via the Internet. The United States citizen, receiving the funds from the victims, then wires the money to the subject.

FRAUD TARGET: SENIOR CITIZENS

Why should Senior Citizens be concerned?

It has been the experience of the FBI that the elderly are targeted for fraud for several reasons:

1. Older American citizens are most likely to have a "nest egg," own their home and/or have excellent credit all of which the con-man will try to tap into. The fraudster will focus his/her efforts on the segment of the population most likely to be in a financial position to buy something.

2. Individuals who grew up in the 1930s, 1940s, and 1950s were generally raised to be polite and trusting. Two very important and positive personality traits, except when it comes to dealing with a con-man. The con-man will exploit these traits knowing that it is difficult or impossible for these individuals to say "no" or just hang up the phone.

3. Older Americans are less likely to report a fraud because they don't know who to report it to, are too ashamed at having been scammed, or do not know they have been scammed. In some cases, an elderly victim may not report the crime because he or she is concerned that relatives may come to the conclusion that the victim no longer has the mental capacity to take care of his or her own financial affairs.

4. When an elderly victim does report the crime, they often make poor witnesses. The con-man knows the effects of age on memory and he/she is counting on the fact that the elderly victim will not be able to supply enough detailed information to investigators such as: How many times did the fraudster call? What time of day did he/she call? Did he provide a call back number or address? Was it always the same person? Did you meet in person? What did the fraudster look like? Did he/she have any recognizable accent? Where did you send the money? What did you receive if anything and how was it delivered? What promises were made and when? Did you keep any notes of your conversations?

The victims' realization that they have been victimized may take weeks or, more likely, months after contact with the con-man. This extended time frame will test the memory of almost anyone.

5. Lastly, when it comes to products that promise increased cognitive function, virility, physical conditioning, anticancer properties and so on, older Americans make up the segment of the population most concerned about these issues. In a country where new cures and vaccinations for old diseases have given every American hope for a long and fruitful life, it is not so unbelievable that the products offered by these con-men can do what they say they can do.

WHAT TO LOOK FOR AND HOW TO PROTECT YOURSELF AND YOUR FAMILY

Health Insurance Frauds

Medical Equipment Fraud:
Equipment manufacturers offer "free" products to individuals. Insurers are then charged for products that were not needed and/or may not have been delivered.

"Rolling Lab" Schemes:
Unnecessary and sometimes fake tests are given to individuals at health clubs, retirement homes, or shopping malls and billed to insurance companies or Medicare.

Services Not Performed:
Customers or providers bill insurers for services never rendered by changing bills or submitting fake ones.

Medicare Fraud:
Medicare fraud can take the form of any of the health insurance frauds described above. Senior citizens are frequent targets of Medicare schemes, especially by medical equipment manufacturers who offer seniors free medical products in exchange for their Medicare numbers. Because a physician has to sign a form certifying that equipment or testing is needed before Medicare pays for it, con-artists fake signatures or bribe corrupt doctors to sign the forms. Once a signature is in place, the manufacturers bill Medicare for merchandise or service that was not needed or was not ordered.

Some Tips to Avoiding Health Insurance Frauds

Never sign blank insurance claim forms.

Never give blanket authorization to a medical provider to bill for services rendered.

Ask your medical providers what they will charge and what you will be expected to pay out-of-pocket.

Carefully review your insurer's explanation of the benefits statement. Call your insurer and provider if you have questions.

Do not do business with door-to-door or telephone salespeople who tell you that services of medical equipment are free.

Give your insurance/Medicare identification only to those who have provided you with medical services.

Keep accurate records of all health care appointments.

Know if your physician ordered equipment for you.

Counterfeit Prescription Drugs

Some tips to avoiding counterfeit prescription drugs

Be mindful of appearance. Closely examine the packaging and lot numbers of prescription drugs and be alert of any changes from one prescription to the next.

Consult your pharmacist or physician if your prescription drug looks suspicious.

Alert your pharmacist and physician immediately if your medication causes adverse side effects or if your condition does not improve.

Use caution when purchasing drugs on the Internet. Do not purchase medications from unlicensed online distributors or those who sell medications without a prescription. Reputable online pharmacies will have a seal of approval called the Verified Internet Pharmacy Practice Site (VIPPS), provided by the Association of Boards of Pharmacy in the United States.

Product promotions or cost reductions and other "special deals" may be associated with counterfeit product promotion.

Funeral and Cemetery Fraud

Some tips to avoiding funeral and cemetery fraud

Be an informed consumer. Take time to call and shop around before making a purchase. Take a friend with you who may offer some perspective to help make difficult decisions. Funeral homes are required to provide detailed general price lists over the phone or in writing.

Educate yourself fully about caskets before you buy one and understand that caskets are not required for direct cremations.

Understand the difference between funeral home basic fees for professional services and any fees for additional services.

You should know that embalming rules are governed by state law and that embalming is not legally required for direct cremations.

Carefully read all contracts and purchasing agreements before signing and make certain that all of your requirements have been put in writing.

Make sure you understand all contract cancellation and refund terms, as well as your portability options for transferring your contract to other funeral homes.

Before you consider prepaying, make sure you are well informed. When you do make a plan for yourself, share your specific wishes with those close to you.

And, as a general rule governing all of your interactions as a consumer, do not allow yourself to be pressured by vendors into making purchases, signing contracts, or committing funds. These decisions are yours and yours alone.

Fraudulent "Anti-Aging" Products

Some tips to avoiding fraudulent "anti-aging" products

If it sounds to good to be true, it probably is. Watch out for "Secret Formulas" or "Breakthroughs."

Don't be afraid to ask questions about the product. Find out exactly what it should do for you and what it should not.

Research a product thoroughly before buying it. Call the Better Business Bureau to find out if other people have complained about the product.

Be wary of products that purport to cure a wide variety of illnesses (particularly serious ones) that don't appear to be related.

Testimonials and/or celebrity endorsements are often misleading.

Be very careful of products that are marketed as having no side effects.

Products that are advertised as making visits to a physician unnecessary should be questioned.

Always consult your doctor before taking any dietary or nutritional supplement.

Telemarketing Fraud

If you are age 60 or older, you may be a special target for people who sell bogus products and services by phone. Older women living alone are special targets of these scam artists. Telemarketing scams often involve offers of prizes, low-cost vitamins and health care products, and travel offers.

There are warning signs to these scams, including promises of "free" or "low cost" vacations and get rich quick schemes. If you hear these—or similar—"lines" from a telephone salesperson, just say "no thank you," and hang up the phone:

"You must act 'now' or the offer won't be good."

"You've won a 'free' gift, vacation, or prize." But you have to pay for "postage and handling" or other charges.

"You must send money, give a credit card or bank account number, or have a check picked up by courier." You may hear this before you have had a chance to consider the offer carefully.

"You don't need to check out the company with anyone." The callers say you do not need to speak to anyone including your family, lawyer, accountant, local Better Business Bureau, or consumer protection agency.

"You don't need any written information about their company or their references."

"You can't afford to miss this 'high-profit, no-risk' offer."

Remember, if you hear the lines above, or similar "lines" from a telephone salesperson, just say "no thank you," and hang up the phone:

Some Tips to Avoiding Telemarketing Fraud

It's very difficult to get your money back if you've been cheated over the phone. Before you buy anything by telephone, remember:

Don't buy from an unfamiliar company. Legitimate businesses understand that you want more information about their company and are happy to comply.

Always ask for and wait until you receive written material about any offer or charity. If you get brochures about costly investments, ask someone whose financial advice you trust to review them. But, unfortunately, beware—not everything written down is true.

Always check out unfamiliar companies with your local consumer protection agency, Better Business Bureau, state Attorney General, the National Fraud Information Center, or other watchdog groups. Unfortunately, not all bad businesses can be identified through these organizations.

Obtain a salesperson's name, business identity, telephone number, street address, mailing address, and business license number before you transact business. Some con-artists give out false names, telephone numbers, addresses, and business license numbers. Verify the accuracy of these items.

Before you give money to a charity or make an investment, find out what percentage of the money is paid in commissions and what percentage actually goes to the charity or investment.

Before you send money, ask yourself a simple question. "What guarantee do I really have that this solicitor will use my money in the manner we agreed upon?"

You must not be asked to pay in advance for services. Pay services only after they are delivered.

Some con-artists will send a messenger to your home to pick up money, claiming it is part of their service to you. In reality, they are taking your money without leaving any trace of who they are or where they can be reached.

Always take your time making a decision. Legitimate companies won't pressure you to make a snap decision.

Don't pay for a "free prize." If a caller tells you the payment is for taxes, he or she is violating federal law.

Before you receive your next sales pitch, decide what your limits are—the kinds of financial information you will and won't give out on the telephone.

It's never rude to wait and think about an offer. Be sure to talk over big investments offered by telephone salespeople with a trusted friend, family member, or financial advisor.

Never respond to an offer you don't understand thoroughly.

Never send money or give out personal information such as credit card numbers and expiration dates, bank account numbers, dates of birth, or social security numbers to unfamiliar companies or unknown persons.

Your personal information is often brokered to telemarketers through third parties.

If you have been victimized once, be wary of persons who call offering to help you recover your losses for a fee paid in advance.

If you have information about a fraud, report it to state, local, or federal law enforcement agencies.

Reverse Mortgage Scams

The FBI and the U.S. Department of Housing and Urban Development Office of Inspector General (HUD-OIG) urge consumers, especially senior citizens, to be vigilant when seeking reverse mortgage products. Reverse mortgages, also known as Home Equity Conversion Mortgages (HECM), have increased more than 1,300 percent between 1999 and 2008, creating significant opportunities for fraud perpetrators.

Reverse mortgage scams are engineered by unscrupulous professionals in a multitude of real estate, financial services, and related entities to steal the equity from the property of unsuspecting senior citizens aged 62 or older or to use these seniors to unwittingly aid the fraudsters in stealing equity from a flipped property.

In many of the reported scams, victim seniors are offered free homes, investment opportunities, and foreclosure or refinance assistance; they are also used as straw buyers in property flipping scams.

Seniors are frequently targeted for this fraud through local churches, investment seminars, and television, radio, billboard, and mailer advertisements.

A legitimate HECM loan product is insured by the Federal Housing Authority (FHA). It enables eligible homeowners to access the equity in their homes by providing funds without incurring a monthly payment. Eligible borrowers must be 62 years or older who occupy their property as their primary residence and who own their property or have a small mortgage balance. See the FBI/HUD Intelligence Bulletin for specific details on HECMs as well as other foreclosure rescue and investment schemes.

Seniors should consider the following:

Do not respond to unsolicited advertisements.
Be suspicious of anyone claiming that you can own a home with no down payment.
Do not sign anything that you do not fully understand.
Do not accept payment from individuals for a home you did not purchase.
Seek out your own reverse mortgage counselor.

APPENDIX 8C

The following is an example of the fraud procedures that are necessary for auditors (http://www.dodig.mil/Inspections/APO/fraud/expectations.html)

UNITED STATES DEPARTMENT OF DEFENSE

Office of the Deputy Inspector General for Policy and Oversight—Audit Policy and Oversight

Audit Planning And Execution

Initial planning stage Early in the initial planning stages of the audit, the auditor should identify and assess any fraud risks factors that could be associated with the specific organization, its environment, its employees, and type of audit. Auditors should also become familiar with and assess the fraud risk factors generally applicable to all audits and upper management.

Figure 8C.1

Next, the auditor designs an audit program that reflects the risk assessment by developing steps to address any risk factors identified as being material or significant to the audit scope, subject matter, or objectives. The team should discuss among themselves and with the supervisor how and where the audited organization might be susceptible to fraud.

Additional planning steps Prior to beginning the field work phase, either at the entrance conference or another time, the auditor should identify the appropriate management officials and ask them what fraud or other criminal activity they are aware of within their organization. The auditor could also inquire as to what fraud risks the organization's management has identified and what actions they have taken. Instead of discussing the fraud risks for each audit separately, the auditor could choose to discuss these issues with the organization's management during the audit organization's annual planning process.

Execution phase The fraud risk assessment process does not end with the development of the audit program. During the execution phase, the auditor should remain alert to potential fraud indicators. Auditors may also decide that, depending on the audit scope, they should make inquiries of other personnel at the audited organization. These inquiries could include what fraud risks could exist and whether the employee has any knowledge or suspicions of fraud. An auditor should not ask every employee or manager these questions; however, based on information or a response to another question from an employee or manager, the auditor could decide that such follow-up questions are appropriate. When an auditor finds fraud indicators during the audit, they should address the indicators by performing additional audit steps or expanding transaction testing. The auditor should revise the audit program accordingly, document the fraud indicators found, and the additional work performed to address them.

Discussions on potential fraud   When an auditor identifies indications of potential fraud, the auditor should discuss the indicators and possibilities of the occurrence of fraud with their supervisor. Auditors may also consult with other auditors, supervisors, or managers who have more experience or knowledge relating to the identified potential fraud scheme or indicators. Additionally, auditors may discuss their concerns and findings with investigators, agency counsel, and other agency staff responsible for fraud prevention or detection programs or activities. Any advice received should be documented in the audit project documentation. Prior to discussing with or notifying a DoD or other Federal government official, except for those mentioned above, of a potential fraud, the auditor should confirm with the appropriate investigative organization that doing so will not compromise an investigation. An auditor should never discuss potential fraud related to a contractor's activities with contractor personnel unless they have obtained approval to do so from the lead criminal investigative organization. A best practice would be to obtain written approval from a manager within the lead criminal investigative organization versus verbally from the investigator.

Documentation   Auditors should document the entire process in the audit project documentation files, to include:

- the fraud risk assessment process,
- any fraud risks factors originally identified,
- how the fraud risk factors were reflected in the audit program,
- any fraud risk factors or potential indicators identified during the audit,
- how the audit program was expanded to address the risk factors,
- any discussions with other parties on whether to make a referral, and
- any fraud referral steps considered or taken.

Auditors should continuously maintain a high level of fraud awareness and appropriately assess fraud risk during the planning and execution of the audit in order to uncover potential fraudulent acts and protect the Government's interests.

Environment Conducive to Fraud

An auditor should understand under what circumstance fraud is most likely to occur. The conditions can be summarized in two words, opportunity and motive, which apply separately and jointly to individuals and the organization, whether government or non-government.

Much emphasis is given to individuals committing fraud against organizations for personal benefit. However, auditors must be able to recognize organizational fraud, fraud committed for the direct benefit of the organization, and, therefore, the indirect benefit of the individual.

Auditors should remember that individuals who commit organizational fraud may be moti- vated differently than those who directly benefit from fraud. In the case of organizational fraud, the individual may benefit through bonuses, raises, promotions, or job retention. A more subtle motivation relates to increased self-esteem, coworker/supervisor praise or envy, a feeling of power, or control over the organization or parts of it as well as staff

Figure 8C.2

Auditor Responsibilities

Auditors who perform independent audits and attestation engagements of DoD organizations, programs, activities, and functions are required by DoD Instruction (DoDI) 7600.02, "Audit Policies," to comply with the GAGAS issued by the Comptroller General of the United States. The GAGAS require auditors when performing financial and performance audits and examination-level attestation engagements (work that requires a positive assurance) to:

- identify risk factors (indicators),
- assess the risk associated with those factors (indicators),
- design and perform appropriate steps and procedures to address the risk areas,
- document the process, and

- include information on any potential fraud that might have a material impact on the audited subject matter in the report.

The auditor must provide reasonable assurance of detecting fraud, illegal acts, violations of provisions of contracts or grant agreements, and abuse that could materially affect the audit or examination. For review-level (work that provides negative assurance) and agreed-upon procedures-level (provides no opinion or assurance) attestation engagements, the auditor is not required to assess fraud risk factors or design steps to address those risks.

The auditor must perform procedures when they find information or indicators that fraud may have occurred that could materially impact the subject matter under review. In those cases, the auditor should determine whether the fraud was likely to have occurred and, if so, determine the effect on the results of the engagement. GAGAS requires auditors to comply with any legal requirements to report known or likely fraud, illegal acts, violations of provisions, of contracts, or grant agreements, or abuse directly to parties outside the audited entity.

DoDI 7600.02, paragraph 6.3, establishes the requirement that auditors shall refer to the appropriate investigative organi-

Figure 8C.3

zation any indications of potential fraud or other criminal acts discovered while performing audit work.

DoD Expectations

DoD expects its auditors to follow the Comptroller General philosophy that GAGAS represents only minimum requirements and audit organizations should strive to exceed them. DoD auditors should implement the standards relating to assessing the risk of fraud, designing and performing appropriate steps or procedures to disclose

Figure 8C.4

fraud indicators, identification of fraud indicators, and referring potential fraud by considering the significance of individual risks or fraud indicators identified as well as the combined total of the risk factors or fraud indicators.

The auditor should not simply use monetary impact, significance, or value when determining risk or evaluating findings. In some situations, the auditor may be unable to determine the materiality or dollar impact of the identified risks or fraud indicators. When the risk factors or fraud indicators relate to the safety, morale, or welfare of service members or civilians, the auditor should use a substantially lower threshold for considering an area high risk. DoD expects its auditors to live up to their fiduciary responsibilities to DoD, the Federal government, and the Public.

Fraud, illegal acts, violations of provisions of contracts or grant agreements, and abuse can occur anywhere, anytime, and in any activity. Auditors should maintain their professional skepticism and mindset that potential fraud could be present regardless of any past experience with the entity or any belief about management's honesty or integrity. However, auditors must not automatically conclude that every entity commits fraudulent acts or that every fraud indicator denotes that fraud has occurred. The auditor must maintain an attitude that includes a questioning mind and critical assessment of audit evidence.

When an auditor identifies indications of potential fraud, the auditor should discuss the indicators and possibilities of the occurrence of fraud with their supervisor and, when warranted, follow their organization's procedures for reporting the potential fraud indicator(s) to the appropriate investigative organization. Additionally, prior to notifying a DoD or other Federal government organization's management of a potential fraud, the auditor should confirm with the appropriate investigative organization that doing so will not compromise an investigation. The auditor should also never include information in their report relating to potential fraud without consulting with the appropriate criminal investigative agency official. Auditors are not responsible for proving fraud, just for reporting indicators of possible fraud; it is the investigator's job to prove whether fraud occurred. For additional guidance on this topic, please see "Fraud Referrals."

Best Practices

Best practices for DoD audit organizations include identifying and assessing potential fraud risks factors during the planning phase for review-level and agreed-upon procedures attestation engagements similar to what the auditor does for other audit services or work. When risk factors are identified during

Figure 8C.5

the planning phase, the auditor should discuss with their supervisor or higher-level management whether the requested or planned review-level or agreed-upon-procedures-level engagement is appropriate.

With audit management approval, the auditor should discuss with the requestor the fraud risk factors and whether an alternative type of audit or attestation engagement would be more appropriate. When the auditor identifies fraud indicators or other information that strongly points to a high probability of fraud during the planning phase, the auditor, after consulting with their management, should raise their concerns to the appropriate oversight or investigative organization.

Best practices also include designing some steps or procedures to address identified risk factors for a review-level attestation engagement. While DoD auditors are required to comply with GAGAS, other auditing standards may provide insight into best practices or other approaches to assessing fraud risks or identifying fraud indicators. The GAGAS incorporates the American Institute of Certified Public Accountants (AICPA) standards for fieldwork and reporting for financial audits and attestation engagements.

The AICPA auditing standards for financial audits and the GAGAS for financial and performance audits provide specific steps that are not included in the AICPA or the GAGAS for attestation engagements such as inquiring of management about potential fraud. Auditors may find these specific steps useful when considering how to best implement GAGAS for attestation engagements. Similarly, audit organizations may learn about other audit organizations' approaches and methods for assessing fraud risks and identifying and detecting fraud indicators and adapt best practices when feasible.

Reporting Audit Results

DoD auditors should coordinate with the lead criminal investigative organization or other appropriate legal authority and obtain their agreement with any disclosure or discussion of potential fraud in their report. This coordination is necessary to avoid any compromise of an ongoing criminal investigation or other legal proceeding and is especially important for publicly available reports.

Figure 8C.6

In certain situations, auditors may have to suspend work or reporting on a particular finding to avoid interfering with a criminal investigation or other legal proceeding. The auditor may incorporate information that is already publicly available. This requirement may supersede GAGAS reporting standards that generally require the auditor to include in their report all instances of fraud and illegal acts unless inconsequential and material violations of contract or grant agreement provisions and abuse.

Auditors should also coordinate with the lead criminal investigative organization and/or appropriate agency attorney or fraud counsel prior to complying with GAGAS external reporting requirements. The GAGAS reporting standards also include requiring auditors to report known or likely fraud, illegal acts, violations of contracts or grant agreements, or abuse directly to parties outside the audited entity when the organization's management does not report such information to external parties as specified in law or regulation. The auditor must first report management's failure to do so to its governance body. When its governance body also fails to take action, the auditor should report the information directly to the appropriate external parties and/or the funding agency.

The auditor's primary objective should be to not compromise any investigation or legal proceeding while still accurately reporting their findings. When an auditor is unable to do so, they should defer issuing the report until it will not impede the investigation or legal proceeding.

Fraud Referrals

Requirements to refer fraudulent activities Executive Order 12731, "Code of Ethics—Principles for Ethical Conduct for Government Officers and Employees," requires all Executive Branch employees to report fraud, waste, abuse, and corruption to appropriate authorities. DoD audit organizations and their auditors have additional requirements. For all audit work, GAGAS requires auditors to comply with any legal requirements to report known or likely fraud, illegal acts, violations of provisions, of contracts, or grant

Figure 8C.7

agreements, or abuse directly to parties outside the audited entity. DoD Instruction 5505.2, "Criminal Investigations of Fraud Offenses," requires the Secretaries of the Military Departments, Heads of DoD Components, the Directors of Defense Agencies, and Commanders of the Combatant Commands to ensure the prompt referral of all allegations of fraud involving DoD personnel or persons affiliated with DoD and any property or programs under their control or authority to the appropriate DoD Criminal Investigative Organizations. DoD Instruction 5505.2 also requires the Director of the Defense Contract Audit Agency (DCAA) to establish procedures to ensure the prompt referral to the appropriate Defense Criminal Investigative Organization (DCIO) of suspicions of irregularity or referrals of suspected fraud arising from DCAA audit activities. The DoD Instruction 7600.02, paragraph 6.3, establishes the requirement that auditors shall refer to the appropriate investigative organization any indications of potential fraud or other criminal acts discovered while performing audit work.

General Fraud Indicators

The scenarios presented in this guidance are organized by types of audits, however, many of the fraud indicators are applicable to other audits as well. The intent of the scenarios is to build on the auditor's knowledge and invoke a sufficient level of awareness for auditors to identify fraud indicators and make referrals when appropriate. Many potential fraud indicators are general in nature or are associated with the structure or operations of upper management.

Figure 8C.8

General Fraud Indicators

General fraud indicators are, as the name implies, applicable to any audit area. During the audit, auditors should always consider the general fraud indicators in addition to indicators specifically related to the audit area under review. The list of general fraud indicators presented below is not meant to be all-inclusive and should not preclude auditors from identifying and considering other indicators.

- Management override of key controls.
- Inadequate or weak internal controls.
- No written policies and procedures.
- Overly complex organizational structure.
- Key employee never taking leave or vacation.
- High turnover rate, reassignment, firing of key personnel.
- Missing electronic or hard copy documents that materialize later in the review.
- Lost or destroyed electronic or hard copy records.

- Photocopied documents instead of originals. Copies are poor quality or illegible.
- "Unofficial" electronic files or records instead of "archived" or "official" files or records.
- Revisions to electronic or hard copy documents with no explanation or support.
- Use of means of alteration to data files.
- Computer-generated dates for modifications to electronic files that do not fit the appropriate time line for when they were created.
- Missing signatures of approval or discrepancies in signature/handwriting.
- Computer report totals that are not supported by source documentation.
- Lengthy unexplained delays in producing requested documentation.

Management-Related Fraud Indicators

Management sets the tone of an organization through its control environment. An organization's control environment is the foundation of all other internal control components. An organization's control environment includes integrity and ethical values, management philosophy, organizational structure, and self-governance. For a DoD contractor, active participation in a compliance program, integrity reporting, and the DoD Voluntary Disclosure Program are key parts of its control environment. The control environment provides both discipline and structure to the organization; therefore, auditors must consider management characteristics and influence over the control environment not only as fraud risk factors but also as fraud indicators along with the general and audit specific fraud indicators. Sometimes general and management fraud indicators are the same due to the control environment being an integral part of every review. Possible management fraud indicators are listed below. This list is not meant to be all-inclusive and should not preclude the auditor from considering other fraud indicators that they might identify.

- Failure to display and communicate an appropriate attitude regarding the importance of internal control, including a lack of internal control policies and procedures; ethics program; codes of conduct; self-governance activities; and oversight of significant controls.
- Displaying through words or actions that senior management is subject to less stringent rules, regulations, or internal controls than other employees.

- Significant portion of compensation being incentive-driven based on accomplishment of aggressive target goals linked to budgetary or program accomplishments or stock prices.
- High turnover of senior executives or managers.
- Hostile relationship between management and internal and/or external auditors. This would include domineering behavior towards the auditor, failure to provide information, and limiting access to employees of the organization.
- Failure to establish procedures to ensure compliance with laws and regulations and prevention of illegal acts.
- Indications that key personnel are not competent in the perform-ance of their assigned responsibilities.
- Adverse publicity concerning an organization's activities or those of senior executives.
- Lack of, or failure to adhere to, policies and procedures requiring thorough background checks before hiring key management, accounting, or operating personnel.
- Inadequate resources to assist personnel in performing their duties, including personal computers, access to information, and tempo-rary personnel.
- Failure to effectively follow-up on recommendations resulting from external reviews or questions about financial results.
- Nondisclosure to the appropriate Government officials of known noncompliances with laws, regulations, or significant contract or grant provisions.
- Directing subordinates to perform tasks that override management or internal controls.
- Undue interest or micromanagement of issues or projects that most knowledgeable individuals would identify with a substantially lower level manager.
- A manager that claims disinterest or having no knowledge about a sensitive or high profile issue in which you would expect manage-ment involvement.
- Constant over usage or inappropriate use of cautionary markings on management or organizational documents such as "Attorney Client Privilege/Attorney Work Product," "For Official Use Only," or other markings indicating an item is business sensitive or has a higher security classification than is appropriate.

CHAPTER 9

AUDITING ISSUES IN INTERNAL CONTROL BIOMETRICS SYSTEMS

"Passwords are not only weak; passwords have a huge problem ... if you get more and more of them, the worse it is"

—Bill Gates, 2007 RSA Conference

The accounting profession has built on a range of control frameworks that identify risks, security, and safeguarding of assets procedures related to organizations' information resources and other assets. Specifically, these control frameworks (e.g., Committee of Sponsoring Organizations [COSO] 1992; SysTrust [AICPA 2002]; COBIT 2002) challenge the accounting profession to design and maintain control systems in a manner that safeguards an organization's information resources. Internal control biometrics systems can potentially reduce control risk in accounting applications and organizational processes, particularly when used in combination with traditional control measures.

Internal control biometrics systems are a growing business opportunity for many organizations. When exploring internal control biometrics systems options, organizations should implement and clearly exhibit effective control of biometrics for users. Without instilling trust for transactions, organizations do not have a chance of succeeding in the internal control biometrics

Biometric and Auditing Issues Addressed in a Throughput Model, pp. 319–344
Copyright © 2012 by Information Age Publishing
All rights of reproduction in any form reserved.

systems arena. Ethical governance enables businesses to inspire that trust, through clearly demonstrated control over the biometrics function.

Information is a commodity in the internal control biometrics systems era, and there are always buyers for sensitive information, including customer data, credit card information, and trade secrets. Data theft by an insider is common when access controls are not implemented. Outside hackers can also use "Trojan" viruses to steal information from unprotected systems. Beyond installing firewall and anti-virus software to secure systems, an organization should encrypt all of its important data.

Internal control biometrics systems threats are just as numerous as internal control biometrics systems opportunities. Perhaps, the most rampant are amplified security threats and vulnerabilities, through information warfare and cyber threats. Hardly ever a day goes by that evidence of hacking or illicit data exploitation is not highlighted in the media. Each innovation comes with a corresponding vulnerability or security concern for internal control biometrics systems transactions. Organizations should continually balance internal control biometrics systems benefits, risks and controls. As organizations experience many uncharted challenges of internal control biometrics systems use, organizations should consider how much capital to invest in security and control, how to remain flexible yet provide a secure environment, and how to plan for an unpredictable future.

FINANCIAL FRAUD

The nature of financial fraud has changed over the years with internal control biometrics systems implementation of advanced information technology. Internal control biometrics system-based financial fraud includes scam e-mails, identity theft, and fraudulent transactions. With spam, con artists can send scam e-mails to thousands of people in hours. For example, victims of the so-called 419 scam are often promised a lottery winning or a large sum of unclaimed money sitting in an offshore bank account, but they must pay a "fee" first to get their shares. Anyone who gets this kind of e-mail is advised to forward a copy to the U.S. Secret Service (419.fcd@usss.treas.gov).

Organizations should review bank statements as soon as they arrive and report any suspicious or unauthorized electronic transactions. Under the Electronic Fund Transfer Act, if victims notify the bank of an unauthorized transaction within 60 days of the date the statement is delivered, they are not liable for any loss. Otherwise, victims could lose all the money in their account, and the unused portion of the maximum line of credit established for overdrafts.

Phishing is a form of identity theft. Spam is sent claiming to be from an individual's bank or credit union or a reputable internal control biometrics systems organization. The e-mail urges the recipient to click on a link to update their personal data. The link takes the victim to a fake website designed to elicit personal or financial information and transmit it to the criminals.

Users should never offer their credit card numbers, PINs, or any personal information in response to unsolicited e-mail. Instead of clicking a link in a suspicious e-mail, call the office or use a URL that is legitimate to verify an e-mail that claims to be from a bank or financial institution. When submitting sensitive financial and personal information in internal control biometrics systems applications, make sure the server uses the Secure Sockets Layer protocol (the URL should be https:// instead of the typical http://).

SECURITY MEASURES

Access privilege and data encryption are good preventive controls against data theft by unauthorized employees who steal for personal gain. The access controls include the traditional passwords, smart-card security, and more-sophisticated biometric security devices. Companies can implement some appropriate controls, including limiting access to proprietary information to authorized employees, controlling access where proprietary information is available, and conducting background checks on employees who will have access to proprietary information. There will, however, always be some risk that authorized employees will misuse data they have access to in the course of their work. Companies can also work with an experienced intellectual property attorney, and require employees to sign incomplete and nondisclosure agreements.

Some of the most common risks associated with internal control biometrics systems transactions include:

1. *Interception.* Since information is usually transferred in unencrypted, plain text, it is possible for information to be inspected and modified at any point between the client and server.

2. *Redirection.* Also known as spoofing, it is relatively easy for individuals to impersonate a web service or act for a web site or organization falsely.

3. *Identification.* It is relatively simple for individuals to take on a different, or fraudulent, identity for internal control biometrics systems. Since there is not yet an internationally accepted standard to establish identity, Web sites must implement unique solutions.

4. *Exploitable program errors.* All computer software, including web servers and browsers, is subject to errors or bugs. These flaws have long

enabled attackers to commit unauthorized actions, including rejection of service and vandalism.

5. *Weak client security*. Even if an internal control biometrics systems provider manages its internal risks, it often is ineffective to do the same for clients. For example, even though vendors regularly issue program patches to correct security problems, only a small portion of internal control biometrics systems users performs the updates. They are then at risk of well-documented problems as well as the Web sites they use.

One of the highest hurdles to overcome is trust among all internal control biometrics systems users. Effective and proactive internal control biometrics systems governance activities undoubtedly demonstrate control over the internal control biometrics systems environment and help organizations inspire trust.

Organizations accomplish their goals through the use of intangible and tangible resources. Many terms denote intangible resources in the literature, such as intellectual capital, knowledge assets, intangible assets etc. (Rodgers, 2007). Since assets indicate ownership or control, we use "resources" since it can come from within as well as outside of a company. Further, the term intangible is used instead of "knowledge," in that these resources can consist of knowledge and nonknowledge items (e.g., internal control biometrics systems software, trademarks, goodwill, etc.). These resources are entrusted to the organization by groups or people outside the organization. Hence, organizations must issue stewardship must establish a strong internal control system for its intangible and tangible resources.

Audit trails are necessary for sound security internal control biometrics systems in order to ensure proper use, maintenance, and control of biometric systems. An audit trail is a sequence of records of computer events, with reference to an operating system, an application, or user activities (Clark, Holloway, & List, 1991). It is generated by an auditing system that monitors system activity. Audit trails have many uses in the realm of internal control biometrics systems security. Audit trails should exist for all transactions implemented in the biometric process as well as providing a means to trace system users and their activity. Finally, audit trail logs should be backed up and protected in an offsite location in order to ensure its security and availability.

Sabotage

A particular security problem is "website defacement," which is the sabotage of internal control biometrics systems-based web pages by hackers placing in or altering information. The altered web pages may deceive unknowing users and represent negative publicity that could affect an organization's image, brand name and credibility. Web defacement is basically a system attack, and the attackers frequently take advantage of undisclosed system vulnerabilities or un-patched systems.

Network firewalls cannot guard against all web vulnerabilities. Organizations should install supplementary internal control biometrics systems application security to mitigate the defacement risk. All known vulnerabilities should be patched to thwart unauthorized remote command execution and privilege escalation. It is also essential that only a few authorized users are permitted root access to a website's contents. Access to different internal control biometrics systems server resources, such as executables, processes, data files, and configuration files, should be monitored.

According to the 2005 CSI/FBI survey, system security episodes were done by insiders than outsiders (http://www.cpppe.umd.edu/Bookstore/Documents/2005CSISurvey.pdf). For security purposes, organizations often concentrate primarily on threats outside of the organization, not the inside. Sabotages by insiders are often acted upon when employees know their termination is coming. In a variety of situations, disgruntled employees are still able to achieve access after being terminated. The 2005 insider-threat case study results by CERT/SEI (http://www.cert.org/contents/contents.html) help identify, assess, and manage sabotage threats from insiders. Their major findings were as follows:

1. A negative work-related episode (e.g., firing, downsizing, or promotion pass-over) generated most insiders' actions.
2. The majority of the insiders had acted out in the workplace.
3. Many of the insiders activities were premeditated.
4. Less than 50% of the perpetrators had authorized access at the time of the incident.
5. Insiders implemented unsophisticated techniques for exploiting systemic vulnerabilities in applications, processes, or procedures; however, a few sophisticated attack tools were also employed.
6. Most insiders compromised computer accounts, produced unauthorized back-door accounts, or used shared accounts.
7. Remote access was utilized in order to perform the majority of the attacks.
8. Many of the insider attacks were discovered only after the damage was already committed.
9. System logs were the most likely ways that the insiders were identified.

The CERT/SEI study indicated that the convenience of remote access facilitates most of sabotage attacks. Another potential threat of unofficial use is when employees quit or are terminated because there is no coordination between the personnel department and the computer center. Some cases indicated that employees still had system access and an e-mail account after they have left an organization. Further, it was not uncommon that employees knew the user identifications and passwords of their colleagues. The study suggests that organizations can adopt some of the following steps to protect against such threats:

1. Disable an employee's system access without delay.
2. Enforce an organization-wide password change on a regular basis, including the day an employee resigns or is terminated. Nonetheless, this control is not practical with large organizations, since people leave every day.
3. Implement biometric access control if possible.
4. Get hold of the password and encryption code to an employee's laptop or encrypted files on the server.
5. Keep a system activity log as a detect control. However, for large organizations, the formation of an activity log may increase system overhead.

AUTHENTICATION, AUTHORIZATION, AND ACCOUNTING (AAA)

Authentication

In most situations, the identity of an individual that an organization deals with is an essential feature in how the internal control biometrics systems handle that interaction. When people go to a bank or through customs into a new country, they have to show identification to prove their identity. *Authentication* is the procedure of identifying a person, generally based on a user name and password. Authentication is predicated on the notion that each individual user will have distinct information that sets him or her apart from other users.

Once a person has been authenticated, the internal control biometrics systems will associate an initial process to the user, and the user will be able to begin other processes. All the processes began by the user accessing resources (intangible assets) by using the identity of the user, which has already been ascertained by the system.

For identification purposes, a biometric tool such as fingerprint or palm print sensors can eliminate the requirement for the user to write down passwords. This can greatly diminish calls to help desks and ensure that only a preenrolled and authorized user gains access to a personal computer or cell phone, the data stored on the device, and the network to which it connects.

Fingerprint sensors can also add convenience features to personal computers and cell phones such enabling functions like fast user switching, speed dialing (each finger is a different phone number) and fast application switching. In addition, in small form factor devices, the sensor can be implemented for device navigation, similar to a joystick.

Authentication consists of the following two activities:

1. the process of supplying evidence of authenticity for the information that is being delivered or stored, and
2. the process of verifying the proof of authenticity for the information that is being received or retrieved.

Authentication allows a method of identifying a user, usually by having the user enter a valid user name and valid password before access is granted. The process of authentication is based on each user having a distinct set of conditions for permitting access. The internal control biometrics systems contrast a user's authentication credentials with other user credentials stored in a database. If the credentials match, the user is allowed access to the network. If there is a discrepancy in the credentials, authentication fails and network access is denied.

The method of providing proof (information integrity) and verifying the authenticity of the identification (identity verification) presented is the two dominant forms of authentication. These two methods of authentications (i.e., providing information integrity and identity verification) are among the most essential security procedures required for allowing access to network users and customers.

It is very essential to create a distinctive abstract object in the form of a user account for each person who will access resources in an internal control biometrics systems environment. This object is implemented to identify the user in the system. In addition, this object is passed on by the system when user access to information assets is defined. Further the system will trace the users' actions and record an audit trail referring to the actual users by their abstract object identification. Therefore, the user identification is the foundation for access control and it also helps to put into practice accountability. Hence, it is essential to have distinct user identification for each user, since each person has precise access requirements.

Authorization

Authorization is the method of allowing or denying a user access to network resources once the user has been authenticated through the username and password or other type of biometric tool such as fingerprint or palm print scanners. The amount of information and the amount of services the user has access is dependent upon on the user's authorization level.

Following authentication, a user must gain *authorization* for performing specific tasks. For example, after logging into a system, the user may attempt to issue commands. The authorization process depicts whether the user has the authority to issue such commands. That is, authorization is the manner of enforcing policies. In addition, it determines what kinds or qualities of activities, resources, or services a user is allowed. Typically, authorization takes places within the context of authentication.

Authentication and authorization are complementary procedures, and it is often complicated to differentiate where authentication comes to an end and where authorization starts. Conceptually, authentication is intended to determine the identity of the user. Authorization, on the other hand, is only responsible for resolving whether or not the user should be permitted access.

After a user is authenticated, he or she may be authorized for different types of access or activity. For example, if a user attempts to access a file that resides on a file server, it will be the responsibility of the file service to verify whether the user will be allowed this type of access. Authorization can make available granular control and may make a distinction between operations such as reading or writing to a file, deleting a file, launching an executable file, etc. Before authorization is initiated, the user must be identified and authenticated. Authorization is built upon identification information to maintain access control lists for each service.

Authorization includes the form and content of media for recording activities and data, and the procedures applicable to data processing duties. Certain internal control biometrics system have built-in controls placed within the computing system that automatically detect errors caused by equipment malfunctioning. They do not detect erroneous data; however, they bring to the forefront erroneous internal handling of data. Examples include parity checks, duplicate circuitry, and "read-after-write" checks.

Parity checks serves to confirm each binary coded character. When characters are transformed into machine code, they are registered as magnetic impressions or "bits." In a binary number system, the code is characterized with zeros and ones. Duplicate circuitry entails a calculation by a computer system simultaneously on two circuits and the results are contrasted to make certain they are identical. Read-after-write checks result with the utilization of dual gap heads on a computer whereby writing occurs at one gap and reading at the other. The writing is then verified by reading immediately afterwards. These programmed controls are an integral component of the internally stored instructions and are controls formulated by the organization to detect erroneous data and erroneous processing.

Accounting

The third piece in the AAA framework is *accounting*, which measures the resources a user utilizes during access. It is the process of maintaining an audit trail for user actions on the system. This can consist of the amount of system time or the amount of data a user has sent and/or received during a session. Accounting is carried out by logging of session statistics and usage information and is implemented for authorization control, billing, trend analysis, resource utilization, and capacity planning activities.

Furthermore, if a user has managed to authenticate successfully and tries to access a resource, both successful and unsuccessful attempts should be monitored by the system; access attempts and their status should appear in the audit trail files. If authorization to access a resource was successful, the user ID of the user who accessed the resource should be provided in the audit trail to allow system administrators to track access.

Accounting measures should be made available, regardless of whether or not successful authentication or authorization has already taken place. A user may or may not have been able to authenticate to the system, and accounting should offer an audit trail of both successful and unsuccessful attempts. From this perspective, accounting can be instrumental from a security viewpoint to determine authorized or unauthorized actions. That is, it can provide information for successful and unsuccessful authentication to the system. In addition, both successful and unsuccessful attempts should be monitored by the internal control biometrics system if a user attempts to access a resource. Access attempts and their status should appear in the audit trail files. If authorization to access a resource was successful, the user identification of the user who accessed the resource should be provided in the audit trail to permit the monitoring personnel to track access.

Accounting is also the method of keeping a report of a user's activity while entering the network resources, including the amount of time spent in the network, the services accessed while there and the amount of data transferred during the session. Accounting data is implemented for trend analysis, capacity planning, billing, auditing, and cost allocation.

For example, the billing and collection capabilities of accounting software are a vital component of its internal control biometrics system features. The software should be able to provide the bill electronically through the website, e-mail, faxing, remote printing, or a third-party portal. The software may also provide billing options, such as discounts based on amount, time, or location; calculation of taxes; automated late-payment charges; and cycle billing.

The payment mechanisms in business-to-customer (B2C) and business-to-business (B2B) internal control biometrics system consist of credit cards, debit cards, electronic cash, and electronic checks. B2B commerce can involve more complicated payment procedures, such as electronic fund transfer (EFT), letters of credit, and bills of exchange. The software may be able to accept common forms of electronic payment and insert this information into the accounting system. (Deshmukh & Romine, 2002).

INTERNAL CONTROL

The following applications are defined for auditing:

1. *Auditing* is the act of confirming the correctness of an invoice submitted by a service provider, or the consistency to the internal control policy of usage policy, security guide, and monitors:
   (a) *cost allocation* is the cost structure associated with voice and data communications segments, and
   (b) *trend analysis* is generally used in forecasting future usage for the purpose of capacity planning.

Auditing is an attest function which fulfills the role of adding to the credibility of representation on internal control biometrics system stewardship and, hence increases the reliance which can be placed on internal control biometrics system transactions. To warrant this assumption of responsibility, the organization must make an examination of the objective evidence underlying the internal control biometrics system transactions.

Etzloni (1964: 1) acclaimed

"Our society is an organizational society. We are born in organizations, educated by organizations, and most of us spend much of our lives working for organizations. We spend much of our leisure time paying, playing, and praying in organizations. Most of us will die in an organization, and when the time comes for burial, the largest organization of all—the state—must grant official permission.

In contrast to earlier societies, modern society has placed a high moral value on rationality, effectiveness, and efficiency. Modern civilization depends largely on organizations as the most rational and efficient form of social grouping known. By coordinating a large number of human actions, the organization creates a powerful social tool. It combines its personnel with its resources, weaving together leaders, experts, workers, machines, and raw materials. At the same time, it continually evaluates how well it is performing and tries to adjust itself accordingly in order to achieve its goals .... All this allows organizations to serve the various needs of society and its citizens more efficiently than smaller and more natural human groupings, such as families, friendship groups, and communities."

A sound internal control system incorporates AAA. This approach supports a sound internal control system relates to at least five basic questions:

1. What am I protecting? The first segment in risk management is to locate assets that must be protected and the impact of their potential loss (see Chapter 3–Internal Control Biometrics Systems).

2. Who are my adversaries? The second segment is to recognize and distinguish unethical acts that may be threatening to these assets (see Chapter 1–Introduction to Auditing and Biometrics Applications and Chapter 6–Ethical Issues addressed in Biometrics Management). The intent and capability of an adversary are the standard criteria for determining the degree of threat to these assets.

3. How am I vulnerable? Segment three includes recognizing and depicting vulnerabilities that would permit acknowledged threats to be realized due to misapplied trust positions (see Chapter 7–Auditing Secured Biometric Transactions: Trust Issues). That is, what distrust issues can lead to a security breach?

4. What are my priorities? The fourth segment includes the assessment of risk and priorities determined for the safeguarding of assets. Risk levels are recognized by assessing the influence of the loss or damage, threats to the asset, privacy and security issues (see Chapter 3–Internal Control Biometrics Systems).

5. What can I do? The last segment requires recognizing countermeasures to reduce or eliminate risks. The advantages and benefits of these countermeasures ought to be weighed against disadvantages and costs (Chapter 7–Biometrics Legal and Ethical Issues and Chapter 8–Fraud and Internal Control).

A system of internal control consists of the plan of organization and all of the coordinate methods and measures embraced within an internal control biometrics system business to safeguard its assets, check the accuracy and reliability of its accounting data, promote operational efficiency, and encourage commitment to prescribed managerial policies.

A strong internal control system is obtained primarily through an efficient and effective information systems and division of work among the employees, which is established by the structure of an internal control biometrics system organization. In order to control the work of an organization, procedural methods and measures are adopted that provide evidence that the tasks specified by the organization structure have been completed.

The concept of structure is a behavioral one that relies heavily on ethical and trust systems of an organization. In an internal control biometrics system environment, there are things one ought to do and those one ought not to do. Individuals sometimes violate these rules, which can weaken established ethical and trust systems.

The characteristics of a satisfactory system of internal control should emphasize the following:

1. A plan of organization that offers suitable segregation of functional responsibilities.
2. Personnel of a quality matching responsibilities.
3. A system of authorization and record procedures sufficient to make available reasonable accounting control over assets (including intangible resources), liabilities, revenues, and expenses.

The 2002 Congress, as a result to accounting and financial scandals, passed the Sarbanes-Oxley Act. This Act compels public companies to assess their internal controls and to publish those findings with their Securities Exchange Commission (SEC) filings. The concepts developed in the COSO Report are generally used as the framework to evaluate internal control. A nonprofit commission established in 1992 called the "Committee of Sponsoring Organizations of the Treadway Commission" (COSO), established a common definition of internal control and created a framework for evaluating the effectiveness of internal controls (Messier, Glover, & Prawitt, 2009).

The concepts developed in the COSO Report are typically implemented as the framework to evaluate internal control. Even though the Sarbanes-Oxley Act is aimed at public companies, many privately owned companies and nonprofit organizations have elected to evaluate their systems of internal control using COSO's framework. The manner in which the parts of the COSO framework are applied to an organization is a function of the nature and size of the organization.

The COSO framework regards internal controls as containing of the following five interrelated components:

1. *Control environment.* The integrity and ethical values of the company, including its code of conduct, involvement of the Board of Directors and other actions that set the tone of the organization.

2. ***Risk assessment.*** Management's process of identifying potential risks that could result in misstated financial statements and developing actions to address those risks.

3. ***Control activities.*** These are the activities usually thought of as "the internal controls." They include such things as segregation of duties, account reconciliations and information processing controls that are designed to safeguard assets and enable an organization to timely prepare reliable financial statements.

4. ***Information and communication.*** The internal and external reporting process and includes an assessment of the technology environment.

5. ***Monitoring.*** Assessing the quality of a company's internal control over time and taking actions as necessary to ensure it continues to address the risks of the organization.

The *control environment* sets the tone of an organization and influences the control consciousness of its people. The control environment is the foundation for all other elements of internal control and provides structure and discipline. The control environment of an organization includes the following aspects:

1. Ethical rules and principles,
2. Commitment to competence,
3. Attention and direction provided by a board of directors or audit committee,
4. Management's philosophy and operating style,
5. Organizational structure,
6. Manner of assigning authority and responsibility, and
7. Human resource policies and procedures.

Risk assessment process involves identifying changed conditions in internal control biometrics system and taking necessary actions. This entails identifying and communicating both external and internal events/activities that may influence the organization's objectives and analyzing the associated opportunities and risks. Risks relevant to the accounting information process may arise due to:

1. Changes in the organization's operating environment,
2. New personnel,
3. New or improvise information systems,
4. Quick growth within the organization,
5. New technology such as biometrics,

6. New and improved lines, products, or activities,
7. Restructuring within the organization;
8. International operations; and
9. New accounting announcements.

Control Activities include establishing policies and procedures to help ensure management directives are carried out. Those policies and procedures symbolize "control activities." Control activities comprise a variety of activities and may include the following:

1. Performance reviews such as comparison of actual results to budgets, forecasts, and previous period performance,
2. Information processing controls such as controls to check the accuracy, completeness, and authorization of individual transactions. Information processing controls consist of automated as well as manual controls,
3. Physical controls includes adequate safeguards over access to assets and records, authorization for access to computer programs and data files, and periodic counting and comparison with amounts recorded in the accounting records,
4. Segregation of duties encompasses assigning the responsibility for authorizing transactions, recording transactions, and maintaining custody of assets to different individuals within the organization.

Control activities typically involve two elements: a policy that establishes what should be done and the procedure that executes the policy. Policies may be communicated either orally or in writing. This depends on the size of the organization and the channels of communication within the organization. Also critical to control activities are the follow-up actions taken in response to identified inconsistencies (for example, investigation by the owner/manager of unexpected variances noted while comparing actual sales to budgeted sales).

Information system consists of methods established to identify, assemble, analyze, classify, record, and report transactions and conditions and to maintain accountability for the internal control biometrics system organization's assets and liabilities. In addition, information systems generate information necessary to carry out many control activities. An information system includes methods and records that:

1. Identify and record all valid transactions,
2. Provide, on a timely basis, sufficient detailed information about transactions to permit proper classification for financial reporting,

3. Allow for the recording of transactions at their proper monetary value on the company's webpage financial information,
4. Provide sufficient information to permit recording of transactions in the proper accounting period, and
5. Appropriately present the transactions and related disclosures on the organizations' webpage financial information.

Communication relates to providing a clear understanding of internal control policies and procedures over financial information, how they work, and the responsibilities of people within the organization related to those policies and procedures. Communication may take the form of policy manuals, memorandums, oral communications, etc., depending on the size and organizational structure of the organization.

Communication also conveys the notion of providing the flow of information upstream in an organization. For control activities to be effective, people must be able to report exceptions to the suitable levels of management. For upstream communication to take place there must be open channels of communication and a willingness on the part of management to deal with problems as they occur.

Monitoring is important due to changes among personnel within an organization. Further, it is essential that internal controls be monitored over time in order to determine whether they are relevant and able to address new risks of the organization. Monitoring is a process that addresses the quality of an organization's internal control over time and involves assessing the design and operation of controls on a timely basis and taking actions as necessary.

Monitoring can be accomplished through:

1. Ongoing activities,
2. Separate evaluations, or
3. A combination of the two.

In determining whether separate evaluations are required, management ought to consider the nature of changes occurring within an organization and its associated risks. In addition, internal control biometrics system-oriented personnel should have the competence and experience of implementing controls, as well as the results of ongoing monitoring. The greater the effectiveness of ongoing monitoring of the internal control biometrics system may result in a decrease need for separate evaluations. Ongoing monitoring embraces management and supervisory activities and other measures that personnel implement in performing their duties. For example, management may question reports that vary notably from their knowledge of operations.

Internal auditors or personnel performing comparable tasks may play a part to an organization's monitoring of controls through separate evaluations. The internal auditing aspect supply information about the functioning of the organization's internal controls by concentrating on evaluating the design and operation of controls. In performing operational audits, internal auditors generally look at business processes regarding the level of efficiency and effectiveness. If, however, they are performing systems audits, they must review controls in the systems inside and outside of the entity, predictive models, the strategic planning processes in business, and nonfinancial applications to facilitate process reengineering.

External parties may provide information to assist an organization in monitoring controls. For example, external auditors may make available recommendations on improving controls as a result of their audit of the financial statements. Customers, by implicitly corroborating billing information through payment of invoices, are another example of external parties that may contribute to management monitoring internal control biometrics system-based activities. Reliable financial reporting and compliance with applicable laws and regulations are the control objectives that are very important to the external auditor. Operational efficiency and effectiveness may also be the external auditor's concern only if they materially affect the reliability of financial reporting or distort the financial picture of the organization.

In sum, internal control is a reliable information system fortified with a suitable division of responsibilities among employees and departments. First, the information system along with the division of responsibilities is based on the organizational structure of the company. Tasks that are important in the internal controls system includes but are not limited to personnel, operations management as well as some duties of the employees in the information processing or computer departments.

An internal control system should provide documentation of all the tasks performed by the management and employees of the company. This documentation takes many forms, such as charts of accounts, purchase requisitions and authorizations, written job descriptions, and formal plans of the internal control biometrics system. The division of responsibility that flows from the structure of the organization includes individual tasks for the information systems. These tasks include the maintenance of the internal control biometrics system web page along with other information systems, and procedural checks on the flow of transaction activity, and records of custody of assets within the organization.

Finally, four primary functions that are necessary for the sound procedures of companies are:

1. accounting (financial reporting),
2. operations,
3. custody (safeguarding of assets), and
4. and compliance.

Typically, in most transaction flows it is better to have a separation of these four functions.

MISUSE OF INTERNAL CONTROL
BIOMETRICS SYSTEM APPLICATIONS

User authentication is the foundation of website application security, and inadequate authentication may make applications vulnerable thereby decreasing the threshold of trust. Organizations should implement a website application firewall to ensure that all security policies are closely followed. The following additional controls can mitigate website application abuses:

1. Installing security patches without delay.
2. Using a website application scanner to discover any vulnerability in the system.
3. Monitoring the server and applications to locate any potential harm and terminate malicious requests.
4. Concealing information that end users do not need to know, as well as the server machine type and the operating system.

ANALYTICAL PROCEDURES USED
IN CONTROL APPLICATIONS

What is ratio analysis? The Balance Sheet, Statement of Income, and the Statement of Cash Flow are essential, but they are only the beginning point for successful internal control systems. Ratio Analysis to financial statements is useful to analyze the success, failure, and progress trends of an organization.

Financial ratios are calculated from one or more pieces of information from an organization's financial statements. For example, the "gross margin" is the gross profit from operations divided by the total sales or revenues of an organization, expressed in percentage terms. In isolation, a financial ratio is an inadequate part of information. In context, however, a financial ratio can provide a manager with an excellent picture of a organization's circumstances and the trends that are developing.

Ratio Analysis enables an organization to spot trends in its operations and to compare its performance and condition with the average performance of similar operations in the same industry. Ratio analysis may provide the all-important early warning indications that allow an organization to solve its problems before bad practices destroyed it.

A ratio gains usefulness by comparison to other data and standards. Taking the previous example, a gross profit margin for an organization of 30% is meaningless by itself. If we know that this organization's competitors have profit margins of 15%, we know that it is more profitable than their industry peer which is quite favorable. If we also know that the historical trend is upwards, for instance has been increasing progressively for the previous few years, this would also be a favorable sign that management has put into practice effective organizational policies and strategies.

Financial ratio analysis groups the ratios into groupings that tell highlights distinct features of a organization's finances and operations. An overview of some of the groupings of ratios is given below.

- **Liquidity ratios** which give a picture of a company's short-term financial situation or solvency.
- **Activity ratios** which use turnover measures to show how efficient an organization is in its operations and use of assets.
- **Profitability ratios** which use margin analysis and show the return on sales and capital employed.
- **Leverage ratios** which show the extent that debt is used in a company's capital structure.
- **Market value ratios** relates to an observable market value, the stock price, to book values obtained from the firm's financial statements.

Liquidity Ratios

Important Balance Sheet Ratios measure liquidity and solvency (an organization's ability to pay its bills as they come due) and leverage (the extent to which the business is dependent on creditors' funding). A complete liquidity ratio analysis can help uncover weaknesses in the financial position of an organization. They include the following ratios:

These ratios indicate the ease of turning assets into cash. They include the Current Ratio, Quick Ratio, and Working Capital.

Current ratios

The Current Ratio is one of the best known measures of financial strength. It is figured as shown below:

$$\text{Current Ratio} = \frac{\text{Total Current Assets}}{\text{Total Current Liabilities}}$$

The main question this ratio addresses is: "Does your business have enough current assets to meet the payment schedule of its current debts with a margin of safety for possible losses in current assets, such as inventory shrinkage or collectable accounts?" A generally acceptable current ratio is 2 to 1. But whether or not a specific ratio is satisfactory depends on the nature of the business and the characteristics of its current assets and liabilities. The minimum acceptable current ratio is obviously 1:1, but that relationship is usually playing it too close for comfort.

If you decide your business's current ratio is too low, you may be able to raise it by:

- Paying some debts.
- Increasing your current assets from loans or other borrowings with a maturity of more than one year.
- Converting noncurrent assets into current assets.
- Increasing your current assets from new equity contributions.
- Putting profits back into the business.

Quick ratios

The Quick Ratio is sometimes called the "acid-test" ratio and is one of the best measures of liquidity. It is figured as shown below:

$$\text{Quick Ratio} = \frac{\text{Cash} + \text{Government Securities} + \text{Receivables}}{\text{Total Current Liabilities}}$$

The Quick Ratio is a much more exacting measure than the Current Ratio. By excluding inventories, it concentrates on the really liquid assets, with value that is fairly certain. It helps answer the question: "If all sales revenues should disappear, could my business meet its current obligations with the readily convertible 'quick' funds on hand?"

An acid-test of 1:1 is considered satisfactory unless the majority of your "quick assets" are in accounts receivable, and the pattern of accounts receivable collection lags behind the schedule for paying current liabilities.

Working capital

Working Capital is more a measure of cash flow than a ratio. The result of this calculation must be a positive number. It is calculated as shown below:

$$\text{Working Capital} = \text{Total Current Assets} - \text{Total Current Liabilities}$$

Bankers look at Net Working Capital over time to determine a company's ability to weather financial crises. Loans are often tied to minimum working capital requirements.

A general observation about these three Liquidity Ratios is that the higher they are the better, especially if you are relying to any significant extent on creditor money to finance assets.

Operating cash flow (OCF) ratio. The numerator of the OCF ratio consists of net cash provided by operating activities from the statement of cash flow. This is the net figure provided by the cash flow statement after taking into consideration adjustments for noncash items and changes in working capital. The denominator is all current liabilities, taken from the balance sheet.

$$\text{OCF} = \frac{\text{Cash Flow from Operations}}{\text{Current Liabilities}}$$

Operating cash flow ratios vary radically, depending on the industry. The operating cash flow ratio can gauge a company's liquidity in the short term. Using cash flow as opposed to income is sometimes a better indication of liquidity since cash is how bills are normally paid off.

Activity Ratios

Inventory turnover ratio

This ratio reveals how well inventory is being managed. It is important because the more times inventory can be turned in a given operating cycle, the greater the profit. The Inventory Turnover Ratio is calculated as follows:

$$\text{Inventory Turnover Ratio} = \frac{\text{Net Sales}}{\text{Average Inventory at Cost}}$$

Accounts receivable turnover ratio

This ratio indicates how well accounts receivable are being collected. If receivables are not collected reasonably in accordance with their terms, management should rethink its collection policy. If receivables are excessively slow in being converted to cash, liquidity could be severely impaired. The Accounts Receivable Turnover Ratio is calculated as follows:

$$\frac{\text{Net Credit Sales/Year}}{365 \text{ Days/Year}} = \text{Average Credit Sales}$$

$$\text{Accounts Receivable Turnover (in days)} = \frac{\text{Accounts Receivable}}{\text{Average Credit Sales}}$$

Accounts payable turnover ratio

A short-term liquidity measure used to quantify the rate at which a company pays off its suppliers. Accounts payable turnover ratio is calculated by taking the total purchases made from suppliers and dividing it by the average accounts payable amount during the same period.

$$\frac{\text{Supplier Purchases/Year}}{365 \text{ Days/Year}} = \text{Average Accounts Payables}$$

$$\text{Accounts Payable Turnover (in days)} = \frac{\text{Accounts Payable}}{\text{Average Accounts Payable}}$$

Profitability Ratios

The following important State of Income Ratios measure profitability:

Gross margin ratio

This ratio is the percentage of sales dollars left after subtracting the cost of goods sold from net sales. It measures the percentage of sales dollars remaining (after obtaining or manufacturing the goods sold) available to pay the overhead expenses of the company.

Comparison of your business ratios to those of similar businesses will reveal the relative strengths or weaknesses in your business. The Gross Margin Ratio is calculated as follows:

$$\text{Gross Margin Ratio} = \frac{\text{Gross Profit}}{\text{Net Sales}}$$

$$(\text{Gross Profit} = \text{Net Sales} - \text{Cost of Goods Sold})$$

Net-profit margin ratio

This ratio is the percentage of sales dollars left after subtracting the Cost of Goods sold and all expenses, except income taxes. It provides a good opportunity to compare your company's "return on sales" with the performance of other companies in your industry. It is calculated before income tax because tax rates and tax liabilities vary from company to company for a wide variety of reasons, making comparisons after taxes much more difficult. The Net Profit Margin Ratio is calculated as follows:

$$\text{Net Profit Margin Ratio} = \frac{\text{Net Profit Before Tax}}{\text{Net Sales}}$$

Return on assets ratio

This measures how efficiently profits are being generated from the assets employed in the business when compared with the ratios of firms in a similar business. A low ratio in comparison with industry averages indicates an inefficient use of business assets. The Return on Assets Ratio is calculated as follows:

$$\text{Return on Assets} = \frac{\text{Net Profit Before Tax}}{\text{Total Assets}}$$

Return on investment (ROI) ratio

The ROI is perhaps the most important ratio of all. It is the percentage of return on funds invested in the business by its owners. In short, this ratio tells the owner whether or not all the effort put into the business has been worthwhile. If the ROI is less than the rate of return on an alternative, risk-free investment such as a bank savings account, the owner may be wiser to sell the company, put the money in such a savings instrument, and avoid the daily struggles of small business management. The ROI is calculated as follows:

$$\text{Return on Investment} = \frac{\text{Net Profit Before Tax}}{\text{Net Worth}}$$

These Liquidity, Leverage, Profitability, and Management Ratios allow the business owner to identify trends in a business and to compare its progress with the performance of others through data published by various sources. The owner may thus determine the business's relative strengths and weaknesses.

Leverage Ratios

This Debt/Worth or Leverage Ratio indicates the extent to which the business is reliant on debt financing (creditor money versus owner's equity):

$$\text{Debt/Worth Ratio} = \frac{\text{Total Liabilities}}{\text{Net Worth}}$$

Generally, the higher this ratio, the more risky a creditor will perceive its exposure in your business, making it correspondingly harder to obtain credit.

The Stockholders' Equity Ratio is the measure of the relative financial strength and long-run liquidity of an organization. A low ratio points to trouble, while a high ratio suggests an organization will have less difficulty meeting fixed interest charges and maturing debt obligations.

Stockholders' equity ratio

$$\text{Stockholders' Equity Ratio} = \frac{\text{Total Liabilities}}{\text{Total Assets}}$$

Market Value Ratios

Price-earnings ratio (P/E ratio)

The Price-Earnings Ratio is calculated by dividing the current market price per share of the stock by earnings per share (EPS). (Earnings per share are calculated by dividing net income by the number of shares outstanding.)

The P/E Ratio indicates how much investors are willing to pay per dollar of current earnings. As such, high P/E Ratios are associated with growth stocks. (Investors who are willing to pay a high price for a dollar of current earnings obviously expect high earnings in the future.) In this manner, the P/E Ratio also indicates how expensive a particular stock is. This ratio is not meaningful, however, if the firm has very little or negative earnings.

$$\text{P/E Ratio} = \frac{\text{Price Per Share}}{\text{Earnings Per Share}}$$

where

$$\text{Earnings Per Share} = \frac{\text{Net Income}}{\text{Number of Shares Outstanding}}$$

Market-to-book ratio

The Market-to-Book Ratio relates the firm's market value per share to its book value per share. Since a firm's book value reflects historical cost accounting, this ratio indicates management's success in creating value for its stockholders. This ratio is used by "value-based investors" to help to identify undervalued stocks.

$$\text{Market to Book Ratio} = \frac{\text{Price Per Share}}{\text{Book Value Per Share}}$$

where

$$\text{Book Value Per Share} = \frac{\text{Total Owners' Equity}}{\text{Number of Shares Outstanding}}$$

CONCLUSIONS

Today environment requires that our personal biometrics implemented in internal control biometrics systems must be protected from misuse. When providing internal control biometrics system services to the public, there are three items that are commonly needed. These are authentication, authorization, and accounting. Authentication is needed to make sure that the person of the service is who he or she claims to be. This is necessary, since the information collected is private and personal to the user. In general, authentication is provided by the implementation of a shared secret or a trusted third party. Associated to authentication is authorization. That is, after the user has been authenticated a technique is required in order to ensure that the user is authorized to do the things he or she is requesting. More often than not authorization is provided by using access control lists or policies. Accounting is the process that the internal control biometrics system service provider brings together information of the network usage for billing, planning and other purposes.

Internal control objectives are the concern of the organization's management. In particular, management must address the highest-level control objective of competitive advantage by means of operational efficiency and effectiveness, unique products and services, or high quality and quick delivery of products and services. Management is also responsible for the organization's system of internal control to ensure reliable webpage financial reporting and compliance with applicable laws and regulations.

Management must address its objective of supporting and facilitating the accomplishment of top management's control objectives by planning, acquiring, maintaining, and monitoring internal control biometrics systems. In this regard, internal control biometrics system strategies should serve to enable the successful implementation of the organization's business strategies.

Internal control biometrics system-based operations can be disrupted by many factors, including system security breaches. System downtime, system penetrations, theft of computing resources, and lost productivity have rapidly become essential system security issues. The financial loss of these security breaches can be significant. Furthermore, system security breaches often contaminate an organization's image and reputation and may compromise its compliance with applicable laws and regulations. A major method of protecting an organization's accounting information system against security breaches is to implement useful biometrics tools for all possible major threats. Further, combination of preventive and detective controls can mitigate security threats.

Finally, to improve internal controls, it is essential to note the significance of the appropriate context for ratio analysis. Similar to computer programming, financial ratio is governed by the GIGO law of "*Garbage In ... Garbage Out!*" A cross industry comparison of the liquidity of stable technology firms and insurance firms would be ineffectual. Investigating a cyclical organization's profitability ratios over less than a business cycle would provide an inaccurate account of its long-term measure of profitability. Implementing historical data independent of basic changes in an organization's condition or forecasts would predict very little about future trends. For example, the historical ratios of an organization that has undergone a merger or had a substantive change in its technology or market position would provide inadequate information pertaining to the organization's prospects.

Although financial ratio analysis is well-developed and the actual ratios are well-known, managers often develop their own measures for particular industries as well as for individual firms. This is especially the case for those ratios that measure intangible assets.

REFERENCES

American Institute of Certified Public Accountants (AICPA). (2002). Trust Services Principles & Criteria. Incorporating SysTrust & WebTrust, Exposure Draft. Available at http://www.aicpa.org/download/ trust_services/ed_princ_criteria. pdf (accessed August 9, 2010).

Clark, R., Holloway, S., & List, W. (1991). *The Security, Audit and Control of Databases*. London: Avebury Technical.

COBIT. (2002). Control Objectives for Information and Related Technology. Available at: http://www.isaca.org/ cobit.htm (accessed September 14, 2002).

Committee of Sponsoring Organizations (COSO). (1992). *The Committee of Sponsoring Organizations of the Treadway Commission*. Available at http://www.coso.org/ (accessed August 9, 2010).

Deshmukh, A., & Romine, J. (2002). The CPA and the Computer, *The CPA Journal*, (November).

Etzloni, A. (1964). *Modern organizations*. Englewood Cliffs, NJ: Prentice-Hall.

Messier, W. F., Glover, S. M., & Prawitt, D. F. (2009). *Auditing & Assurance Services: A Systematic Approach*. New York, NY: McGraw-Hill/Irwin.

Rodgers, W. (2007). Problems and resolutions to future knowledge-based assets reporting. *Journal of Intellectual Capital 8*, 205–215.

CHAPTER 10

CONCLUSIONS

"The longer I live, the more I realize the impact of attitude on life. Attitude.
To me, is more important than facts. It is more important than the past,
than education, than money than circumstances, than failures.
Than successes, than what people think or say or do.

It is more important than appearance, giftedness or skill. It will make or break a
company ... a church ... a home. The remarkable thing is we have a choice every day
regarding the attitude we will embrace for that day.

We cannot change our past ... we cannot change the fact that people will act a certain
way. We cannot change the inevitable. The only thing we can do is play on the string
we have, and that is our attitude.

I am convinced that life is 10% what happens to me and 90% how I react to it. And so
it is with you ... we are in charge of our Attitude."

—"Attitude" by Charles Swindoll

This book proposes a *Throughput Modeling* framework that draws from the cognitive psychology literature to model perceptual and judgmental processes where biometrics might be used to reduce fraud and internal control risk.

Biometric technologies measure and analyze human physiological and behavioral characteristics.

Identifying or verifying an individual's physiological characteristics is based on direct measurement of a part of the body such as fingertips, palm print, hand geometry, ear recognition, facial recognition, and eye

Biometric and Auditing Issues Addressed in a Throughput Model, pp. 345–359

retinas and irises. The corresponding biometric technologies are finger-print and palm print recognition, hand geometry, ear image, facial, retina, and iris recognition. Identifying behavioral characteristics is based on data derived from actions, such as gait, speech and signature, the corresponding biometrics being walking strides, speaker recognition and signature recognition.

Biometrics can theoretically be very effective personal identifiers since the features they measure are thought to be unique to each individual. Unlike conventional identification techniques that use something you have, such as an identification card to obtain access to a building, or something you know, such as a password to log on to a computer system, these features are at the heart of to something you are. Since they are tightly bound to a person, they are more reliable, cannot be forgotten, and are less easily lost, stolen, or guessed.

Fraud is a crime and the most excellent means of prevention is to understand why it occurs. Fraudsters usually identify an opportunity for taking advantage of a weakness in the control procedures and then assess whether their potential rewards will outweigh the penalties should they be caught. Ethics policies should clearly detail what you consider to be illegal, improper and fraudulent behavior.

Prevention of fraud is a two-stage process:

1. make sure that opportunities for fraud are minimized, (fraud prevention), and
2. make sure that potential fraudsters believe they will be caught (fraud deterrence).

Simply recognizing and reacting to fraud is insufficient. Organizations must eliminate the so-called the "fraud triangle," which involves a potential scammer's immediate financial needs (*pressure*), *opportunity* to meet those needs and ability to *rationalize* the crime.

To deter such activities, organizations should establish fraud-prevention guidelines, ethics codes and internal controls. Background checks on low- and high-level recruits can weed out possible criminals, while tip hotlines encourage employees to police themselves and coworkers. Requiring employees to take time off and separating financial responsibilities can eliminate temptation, while promising offenders they will be terminated, prosecuted and otherwise disciplined will make it clear that the organization does not tolerate fraud.

The first line of defense against fraud is a strong system of internal controls. While a lack of internal control does not guarantee fraud will take place, it does open the door a bit wider. If people intent on committing fraud think they may be blocked by strong internal controls, they will be deterred.

Despite its potential strengths, biometric technology is not a panacea and represents one element in a portfolio of security mechanisms needed to protect information resources and other intangible assets. The book discusses challenges in implementing biometric technology and identifies avenues for future research.

Despite the many challenges facing biometrics development, this market is continually emerging and several large deployments to massive sections of populations are taking place, or are about to take place. These include the application of biometrics in identity card and document programs, passports, and other travel documentation. Next, the management and delivery of services in health, education and transport is increasing in biometrics deployment. In addition, biometrics is emerging as a valuable technology for organizational security and safeguarding of assets in the commercial sector, for establishing the identity of employees as well as customers and suppliers. The financial services industry is also an adopter of this technology, a number of projects are now springing up around the world that are developing biometrics for the delivery of financial services.

Although the biometric tools are fragmented in the technologies they analyze, each end product operates essentially in the same manner. The first critical step in building any biometric system is to obtain a sample of the biometric feature during an enrollment process. This step is essential in the effectiveness of the internal control biometrics system, since this is when the initial features of an individual are determined. During the enrollment process, each person supplies samples of the internal control system's specific biometric characteristic. This is achieved by interacting with the scanning hardware that the system make available. The distinct characteristics of the sample are then extracted and transformed by the system into a mathematical code and the sample is then saved as the biometric template for that user. The biometric template that is saved may be located in the internal control biometrics system itself, or in any other form of memory storage, such as a computer database, a smart card, or a bar-code.

A typical internal control biometrics systems use a method that includes of four stages: capture, extraction, comparison, and matching. The only difference is the procedures that each internal control biometrics system implements to deal with an individual feature involved. The capture stage denotes the physical or behavioral sample that is encapsulated during the enrollment process. The extraction stage represents the extraction of distinctive data from the captured sample and then utilized in the generation of a template. The comparison stage involves comparing of a new sample with that of the original sample imprinted on the template. Finally, the matching stage entails the process in which the internal control biometrics system will ascertain whether the new sample precisely matches the original sample or not.

IMPLEMENTATION OF AN INTERNAL CONTROL
BIOMETRICS SYSTEM

Ethics is essential in an effective internal control program for without it the words and actions of internal control are meaningless. The internal controls are all measures taken by an organization for the function of (1) protecting its resources against waste, fraud, or inefficient use; (2) making certain the reliability of accounting data; (3) obtaining compliance with management's policies; and (4) appraising the performance of all employees, managers, and departments within the organization.

Therefore, all measures and procedures intended to assure management that the entire business is operating according to management's plans and policies may be depicted as internal controls. Collectively, the internal controls applicable throughout the organization are called the internal control system. The objective of the internal control system is to keep an organization "on track," operating in accordance with the policies and plans of management.

There are five significant elements of internal controls. Each element is an essential component of the control system as a whole. Without all of these fundamentals present, the internal control system simply won't work.

Environmental Control

Environmental control pertains to the attitude and behavior of management and employees. It is the responsibility of management to endorse the policies and procedures that will drive employee behavior and attitude. Management sets the example; if senior managers are negligent about adhering to policy, then employees will tend to follow suit. A critical piece of environmental control is independent oversight, whether from a board of directors or an audit committee.

Risk Assessment

Risk assessment depicts an organization's capability to evaluate business risks, determine their gravity, and act (or react) accordingly. Risk assessment usually falls under the purview of management; however, it can be incorporated with day to day scrutiny from employees.

Control Procedures

Control procedures are the policies and procedures that are establish for executing the environmental controls, the risk assessment, the monitoring, and the communication necessary to keep the internal control system functioning. When appropriately endorsed, control procedures can diminish the likelihood for procedural errors and reduce the threat of theft or fraud. By implementing policies that segregate duties and require independent verification, management can generate a series of checks and balances that will keep operations running smoothly and efficiently.

Monitoring

Monitoring does not refer to the actions of the employees in and of themselves. This process should be effectively covered under control procedures. Instead, monitoring refers to the metrics put in place to ascertain that the internal controls themselves are functioning as expected. If an organization does not appropriately monitor its internal control system, it has no way of acknowledging whether or not the system is working. With suitable monitoring, problematic control procedures can be readily identified and retooled, replaced, or eradicated to keep the internal control system (and operations as a whole) running smoothly.

Communication

Finally, no internal control system can perform without the communication of essential information. Communication should flow downward within each department, laterally between departments, as well as upward to management. The checks and balances established by the internal control procedures make certain that each department will provide information that is timely, accurate, and complete.

Guidelines for an effective internal control system include make sure that:

a. An organization has well-written policies and procedures manual that address its significant activities and unique issues. In addition, employee duties, limits to authority, performance standards, control procedures, and reporting guidelines should be clear.
b. Employees are well familiar with the organization's policies and procedures that are relevant to their job responsibilities.
c. Discussion of ethical issues with employees take place. If employees need supplementary guidance, issue standards of conduct.
d. Employees comply with the conflict of interest policy and reveal possible conflicts of interest (e.g., ownership interest in companies doing business or proposing to do business with the organization).
e. Job descriptions are in existence, plainly affirm responsibility for internal control, and appropriately translate desired competence levels

into requisite knowledge, skills, and experience; make sure that hiring practices result in hiring qualified employees.

f.   The organization has a satisfactory training program for employees.
g.   Employee performance evaluations are carried out periodically. High-quality performance should be valued favorably and acknowledged in a constructive manner.
h.   Suitable disciplinary action is taken when an employee does not abide by with policies and procedures or behavioral standards.

NATURE OF AN INTERNAL CONTROL BIOMETRICS SYSTEM

An internal control biometrics system modifies data derived from behavioral or physiological features into templates, which are used for succeeding matching. This process takes the following several stages.

Enrollment is the process whereby an individual's first biometric sample or samples are collected, evaluated, developed, and stored for continuing use in an internal control biometrics system. Enrollment occurs in both 1:1 and 1:N systems. If users are experiencing difficulties with an internal control biometrics system, they may be required to re-enroll to gather superior quality data.

Submission is the process whereby an individual supplies behavioral or physiological data in the form of biometric samples to a biometric system. A submission may necessitate glancing in the direction of a camera or placing a finger on a platen. Depending on the internal control biometrics system, a user may have to do away with eyeglasses, remain motionless for a number of seconds, or recite a pass phrase in order to provide a biometric sample.

Acquisition devices embody the hardware utilized to acquire biometric samples. The following acquisition devices in Table 10.1 are connected with each biometric apparatus:

Biometric sample is the particular, unprocessed image or recording of a physiological or behavioral feature, obtained during submission, implemented to generate biometric templates. Table 10.2 exemplifies the sample types that are linked with each biometric apparatus:

Feature extraction is the programmed process of locating and encoding inimitable features from a biometric sample in order to produce a template. The feature extraction process may consist of sundry gradations of image or sample processing in order to locate a sufficient amount of precise data. For example, voice recognition tools can separate out certain frequencies and patterns; while palm print technologies can thin the ridges present in a palm print image to the width of a single pixel. Furthermore, if the sample made accessible is inadequate to perform feature extraction, the internal

Table 10.1.   Acquisition Devices

Technology	*Acquisition Device*
Fingerprint	Desktop peripheral, PCMCIA card, mouse, chip or reader embedded in keyboard
Palm print	Desktop peripheral, PCMCIA card, mouse, chip or reader embedded in keyboard
Hand geometry	Proprietary wall-mounted unit
Vein analysis	Desktop peripheral, PCMCIA card, mouse, chip or reader embedded in keyboard
DNA	Can be collected from any number of sources: blood, hair, finger nails, mouth swabs, blood stains, saliva, straws, and any number of other sources that has been attached to the body at some time.
Retina-scan	Proprietary desktop or wall-mountable unit
Iris-scan	Infrared-enabled video camera, PC camera
Facial recognition	Video camera, PC camera, single-image camera
Facial thermography	Infrared camera
Ear recognition	Video or infrared-enabled camera, commercial application is in the developmental stage
Body odor (scent) recognition	odor-sensing instrument (an electronic "nose"), commercial application is in the developmental stage
Speaker recognition	Microphone, telephone
Gait	Video camera
Dynamic signature	Signature tablet, motion-sensitive stylus
Keystroke dynamics	Keyboard or keypad

control biometrics system will usually instruct the user to provide another sample, often with some sort of advice or feedback.

The mode in which internal control biometrics systems obtain features is patented is at variance from vendor to vendor. Table 10.3 portrays customary physiological and behavioral characteristics implemented in feature extraction.

As technological advancements are increasingly immersed in routine human endeavors, the criticality for parallel and proportional achievements in internal control biometrics systems is a reality for security and asset protection. Contextually, those engaged in nefarious information technology activities is on the rise. When information assets are deemed valuable, authorization through a single access scheme appears woefully inadequate compared to the estimated number of "hackers" or "crackers"

Table 10.2.   Biometric Sample

Technology	Biometric sample
Fingerprint	Fingerprint image
Palm print	Palm print image
Hand geometry	3-D image of top and sides of hand and fingers
Vein analysis	Near-infrared light
DNA	Oral swab (or needle) to collect
Retina-scan	Retina Image
Iris-scan	Iris Image
Facial recognition	Facial image
Facial thermography	Infrared image of face
Ear recognition	Infrared image of ear
Body odor (scent) recognition	Capture the volatile chemicals that skin pores emit
Speaker recognition	Voice recording
Gait	Sequence of images to derive and analyze motion characteristics
Dynamic signature	Image of signature and record of related dynamics measurements
Keystroke dynamics	Recording of characters typed and record of related dynamics measurements

probing information technology operational defenses. Two or more authentication factors will inevitably become the security deployment norm, with one architectural authentication factor relying on a biometrically based process; unless superior alternative access control remedies are devised.

Privacy is central to any organization deployment of biometrics. Issues such as data collection, storage and retention, linking and common identifiers, physical and logical access controls, and consent and control over information must be thoroughly addressed to guarantee that installments are consistent with legal and societal rules and principles.

An organization's internal control, no matter how well designed and operated, can only provide reasonable assurance as to the achievement of the organization's objectives. These limitations are present due to cost-benefit matters and such aspects such as faulty individuals' judgment in decision making or simple errors or mistakes. Furthermore, controls can be overridden by management or circumvented by collusion by two or more people. The effectiveness of an organization's internal control could also be affected by changes in ownership or management, turnover in other personnel, or modifications in the organization's business or operating environment.

Table 10.3. Feature Extraction

Technology	Feature extracted
Fingerprint	Measuring the pattern, ridge endings and splits in ridge paths of the raised portion of the print.
Palm print	Measuring the pattern, ridge endings and splits in ridge paths of the raised portion of the print
Hand geometry	Height and width of bones and joints in hands and fingers
Vein analysis	The pattern of blood vessels in the vein
DNA	Double helix structure present in every human cell
Retina-scan	Blood vessel patterns on retina
Iris-scan	Furrows and striations in iris
Facial recognition	Relative position and shape of nose, position of cheekbones
Facial thermography	Heat patterns shaped by the sectioning of blood vessels and emitted from the skin
Ear recognition	Outer ear and ear lope; however, the entire ear structure and shape can be captured
Body odor (scent) recognition	A scent that is made up of traces of chemicals that evaporate off the body (called thermal plume)
Speaker recognition	Frequency, cadence and duration of vocal pattern
Gait	Periodic activity with each gait cycle covering two walking strides
Dynamic signature	Speed, stroke order, pressure, and appearance of signature
Keystroke dynamics	Keyed sequence, duration between characters

The nature of internal control biometrics system for convenience and flexibility for website applications can produce vulnerability and abusing of users' rights. Hackers can circumvent traditional network firewalls and intrusion-prevention systems and assault website applications directly. They can inject commands into databases through the website application user interfaces and surreptitiously steal data, such as customer and credit card information.

The day has come that biometrics is real technology for internal control biometrics system use. Spurred by the size and cost advantages of fingerprint sensors and a growing need for security, biometric technology is being integrated into more and more devices, including laptop personal computers from the leading manufacturers around the world, cell phones, and home door locks being sold at major home improvement retail centers.

Internal control biometrics systems can be implemented in two ways: for verification or for identification. When a biometric is utilized to verify whether individuals are who they claim to be, that verification is frequently referred to as "one-to-one" matching. Almost all systems can determine whether there is a match between a person's presented biometric and biometric templates in a database in several seconds.

Identification, by contrast, is known as "one-to-many" matching. In identification, an individual's presented biometric is compared with all of the biometric templates within a database. There are two categories of identification systems: positive and negative. Positive systems anticipate there to be a match between the biometric presented and the template. These systems are designed to make sure that an individual is in the database. Negative systems are set up to make sure that an individual is not in the system. Negative identification can also take the form of a watch list, where a match generates a notice to the suitable authority for action.

Neither verification systems nor identification systems produce perfect matches. Instead, each comparison creates a score of how close the presented biometric is to the stored template. The internal control biometrics system compare the score with a predefined number or with algorithms to determine whether the presented biometric and template are sufficiently close to be considered a match.

Most biometric systems necessitate an enrollment process in which a sample biometric is captured, extracted, and encoded as a biometric template. This template is then captured in a database against which future comparisons will be made. When the biometric is implemented for verification (e.g., access control), the internal control biometrics system confirms the validity of the claimed identity. When used for identification, the biometric tool compares a precise user's biometric with all of the stored biometric records to see if there is a match. For biometric technology to be successful, the database must be specific and reasonably comprehensive.

Identification and verification are an essential part of security in most internal control biometrics systems. There are many technologies and protocols supporting this functionality. Biometrics is considered promising because of ease of use from an individual's viewpoint. They are also helpful if a physical user presence has to be guaranteed. The day is coming soon when the everyday consumer will use biometrics on at least one device and may end up using biometrics all day long, from home to transit to work to shopping and more.

In an internal control biometrics system environment, it is common to have three main security processes working together to provide access to assets in a controlled manner. These processes are:

1. *Authentication* determines and validates the user identity.
2. *Authorization* provides users with the access to resources that they are allowed to have and avert users from retrieving resources that they are not allowed to access.
3. *Accounting* provides an audit trail of user actions.

Authentication, authorization, and accounting (AAA) is framework for prudently controlling entrance to internal control biometrics system resources, enforcing policies, auditing usage, and providing the information necessary to bill for services. AAA provides in the structure of a network architecture that assists in the protection of the network operator and its customers from fraud, attacks, inappropriate resource management, and loss of revenue. These combined processes are regarded as essential for effective internal control biometrics system management and security.

INTERNAL CONTROL BIOMETRICS SYSTEMS

Internal control biometrics systems use parts of the human body for recognition and identification. Iris of the eye, facial recognition, fingerprints and palm prints are a few of the more common body parts utilized. There are no external credentials such as magnetic swipe cards, proximity keys, PIN numbers, etc. Utilizing parts of the human body eradicates stolen or lost credentials as well as identification fraud.

Internal control biometrics systems can be use in all organizational environments. Large corporations and small entities alike can greatly benefit from using biometrics. It eliminates re-keying, provides a full audit trail for each user in the system, and purges credential sharing between employees.

Internal control biometrics systems immensely enhance the security and efficiency of "time and attendance systems." Employees can no longer "clock in" or "clock out" their friends and colleagues which do away with the chance of them being paid for hours they did not work.

Internal control biometrics systems provide a complete log of all users who enter and exit through the system. The system logs time, date, user, department, etc. Surveillance can be included with the access control system to provide a video snapshot of the individual in real time as they are interfacing with the system.

Biometrics can be used to control access in and out of certain departments within a facility. Certain employees may have access to the information technology department or the warehouse. After hour's access to the front office can be disallowed to production workers, parts and inventory departments can be denied to all employees between certain hours of the day. The options are virtually unlimited.

In summary, internal control biometrics systems are the most cost-effective way of controlling the security of an organization. Biometrics complements full audit trail capabilities, instant administration using system software, total accountability with no credential sharing, integration with surveillance systems, alarm systems, time and attendance systems and lighting/automation systems.

Most Internal control biometrics systems restrict entry by time of day, day of week, and door accessed. Access is granted when the person presents the correct card, keypad code or both. Internal control biometrics systems spell heightened security for employees, assets, and this organizational knowledge creates a more productive workplace. Turnover decreases, costs drop, and those who would take advantage of an organization's assets will seek easier targets elsewhere. Other benefits include:

For employers

Reduced expenses—password maintenance
Reduced expenses—no buddy punching
Increased security—no shared or compromised passwords
Increased security—discourage and detect fraudulent account access
Increased security—no badge sharing in protected areas
Competitive advantage—familiarity with advanced technology

For employees

Convenience—no passwords to remember or reset
Convenience—quicker login
Security—confidential files can be put in storage securely
Nonrepudiation—biometrically transactions not easy to contest

For consumers

Convenience—no passwords to remember or reset
Security—personal files, comprising of emails, can be protected
Security—online purchases more secure when facilitated by biometric
Privacy—capability to execute anonymously

For retailers (online and point-of-sale)

Reduced expenses—biometric users less likely to perpetrate fraud
Competitive advantage—first to provide secure transaction method
Security—account access much more secure than by the use of password

For public sector usage

Reduced expenses—most robust method to discover and discourage
      benefits fraud
Increased trust —diminished entitlement abuse

Internal control biometrics systems can assist decision-makers to confirm identity or verify a particular person. Using biometric information on a routine basis could help create a more facilitative internal control system, by allowing more efficient and effective decision making for employees, customers, suppliers and others. It would also create a more robust system for preventing identity fraud and detecting deterring persons who should not be accessing an information system.

The implementation of internal control biometrics systems for increasing security and safeguarding of assets raises an abundant of practical and policy questions. It is essential that the right type of technology is selected to meet the purpose and privacy requirements of a particular use. In order for internal control biometrics systems to provide security, it is necessary that people not have a false sense of security about them. The weaknesses and flaws of the technologies must be acknowledged and countermeasures need to be considered. The internal control biometrics systems cannot be seen as the ultimate security tool, and thus the perfect solution. To a certain extent biometrics are simply another tool in a layered approach to security and assets safeguarding. They are not a magic potion; however, they can play a principal role in protecting organizations and should not be demonized as unacceptable technology.

A growing number of novel *real-world* biometric technologies have begun to take the place of our most commonly used identification systems, ushering in a new era of security, convenience and user friendliness. Modern biometrics are more flexible then their predecessors, capable of being integrated into internal control systems unimagined in the past.

Internal control biometric systems have many complex algorithms to identify people, but all of these systems have similar procedures and steps. Although this technology is still new and developing, biometrics is quickly becoming the trustworthy, appropriate and most accurate means for identification and verification. Hence, there are many reasons to believe that internal control biometrics systems will change the life of people in the near future more often than not since its use will be much more convenient than other techniques in use today for identification and verification purposes. This is already apparent today, particularly in connection with applications such as physical and logical access control, transportation, as well as in the financial industry.

Present and Beyond

Effective security cannot be obtained by relying on technology alone. Technology and people must work together as part of an overall internal control biometrics system. Weaknesses in any of these areas weaken the effectiveness of an internal control biometrics system. The internal control biometrics system needs to account for limitations in biometric tools. For instance, some individuals cannot enroll in a biometrics system. Likewise, errors sometimes come about during matching operations. Procedures need to be made available in order to handle these situations.

Three fundamental considerations need to be addressed before a decision choice is implemented to design, develop, and implement biometrics into an internal control biometrics system:

1. Decisions must be made on how the technology will be utilized.
2. A comprehensive cost-benefit analysis must be performed to determine that the benefits derived from a system outweigh the costs.
3. A trade-off analysis must be accomplished between the increased security, which the biometrics implementation would provide, and the effect on areas such as privacy and convenience.

Many organizations continue to advance the present biometric tools as well as searching the frontier for the next biometric that shows potential of utilization in the private and public domains. Emerging biometric is a biometric that is in the infancy stages of proven technological maturation (e.g., ear, odor etc.). Once proven, an emerging biometric will undoubtedly evolve into that of an established biometric tool.

In sum, a high-quality internal control biometrics system must ensure that the biometric information

1. comes from a live person at the time of verification, and
2. matches the master biometric data on file.

Internal control biometrics systems can aid in:

*   Reducing the risk of breaches.
*   Add Profits—new revenues, lower expenses.
*   Bring convenience and simplicity.
*   Increase employee, customer, and supplier satisfaction.
*   Surpass regulatory compliance.
*   Minimize service and support.
*   Facilitate organizational synergies.
*   Provide marketing and public relation opportunities.
*   Improve image, reputational, and brand value.

Internal control biometrics systems future will eventually include e-commerce applications for extra security on the checkout page, and biometrics will safeguard against unauthorized access to cars and cell phones. In the future, biometric technology will further develop 3D infrared facial recognition access control, real-time facial recognition passive surveillance, and visitor management authentication systems.

Further development of biometric technologies may change the world considerably. These technologies not only have the making of a simpler life, but also for more perfect invigilation. This will not encumber the development of these techniques. Almost every technology can be implemented for good and bad purposes, which depends on the people using it.

ABOUT THE AUTHOR

Waymond Rodgers is a CPA and a Professor and in the School of Business at the University of California in Riverside. He received his BA from Michigan State University, his MBA from the University of Detroit Mercy, his, PhD in accounting information systems from the University of Southern California, and an experimental psychology post-doctorate from the University of Michigan. His experiences include working as an auditor with Ernst & Young and Price Waterhouse Coopers, as well as a commercial loan officer with Union Bank. His primary research areas are auditing, commercial lending decisions, decision modeling, ethics, trust issues, intellectual capital, and knowledge management. Professor Rodgers has published in the Auditing: A Journal of Practice & Theory Communications of the ACM, European Accounting Review, Journal of Business Ethics, Journal of Applied Social Psychology, Journal of Economic Psychology, Journal of the Association of Information Systems, Management Science, Organization Studies among other journals. Finally, he is the recipient of major research grants from the Ford Foundation, National Institute of Health, National Science Foundation, Department of Defense, and the Navy Personnel Research and Development Center.